## Close Encounters of All Kinds

**S0-BYT-490**

UFO encounters are classified according to the proximity and interaction between the observer and the UFO. Different groups of UFOlogists use different classification systems, but the more-or-less standard one breaks down like this:

➤ *A Sighting.* Where the observer has seen an object in the sky that he or she cannot identify and that, either through appearance or activity, seems unlike a normal aircraft—that is, if it's close enough to see clearly and it doesn't look like any object the observer is familiar with, or it maneuvers in a fashion that the observer believes normal aircraft are incapable of doing.

The value of a "sighting" report increases with the knowledge and trustworthiness of the observer. A bishop who is also an airline pilot would make a first-class observer.

➤ *A Close Encounter of the First Kind.* The observer sees the UFO at close range, and possibly hears it, but there is no physical contact. When the UFO departs, it leaves behind no physical trace of its presence. Even this no-contact sort of encounter can be very psychically stressful for the observer.

➤ *A Close Encounter of the Second Kind.* Take a close encounter of the first kind, and add to it some sort of physical evidence of the UFO's presence, such as scorched ground where the vehicle took off, or broken tree limbs, or some physical action-at-a-distance, like a car's ignition system failing, and you have a close encounter of the second kind.

➤ *A Close Encounter of the Third Kind.* Have Steven Spielberg make a movie—no, no—this is an encounter where the observer actually sees alien beings emerge from a (usually landed) UFO. It can include touching or being touched by an alien, talking to an alien, often by telepathy, or even being invited aboard the alien spacecraft.

➤ *A Close Encounter of the Fourth Kind.* This, the most intimate of the close encounters, is a case of "alien abduction," where a person is forcibly taken aboard a UFO to be examined medically, physically, or mentally, and then returned. The abduction is usually accompanied by amnesia blocking memory of the event, and the only sign is a block of time that seems to be missing from the person's past. The memory is sometimes recovered spontaneously, or more often while under hypnosis.

alpha
books

*tear here*

## The Ten Signs Said to Indicate That a Person May Have Had a Close Encounter of the Fourth Kind

- ➤ Missing periods of time
- ➤ Frequent nightmares about aliens and/or UFOs
- ➤ Sleep disorders
- ➤ Unusual body sensation upon waking
- ➤ Unexplained marks or scars on the body
- ➤ A feeling of being watched
- ➤ Repeated sightings of UFOs
- ➤ Partial memory of an alien encounter
- ➤ Sudden spontaneous healing of a long-term illness or affliction
- ➤ Phobic reaction to discussions about UFOs or extraterrestrials

## A Few Selected Divination Techniques

Humans have devised hundreds of ways to predict the future by studying the alignment of inanimate objects or the behavior of animate ones (for a list of something over a hundred of them, see Appendix D, "Divination Techniques"). A few of the more common or more interesting ones are …

- ➤ **Astrology:** Studying the positions of the planets in the Zodiac in a belief that they influence human character and behavior (see Chapters 13, "It's In Your Stars," and 14, "An Astrology Primer").
- ➤ **Bibliomancy:** The art of divining the future by picking a random passage in a book, often the Bible.
- ➤ **Chresmomancy:** Divination by listening to the babble of a madman and creating meaning from the verbal chaos. Madmen and –women were supposed to have been touched by the gods.
- ➤ **Dowsing:** The art of finding water, metal ores, or minerals by focusing on the ground (or a map) using a bent twig, often of hazel, or a metal rod.
- ➤ **Numerology:** Using the numbers in a birthday or other date, or the number equivalent of the letters in names or other words, to predict the future.
- ➤ **Oneiromancy:** Interpreting the prophetic meaning of dreams.
- ➤ **Scrying:** Peering into crystal balls or polished mirrors to see into the future.

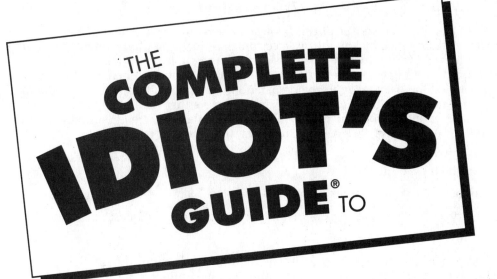

# THE COMPLETE IDIOT'S GUIDE® TO

# Unsolved Mysteries

by Michael Kurland
with Linda Robertson

**alpha
books**

Macmillan USA, Inc.
201 West 103rd Street
Indianapolis, IN 46290

A Pearson Education Company

**Publisher**
*Marie Butler-Knight*

**Product Manager**
*Phil Kitchel*

**Managing Editor**
*Cari Luna*

**Acquisitions Editor**
*Randy Ladenheim-Gil*

**Development Editor**
*Michael Thomas*

**Production Editor**
*JoAnna Kremer*

**Copy Editor**
*Amy Lepore*

**Illustrator**
*Jody P. Schaeffer*

**Cover Designers**
*Mike Freeland*
*Kevin Spear*

**Book Designers**
*Scott Cook and Amy Adams of DesignLab*

**Indexer**
*Angie Bess*

**Layout/Proofreading**
*Darin Crone*
*Terri Edwards*
*Steve Geiselman*
*Donna Martin*

# Contents at a Glance

**Part 1: Disappearances**                                          **1**

  1 Solved and Unsolved                                         3
    *What makes a mystery?*

  2 Disappearing Ships and Planes                              11
    *They sailed or flew to nowhere.*

  3 Disappearing People                                        23
    *Now you see them, now you don't.*

  4 Travelers to Nowhere                                       33
    *Whole colonies just disappeared.*

**Part 2: People Power, Past and Present**                          **49**

  5 A Mind Is a Difficult Thing to Read                        51
    *ESP explains it, but what explains ESP?*

  6 They Delved Into the Future                                63
    *What did they know, and when did they know it?*

  7 The Great Medieval Prophets                                75
    *Mother Shipton and Nostradamus predict ...*

  8 Recent Prophets                                            89
    *Uncanny predictions from unusual people.*

  9 Monumental Mysteries                                      101
    *Great stone monuments keep their secrets.*

**Part 3: The Big Questions**                                       **115**

  10 Beginnings and Endings                                   117
    *Where we came from, where we're going.*

  11 Beneath the Waves                                        129
    *The rise and fall of Atlantis.*

  12 We Are Not Alone                                         143
    *The search for extraterrestrial intelligence.*

  13 It's In Your Stars                                       157
    *The history of astrology.*

  14 An Astrology Primer                                      169
    *How astrology works.*

## Part 4: Human Events     **183**

15 Well Done, Rare Old Medium     185
*The continuing story of spiritualism.*

16 Gurus or Charlatans?     197
*Saint-Germain, Cagliostro, and Rasputin.*

17 The Lindbergh Baby Kidnapping     209
*Still not satisfactorily solved after 70 years.*

18 It's a Crime     223
*Several unsolved—or wrongly solved—crimes.*

19 Did Lizzie Borden Take an Axe?     237
*What really happened on August 4, 1892?*

20 The Mysterious Mata Hari     249
*The most famous spy who never spied.*

## Part 5: Inhuman Events     **263**

21 Saucers That Fly     265
*The birth of flying saucer stories.*

22 The Roswell Incident     279
*The most famous UFO case continues to develop.*

23 Those Who Got Carried Away     291
*Sightings, close encounters, and abductions.*

## Part 6: Unanswered Questions     **301**

24 The Undead and the Inhuman     303
*Vampires, werewolves, and ghouls.*

25 The Crypto-Zoo     315
*Nessie, Bigfoot, and—Ogopogo?*

26 Will the Real William Shakespeare Please Stand Up?     327
*The many people who may have been William Shakespeare.*

## Appendixes

A Glossary     341

B Astrological Information     345

C Reporting UFOs     349

D Divination Techniques     353

E Selected Bibliography     357

Index     361

# Contents

**Part 1: Disappearances**     **1**

**1 Solved and Unsolved**     **3**

The Mark of a Mystery ...................................................3
   *The Universal Question* .........................................4
I Love a Mystery .............................................................4
   *The Great Story* ......................................................5
   *The Great Mystery* .................................................5
   *The Unknown vs. the Unknowable* ......................6
   *Shakespeare's Plays* ..............................................7
   *The Laws by Which the Universe Works*..............7
   *The Mysterious Past* ..............................................8
A Little Help for My Friends ........................................8
   *A Really Good Story* ..............................................9

**2 Disappearing Ships and Planes**     **11**

*De Vliegende Hollander* ..............................................12
The *Mary Celeste*.........................................................13
   *The Story* ...............................................................13
   *Final Voyage* .........................................................14
   *Fancy Free* .............................................................15
   *The Inquiry* ...........................................................15
   *Looking at the Facts*.............................................16
   *A Couple of Possibilities* .....................................17
More Missing Men .......................................................17
The Eternal Bermuda Triangle ...................................18
   *The Disappearing Avengers*..................................18
   *"The Devil's Triangle"* ..........................................19
   *Flight 19* ................................................................20
   *Other Bermuda Triangle Mysteries* .....................20
The *Scorpion* ...............................................................21

**3 Disappearing People**     **23**

The Mystery of Benjamin Bathhurst............................24
Poor Charlie Ross.........................................................25
The First Missing Ambrose ........................................26

A Small Story: The Second Missing Ambrose ....................26
The Flying Officers..............................................................27
The Double Disappearances of Pauline..........................28
The Disappearing Judge.....................................................29
Jimmy Hoffa.........................................................................30
The Unfound ........................................................................32

## 4 Travelers to Nowhere 33

Where Went the Norse? ....................................................33
*The Little Ice Age* ...........................................................34
*Where Did They Go?* .......................................................35
The Roanoke Colony ..........................................................36
*Ecstatic Reports* .............................................................36
*The First Indian Fights*....................................................36
*Gone, All Gone* ...............................................................37
*White's Turn* ...................................................................38
*Fernandez Splits* .............................................................39
*All Gone—Again* .............................................................39
*The Mystery Persists*........................................................40
The Franklin Expedition .....................................................42
*The Expedition*.................................................................42
*The Ships Disappear* .......................................................43
*The First Hints*.................................................................44
*Dragging Their Boat Behind Them* .................................44
*No End to the Searching* ..................................................46
Bad Luck................................................................................47

## Part 2: People Power, Past and Present 49

## 5 A Mind Is a Difficult Thing to Read 51

What Is This Thing Called ESP? .......................................52
*The Case Against ESP* .....................................................53
*The Case For ESP*.............................................................53
Anecdotal Evidence ............................................................55
*By the Mark, Twain* .........................................................55
*Abraham Lincoln and Mrs. Julia Grant* ..........................55
Morgan Robertson, the Unwitting Seer ...........................56
*Unsinkable*.......................................................................57
*Speed, Passengers, and Lifeboats*....................................58
*And So to Sink* .................................................................58
*And Furthermore* .............................................................58

Doctor Rhine ............................................................58
   *The Rhine Deck* ...............................................59
   *Hitting the Deck* ..............................................59
The Ganzfeld Technique ........................................60
You Read My Mind ................................................61

**6 They Delved Into the Future**       **63**

Predicting the Future .............................................64
The Greek Oracles .................................................64
Croesus and the Delphic Oracle ..........................66
   *How to Pick an Oracle* ....................................66
   *"A Great Empire Will Be Destroyed"* ............67
The Sibylline Books ...............................................67
Medieval Prophecy ................................................68
   *Merlin Predicts* ...............................................68
   *St. Malachy Predicts the Popes* .....................69
   *The List Recovered* ........................................70
   *The Listed Popes* ............................................71
   *The Last Few* .................................................72
   *The Last Bit* ..................................................72

**7 The Great Medieval Prophets**       **75**

Mother Shipton .....................................................76
   *"Wolsey Shall Not Reach York"* .....................76
The Prophetic Rhymes of Mother Shipton ...........77
   *The Verse She Could Do* .................................77
   *One More Paragraph* ......................................79
   *The Added Verse* ............................................79
Nostradamus ..........................................................80
   *The Wanderer* .................................................81
   *Obscure and in Verse* .....................................81
   *The Golden Cage* ............................................83
   *Ancient Egyptian Books* ..................................84
But What of the Quatrains? ..................................84
   *What Did He Say?* ..........................................85
   *You're On Your Own* ......................................86
   *124c41* ...........................................................88

**8 Recent Prophets**       **89**

The Events at Fatima ..............................................90
   *A White Mist* ..................................................90

*A Glowing Globe* ........................................ 91
The Final Proof ........................................... 91
*The Sky Cleared* ........................................ 92
The Three Secrets ........................................ 92
*A Glimpse Into Hell* .................................... 92
*An Unknown Light* ...................................... 93
*The Third Prophecy Revealed* ....................... 94
*The Doubters* ........................................... 95
Our Lady of Medjugorje ............................... 95
Edgar Cayce ............................................... 96
*The Sleeping Prophet* .................................. 96
*Diagnoses and Treatments* ........................... 98
*On to Atlantis* .......................................... 99

**9  Monumental Mysteries                             101**

The Greatest Pyramid .................................. 102
*What a Wonder* ........................................ 102
*The Pyramid Inch* ..................................... 104
*From Creation to the Judgment Day* ............... 105
A Japanese Pyramid .................................... 106
*Very Big and Very Old* ............................... 106
*Smaller Steps* .......................................... 107
*We Inherited Their Brains* ........................... 107
The Sphinx ............................................... 107
*Older Than That* ....................................... 108
*The Stars at Night* ..................................... 108
Stonehenge and All the Little Henges ............... 110
*Moving the Stones* .................................... 110
*Whatever For?* ......................................... 111
Gilgal Refaim ............................................ 112
*The World's Largest, Heaviest Calendar* .......... 112
*It Stands Alone* ........................................ 112
*Did Giants Walk the Earth?* .......................... 113
Ancient Astronauts or Just Us? ....................... 113

**Part 3:  The Big Questions                          115**

**10  Beginnings and Endings                          117**

How Did the Universe Begin? ......................... 118
*The Conceptual Framework* ........................... 118
*Great Balls of Gas* ..................................... 119

It's In the Stars .................................................120
*The Redder the Shift* .........................................*121*
*The Balloon Analogy* ..........................................*122*
The Big Bang ....................................................122
*A Steady State* ................................................*122*
*And the Winner Is* ............................................*123*
The Fate of the Universe ........................................123
*The Role of Gravity* ..........................................*124*
*The First Mystery* ............................................*124*
An Incident in the Cretaceous ..................................125
*The Geologic Eras* ............................................*125*
*Mass Extinctions* .............................................*126*
*The Age of the Dinosaur* .....................................*126*
*The Crashing Asteroid* .......................................*127*
*Chicxulub* ....................................................*127*
Nemesis ..........................................................127

**11  Beneath the Waves                                    129**

How It Began ...................................................130
*The First Mention of Atlantis* ...............................*130*
*And the Next Mention* .........................................*131*
Straight from the Source's Mouth ..............................132
Thank You, Columbus ...........................................134
Ignatius T.T. Donnelly Discovers Atlantis ....................135
*No Lack of Evidence* .........................................*137*
*Donnelly's Facts* ............................................*138*
The Post Donnelly Seekers .....................................138
*Helena Petrovna Blavatsky* ...................................*139*
*Edgar Cayce* .................................................*139*
The Santorini Connection ......................................140

**12  We Are Not Alone                                     143**

They Thought They Were Alone ..................................143
Most Stars Are Big Mothers ....................................144
*The Dance of the Planets* ....................................*145*
*We Find the Big Ones* ........................................*146*
Yes, But Is There Life? .......................................146
*The Mix Must Be Just Right* ..................................*147*
*Generations* .................................................*147*
The Fermi Paradox .............................................147

Doctor Drake's Equation ..................................................150
*The Equation of Life* ...............................................*151*
*Is It Intelligent or Ain't It?* ....................................*152*
*The L You Say* .....................................................*153*
*The Truth Is Out There* ............................................*154*
Now We're Listening ......................................................154
*Project Phoenix* ...................................................*154*
*The SETI League* ...................................................*155*
*SERENDIP* ..........................................................*155*

**13  It's In Your Stars                                         157**

The "Science" of Astrology ...............................................158
*They Have It Down Cold* ............................................*158*
*"How Did He Know?"* ................................................*159*
The Ancient Astrologers ..................................................159
*The Astrologer-Priests* ............................................*160*
*Post Hoc Ergo What?* ...............................................*160*
*Chaldean Astrology* ................................................*161*
*The Chaldean Zodiac* ...............................................*162*
Astrology in the Medieval World ..........................................162
*The Royal Astrologers* .............................................*162*
*The Learned Astrologers* ...........................................*163*
The New Astrology ........................................................167
Hitler's Astrologers .....................................................167

**14  An Astrology Primer                                        169**

Jeane Dixon ..............................................................170
*The Jeane Dixon Effect* ............................................*170*
*An Astrologer for the FBI* .........................................*170*
An Amazing Parallel ......................................................171
The Basic Rules ..........................................................172
*The Signs of the Zodiac* ...........................................*173*
*Character Traits* ..................................................*174*
*Cusps* .............................................................*177*
Casting a Horoscope ......................................................178
*The 12 Houses* .....................................................*180*
*Drawing the Lines* .................................................*181*
Digging Deeper into Astrology ............................................181

## Part 4: Human Events                                    183

### 15  Well Done, Rare Old Medium                          185

The Hydesville Sisters ...................................................186
*Dig We Must* ...............................................................*187*
*Leah Holds a Lecture* ................................................*188*
An Early Seance ............................................................189
Swedenborg, Mesmer, and Davis.................................190
*Conversing with the Dead* .......................................*190*
*Animal Magnetism* ...................................................*191*
*The Poughkeepsie Seer* .............................................*192*
The Physical Medium ...................................................193
*Daniel Dunglas Home* ..............................................*193*
*The Levitating Man* ..................................................*194*
To Cheat or Not to Cheat ...........................................196

### 16  Gurus or Charlatans?                                197

The Count de Saint-Germain .......................................197
*The Mystery Grows* ...................................................*198*
*Life After Death* .........................................................*199*
Alessandro, Conte di Cagliostro .................................200
*Balsamo Becomes Cagliostro* ....................................*200*
*The Fleecer Fleeced* ...................................................*201*
*Paris* ...........................................................................*203*
Rasputin ........................................................................205
*The Miracles of Rasputin* ..........................................*205*
*The Final Miracles* .....................................................*207*

### 17  The Lindbergh Baby Kidnapping                     209

The Kidnapping..............................................................210
*The Ransom Note* .......................................................*210*
*The Evidence* ..............................................................*211*
The Colonels .................................................................211
More Notes.....................................................................212
Jafsie to the Rescue .....................................................213
*Condon Is Accepted* ...................................................*213*
*The Kidnappers Communicate* ...................................*214*
*Jafsie Grows Restless* .................................................*215*
The Drop ........................................................................215

The Body ...................................................216
   *The Old Fox*.............................................217
   *The Old Fox Rebuffed*..........................217
Jafsie Rejected ........................................218
A Few Bills Turn Up ..............................218
Bruno Richard Hauptmann ...................219
The Trial ..................................................219
   *The Evidence Is Presented*....................220
   *The Conviction* .....................................221
Are You the Lindbergh Baby? ................221

**18 It's a Crime**                 **223**

Death to the Anarchists..........................224
   *The "Expert" Witnesses* .........................224
   *A Review of the Case* .............................225
The New Orleans Axeman.......................226
   *The Axeman Cometh* ..............................226
   *Polish Grocer or Spy?* .............................227
   *Broad-Jumping to Conclusions* ............227
   *One Victim Is Saved* ...............................228
   *A Dark, Tall, Heavy-Set Man* ...............228
   *Rosie Changes Her Story* ........................229
   *The Jazz Lover* .......................................229
   *The Next Few Chops* ..............................231
   *The Murder of Mumfre* ..........................231
The Sam Sheppard Case .........................233
   *The Bushy-Haired Man* ..........................233
   *The "Surgical Instrument"* .....................234
   *Dr. Kirk's Version* ..................................234
   *The Ohio Courts Vacillate* .....................235

**19 Did Lizzie Borden Take an Axe?**     **237**

The Borden Family ..................................237
The Crime ................................................238
   *"Father is dead."* ....................................240
   *There Is Another* ....................................241
The Investigation.....................................242
   *Clues and Suspects Galore* .....................242
   *Just the Facts* .........................................243
   *The Borden Burglary* .............................244

The Trial ................................................................244
  *A Burning Question* ........................................245
  *The Lawyers Fight It Out* ...............................246
The Unanswered Questions...............................247

**20  The Mysterious Mata Hari                          249**

Mata Hari's Story ...............................................250
Margaretha's Story .............................................250
The Dance Begins ...............................................251
  *The Lovers* .......................................................252
  *The Offer* ..........................................................252
  *To Spy or Not to Spy*.......................................253
Mistaken Identity................................................254
In Madrid On Her Own ......................................255
A German Conquest ...........................................255
  *A Chance Meeting* ...........................................256
  *Back to Paris and Disaster* .............................257
  *Arrested* ............................................................257
  *The Intercepts* ..................................................257
Mata Hari—the Myths ........................................260

**Part 5:  Inhuman Events                                263**

**21  Saucers That Fly                                     265**

What the Ancients Saw .......................................266
  *Ezekiel* ...............................................................266
  *The Pharaoh Sees a Circle of Fire* ..................267
  *The Great Pearl* ...............................................267
  *The Prefect*........................................................267
Flying Silver Cigars ............................................268
  *Alex Hamilton Loses a Cow* ...........................269
  *Space Ship Hits Windmill*...............................269
The Very First Flying Saucers.............................270
  *Kenneth Arnold Sees Skipping Saucers*...........270
The Mysterious Death of Captain Thomas Mantell .......271
The UFO Blitz......................................................273
  *The Air Force Investigates*...............................273
  *Flying Saucers Over the Capital* .....................274
Project Blue Book................................................275
  *The Robertson Committee* ...............................275
  *Bye-Bye, Blue Book*..........................................277

## 22  The Roswell Incident    **279**

The Air Force Takes a Look .............................................280
*Meanwhile, Back at Headquarters ...* .........................280
Roswell Rekindled ..........................................................281
The Plot Thickens ...........................................................282
*Articles of Faith* .........................................................282
*A Different Truth* ........................................................283
*Roswell Reading* .........................................................283
The Body Is the Evidence ...............................................284
Majestic-12.......................................................................284
*A Closer Look* .............................................................288
*Other Questions* .........................................................288
*The Continuing Story* .................................................290

## 23  Those Who Got Carried Away    **291**

The Interrupted Journey of Betty and Barney Hill .........291
*Close Encounters of the Fourth Kind*...........................292
*Enter the Air Force* ....................................................292
*Two of Our Hours Are Missing* ..................................293
*Examined by Aliens* ....................................................294
The Abductee Parade ......................................................296
*At the Sound of My Voice* ...........................................297
*Try to Remember* ........................................................298
The True UFO....................................................................299

## Part 6:  Unanswered Questions    **301**

## 24  The Undead and the Inhuman    **303**

Vampires ..........................................................................304
*By Their Names Shall You Know Them* ........................304
*The Lamia* ...................................................................305
Welcome, Vampire............................................................306
*Arnold's Story* ............................................................306
*Arnold Wanders in Death* ..........................................307
*Buried Secrets*.............................................................307
Werewolves? Here Wolves! ............................................308
*The Miraculous Salve* .................................................309
*A Horrible Illness* .......................................................310

Real Live Ghouls ................................................311
  *Ed Gein* .......................................................*311*
  *Jeffrey Dahmer* ..........................................*313*

**25  The Crypto-Zoo**                                        **315**

Cryptids ............................................................316
Leviathans in the Lakes ....................................316
  *The Loch Ness Monster* ...............................*316*
  *Lake Serpents of North America* ..................*318*
  *Lake Monsters in Scandinavia* .....................*319*
The Rest of the World .......................................320
The Tasmanian Tiger and Other Big Cats ........321
Missing Links ....................................................322
  *Yeti* .............................................................*323*
  *Bigfoot* .........................................................*324*
  *The Patterson Picture* ..................................*325*
  *Bigfeet Elsewhere* .........................................*325*
Chupacabra .......................................................326
Examining the Unknown ..................................326

**26  Will the Real William Shakespeare
Please Stand Up?**                                            **327**

Why the Fuss? ..................................................328
Why Not Shakespeare? .....................................329
  *And Besides ...* ............................................*330*
Sir Francis Bacon .............................................331
  *The Cipher* ..................................................*333*
The Earl of Oxford ...........................................335
Christopher Marlowe .........................................336
  *Dead Is Dead—or Is It?* ...............................*337*
The Case for Will ..............................................338

**Appendixes**

**A  Glossary**                                               **341**

**B  Astrological Information**                               **345**

The Signs of the Zodiac ....................................345
The Qualities Attributed to the Signs of the Zodiac ........346

The Planets and What They Represent ..........................346
The 12 Houses and What They Represent ......................347

**C  Reporting UFOs**                                    **349**

**D  Divination Techniques**                             **353**

**E  Selected Bibliography**                             **357**

General..............................................................357
Archaeology and Crypto-Archaeology ..........................357
Astrology ..........................................................358
Atlantis.............................................................358
Mata Hari ..........................................................358
Prophecy ...........................................................358
Shakespeare Authorship ..........................................359
Spiritualism ......................................................359
Strange Happenings...............................................359
UFOs..................................................................359

**Index**                                                 **361**

# Foreword

Everyone loves a mystery.

Some prefer the fictional variety—fortunately for me, since it happens to be my stock-in-trade—in which clever sleuths both amateur and professional unravel and explain seemingly insolvable riddles. Generations of people worldwide have been entertained, in print and on film, by the exploits of Sir Arthur Conan Doyle's Sherlock Holmes, Dashiell Hammett's *Thin Man* series, and the work of such popular puzzlemakers as Agatha Christie, Ellery Queen, Tony Hillerman, and Sue Grafton.

Real-life mysteries, especially those in which there appears to be no attainable solution, hold an even greater appeal. No person with an imagination and a sense of wonder can fail to be fascinated by such enigmas as the Bermuda Triangle, the lost world of Atlantis, UFOs, and the existence of alien life forms. Or by the question of whether Lizzie Borden did or did not take an axe and give her parents forty whacks. Or by such legendary individual disappearances as those of Ambrose Bierce, Judge Crater, and Jimmy Hoffa.

Nor can any such person, in possession of all salient facts in a particular case, fail to formulate a possible solution no matter how sketchy or far-fetched. (A case in point is the widespread speculation a few years ago that Jimmy Hoffa was murdered and buried in the New Jersey Meadowlands, on the site where Giants Stadium now stands and perhaps in the vicinity of one of the football field's end zones; and the oft-quoted remark of Sean Landetta, the New York Giants' kicking specialist, that if the rumors were true, it gave a whole new meaning to the term "coffin corner punt.")

*The Complete Idiot's Guide to Unsolved Mysteries* takes the reader on a tantalizing exploration of all the principal conundrums through the centuries. Each entry is concisely arranged so that it may be read as pure entertainment, as a mini history lesson, as a puzzle to be pondered and "solved," or as all three. Michael Kurland and Linda Robertson deserve kudos not only for creating a memorable look at mystification, but for making it fun in the process. You'll find no dry pontifications here, just impeccable research, clear, meaty prose, and an innate sense of pleasure that infers the authors had a grand time in its compilation.

I had an equally grand time reading it, and in developing my own theories on such matters as whether ghosts and vampires and flying saucers actually exist, Edgar Cayce did in fact discover Atlantis, and Merlin was a true medieval wizard capable of foretelling the future. When I reached the last page, I was sorry to see the book end—one true test of the worth of any piece of fiction or nonfiction. I'm confident that you'll feel the same when you've finished this delightful compendium.

—Bill Pronzini

*A full-time professional writer since 1969, Bill Pronzini has published 50 novels, including three in collaboration with his wife, novelist Marcia Muller, and 26 in his popular "Nameless Detective" series. He is also the author of four nonfiction books, six collections of short stories, and scores of uncollected stories, articles, essays, and book reviews; and he has edited or co-edited numerous anthologies. His work has been translated into 18 languages and published in nearly 30 countries. He has received three Shamus awards and the Lifetime Achievement Award (presented in 1987) from the Private Eye Writers of America; and six nominations for the Mystery Writers of America Edgar award. His novel* Snowbound *was the recipient of the Grand Prix de la Litterature Policiere as the best crime novel published in France in 1988. And his* A Wasteland of Strangers *was nominated for best crime novel of 1997 by both the Mystery Writers of America and the International Crime Writers Association.*

# Introduction

Albert Einstein once said that there is nothing more beautiful than a mystery. If so, this is a most beautiful book, for it is full of mysteries.

We humans are surrounded by mysteries, which is another way of saying that there are many, many things we do not know; many, many questions to which we do not have the answers. After all, the universe has had about 15 billion years to form itself in ways that we must try to understand, and we've only been attempting to understand for, perhaps, the past five thousand years. We don't know how old the universe is (15 billion years is just an educated guess), how it came into being (the Big Bang Theory, even if it's right, leaves a lot of unanswered questions), why its various laws work the way they seem to, how life was created, why it always rains right after you wash your car, or how ants know when you're having a picnic.

And to compound the problem, humans seem determined to go out of their way to create mysteries for other humans. Our ancestors left the Sphinx, the Pyramids, Stonehenge and a bunch of little henges, and various structures, symbols, stories, writings, carvings, and happenings for us to ponder about, mull over, and try to understand with insufficient information and overactive imaginations. And to further complicate the story, they may have been aided by visitors from some distant planet—aliens, with or without flying saucers. But that's, well, an unsolved mystery.

## In This Mysterious Book

In this book you'll be introduced to mysteries of all sorts: mysteries of the universe itself, mysteries of early earth, mysteries of our own ancient past, mysterious disappearances, mysterious happenings, accidental mysteries, and mysteries created by design.

We hope this gives you a feeling for the mysterious, for understanding what makes a mystery and why we are so fascinated by them. In a real sense you and I are the greatest mysteries of all. Each of us encompasses a triple mystery: the mystery of life, the mystery of intelligence, and the mystery of our own awareness and introspection. And of course there is the eternal mystery of sex, with all its permutations and puzzles and pleasures. But that needs an entire book, or perhaps an entire library, to itself.

## How to Use This Book

This book is divided into six parts.

**Part 1, "Disappearances,"** introduces you to unexplained disappearances. Some are people who left home but never arrived where they were going. Some are planes or ships that headed into the unknown and never returned; or even stranger, ships that returned but were completely deserted. Some are whole colonies of people, men, women, and children, that disappeared and have never been heard from since.

**Part 2, "People Power, Past and Present,"** looks at the phenomena lumped together as ESP: powers of the mind such as telepathy, telekinesis, clairvoyance, and prophecy that some people seem to possess and science cannot explain. Most prophecies are deliberately vague, and their meaning cannot be understood until after the event they prophesy; but some are frighteningly precise and accurate.

**Part 3, "The Big Questions,"** discusses the big questions of the age of the universe and where it came from and whether there is intelligent life elsewhere in the universe. We'll also delve into the riddle of Atlantis, and how Plato's casual mention has caused 20 centuries of speculation. And we'll trace the history of astrology and provide some insight into how horoscopes work.

**Part 4, "Human Events,"** begins with the story of spiritualism, and goes on to tell the stories of some extraordinary people like the Count of Saint-Germain, Count Cagliostro, and Rasputin. Then we'll delve into some unsolved crimes, or crimes where the solution is in doubt, like the Lindbergh baby kidnapping, and the deaths of Lizzie Borden's mom and dad. There's also the strange case of Mata Hari, who was executed as a spy, but who seems to have spied only for the side that executed her.

**Part 5, "Inhuman Events,"** is devoted to UFOs and the people who have seen them, talked to their crews, or been abducted by them. We will look at biblical and other ancient references of strange sightings that some today are interpreting as early UFOs. We'll explore the continuing Roswell phenomenon and the different explanations of what really went on in the New Mexico desert. We'll look at the people who believe they've been abducted by aliens and examine their frightening stories.

**Part 6, "Unanswered Questions,"** tackles the mysteries of people who think they're animals, and examines the tales of werewolves and vampires to see how they might have originated and how much truth there might be in them. Then we look at the tales of the shyest sorts of animals that seem to disappear whenever anyone takes a serious look for them, like the Loch Ness monster, and Bigfoot, and their cousins around the world. We round it off with one of our favorite mysteries: Who really wrote the plays attributed to William Shakespeare? If you think the answer is obvious, read Chapter 26 and be surprised.

## Extras

There are five types of sidebars scattered throughout this book that convey bits of information to enhance, explain, expand on, or otherwise improve your understanding of the subject at hand.

### No Mystery Here

When you see this sidebar, be prepared to learn a little more about whatever mystery we're talking about in the main text.

### Here There Be Dragons

These distinctive sidebars are reserved for warnings and alerts about the information in the text.

### What Does This Mean?

These sidebars define unfamiliar terms.

### The Mystery Deepens

This sidebar gives more details about some point in the text, or presents some interesting point related to, but not part of, the subject we're discussing.

### Mysterious Comments

In these sidebars, you'll find what other people had to say about the subject.

# Acknowledgments

As John Donne remarked almost 300 years ago, "No man is an island, entire of itself." We admit that, singly or collectively, we are no better than a peninsula. We would like to give credit here to those people without whose assistance this book would be other than it is.

Our thanks to:

Michael Conant, who had the word.

Randy Ladenheim-Gil, who was patient.

Kathryn Lennon, who was supportive.

Dick Lupoff, who was unstinting with his aid and advice.

Max Maven, who, as usual, knew the answer.

Tom Ogden, who gave us a starting place.

# Trademarks

All terms mentioned in this book that are known to be or are suspected of being trademarks or service marks have been appropriately capitalized. Alpha Books and Macmillan USA, Inc. cannot attest to the accuracy of this information. Use of a term in this book should not be regarded as affecting the validity of any trademark or service mark.

# Part 1
# Disappearances

*When someone disappears, it gives us a frightening glimpse into the unknown. In some cases, as with the disappearance of Ambrose Bierce, we could come up with a dozen logical explanations, and the problem would be to pick among them. In other cases, such as the disappearance of Benjamin Bathurst or the crew of the* Mary Celeste, *there is no reasonable explanation. And what are we to make of the English colony at Roanoke, which explorers returning after two years discovered had completely vanished?*

# Chapter 1

# Solved and Unsolved

## In This Chapter

➤ Defining the mystery

➤ Universal significance and a good story

➤ Mysteries with questionable solutions

➤ Mysteries with many mutually exclusive solutions

➤ Curiosity: the mystery behind mysteries

Welcome to *The Complete Idiot's Guide to Unsolved Mysteries*. In these pages, you'll find mysteries of all sorts—disappearing ships and airplanes, disappearing people, mysterious events, unexplained tragedies, strange objects, unsolved crimes, secrets from the past, and possible visitors from distant planets. We'll also discuss the origins of the universe, the origins of life, and the origins of people.

## The Mark of a Mystery

Let's start by deciding just what a mystery is. What follows is one possible definition, but it isn't the only one. You might have your own ideas about the mysterious that make it definable in other ways that are important to you. If you have a different answer, your definition is the right one, too.

## What Does This Mean?

The word **mystery** comes from the Latin *mysterium,* which refers to the secret rites and hidden truths known only to the initiates of various religions, and further back from the Greek *muein,* which means to close the eyes or lips.

## *The Universal Question*

There are two things that turn a question or a problem into a *mystery*. First, the question should be of universal interest. Not only is it a question that's likely to be important to each of us, it's the sort of problem that not knowing the answer is liable to make one worry—like the question of what happens when we die or when the next *Star Wars* movie is coming out.

Extinct dinosaurs are one such mystery. When the fossil record revealed that giant dragon-like creatures dominated the planet for tens of millions of years but then suddenly disappeared, the question of what happened to them became one of the most popular scientific mysteries. (For more on the story of dinosaur extinction, see Chapter 10, "Beginnings and Endings.")

The sobering fear that whatever happened to the dinosaurs could also happen to us is what makes this such a compelling mystery. Universal problems include problems of life and death, of spirituality, of people who were representative of ourselves. The universal problem is one that will affect *you*.

## Mysterious Comments

"There are more things under heaven and earth than are dreamed of in your philosophy."
—William Shakespeare

# I Love a Mystery

There was a radio program called *I Love a Mystery* in the distant past, when radio was what people listened to for entertainment and television was just a science fiction device used in Saturday-morning movie serials. In the show, the three protagonists—Jack, Doc, and Reggie—went around the world solving mysteries. And when they solved a mystery, that mystery was *solved!*

Well, we, too, love a mystery. And we will present a lot of them to you in the next few hundred pages. Unfortunately, as you can tell by the title of this book, few of them have definitively and absolutely, cross-our-heart-and-hope-to-die been solved.

## The Great Story

The second part of what makes something a mystery has to do with the human fascination with and need for stories and storytelling. Above all, we need to know how a story ends.

A story becomes a mystery when it doesn't have an ending or when the facts of the ending are in dispute. Every story needs an ending—preferably a happy ending, but at least *some* sort of ending. When there is no known ending to a story, human beings will search for one—and we have a mystery.

## The Great Mystery

The saga of Lizzie Borden is a story that combines a universal question with a riveting storyline. In Fall River, Massachusetts, in 1892, somebody killed Lizzie's father and stepmother, hacking at them both savagely about the head with an axe. Lizzie was tried for the murders and acquitted.

Now, worse crimes have been committed and continue to be committed—crimes that go unremarked upon (except in the town or area in which they take place). But 100 years later, the Borden case continues to fascinate us. Could a proper Victorian young lady, with no known history of violence and no real motive, viciously chop her father and stepmother to death with an axe? How could she have done it without getting a drop of blood on her dress? If Lizzie didn't do it, who did? Could a mad fiend have snuck down Second Street in the middle of a hot summer day with neighbors sitting out on their porches all around to catch the breeze? And then snuck away again unseen, bloody axe in hand—an axe that was never found?

Why has this story—of Lizzie and her parents, her sister Emma, her Uncle John, and Bridget the serving girl—been told and retold, become the subject of books, TV shows, poems, songs, an opera, and a ballet? It's the *mystery* of it, to be sure! (For more on the story of Lizzie Borden, see Chapter 19, "Did Lizzie Borden Take an Axe?")

**Mysterious Comments**

"Lizzie Borden took an axe
And gave her mother forty whacks.
When she saw what she had done,
She gave her father forty-one!"

—Anonymous rhyme

# The Unknown vs. the Unknowable

Believe it or not, there are different types of "unsolved" mysteries. In some cases, the mystery is unsolved in that nobody knows, or even thinks he knows, the solution. Some of the deeper philosophical questions that have bothered human beings since we first developed the ability to think fall into this category. Where did the universe come from? How did life begin? Is there intelligent life anywhere else in the universe? People have "answers" in the form of opinions—many if not most astronomers now believe that there *is* intelligent life elsewhere, for example—but nobody *knows*.

### Mysterious Comments

Faustus: Then where is hell and how came you out of it?

Mephistopheles: Why this is hell, nor am I out of it.

—Christopher Marlowe, *Doctor Faustus*

Also in the category of completely unsolved, and possibly unsolvable, mysteries are lesser but still fascinating problems. What happened to Judge Crater? Where did Ambrose Bierce disappear to? Just what (or where) did Plato have in mind when he wrote about an ancient kingdom called "Atlantis"?

In other cases, the mystery is both solved and unsolved—solved in the opinion of most people concerned but unsolved in the opinion of a small but insistent minority. Most of us, for example, believe that humankind reached the moon with the Apollo spacecraft and even brought home samples of moon rocks, which have given scientists great insight into how the moon was created. But there are people who firmly believe that the Apollo missions were faked—that the scenes of astronauts walking on the moon were actually shot in a huge underground cavern somewhere in the Nevada desert. Mystery can definitely be in the eye of the beholder.

Likewise, the majority may think of some mysteries as being unsolved, while a select few know—or think they know—"the truth." UFOs—unidentified flying objects—fall into this category. Many people have seen strange-looking flying objects that they were unable to identify. In some cases, the viewer was a pilot or a professional observer who was familiar with all sorts of airborne objects and who was convinced that what he saw was none of them.

Most of the professionals—Air Force experts, physicists, meteorologists, psychologists, and others—who have analyzed these sightings have found that some few of them are, indeed, mysterious and remain unexplained. There are many possible explanations, all of them intriguing, and some experts favor one explanation over another. But they don't know which, if any, is the true one, and they continue to wait for better evidence.

There are people, however, for whom the mystery of the UFOs is no mystery at all. They "know" that flying saucers are visitors from another planet whose alien crews have come to earth to experiment on human subjects, or to lead us in the paths of righteousness, or to save 144,000 of the "elect" during the coming Armageddon, or to make secret deals with certain high-placed officials for reasons of their own. (For what's known, what's merely supposed, and what remains to be known about UFOs, see the chapters in Part 5, "Inhuman Events.")

## Shakespeare's Plays

Some mysteries have been "solved" by several different groups with several different solutions. The problem of who really wrote Shakespeare's plays falls into this category. Was it Shakespeare himself? Was it Christopher Marlowe? Was it Edward de Vere, the Seventeenth Earl of Oxford? Was it Sir Francis Bacon? Or was it, as some have suggested, another man named William Shakespeare?

There are adherents in each of these camps, and they adhere to their point of view with a sticky insistence, ignoring facts that are distasteful to them and chewing heartily on "facts" that are more pleasing to their palate. If you study the theories put forth by these groups, you are likely to come to the opinion that the plays couldn't have been written by anyone. (For more on Shakespeare, whoever he was, see Chapter 26, "Will the Real William Shakespeare Please Stand Up?")

## The Laws by Which the Universe Works

Ironically, some mysteries, with each solution, become more mysterious. The workings of the physical universe—involving gravity, acceleration, and inertia—fall into this category. Back in the seventeenth century, Sir Isaac Newton devised a set of "laws" to explain these concepts, and his explanation seemed to cover the observed facts very well for a couple hundred years. Then, in 1905, Albert Einstein theorized that, over very large distances and at very high speeds, Newton's laws wouldn't work. Some very clever tests were performed, and Einstein's proposed laws were shown to be valid.

Now it seems that, over very tiny distances and with very tiny particles, a whole new set of laws comes into play. Physicists are still working on them; one more layer of the onion is being peeled away. There may be—and probably are—still more layers that we will peel away in turn as our understanding increases.

We have a couple of friends who are physicists. They use a gadget called a particle accelerator to question the universe. A particle accelerator is bigger than a couple of football fields, and it whirls pieces of atoms around at extremely high speeds to smack them into things. This is their way of asking some basic questions about the universe and how it works. And now they know—or think they have a pretty good idea—of how and when the universe was created and what might happen to it in the future.

But for all the knowledge that scientists and philosophers have gained since humans began to ask questions, the wise ones will admit that there are still many more things out there that we don't understand. And the really wise scientists and philosophers will admit that many of the things we do "know" are probably wrong.

## The Mysterious Past

Some mysteries are mysteries because their answers have been lost somewhere in the past. Some of these are what we might call cosmic mysteries, in which the hand of humanity is absent from the event, like how the moon was created or what killed the dinosaurs. Some are mysteries out of ancient human past, like who built Stonehenge and why or what secrets are encoded into the Great Pyramid of Khufu.

**No Mystery Here**

For a look at Stonehenge and the Great Pyramid, see Chapter 10. For a look at mysterious disappearances, check out Chapters 2, 3, and 4. For the criminal mysteries, see Chapters 17, 18, and 19.

Then there are mysteries that stem from a lack of eyewitnesses, like what happened to the brig *Mary Celeste*. And there is another sort of mystery, the cover-up, in which someone very much didn't want anyone to know what really happened or who was behind it. What really happened to James Hoffa? In other cases, the authorities *think* they know what happened, but there is strong reason to doubt the official verdict. Who kidnapped the Lindbergh baby is one of these, as is who killed Sam Sheppard's wife and who committed the murder for which Sacco and Vanzetti were executed.

## A Little Help for My Friends

I'm going to present the most balanced view I can of our various mysteries and their possible solutions. In some cases, when the weight of evidence or scientific knowledge comes down strongly on one side of an argument, I'll say so. In cases in which I have a strong opinion about what happened or believe that one group's opinions are questionable, I'll exercise my authorly prerogatives and tell you what I think. You're free to disagree (although I should point out that, as Sam Goldwyn is reputed to have said, "I may not always be right, but I am *never* wrong").

# A Really Good Story

We've been reading about and collecting information on all sorts of mysteries for many years. When we began writing *The Complete Idiot's Guide to Unsolved Mysteries*, we had to decide which mysteries to include. So we asked ourselves the following questions, which became the criteria for inclusion:

➤ Is the mystery really a *mystery?*

➤ Is the underlying story either interesting enough or important enough for the reader to care about?

➤ Is there at least a reasonable probability that the story is true?

➤ If a solution to the mystery has been offered, is there room for reasonable doubt?

➤ If the mystery has almost certainly been solved, is the solution questionable enough that people still consider it a mystery?

If you are a connoisseur of the unsolved mystery, you have your own favorites, and you might not find them in this book. But we're sure you'll enjoy reading about the ones we've chosen for you. After all, what can make better reading than a good mystery?

---

### The Least You Need to Know

➤ An unsolved problem or unanswered question becomes a mystery because of two factors: its importance and relevance to us and its fascinating storyline.

➤ There are many types of mysteries—mysteries of the natural world, mysteries of authorship, mysteries of the cosmos, mysteries of the human.

➤ Sometimes the solution only deepens the mystery.

➤ Humans are very adept at creating their own mysteries including disappearing ships, airplanes, and people and mysterious monuments built for unknown purposes.

➤ Humans, like cats, are creatures of curiosity. This, ultimately, is what makes for mystery.

---

# Chapter 2

# Disappearing Ships and Planes

---

**In this Chapter**

➤ The *Flying Dutchman*—doomed to sail for an eternity

➤ The mystery of the *Mary Celeste*

➤ The Bermuda Triangle

➤ The disappearing Avengers

---

Ships sink and airplanes crash. The *Titanic*, brand new and "unsinkable," hit an iceberg and sank on her maiden voyage in 1912 with 1,513 casualties. The greatest airplane disaster occurred on 27 March 1977 at Santa Cruz de Tenerife in the Canary Islands, when a Pan American 747 trying to land collided with a KLM 747 already on the runway, killing 582 people. (The miracle is that 61 people survived.)

Such accidents are certainly tragedies, but they aren't mysteries. We know what happened, we know (usually) who the victims were, and given enough time, we usually figure out why it happened. It took about 80 years in the case of the *Titanic*, but now we know the iron plates that made up the ship's sides were brittle—not really anyone's fault, they didn't understand quality control very well back then—and the rivets were strained. So the first good hit by an iceberg did her in.

But what happens when a ship or an airplane just disappears—when we don't know whether the ship sank or the plane crashed, where it happened, why it happened, or whether there were any survivors? In contemporary language, the event lacks closure. And that, along with the mystery of just what happened, is why such stories become *legends*.

Let's look at a few of these vanishings and unexplained events at sea or in the air and see what we can make of them.

# De Vliegende Hollander

The *Flying Dutchman* (or *De Vliegende Hollander,* as the Dutch say) is a legendary ghost ship often said to be seen sailing off the Cape of Good Hope during stormy weather. Seeing her is supposed to bring the worst sort of bad luck—particularly to sailors rounding the Cape.

The legend is that, with a heavy wind against him and unable to make headway around the Cape, Captain Van der Decken swore a powerful oath that his ship would round the Cape if it took an eternity. He apparently is being given his chance. Some people who claim to have seen the ghost ship say that its crew consists of just four people: the captain, the boatswain, the cook, and one sailor. They all have long beards and staring eyes. If the ship is hailed and asked its name or destination, it immediately disappears. Or so they say.

The novelist Sir Walter Scott, in a note to his poem "Rokeby," says that the legend of the *Dutchman* was based on a ship that was carrying a cargo of precious metal. According to Scott, a horrible murder happened on board, and then the plague broke out among the crew; the result was that the ship was forbidden to land at any port. The 1839 novel *The Phantom Ship* by Captain Frederick Marryat tells of Captain Van der Decken's son Philip spending his life searching for his father and the *Flying Dutchman.*

The legend is best known today because of Richard Wagner's 1843 opera *Derfliegende Holländer* (*The Flying Dutchman,* this time in German), most of which he adapted from a tale by Heinrich Heine. Wagner has Captain Van der Decken under a curse to sail for all eternity unless he can find a wife willing to sacrifice everything for his sake. The captain wants desperately to give up his cursed immortality and accept death, and he is finally redeemed by the love of Senta, a Norwegian maiden.

Is there any truth to the legend of the *Flying Dutchman?* Some mythologists claim that all legend is based on some sliver of truth, however thin. Certainly, many ships were lost in the early days trying to round the Cape of Good Hope with its bad weather and its unmarked shoals. But which of them the story is based on is unknown. I'm open to suggestions.

# The *Mary Celeste*

There is no doubt that there really was a ship named *Mary Celeste,* and the facts concerning what happened to her were taken down by a British Vice Admiralty Board of Inquiry shortly after the events occurred. The stories created from these facts vary greatly from storyteller to storyteller, becoming wilder and more remarkable with each retelling. Even the most conservative account of the events, however, presents us with a tale of true mystery with no easy or truly satisfactory solution.

### What Does This Mean?

Probably the greatest loss of life in a shipwreck was on 3 December 1948, when a Chinese Nationalist troop ship evacuating troops from Ying-k'ou, Manchuria, sank with an estimated loss of 3,000 lives.

### Mysterious Comments

We met the Flying Dutchman,
By midnight he came,
His hull was all of hell fire,
His sails were all aflame;
Fire on the main-top,
Fire on the bow,
Fire on the gun-deck,
Fire down below.

Four-and-twenty dead men,
Those were the crew,
The devil on the bowsprit,
Fiddled as she flew,
We gave her the broadside,
Right in the dip,
Just like a candle,
Went out the ship.

—Charles Godfrey Leland, "The Flying Dutchman," 1877

## The Story

The *Mary Celeste* was a 104-foot-long *brigantine* displacing 282 tons of water. When she was first launched in a Spencer Island, Nova Scotia, shipyard in 1860, she had a single deck with a cabin, and her name was the *Amazon.* After a decade of undistinguished service during which she had been run aground in Glace Bay, Prince Edward Island, she was sold at auction in New York City for $2,600. Her new owners spent about $14,000 rebuilding her, adding an upper deck and outfitting her for the Atlantic service. They renamed her the *Mary Celeste.*

### What Does This Mean?

A **brigantine** is a two-masted sailing ship in which the forward mast is square-rigged (with square sails) and the main mast is schooner-rigged (with triangular sails).

Captain Benjamin Briggs, one of the new owners, took over as captain of the *Mary Celeste*. He was 37 years old and was well-regarded both as a skipper and as a man. This would be his fourth command; he previously captained the three-masted schooner *Forrest King,* the bark *Arthur,* and the brig *Sea Foam.* But *Mary Celeste* was the first ship he commanded in which he had an ownership interest.

## Final Voyage

On 7 November 1872, the *Mary Celeste* left New York harbor with a crew of seven in addition to Captain Briggs; the captain's wife, Sarah; and their two-year-old daughter Sarah Matilda. They were headed for Genoa, Italy, with a cargo of 1,700 barrels of unrefined alcohol.

Eight days later, on 15 November, the British Brig *Dei Gratia,* commanded by a Captain Moorhouse, set sail from New York for Gibraltar. On 4 December, not quite three weeks into her voyage, the *Dei Gratia* caught up with the *Mary Celeste.* Their position, as recorded in the log of the *Dei Gratia,* was 38 degrees 20 minutes north latitude, 17 degrees 15 minutes west longitude, which would put them about 590 miles west of Gibraltar.

The *Mary Celeste* was sailing with the wind, and three sails were set, but something about her didn't look right to Captain Moorhouse. He sailed within hailing distance and hailed and hailed. There was no answer, no evidence of life aboard the *Mary Celeste.* Moorhouse sent a boarding party headed by his mate Mr. Deveau across to investigate. What they found was a ship in perfect sailing order, fully stocked with food and water, cargo intact—and no crew.

### No Mystery Here

Santa Maria Island, the southeasterly island of the Azores group, was known as St. Mary's Island during the nineteenth century.

Captain Benjamin Briggs, his wife, their two-year-old daughter, First Mate Albert Richardson, Second Mate Andrew Gilling, Cook E.W. Head, and seamen Arien Harhens, Gotlieb Goodschoad, Bos Larensen, and Volkert Lorenzeau were not on board the *Mary Celeste,* and there was no sign of why they left or that they had in any way prepared to go. The yawl boat, a small four-oared boat carried over the main hatch, was gone, so the missing crew presumably had left in that. But why?

The ship's log was lying open on Mate Richardson's desk, and the last entry was dated 24 November 1872, 10 days before. The entry read: "Weather, fine, wind, light; St. Mary's Island distant about six miles. Latitude 37 deg. N, Longitude 25 deg. O2" W." This is about 600 miles from where the ship was found.

Except for the ship's logbook, the ship's papers were missing as were the sextant and whatever other navigation instruments Captain Briggs might have had. But the captain's and the crew's possessions were present and apparently untouched, and there were toys on the bed as though two-year-old Sarah Matilda had been playing with them up until the moment she left.

On closer inspection of the ship, Mr. Deveau found that two of the sails, the upper topsail and the foresail, had blown away. Three sails, the lowertopsail, foretopmast staysail, and the jib, were set. The remaining sails were all furled save the main staysail, which was loose on top of the forwardhouse. The missing sails had probably been lost after the crew had departed, but why were some sails furled and some set? Water was in the forwardhouse, and the main cabin looked as though there had been water in it; some things in it were still wet. There was three and a half feet of water in the lower hold, which is not as bad as it sounds since, with the hold packed with barrels, any incoming water would rise quickly.

## Fancy Free

So far, the details are pretty much agreed upon by all accounts. Now, however, we get to some "facts" that may or may not be strictly accurate. They are the sort of embellishments that writers over the past 130 years would be sorely tempted to put in to add an air of romance and mystery to what is already a pretty romantic and mysterious tale.

Some accounts have it that the table was set for breakfast with plates of bacon and eggs, bread and butter, and cups of coffee laid out. One account has the coffee still warm in the cups, but since the last log entry was a week old, that is highly unlikely. A phial of oil is said to have been sitting, unspilled, on top of Mrs. Briggs' sewing machine, which would indicate calm seas in the 10 days since the disappearance of the crew.

And then there's the sword. A naval dress sword was found under Captain Briggs's bed, or perhaps it was hanging on the wall. It was covered with bloodstains, or perhaps they were rust stains. Some accounts mention no stains at all.

## The Inquiry

A salvage crew headed by Captain Moorhouse's mate, Mr. Deveau, took the *Mary Celeste* into Gibraltar. The court of inquiry questioned the salvors at length and pondered what had happened to Captain Briggs and his family and crew. They were able to come to no conclusions. "Every part of the vessel, inside and outside, was in good order and condition," the salvors testified.

There were rumors of plotting and evil in the wake of the trial. It was said that Captain Moorhouse had planted some crew members aboard the *Mary Celeste* to murder the rest of the crew and wait for the *Dei Gratia* to catch up so that the *Mary Celeste* could be claimed for salvage. There was no indication that this could be so, and it hardly seemed worth the trouble for a cargo of raw alcohol.

### The Mystery Deepens

In the January 1884 issue of *The Cornhill Magazine,* there was a story called "J. Habakuk Jephson's Statement," which explained the whole mystery of the "*Marie Celeste.*" An elaborate and romantic adventure yarn loosely based on the *Mary Celeste* case of 12 years before, it convinced much of the readership that it had been written by the most popular writer of the day, Robert Louis Stevenson (*Cornhill Magazine* stories were traditionally unsigned), and the rest of the readers that it was a true account of the *Mary Celeste.* The British advocate general in Gibraltar even sent a long telegram insisting that "Jephson" had his facts wrong. The author was in fact a young and still unknown Arthur Conan Doyle, who would not write his first Sherlock Holmes story for another four years.

Speaking of raw alcohol, another of the popular theories of the day was that demon rum had done in the crew. The temperance movement was in full swing in the United States, and the evils of alcohol were being viewed with alarm everywhere. Surely the fact that the *Mary Celeste* was carrying a cargo of alcohol must be the cause of the tragedy. Secretary of the Treasury William A. Richard stated the case in a letter published on the front page of the *New York Times* on 25 March 1873:

> The circumstances of the case tend to arouse grave suspicion that the master, his wife, and child, and perhaps the chief mate, were murdered in the fury of drunkenness by the crew, who had evidently obtained access to the alcohol with which the vessel was in part laden.

## Looking at the Facts

Here is one analysis of the facts, which may not solve the mystery but will trim down the number of possible solutions a bit. If you don't like our analysis, you are of course free to develop your own.

➤ The fact that the yawl boat was gone indicates that the crew used it to depart the ship.

➤ The fact that they apparently took nothing with them indicates that they left in a hurry and that they probably expected to be able to return to the ship later.

➤ The fact that Captain Briggs was an experienced shipmaster and that he had his wife and child aboard eliminates some of the sillier suggestions such as (We're not making this up, someone else did) the mate challenging the captain to a swimming race around the ship. Supposedly, a shark came and ate them, and more sharks ate the people trying to rescue them until there was no one left.

➤ The fact that the *Mary Celeste* was not burned and sunk shows that the events were not an elaborate plot to destroy the ship for the insurance.

## A Couple of Possibilities

So what *is* a reasonable explanation? One of the forehatch covers was found open. This raises the possibility, suggested by some people at the time, that alcohol fumes blew the cover off.

Perhaps the noise startled the crew, and seeing the vapors rising from the hatch like smoke, they thought a fire had started below. With a cargo of alcohol, they would have boarded the yawl boat and gotten as far away from the ship as quickly as possible. They should have attached a line between the boat and the ship, but the line might have parted, or they might have neglected to attach it in their haste to get away. Then the ship refused to catch fire, blithely sailing away before the passengers could return to it.

Among the other suggestions that are at least plausible are a waterspout or a sea quake that bounced the ship around so much that the crew panicked and abandoned ship. But what actually happened nobody knows, and now after more than a century and a quarter, it is probable that nobody ever will.

What happened to the crew and the captain and his family, crowded on the little yawl, can only be guessed at. Perished in a storm? Died of thirst at sea? Taken prisoner on a UFO? Again, your guess is as good as ours.

# More Missing Men

The *Mary Celeste* is not the only ship to mysteriously lose its crew. On 6 November 1840, the *London Times* reported the discovery of the French ship *Rosalie,* which had departed Hamburg and was on its way to Havana. The *Rosalie* was discovered sailing the Atlantic with all her sails set and no crew on board. Her cargo, which was reported to be valuable, was intact, and the only living things aboard were several half-starved canaries in their cages.

On 21 June 1921, the *New York Times* reported that the *Carroll A. Deering*, a five-masted schooner sailing from Rio de Janeiro to Norfolk, Virginia, had run aground near Diamond Shoals, North Carolina. The 11-man crew that had been aboard when the ship left Barbados, British West Indies, her last port of call, was nowhere to be found. Like the *Mary Celeste* before her, the *Carroll A. Deering* had been mysteriously abandoned. The table was set for a meal, the meal was ready in the galley, but there was nobody to eat it. The ship's cat was found in the captain's cabin.

**17**

### The Mystery Deepens

A couple of days after the *Carroll A. Deering* ran aground, a bottle was cast up on shore with a message inside it: "An oil-burning tanker has boarded us and placed our crew in irons. Get word to headquarters of the Company at once." It was supposedly signed by the ship's mate. In all probability it was a hoax because, if pirates *had* captured the ship and intended to kill the crew (none of whom were ever found), why would they delay? Why the irons? And if the mate were in irons, how did he write the message, procure the bottle, and toss it off the ship? Besides, wouldn't he want the police or the coast guard notified rather than the company?

### What Does This Mean?

**The Bermuda Triangle** is an area in the Atlantic Ocean bounded by Bermuda and the coast of North America from Florida to as far north as whoever is using the term chooses to claim. Ships and planes are said to disappear at an above-average rate in this region.

# The Eternal Bermuda Triangle

The legend of *the Bermuda Triangle* was born in December 1945 when a flight of five Navy aircraft left their Florida base on a routine training mission and was never seen again. The story is usually told something like this:

## *The Disappearing Avengers*

Shortly after 2 P.M. on Wednesday, 5 December 1945, Flight 19, a training flight of five Grumman TBM-3 Avenger torpedo bombers, took off from Fort Lauderdale Naval Air Station on a practice bombing and navigation run. The scheduled route of Flight 19 was simple: 160 miles due east, 40 miles north, and then back to base. The Avengers had three-man crews consisting of a pilot, who was an officer, and two enlisted men. On this flight, however, one of the enlisted men was missing—he had a premonition of impending doom and had requested removal from flying status.

All the pilots and crews were highly experienced. It was a simple, almost routine drill, the weather was fine, and since World War II had been over for about four months, there was no threat of enemy interference. About an hour and a half into the mission, the radio man at the Naval Air Station tower received a message from the flight leader:

LEADER: Control tower, this is an emergency. We seem to be off course. We cannot see land ... Repeat ... We cannot see land.

TOWER: What is your position?

LEADER: We are not sure of our position. We can't be sure of just where we are. We seem to be lost.

TOWER: Assume a heading of due west.

LEADER: We don't know which way is west. Everything is wrong ... strange ... We can't be sure of any direction. Even the ocean doesn't look as it should.

At around 4 P.M., a different pilot called in as flight leader. This was an indication that the original flight leader had turned over his command, being either confused or panicked, neither of which was encouraging.

[NEW] LEADER: We're not certain where we are. We must be about 225 miles northeast of base ... It looks like we're ...

And then the signal cut out.

The Naval Air Station promptly sent out a search plane, a huge Martin Mariner with a crew of 13. After several radio transmissions, the Mariner went strangely silent. None of the planes from training Flight 19 nor the Martin Mariner was ever seen again.

At 7 P.M., a radio operator in the Miami tower heard a faint call: "FT FT FT ..." And then nothing. Those were the call letters of Flight 19, but the Avengers of Flight 19 didn't have enough fuel to still be airborne after five hours.

## "The Devil's Triangle"

The six planes were lost over a section of the Atlantic Ocean that has become known as "The Devil's Triangle" or "The Graveyard of the Atlantic," among other colorful names. Hundreds of ships and planes have been lost in this area in the past 300 years, many of them in the years since the tragedy of Flight 19. It was only after Flight 19, however, that anyone began treating the Bermuda Triangle as an area of the Atlantic with unique dangers that were greater, more frequent, and more mysterious than elsewhere.

Is an evil presence emanating from an area of the sea bounded by Bermuda to the north, the coast of Florida to the west, and Puerto Rico to the south? Is there a portal into another dimension there through which passing craft are occasionally flung? Is the area a UFO landing base? Are people unlucky enough to be close enough to see UFOs coming in casually destroyed? Is there another and even stranger explanation? Or is the whole thing just a myth?

Let's look more closely at the story of the Avengers.

# Flight 19

The preceding facts are fairly accurate but with several twists or distortions that together can turn a tragedy into a mystery. Flight 19 did take off a little after 2 P.M. on that Wednesday. There was one crew member missing, but he didn't have a premonition—he had only four months left to serve and had asked to be relieved of flight duty. The pilots and crew were not highly experienced; all the pilots but the flight leader, Lieutenant Charles Taylor, and all the crew but one were in training.

The provocative dialogue quoted (including the eerie, "Everything is wrong … strange … We can't be sure of any direction. Even the ocean doesn't look as it should.") is nowhere in the investigative report, although it shows up in several books on the Bermuda Triangle.

The weather had been fine when the planes took off, but it steadily deteriorated as the day progressed. The radio transmissions were so bad that they broke up constantly; the tower couldn't be sure what the pilots were saying. Taylor, who was an experienced pilot, was new to the area and apparently believed that he and his flight were over the Gulf of Mexico when they were actually north of the Bahamas. His decision was to fly east, which took him farther and farther from land. By the time the direction-finding stations had located the flight in the Atlantic, he was out of radio contact. The planes ran out of gas while far east of the coast and crashed at sea. At least this is the best guess of aeronautical experts who have studied the case.

The Martin Mariner did disappear while hunting the lost flight, but a great explosion was heard and a fireball was seen by several land-based observers right where the Mariner should have been at that moment. The planes were known to leak gas fumes, and a spark or a crewman sneaking a cigarette could have caused the explosion.

So what we have is not so much a mystery but a compounded tragedy. Only to those who would make it a mystery does it remain mysterious.

# Other Bermuda Triangle Mysteries

Not all of the disappearances in the area have been so amenable to explanation. Let's look at a few of the other tragedies that have enabled the Bermuda Triangle to keep its evil and eerie reputation.

## The H.M.S. Atalanta

On 31 January 1880, the British training ship H.M.S. *Atalanta* left Bermuda for a trip back to her home port of Portsmouth with a crew of 290 cadets and officers. She was never seen again. The weather on the return trip was heavy, however, the ship was balky, and the crew was untrained. A seaman who was invalided off the *Atalanta* before her last voyage reported that, in his opinion, most of the officers were no better trained than the cadets.

### The U.S.S. Cyclops

On 4 March 1918, the Navy collier U.S.S. *Cyclops* left Barbados in the West Indies with a crew of 309 men and a cargo of manganese ore. She was one of the largest ships in service at that time, with a length of 542 feet and a displacement of 19,600 tons. She never arrived at Norfolk.

Since World War I was still active at that time, it was at first thought that the *Cyclops* had been sunk by a German U-boat, but after the war it was established that no German U-boats had been anywhere near her probable course. If she had hit a mine or been sabotaged, the ocean would have been littered with debris from the sinking, and the men would have had time to get off in the lifeboats. The Navy continued searching the area until May of that year but found nothing. President Wilson was quoted as saying, "Only God and the sea know what happened to the great ship."

### A Missing DC-3

On the morning of 28 December 1948, a chartered DC-3 was en route from San Juan, Puerto Rico, to Miami, Florida. The pilot, Captain R.E. Linquist, radioed that he was 50 miles south of Miami at 4:13 A.M. The plane never arrived. No debris from it was ever found.

# The *Scorpion*

Around midnight on 21 May 1968, the atomic submarine *Scorpion* radioed a routine position report to her base at Norfolk. At the time, she was just off the Azores. She never made it home. She was eventually found 400 miles southwest of the Azores, broken in two and lying in water over two miles deep. This is far from the usual border of the Bermuda Triangle, but mythmakers are always willing to expand the boundaries to add a good wreck to their collection.

If you are fascinated by the Bermuda Triangle, any good book on the subject will list a hundred incidents we haven't mentioned here. Another book will probably list a different hundred.

So is the Bermuda Triangle particularly dangerous, especially cursed, the site of a secret UFO base, or the location of a portal to another dimension? I won't scoff at anyone's beliefs, but we think that humans and their devices are fallible enough to explain the tragedies without the need to invoke the supernatural.

## The Mystery Deepens

The atomic submarine *Thresher* had been lost in a similar inscrutable accident in 1963, but her location 220 miles east of Cape Cod made it hard to blame the Bermuda Triangle. In the same year the Scorpion went down, the French submarine *Minerve* and the Israeli submarine *Dakar* disappeared in the Mediterranean. Two years later, the *Eurydice*, another French submarine, likewise vanished in the Mediterranean. Part of the *Eurydice* was eventually located, but no cause for the tragedy could ever be determined.

## The Least You Need to Know

➤ The story of the *Flying Dutchman,* doomed to sail for an eternity, is a legend that might be based on some morsel of fact.

➤ In 1872, the brigantine *Mary Celeste* was found adrift without her captain, his wife and child, or the crew, although the ship was in perfect condition.

➤ In 1920, the *Carroll A. Deering,* a five-masted schooner, ran aground near Diamond Shoals, North Carolina. The 11-man crew had vanished.

➤ In 1945, five Grumman Avenger airplanes disappeared at sea off the coast of Florida. A rescue plane sent to look for survivors also vanished. This gave birth to the Bermuda Triangle legend.

➤ Hundreds of shipwrecks, plane crashes, and disappearances have been attributed to the malevolent influence of the Bermuda Triangle. A skeptic might say that they are no more than the workings of chance.

# Chapter 3

# Disappearing People

### In This Chapter

➤ Now you see them, now you don't

➤ The mystery of Benjamin Bathurst

➤ Charlie Ross: the first notable American kidnap victim

➤ Ambrose Bierce and Ambrose Small

➤ The girl who disappeared twice

➤ A disappearing judge and a disappearing crook

I once knew a lady who met a man on a subway while on her way from her classes at Barnard College in Manhattan to her home in Queens. Before she reached her stop, she and her new acquaintance got off and went away together (if I remember correctly, they got off at Queens Plaza and then took the F train back down to West Fourth Street in Greenwich Village), she leaving her husband and he his wife. Nobody knew what had happened to them. Two weeks later, they got around to calling their respective spouses and the mystery of their disappearance, for better or worse, was solved.

People disappear every day for all sorts of reasons. They are abducted, get amnesia, have wanderlust, or become fed up and walk away from their normal lives. Some of them don't return.

## Here There Be Dragons

In March 1895, a painter named John Osborne was walking down a country road in England when he heard the hoofbeats of a horse behind him. He turned and saw a rider approaching. The rider seemed to be having some trouble controlling his mount, so Osborne jumped aside. Abruptly the hoofbeats ceased, and when he looked again, both horse and rider had disappeared. This is the sort of experience that can cause a person to doubt not only their own senses, but the basic physical structure of the universe.

Some disappearances truly are mysterious. Either the person who went "poof!" was someone prominent or important enough that you would think somebody would have seen him or her, or the circumstances were such that the disappearance itself seemed impossible. Let's look at a few of these.

# The Mystery of Benjamin Bathhurst

In 1809, Sir Benjamin Bathurst was sent as the British ambassador to the court of the Austro-Hungarian Empire in Vienna. Britain and Austria were forming an alliance against Napoleon, and Bathurst was helping to draft the terms of the alliance.

On 25 November 1809, Bathurst was returning to Britain, crossing the continent by coach, when he stopped at an inn in the little German town of Perleberg. As his valet and his secretary stood by the door of the coach, Bathurst went forward to examine the horses to make sure they were fit to continue the journey.

After seeing to the ones on the near side, he stepped around in front of the horses to inspect the other side. At that point, Benjamin Bathurst, Ambassador Plenipotentiary of the British Empire, disappeared from history. He did not return from the far side of the coach. He did not walk away from the coach because he would have been seen by someone in the inn yard. He simply vanished.

### The Mystery Deepens

To add to the Bathurst mystery, two months after he disappeared, on 23 January 1810, a notice appeared in a Hamburg newspaper saying that Bathurst was safe and well and that his friends had received a letter from him. It was not true, however; his friends had not heard from him at all, and they never did. Who put the notice in the paper and why is not known either.

One theory that went around at the time was that Bathurst had been abducted by agents of Napoleon to make things difficult for the British-Austrian alliance. When asked about this in later years, Napoleon denied it. And besides, it doesn't make the disappearance any less a mystery. If Bathurst was abducted against his will, why didn't he cry out? Why didn't anyone hear anything? And how could it have been done without someone noticing? No, that "solution" didn't solve anything. Benjamin Bathurst disappeared 200 years ago, and we have yet to understand how it happened, why it happened, or what became of him.

# Poor Charlie Ross

The first kidnapping in the United States to become a cause celebre was the abduction, on 5 July 1874, of Little Charles Brewster Ross. Charlie and his six-year-old brother were taken into a buggy by two men and were driven from their home in Philadelphia to a place about two hours to the north, where the brother was let out of the buggy and Charlie was carried off.

Charlie's father, Christian K. Ross, immediately posted a $300 reward for the child's recovery or for information regarding the abduction. But the sum mentioned did not meet with the kidnappers' notions; they sent Ross a letter demanding a $20,000 ransom, along with a threat to kill the child if the money was not forthcoming.

Newspapers across the country followed the case—on which there was little substantial progress—and wrote editorials denouncing the practice of kidnapping. As the *New York Times* put it in an article on 14 July:

> Must it, then, be accepted as true that any of us are liable to have our children stolen from the public streets and in open day? It is extremely unlikely that the child of any reader of this article will be stolen from him, but this Philadelphia business shows that any of us is liable to such a loss; for what may be done in one instance, and in one place, may be done in another instance and in another place.
>
> Of perils by night we are careful enough, with our combination locks, burglar-alarms, and private watchmen, but that there are perils by day which also demand our serious attention this Philadelphia business is striking evidence.

Christian Ross tried to pay the ransom several times, but each time the kidnappers failed to show up. Then, two weeks after the kidnapping, the New York Police received word from an informer that the kidnappers were William Mosher and Joseph Douglass. Both men had long criminal records and were currently AWOL from a local jail where they had been waiting to stand trial for burglary.

The police began an intensive manhunt for the two, spurred on by the $20,000 reward being offered by the mayor and city fathers of Philadelphia. They had no success until December 14, when Mosher and Douglass were apprehended trying to burglarize a home on Long Island. Mosher was shot and killed; Douglass was mortally wounded but lived long enough to admit to the kidnapping, though not long enough to reveal the fate of poor Charlie.

Reported sightings of Charlie Ross came in from all over the country and continued to come for 50 years after the event, but none of them proved true. The only person ever tried for the crime was William Westervelt, Mosher's brother-in-law, who was charged with aiding in the kidnapping, writing the ransom note, and concealing the child. He was convicted and sentenced to a prison term of seven years and a fine of $1. If he knew what happened to poor Charlie Ross, he never told.

# The First Missing Ambrose

Ambrose Bierce was a sardonic misanthrope who, after serving in the Civil War, where he was promoted to the rank of major and was twice wounded, moved to California to become a journalist like his contemporaries Bret Harte and Mark Twain. Later, he turned to short-story writing and produced some notable stories that blended fantasy with realism. Perhaps the best known of these is "An Occurrence at Owl Creek Bridge," a story of a spy's hanging during the Civil War. This story has one of the strongest and most wrenching surprise endings you'll ever run across.

Bierce is remembered as the author of the *Devil's Dictionary,* which he originally published in 1906 as the *Cynic's Word Book*. It contains definitions such as these:

➤ **belladonna**   In Italian, a beautiful lady; in English, a deadly poison; thus showing the essential similarity of the two languages.

➤ **peace**   A period of stealing between two wars.

In 1893, Bierce wrote a story, "Charles Ashmore's Trail," about a man who disappears, passing into another dimension. In 1914, Bierce himself disappeared while traveling through Texas on his way to Mexico. It is believed that he was planning to join Pancho Villa, a revolutionary who was fighting the Mexican government at the time. Neither Villa nor the Mexican government ever admitted to seeing Bierce.

# A Small Story: The Second Missing Ambrose

On 2 December 1919, Canadian stockbroker and real estate dealer Ambrose Small disappeared from his office in the Grand Opera House in Toronto, Canada, a building that he owned. He was last seen in his office somewhere between five and six in the evening, and none of the secretaries in his outer office saw him leave. He was believed to be happily married, and he had no money problems. Indeed, he left over a million dollars in securities behind, and in those days, a million dollars was real money.

Newspapers all around the world carried the story of Small's disappearance, and a reward was offered for information regarding his whereabouts. There were no takers.

Then, a few days later, John Doughty, who had been Small's private secretary, also disappeared. With that, Small's wife, accompanied by the appropriate authorities, had Small's safe deposit boxes opened. In them were over a million dollars in securities, but $105,000 worth of bonds were missing and couldn't be accounted for. The police instigated a search of all appropriate places, and the missing bonds were found hidden in the home of John Doughty's sister. Doughty was eventually found hiding in a town in Oregon under the name of Cooper. He was brought back to Toronto, where he was charged with the theft of the bonds and having done away with his boss to cover the theft.

The logic was sound: Small had no reason to disappear that anyone knew about, and Doughty did have a reason to get rid of him. But how could he have done it? A newsboy testified that he had seen the missing Small sometime after five o'clock, but the boy's own father said the boy was making it up. Another newsboy claimed to have sold Small a paper sometime after six, but when he was cross-examined, it became clear that he wasn't sure of the date. Doughty was found guilty of embezzlement, but the jury concluded that nobody had any idea what had happened to Ambrose Small.

### Mysterious Comments

"Before I looked into the case of Ambrose Small, I was attracted to it by another seeming coincidence. That there could be any meaning in it seemed so preposterous that, as influenced by much experience, I gave it serious thought. About six years before the disappearance of Ambrose Small, Ambrose Bierce had disappeared. Newspapers all over the world had made much of the mystery of Ambrose Bierce. But what could the disappearance of one Ambrose in Texas have to do with the disappearance of another Ambrose in Canada? Was somebody collecting Ambroses?"

—Charles Fort, *Wild Talents*

# The Flying Officers

On 24 July 1924, a reconnaissance aircraft was sent out on a routine patrol from the British airfield in Mesopotamia. The patrol shouldn't have lasted more than a couple hours. When the plane failed to return, search aircraft were sent out to find it.

No, this isn't a story of a disappearing aircraft. The searchers found the airplane sitting in the desert, but the two men who had flown it, Flight-Lieutenant W.T. Day and Pilot Officer D.R. Stewart, were nowhere to be found. Why the plane had landed was

a mystery. There were no weather problems reported. There were no signs that the airplane had been shot at. But there it sat. The plane had fuel in it; it was even flown back to base with no problems.

But the men—what had happened to the men? The footprints of Flight-Lieutenant Day and Pilot Officer Stewart were in the sand all around the plane. They went off together for a distance of some 40 yards. And then they abruptly stopped.

Perhaps, authorities thought, hostile natives had captured the two and then brushed away their footprints as they escaped. Airplanes, armored cars, and horse patrols searched the desert for four days. Nothing was found. Nowhere did the tracks of the two men resume. There were no hostile natives, or natives of any other kind, in the area. The two men were never found.

### No Mystery Here

The story of Day and Stewart is taken from Charles Fort's book *Wild Talents*. According to Fort, the last reference to the missing airmen was in the *London Sunday News* of 15 March 1925, which reported that they were still missing.

## The Double Disappearances of Pauline

On 6 April 1922, a 12-year-old girl named Pauline Picard disappeared from her home, a farm near the city of Brest, France. Two days later, a child was found wandering in the streets of Cherbourg, 230 miles from Brest. The child had no idea who she was or what she was doing there.

The authorities, connecting the missing child with the newly found child, sent for the Picards, who traveled to Cherbourg and identified their daughter. Pauline seemed to be suffering from traumatic amnesia and did not recognize them. They took their daughter home.

Three weeks later, on the first of May, Pauline disappeared again. This time, her parents didn't hear from or about her for almost three weeks. Then came the shocking news.

On 26 May, a bicyclist was passing near the Picard farm when he saw what looked like a bundle out in the field. He went to investigate and found the body of Pauline Picard. She was naked and her head, hands, and feet were missing. Her clothes were folded neatly by her naked torso.

The inquest decided that she had wandered away from home and died of exhaustion. After all, she had wandered away once before. And what of the missing head, hands, and feet? Eaten by rodents and foxes, it was decided.

The inquest verdict makes no sense as far as I can see. Perhaps you had to be there, but here are some questions that should have at least been asked, if not answered. If the body was seen so easily from the road, it couldn't have been there for very long without being noticed. The "neatly folded clothes" would also indicate that the body hadn't been there for very long. So how did it get there? Just how did Pauline die? And perhaps the most interesting question of all, where was she for the three weeks before she was found? And just as a side question, if rodents and foxes ate the head, hands, and feet, how come they didn't so much as touch the rest of the body?

One could decide that Pauline's head had been removed and her body mutilated to make identification difficult. But then to leave the body right next to her home? And leave her easily identifiable clothes beside it? No explanation that fits the facts, including Pauline's earlier disappearance, comes to mind.

# The Disappearing Judge

A justice in the New York Supreme Court in New York City, Judge Joseph Force Crater, created one of the country's abiding mysteries on Wednesday, 6 August 1930, when he walked out of a restaurant on Manhattan's West 45th Street and hailed a cab. He climbed into the taxi, rode off, and was never seen again. His disappearance was kept quiet for a month, but when it was clear that he was not going to reappear, District Attorney Thomas C.T. Crain launched an all-out search for him and a Grand Jury investigation into his disappearance.

Crater, a graduate of Lafayette College and Columbia Law School, had a successful New York City practice before his appointment to the bench in April 1930, some four months before his disappearance. His presidency of the Cayuga Democratic Club, an important adjunct to the city's Tammany Hall political machine, had certainly been a material consideration in New York Governor Franklin D. Roosevelt's selection of Crater, but the choice wasn't purely political as shown by the fact that Crater had been endorsed by the New York Bar Association.

### The Mystery Deepens

In 1829, 101 years before Judge Crater disappeared, John Lansing, a justice on the Court of Chancery of the State of New York, left his hotel to mail a letter on the steamer for Albany. He was never seen again. It is probably no more than an interesting coincidence that Joseph Crater also served on the Court of Chancery.

Crater had cut short a vacation at his summer camp in Maine to return to the city and had spent part of Tuesday and Wednesday in his court chambers. His wife, Stella, who had remained in Maine, could shed no light on the reason for Crater's return to New York, and she professed absolute bewilderment as to his disappearance. It was shown that he had withdrawn several thousand dollars from two bank accounts and had sold $16,000 worth of stock shortly before he vanished. There was speculation that his disappearance was somehow connected to an investigation into corrupt city officials being conducted by State Attorney General Hamilton Ward. The events spurred the broader Seabury investigation that followed, but no allegation of misconduct was ever brought against the absent judge.

After seeing many witnesses and taking hundreds of pages of testimony, the Crain Grand Jury disbanded on 9 January 1931 without discovering anything of significance to explain the judge's disappearance. Two weeks later, on the 20th, Stella Crater announced that she had found in a desk drawer $6,690 in cash, a bundle of securities, and a written list of debts owed to the absent judge. On the bottom of the list was penned a note: "Am very weary. Love, Joe."

Since the police had searched the apartment several times since the judge's disappearance, including the drawer that now held the newly discovered documents, this merely deepened the mystery. Sightings of Judge Crater were reported all over the country, and for a while, the police followed up every lead. But they all came to naught. Seven years after he disappeared, he was declared legally dead and Stella remarried, but she never gave up looking for her missing first husband. And she never found him.

# Jimmy Hoffa

On 30 July 1975, James Hoffa, erstwhile boss of the Teamsters Union (1957–1967) and erstwhile convict (1967–1971), walked out of the Manchus Red Fox restaurant in Detroit and was never seen again. Like Judge Joseph Crater, Hoffa left the world of the mundane and entered American myth.

Hoffa fought his way to the top of the Teamsters Union in the 1930s, organizing Detroit locals in an atmosphere that approached physical war between union and management. His brother was shot. Their cars were bombed and their offices wrecked. Strikebreakers and police assaulted them on the street. It was a time that blurred the distinction between the unions, management, and organized crime. Mafia figures worked for both sides, and the Teamsters proved more adept than most at using violence as an organizational tool.

When Hoffa took over from Dave Beck as Teamster president, the intertwining of the union and organized crime was an established fact. The union leadership needed the gangsters to supply muscle in strike situations and to keep the faithful in line during local elections. Hoffa, with the mob's help, used the power of the union as a whip to extort money from companies employing teamsters. He used the union's pension funds as his own private bank, buying political favors with the money.

### Mysterious Comments

"Everybody has his price" was the credo by which Jimmy Hoffa managed the union. That policy resulted in payoffs for some and promises of political support or special favors for others. He kept no bank accounts, drew no checks, and when he traveled he carried an attaché case that contained up to $500,000 in cash ...

"Each month of every one of the ten years he steered the Teamster steamroller through the nation's Upper and Lower Houses, some of Hoffa's most trusted intimates would enter the offices of the representatives and senators who were on the union's 'friendship rolls' and plunk down a large manila envelope on each of those lawmakers' desk. 'Here's your copy of the magazine,' Hoffa's emissaries said. Indeed, that month's issue of *International Teamster* was in the envelope—but so were $500 to $1,000 in crisp legal tender of $50- or $100-bill denominations."

—William Balsamo and George Carpozi, *Under the Clock*

When Robert Kennedy became chief counsel to the Senate Select Committee on Improper Activities in the Labor or Management Field—more generally known as the McClellan Committee—he targeted Hoffa for special attention, describing the Teamsters' leadership as a "conspiracy of evil." Kennedy continued the attention when his brother, newly elected President John F. Kennedy, appointed him attorney general.

In 1962, Hoffa went on trial for extortion and managed to get a hung jury. How he accomplished this was revealed when he subsequently was put on trial for jury tampering. This time, he was convicted and drew an eight-year sentence. In 1964, he was put on trial again and was convicted of defrauding the union pension fund of close to two million dollars. In 1967, when his lawyers ran out of appeals, he began serving his sentence in the federal penitentiary at Lewisburg, Pennsylvania. Hoffa wanted to keep his hold on the union from Lewisburg and had his protégé Frank Fitzsimmons appointed president in his place.

But Fitzsimmons showed an unexpected stubbornness and refused to take orders from the imprisoned Hoffa. If Fitzsimmons was the president, then he was going to be the president. A very annoyed Hoffa vowed that, when he got out of prison, he would regain the union leadership.

In 1971, President Richard Nixon agreed to commute Hoffa's term to time served—but with the proviso that Hoffa must agree to renounce the Teamsters' presidency and stay out of union politics, including any seat on the ruling councils, for 10 years.

Four years later, at 2 P.M. on 30 July 1975, Hoffa went to the Manchus Red Fox restaurant in Detroit to meet three men. Half an hour later, he called his wife to say that the men hadn't arrived yet. Shortly after that, he was seen entering a car in the restaurant parking lot with a couple other men. Who the other men were is not known. Whether Hoffa ever got out of that car alive is not known. The FBI later found traces of hair and blood in the car, but no trace of Hoffa has ever been found.

# The Unfound

Many people disappear in any given year. Most of them return or are found, and the story may turn into a tragedy but is no longer a mystery. But there are many mysterious disappearances that we haven't had room to cover in this chapter. A mystery, we feel, is a disappearance with no easy solution. The world's leading lady pilot, Amelia Earhart disappeared without a trace while trying to fly the Pacific Ocean in 1937. An extensive search was carried out by the Navy, and they should have found something, but they didn't. Band leader Glen Miller was in a light plane which disappeared over the English Channel during World War II. The weather was not that bad, and again some trace of wreckage should have been found, but it wasn't. There is a question, as you will see in Chapter 17, "The Lindbergh Baby Kidnapping," as to whether the body found in the kidnapping of the Lindbergh baby was really that of the baby, in which case some septuagenarian may, all unknowing, be the eldest son of flying ace Charles Lindbergh. It's possibilities like that that make these unsolved mysteries so fascinating.

---

### The Least You Need to Know

➤ Sir Benjamin Bathurst disappeared while examining the horses pulling his carriage.

➤ Little Charlie Ross was the first American kidnap-for-ransom victim.

➤ Ambrose Bierce was headed to Mexico when he walked off the face of the earth.

➤ Ambrose Small left his office and business and was never seen again.

➤ Flight-Lieutenant Day and Pilot Officer Stewart left their aircraft in the desert and disappeared.

➤ Poor Pauline Picard disappeared twice, and the second time was not the charm.

➤ Judge Joseph Force Crater left a Manhattan restaurant, climbed into a taxicab, and rode into limbo.

➤ Teamster boss Jimmy Hoffa went to meet some men in a Detroit restaurant and never came home.

---

# Chapter 4

# Travelers to Nowhere

---

### In This Chapter

➤ Eric the Red settles Greenland—and two colonies disappear

➤ The Roanoke colony: vanished without a trace

➤ The Franklin expedition—a Northwest Passage to the unknown

---

The desire to explore, to "boldly go where no one has gone before," is one that humans delight in. Throughout history, brave people (and sometimes people who couldn't get along with their neighbors) have followed this desire, leaving for unexplored lands. Some of these explorers never came back.

Perhaps they sailed off the edge of the earth. Perhaps they were eaten by sea serpents. Or perhaps a cyclone whisked them to Oz. Whatever happened to them, we know where they ultimately wound up: in the world of the unexplained.

## Where Went the Norse?

By the tenth century A.D., the Vikings, those famous seagoing raiders from Scandinavia, had explored and colonized a number of islands to the west of their homeland including Iceland and the northern part of Scotland. It was around that time that Eric the Red, a Viking chieftain in Iceland, got into trouble for feuding with his neighbors, and he and his followers took to the longboat to search for another, less settled place to live. On the southern coast of a large island west of Iceland, he

### Here There Be Dragons

Eric seems to have been a troublemaker, even by the quarrelsome Viking standards. He had a quick temper and was unduly eager to draw his two-handed long sword. Finally, the Thorsness Thing—Norse for the ruling council—had enough of him and declared him an outlaw. This effectively meant, "Get out of here and don't come back for a long, long time."

### No Mystery Here

The son of Eric the Red, Leif Ericsson, followed in his father's footsteps as an explorer. Leif is believed to have been the first European to land in North America, sailing to Newfoundland early in the eleventh century.

found a relatively hospitable and uninhabited country with deep fiords bounded by green meadows that would make good pastures for sheep and cattle. To Eric, it must have looked a lot like home.

He decided to start a colony of his own there. To attract prospective settlers from Iceland, he named his new territory Greenland.

Eric returned to Iceland with stories of the new land he had found. Around 986 A.D., he went back to Greenland with about 30 ships full of Norse settlers and their livestock. More people followed, and two colonies were formed, the Western Settlement and the Eastern Settlement, a few hundred miles apart.

For several hundred years, the settlers on Greenland (there may have been as many as five or six thousand) subsisted by farming, raising sheep and dairy cattle, and hunting walrus, seal, and caribou. They traded walrus hides, ivory, and sealskins with their mainland kinsmen for timber and other materials they could not grow on the island. The settlements had their own government, many churches, and even a bishop appointed by the pope.

## The Little Ice Age

Around 1300 A.D., the climate of Europe and North America grew considerably colder. This cold spell, called the Little Ice Age, lasted about 500 years. Drift ice filled the sea around Greenland, making it difficult for ships to get to the island, and gradually regular trade with the settlements stopped.

We know that, around 1350, a priest from the Eastern Settlement took a trip to the Western Settlement. He found it eerily deserted except for some cattle and sheep running wild. The Eastern Settlement, which was farther south, apparently lasted longer, although no written records exist of contact with it after around 1408. The popes continued to appoint bishops for Greenland for another 200 years or so, but the bishops stayed in Rome rather than hazard the dangerous journey to their remote and ice-locked parish.

In 1721, a Danish missionary, Hans Egede, sailed to Greenland, hoping to convert the Catholic settlers to the Protestant faith. He found only abandoned buildings; their inhabitants had disappeared.

No one knows what became of the Norse settlers during those centuries of silence. As the weather grew colder and the people waited out the dark and seemingly endless winters in their sod houses, as they watched through the brief summers for merchant ships that seldom came, they must have felt increasingly isolated and hopeless. Some probably died of starvation or illness brought on by poor nutrition and harsh living conditions, but at the end, the settlers seem simply to have vanished.

## Where Did They Go?

Some people believe the last settlers may have been carried off by Basque pirates. Some believe they may have been massacred by the Thule Eskimos, who had migrated to Greenland from northern Canada as the weather became colder. But the abandoned houses and farms showed no signs of violence. Instead, they looked as though their inhabitants simply packed up and moved away, taking their important possessions with them. No one knows where they went, and no record exists that refugees from Greenland ever surfaced in Europe.

It has been suggested that the last settlers may have gone to live among the Eskimos and may eventually have been absorbed into their culture, but this doesn't seem likely either. Archaeologists who have studied the Greenland settlements have found no indication that the Norse intermarried with the Eskimos or adopted any of the Eskimos' technology or clothing, even though they were superior to the methods and materials brought by the Norse from their homeland.

Some archaeologists believe that the settlers starved to death, victims of the cold climate and the failure to adopt the Eskimos' survival techniques. Others suggest a more mundane explanation that occasional whaling and trading ships found their way to Greenland even during the Little Ice Age, and the settlements dwindled as young people left, hoping for a better life somewhere else. The lack of written records about the settlements can be explained, they say, by Renaissance Europeans having more momentous things to write about than the migrations of a few Greenlanders.

The archaeological record, however—the farmhouses and *middens* and the bodies buried in the churchyards—can only explain so much. The question of what actually happened to the Greenland Norse will probably never be answered with certainty.

### What Does This Mean?

A **midden** is what an archaeologist calls a trash heap. In the centuries before modern sanitation and garbage collection, people who lived in farms and villages often tossed their kitchen garbage, broken household objects, and other trash onto a heap on their property. For archaeologists, these piles provide valuable information about what ancient people ate and the tools and materials they used in their daily lives.

# The Roanoke Colony

The sixteenth century is often, and justifiably, called the Age of Exploration. Adventurers from Europe were sailing to far-off lands whose existence had been unknown a century before. Spain, France, and Portugal were staking claims right and left to territories in Asia, Africa, and the New World.

Queen Elizabeth encouraged her adventurous subjects to join the land rush by granting charters to men who were willing to finance expeditions to explore North America and start colonies there. Elizabeth wanted to claim some of the new country for England before Spain or France could occupy it, and she wanted to do it with private money rather than with funds from England's perpetually cash-strapped treasury. What was in it for the investors? The chance to become large landholders, gentleman farmers, in a time when arable land was a source of wealth and status. But the opportunity, as many of them learned, came with enormous risks.

## Ecstatic Reports

In 1584, Elizabeth granted a charter to one of her favorite courtiers, Sir Walter Raleigh. Raleigh quickly organized a voyage and appointed Philip Amadas and Arthur Barlowe to captain the expedition's two ships. Amadas and Barlowe left England in April of 1584.

They landed on one of the islands on the outer banks of what is now North Carolina and stayed a couple months, exploring the area. During their stay, they were generously entertained by a tribe of natives on Roanoke Island, a small island between the Outer Banks and the mainland. They returned to England with two Indians named Towaye and Manteo and with ecstatic reports of a fertile land full of useful timber and wild fruit and teeming with game and fish. The Queen, thoroughly impressed, named the new country "Virginia."

The next spring, Raleigh sent seven ships, carrying 108 men, back to Roanoke Island. Their mission was to establish a permanent English presence in the area and possibly to serve as a base of operations for attacks on Spanish ships. (England and Spain were nearly at war.) Sir Richard Grenville, the leader of the expedition, dropped the colonists at Roanoke and returned immediately to England to get more supplies. Ralph Lane was left to govern the settlement.

## The First Indian Fights

Lane and his men built a fort at the north end of the island. There they waited for more supplies, surviving by freeloading off the Indians. At first, the Indians were as generous as they had been to Amadas and Barlow, but eventually, they started running out of food to share. Lane and some of his men, angered at being turned down, reacted with violence. In what would become typical of the Europeans' idea of diplomatic negotiations, the settlers raided the Indians' villages, burned their houses, and killed several of them including a chief who had befriended them. Surprisingly, the Indians did not retaliate except by robbing and stealing the settlers' fish traps. But the friendly and mutually respectful relations established by Amadas and Barlowe the year before were badly damaged.

*An early chart of the Roanoke settlement.*

Grenville's return with supplies for the colony was delayed, and he didn't leave England until the spring of 1586. In June, while Grenville was still making his way across the Atlantic, Sir Francis Drake happened to anchor his fleet off the barrier islands, and some of his ships sailed in to Roanoke. There they found the English colonists, as a contemporary historian described them, "in great Penury and want, and out of Hope of Provisions out of England, their Number also much diminished." Without the Indians to exploit, they were hungry, miserable, and desperate. They were also afraid that the Indians were planning to attack them and destroy their fort. Drake offered to take them all back to England. After some dithering about whether they should wait to see if Grenville arrived, they took Drake's offer and left with him for home.

## Gone, All Gone

Two weeks later, Grenville arrived with the supply ships and found the fort deserted. Unwilling to risk losing England's claim to the country, and unaware of how Lane's crew had treated the Indians, he left only 15 men at the fort with two years' supplies and sailed again for home.

Meanwhile, back in England, Raleigh, unfazed by the poor development of the Grenville-Lane colony, was lining up volunteers for another one to be established near Chesapeake Bay. To attract settlers, he promised them grants of 500 acres or more of land. Raleigh appointed John White governor of the colony and designated 12 men as his assistants. White was an experienced sailor who had been in Lane's colony. A gifted artist, on his previous trip to Roanoke, White had made a series of sensitive, naturalistic drawings of Indian life. The few that survive are among the best records we have of how the natives on the island dressed, hunted, fished, and cooked their food.

### No Mystery Here

Raleigh, with creative flair, decided to call the new settlers "planters" and their holdings "plantations." The terms caught on.

### What Does This Mean?

**Privateering,** a form of legal piracy, allowed privately owned ships to attack and capture the merchant ships of an enemy country and confiscate the cargo.

## White's Turn

On 8 May 1587, White and the colonists sailed from England on three ships. There were by one count 91 men, 17 women, and 9 children. Among them were White's own daughter, Elynor, and her husband, Ananias Dare. The two Indians, Towaye and Manteo, who had been brought to England by Amadas and Gilbert, sailed with the new colonists. White's pilot was Simon Fernandez, a Portuguese navigator who had been on the 1584 voyage. The voyage from England to Virginia, with a stop in Puerto Rico, took about two and a half months. At least two of the women, Elynor Dare and Margery Harvey, were pregnant throughout the long and uncomfortable trip.

On 22 July 1587, before sailing to Chesapeake Bay, White and his ships stopped near Roanoke Island, probably to check on the men Grenville had left there the previous year. They would go no farther. There had been tensions between White and Fernandez during the trip from England, and Fernandez, possibly anxious to get back to England and maybe to do some *privateering* along the way, refused to take the colonists to Chesapeake Bay. So the settlers were stranded on Roanoke Island.

They were greeted almost immediately by ominous signs. The fort built by Lane's colonists had been torn down. Of Grenville's 15 men, no trace remained except the skeleton of one in the ruined fort. Less than a week after their arrival, one member of the group, George Howe, was ambushed and killed by Indians while fishing for crabs. The English retaliated by attacking a village supposedly belonging to the Indians who had killed Howe, but they shot a member of a friendly tribe, the Croatoans, instead. The Indian Manteo, who was a Croatoan, interceded to prevent further hostilities.

It took over a month for the settlers to unload their supplies from the ships. During that time, they rebuilt the fort and the little village of houses that the previous colonists had constructed around it. On 18 August 1587, Elynor Dare gave birth to a daughter, the first English child born in the New World. She was named Virginia in honor of her new homeland.

## Fernandez Splits

As the fall hurricane season approached, Fernandez became anxious to get on his way back to England. It was too late in the year to plant food crops, and the colonists had only a few months' worth of supplies. Some of the leaders would have to go back to England with Fernandez to arrange to bring supplies back to the colonists. The colonists asked White to take the responsibility. Reluctantly, he agreed and sailed for England with Fernandez, leaving his daughter, son-in-law, and granddaughter behind. Before he left, he arranged with the colonists that, if they moved their settlement away from the fort, they would carve their destination on a tree. If they had to leave because of an attack, they would add a Maltese cross.

Bad weather kept White from reaching England until November. Once there, he hurried to gather supplies, and within four months he had a fleet of ships together. Just then, however, the English learned that the Spanish king was organizing an armada of warships to attack England. The fleet of ships White planned to take to Virginia was needed by the English Navy, and White was left with only the two smallest. On the way to Virginia, the captains of the two ships tried, foolishly, to privateer and were attacked by larger French ships. Damaged, they were forced to return to England.

Over the next year and a half, White tried repeatedly and unsuccessfully to organize a fleet to relieve the Roanoke colony. One can only imagine what his feelings must have been as he thought of his family, stranded and short of provisions, thousands of miles away in the wilderness. It was 1590 before White was finally able to buy a passage to Roanoke with a fleet of privateers.

## All Gone—Again

The fleet anchored off the outer banks on 15 August 1590. From their anchorage, they saw smoke rising on Roanoke Island and became hopeful that the colonists were still alive. The next day, White and a party of men set out for the island in two boats. On the way, they saw another smoke column on a different island. They went ashore to investigate but found it was only a brush fire.

The next day, on the trip to Roanoke Island itself, one of their boats capsized, and six men drowned. White and the rest landed on Roanoke Island that night. At the north end of the island, they saw a light, but when they walked to it in the morning, it turned out to be only another woods fire.

On August 18, three years to the day after the birth of his granddaughter, White finally found the settlement. All the houses had been pulled down, and the area had been enclosed by a palisade made of tree trunks. Inside the enclosure, some heavy objects lay overgrown with grass, suggesting that the fort had been abandoned long before. Carved on a tree near the settlement, they found three letters, "CRO." On one of the posts of the palisade, someone had carved the word "CROATOAN." No Maltese cross had been carved with the word. White must have felt some relief at this: At least the colonists had not left in flight from an attack.

White and his search party went to Town Creek, south of the settlement, where the settlers' boats had been kept in an area fortified with small cannon, but both the boats and guns were gone.

White was forced to go back to England without learning any more of what had become of his family and the rest of the colony. White could not raise the money to return again to Roanoke and had to give up trying to find the lost colonists. In 1593, he wrote sadly to a friend, "And wanting my wishes, I leave off from prosecuting that whereunto I would to God my wealth were answerable to my will." He died in 1606 without ever knowing the fate of the family he had left so far away in the New World.

**The Mystery Deepens**

In 1602, Sir Walter Raleigh sent a couple of ships, under the command of Samuel Mace, to search for Roanoke. Mace never reached the colony but spent his time near Cape Fear gathering sassafras, which he could sell at a high price in London. The next year, Raleigh sent two ships on another expedition, which also failed to reach Roanoke. Soon afterward, Raleigh was arrested and imprisoned in the Tower of London by King James I. From that point on until he was executed in 1618, he was too preoccupied by his own problems to have anything more to do with the lost colony.

## The Mystery Persists

Jamestown, the first successful English colony in Virginia, was established in 1607. Its settlers made several attempts to find the Roanoke colonists, figuring that, with 20 years of experience surviving in the New World, they would be a valuable source of information about the area. They found no physical evidence of the colonists. In 1608, John Smith, Jamestown's governor, reported a chilling story told to him by Powhatan, an Algonquin chief. According to Powhatan, the Roanoke colonists had lived with the Chesapeake tribe for 20 years but had then been massacred by a confederacy of Indians led by Powhatan himself. Powhatan showed Smith a few metal items that he said had belonged to them.

The true fate of the Roanoke settlers has never been discovered. No physical trace has been found of their journey from the fort on Roanoke Island. Over the centuries, the lost colony became a legend, and stories, largely unfounded, were told of blue-eyed Indians with English names living the backwoods of North Carolina.

Historians have proposed a number of theories about where the colonists went after leaving Roanoke Island and what happened to them. One, of course, is that John Smith was telling the truth, and Powhatan's Indians really did massacre the settlers. Another theory is that the colonists were taken in by a tribe of Indians and were eventually assimilated by them. Some people suggest that the Indians who helped them were the friendly Croatoans, Manteo's kinsmen—a theory that fits John White's story of finding "Croatoan" carved on a tree in the fort. But others have questioned this theory because White had noted in 1587 that the Croatoans were afraid the English would take their already limited supplies of corn—which suggests they had too little food to support a hundred people in addition to their own tribesmen. They speculate that the colonists, instead of staying with the Croatoans on North Carolina's Outer Banks, may have moved to the mainland and joined one of the larger tribes there.

### The Mystery Deepens

Virginia Dare won a place in the history books by being the first child of English parents born in the New World. After Virginia's birth and before Governor John White returned to England, another baby was born in the colony. The parents were Margery and Dionys Harvey (or Harvie—the spelling of names in Elizabethan accounts lacks consistency). As little as we know about the fate of Virginia Dare, we know even less about this second English baby: No record exists of its first name or even whether it was a boy or a girl.

Another theory is that a group of Indians attacked the colonists in their fort or after they left, killed the men, and took the women and children with them. Yet another theory suggests that a company of Spanish soldiers found the fort, took the colonists hostage, and later killed them. But this does not explain why no Maltese cross, the agreed-upon sign of attack or peril, was carved on the tree.

Historians still hope that someone, someday, will find the missing pieces to the puzzle of the colonists' disappearance: Elizabethan tools and keepsakes on the site of an Indian village, for example. But nothing like that has been found as of yet.

The mystery of the disappearance of the men, women, and children of the colony remains unanswered, a haunting footnote in American history.

# The Franklin Expedition

For 300 years after Columbus sailed to America, European explorers hunted for a route around the new continent with its savage natives and miles and miles of empty wilderness. The goal was to get to China, India, and Japan with their silks and teas and spices. The route had to be to the north; the explorers already knew that there was no passage to the south. The Northwest Passage—the hoped-for sea route from the Atlantic to the Pacific Ocean over the top of North America—became the Holy Grail of arctic exploration.

In the eighteenth and nineteenth centuries, as England became a worldwide empire and a great sea power, it also became the leader in the search for the Northwest Passage. The British Navy organized and financed a series of land and sea expeditions to survey the northern coast of Canada and to explore the channels among the maze of islands above it.

By the 1840s, all but about 900 miles of the area had been explored and mapped. The Northwest Passage seemed within reach—perhaps only one more voyage away. Several eminent arctic explorers proposed a Navy expedition to survey the unmapped area and to make other scientific observations. They estimated that it could be completed in a year. After hearing their plans, Sir Robert Peel, the Prime Minister, agreed to let the Admiralty organize a voyage.

## The Expedition

The man chosen to lead the expedition was Sir John Franklin. Franklin had been knighted for leading two prior exploratory trips overland through Northern Canada to the Arctic Ocean. Even though Franklin was nearly 60 years old, he was still considered a natural for the expedition because of his experience, his leadership ability, and his interest in the scientific aspects of exploration. (He was a vice-president of the Royal Geographic Society.)

The expedition consisted of 129 men in two ships, the *Erebus* and the *Terror*. Both ships had been specially fitted for polar travel, reinforced for sailing in sea ice, and insulated against the extreme cold. Under the command of another explorer, Sir James Clark Ross, they had sailed around the continent of Antarctica in 1836–37. For Franklin's expedition, they had also been outfitted with steam engines so that they would not have to rely completely on sail to navigate the icy waters north of the North American mainland. Three years' supplies were loaded onto the ships.

**No Mystery Here**

After leading the two expeditions to the arctic, Franklin had gone south, becoming colonial governor of Van Diemen's Land (now Tasmania). He and his wife, Lady Jane Franklin, were very popular there.

*Sir John and Lady Jane Franklin.*

It was expected that the ships would have to spend the winter of 1845 to 1846 anchored off one of the remote islands above North America and that they would finish their explorations the next summer when channels would open up again in the sea ice. If the company found a waterway through the Passage, they would sail on to the Pacific. If not, they would turn around and return to England. Either way, they would get back to something like civilization by the end of 1846.

The two ships set sail down the Thames on 19 May 1845. In early July, they stopped in Greenland to take on more supplies and to send last letters home. At the end of the month, they were seen by two whaling ships and were never seen again.

## The Ships Disappear

Relatives and friends of the crew became concerned and then alarmed when 1847 came without a sighting of the *Erebus* and the *Terror*. Plans were made to send relief parties to look for them and to leave behind caches of supplies so they wouldn't starve on the barren islands, but a bad winter kept the rescue parties from starting out until the beginning of 1848.

The first parties to search the area found no sign of the missing company. As months went by with no word of their fate, the scope of the tragedy began to sink in. About 40 search parties were organized over the next 10 years. Sailing into the Passage from the Atlantic or the Pacific or searching the North American coast on land, they crisscrossed the area where the lost ships were believed to have sailed, seeking any word or sign of them or their crews.

## The First Hints

It was five years before a search party found evidence of the missing expedition, the base on Beechey Island where Franklin and the men had spent their first winter. All that remained were some ragged clothes and food tins and the graves of three seamen: John Hartnell, W. Braine, and John Torrington. Their wooden headstones told when they had died, two of them in January 1846 and the third in April of that year. But no message had been left saying where the ships had gone after leaving the island.

## Dragging Their Boat Behind Them

Four more years passed before additional clues were found. In 1853 and 1854, John Rae, a trader with the Hudson's Bay Company, led an overland search along the coast of the mainland. Twice along the way, he met Eskimos who told him about some white men who had been seen several years earlier. In the spring of 1850, they told him, a party of about 40 white men were seen traveling southward, dragging a boat with them. By signs, the Eskimos were made to understand that the white men's ships had been crushed by ice and that the men were now going to where they expected to find deer to shoot. From their appearance, the Eskimos supposed the men were getting short on provisions. They purchased a small seal from the natives.

Rae continued the Eskimos' story in his report to the Hudson's Bay Company:

> At a later date, the same season ... the bodies of about thirty white persons were discovered on the continent, and five on an island near it .... Some of the bodies had been buried (probably some of the first victims of famine), some were in a tent or tents, others under a boat that had been turned over to form a shelter, and several lay scattered about in different directions. Of those found on the island, one was supposed to have been an officer, as he and a telescope strapped over his shoulder and his double-barreled gun lay underneath him.

> From the mutilated state of many of the corpses, and the contents of the kettles, it is evident that our miserable countrymen had been driven to the last resource, cannibalism, as a means of prolonging life.

The Eskimos Rae met had a number of articles from the site, including pieces of watches, telescopes and compasses, and silver spoons and forks monogrammed with the initials of some of Franklin's officers. Rae bought as many of them as he could. Bad weather kept him from traveling to the place where the Eskimos said the bodies had been found. That fall, Rae went to England to bring the relics he had purchased to the Admiralty and Lady Franklin.

### Mysterious Comments

Back in 1828, after his second overland journey along the shore of the Arctic Ocean, Franklin had urged England to continue exploring the Arctic and searching for the Passage. Ironically, one of the factors he cited was how safe an undertaking it was. "It is, moreover," he wrote, "pleasing to reflect that the loss of life which has occurred in the prosecution of these discoveries does not exceed the average number of deaths in the same population at home under circumstances the most favorable."

The English public greeted Rae's news with indignation and denial. In the romantic spirit of the day, they couldn't accept that the heroic men of Franklin's company could have stooped to something so terrible as cannibalism. To suggest it was to desecrate their memory. Charles Dickens wrote an irate and racist editorial in which he suggested that the Eskimos had massacred the men and lied about it.

Rae responded with a defense of the Eskimos and explained his reasons, from long experience in the arctic, for believing what they had told him. In the end, after some hesitation, the Admiralty gave him the reward of $10,000 it had promised for information about the fate of the Franklin expedition.

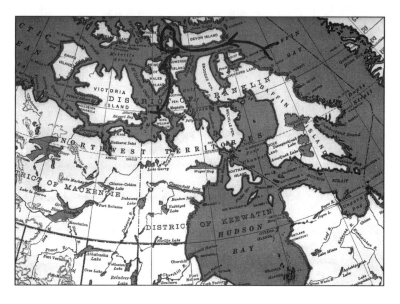

*The approximate route of the Franklin expedition.*

# No End to the Searching

After Rae's news, the British government financed no more searches for Franklin. In 1857, a privately funded expedition led by Captain Francis McClintock made another voyage to the Canadian arctic in a yacht, the *Fox*, paid for by Lady Franklin. In the spring of 1859, they met some Eskimos who had articles from Franklin's ships. The Eskimos said the items had "come from some white people who were starved upon an island." One of them also told of a ship that had been crushed by the ice in the sea off King William Island after its crew had left it.

McClintock organized two parties of men to search along the west coast of King William Island. They soon found relics: the remains of a campsite with tents, bedding and fire pits, and a series of stone *cairns*. The fourth cairn was at the place where it appeared the crew had left its ship. The ground was heaped with discarded clothing and was strewn with stoves, pickaxes, curtain rods, shovels, a medicine chest, and other articles. In two cairns, they found printed forms with handwritten entries on them. The first one, written in the spring of 1847, said that the two ships had wintered in the ice and described the route they had taken from their first base on Beechey Island. The second record told far more of the story:

### What Does This Mean?

**Cairns** were towers of stones that the Eskimos, and later the Europeans, built as a sort of signal to other people who might travel along the same route. In the treeless arctic, a cairn built on a spot of high ground could be seen from a long distance. European explorers, including Franklin, often left messages inside cairns as a way of letting others know where they had been and where they were planning to go.

1848 H.M. Ships Terror and Erebus were deserted on the 22d April ... having been beset since 12 Septr. 1846. The Officers and Crew consisting of 105 souls, under the command of Captain F.R.M. Crozier landed here ... Sir John Franklin died on the 11th of June 1847 and the total loss by deaths in the Expedition has been to this date 9 Officers and 15 Men.

James Fitzjames, Captain H.M.S. Erebus

F.R.M. Crozier, Captain and Senior Officer

Below the entry, another note had been added: "and start on tomorrow 26th for Backs Fish River."

The Great Fish River, now known as Back's River, was on the North American mainland south of King William Island; the entry confirmed the story the Eskimos had told John Rae of seeing white men dragging a boat southward on the island. As the searchers explored the island's west coast along the route the crew would probably have taken, they found more evidence: the skeleton of a crew member, his steward's uniform still recognizable, lying face down in the snow. Later they also found a boat on runners with two bodies in it. It appeared that the boat was being dragged to its destination, presumably the Fish River, but it was turned, strangely, back toward the place where the ships had landed. The only food in the boat was 40 pounds of chocolate, an empty pemmican tin, and a little tea.

After McClintock's party, a number of other expeditions explored the area around King William Island and found more relics and bodies, but they no more records to explain what finally happened to the officers and men who left the ships on that April day in 1848.

### The Mystery Deepens

The boat was 28 feet long and must have weighed 1,400 pounds. In addition to the corpses and a pile of clothing, the boat contained a strange array of objects—some heavy, some useless—including five watches, two double-barreled shotguns, slippers, towels, silk handkerchiefs, hair combs, two rolls of sheet lead, and 26 silver spoons and forks. No one knows why they took with them such strange articles while leaving warm clothing and medicines behind.

# Bad Luck

The tragedy and its bizarre ending have led to a lot of speculation about what might have happened to the ships and their crews. Franklin's expedition was the victim of some undeniable bad luck on at least two counts.

First, it set out at a particularly bad time for polar exploration. The mid-nineteenth century was one of the coldest periods in the Canadian arctic in the last several hundred years. The monumental packs and floes of ice that trapped Franklin's ships and diverted those of his rescuers were much worse than they had been 50 years earlier or would be 50 years later. Second, the west side of King William Island, where his men had to leave the ships, was an area with very little wildlife and game to hunt. Had they landed on any of a number of other places in the area, they might have been able to shoot enough caribou and geese and catch enough fish to survive for considerably longer than they did.

The company that provided the canned meat for the expedition was the subject of an investigation not long afterward, when canned meat it had sold to the Navy was found to be poor in quality and rotted in the tins. Some of the tinned meat brought along by Franklin may have been inedible, leaving the company with a shortage of provisions. Another problem may have been the fact that canned goods at the time were sealed with solder with lead in it. If the seals were not done correctly, they could leach lead into the canned food, slowly poisoning the people who ate it.

There is evidence that this may have happened to Franklin's men. In the 1980s and 1990s, the bodies of the men buried on Beechey Island and some bones of other crewmen buried on King William Island were analyzed and were found to contain unusually high levels of lead. Lead poisoning can cause mental symptoms including confusion and disorientation.

No one knows, or probably will ever know, just why or how Franklin's men met their end, scattered along the wind-scoured coasts of arctic Canada. The reasons for the tragedy of the lost expedition remain locked in the silence of the arctic and the bones of the 129 men who died in it.

---

### The Least You Need to Know

➤ The Vikings settled Iceland and then, around the tenth century A.D., Eric the Red moved on to Greenland. What happened to the colonists is still a mystery.

➤ The Island of Roanoke was settled by English colonists in 1584. No verifiable sign has ever been found of what happened to the Roanoke colonists.

➤ In 1845, Sir John Franklin headed an English expedition to find the Northwest Passage. By 1847, it was clear that he and his men were missing.

➤ Franklin's men may have died of starvation, they may have turned to cannibalism, or they may have been poisoned by their own food.

---

# Part 2

# People Power, Past and Present

*Some people just seem to know more than the rest of us, whether it's mathematics, or history, or how to make five-pointed stars with folded paper and a pair of scissors. We may not be able to equal their ability, but at least we understand how they could develop it.*

*But when someone seems able to read your mind, or to diagnose your illness by just looking at you or by closing his eyes and thinking about you even though you're hundreds of miles away—we have no rational explanation for how they accomplished that. It could be a trick—there are some very clever tricksters out there—but suppose it's the real thing?*

# Chapter 5

# A Mind Is a Difficult Thing to Read

## In this Chapter

➤ Extra-sensory perception defined

➤ The (anecdotal) evidence

➤ A titanic prediction

➤ The Rhine deck and the Ganzfeld technique

*Extrasensory perception (ESP)* is the ability to know things or to influence behavior by means of special senses beyond the normal five. Many people believe that we possess this ability (or that at least some of us do) and that with practice and training we can learn how to use it. Wouldn't it be nice if it were so.

We've probably all had moments when it seemed as if a flash of ESP had come into play. The phone rang, and we absolutely knew who was calling. Someone starts to say something, and we know exactly what he or she's going to say before it is said. We have a sudden feeling that we should call someone we love, and it turns out that, for some reason, the person really needed that phone call.

A friend of ours recalls that, when he was eight years old, his parents came home one evening, and his mother was carrying a black handbag he had never seen before. It suddenly flashed through his mind that his Aunt Celia was dead. Why he even noticed that his mother was carrying a different handbag he doesn't know; it's not the sort of thing that an eight-year-old boy normally notices.

### What Does This Mean?

The term **ESP** was invented by Dr. Joseph Rhine in the late 1920s. Rhine wanted to make the field of psychic research more respectable. (We'll talk more about Dr. Rhine later in this chapter.) ESP is also known as psi, after the 23rd letter of the Greek alphabet, the one that looks sort of like a trident: ψ.

We could add a few more whys to the list: Why should he connect the alien handbag with his Aunt Celia? Why should he conclude that she, who as far as he knew had been alive and healthy only the day before, was dead? But it was true. She had died earlier that afternoon of a sudden heart attack. He has no idea how the knowledge came to him; it could have been any of the various ESP abilities or merely an accurate subconscious reading of his parent's mood combined with a wild hunch as to what had caused it. After all, if he had guessed wrong, he would long ago have forgotten the story. It's only the times when we guess right that we remember.

## What Is This Thing Called ESP?

Several different abilities come under the general definition of ESP:

➤ **telepathy**   The ability to become aware of the thoughts of another person; the ability to converse with another person mind to mind, with nothing being said aloud.

➤ **clairvoyance**   The ability to know what is happening at a distance with no connection other than mental power.

➤ **clairaudience**   The ability to hear things that are not audible to anyone else.

➤ **precognition**   The ability to know what is going to happen in the future.

➤ **telekinesis**   The ability to move objects at a distance through mental power.

➤ **dowsing**   The ability to find water, precious metals, lost objects, or various other things using a forked stick or a pair of metal rods to focus the mental powers.

### No Mystery Here

Clairvoyance, clairaudience, and dowsing are also described as occult powers and are discussed from that point of view in Chapter 8, "Recent Prophets," and Chapter 15, "Well Done, Rare Old Medium."

These are the main powers or abilities that are classed as variants of ESP. Telekinesis is not, strictly speaking, a form of perception, but it is included in the list as a variant mental ability that seems to go with the others in that it is unexplained by any standard science, it is uncontrolled, and there is doubt as to whether it really exists.

## The Case Against ESP

We hear through our ears, see through our eyes, smell through our nose, taste with our tongue, and feel with the nerve ends distributed throughout our skin. In each case, the perception is fed to the brain, where we interpret what we have perceived through a system of nerves.

We actually do have a bunch of other senses beyond the favored five. We can sense heat or cold, we have a sense of balance, and we have a sense of our body's position (which is why you can touch the tip of your nose with the tip of your forefinger with your eyes closed). All of these involve the nervous system in transmitting the information to the brain from the sensors that are themselves specialized nerves.

We speak of other senses that don't involve sensory apparatus; we have a sense of right and wrong, a sense of fair play, a sense of responsibility, and some of us have a sense of humor. But all of these are completely internal, describing our mind's reaction to information brought to it by the other senses.

**No Mystery Here**

If another sense involving the input of information exists, such as telepathy, that information must arrive at the sensory organ in some fashion. The eyes see by reacting to photons of light; the ears hear by recognizing sound waves; the nose picks up and interprets odor particles in the air. If there is a wave or particle involved in telepathy, it is one completely unknown to science and completely undetectable by any known device.

To call something "extrasensory perception" is to imply that the perception is received by some sense of which we are not aware—not that there is no sense involved. If we do possess the ability to "read" someone else's mind, to know what he or she is thinking without any verbal or aural cues, then we must have evolved some sensory organ to accomplish this. We have explored the human body thoroughly, inside and out, and have yet to run across such an organ. If such extrasensory senses exist, it is unlikely that they are restricted to humans only. Some other mammals must also possess this ability.

## The Case For ESP

Let us start with a list. Do you know what all these items have in common?

➤ Ball lightning

➤ Meteors

➤ Continental drift

➤ Fossils

➤ Troy

➤ Hypnotism

➤ Heavier-than-air flying machines

➤ Space flight

At some point in the past, perfectly respectable and highly regarded scientists of the times have refused to admit the existence or the possibility of any of the above. Just because science can't see how something could be possible today, this doesn't mean it doesn't exist or won't be possible 20 years from now.

There is heavy anecdotal evidence for the existence of some sort of telepathy. Many of the stories may be apocryphal, a few are downright lies, but others are well-documented, well-authenticated, and told by people whose honesty is above reproach. Mark Twain experienced at least one instance of precognition: He reported a dream in which he saw his brother's death, not the sort of thing one would make up. Abraham Lincoln foretold his own assassination.

### The Mystery Deepens

During World War II, Prime Minister Winston Churchill was having dinner with some officials at 10 Downing Street when he suddenly got up and went into the kitchen. He directed the staff to bring the dinner out and then leave the building and go to the air raid shelter. Then he went back to the dining room and resumed eating. Before he had finished dinner, a bomb fell on the back of the house, destroying the kitchen area. The dining room was not disturbed in the slightest.

To quote mentalist Max Maven:

> It is a biological fact that most human beings have trace elements of iron in their nasal linings, the vestigial remains of what was once an ability to orient one's sense of direction using the magnetic poles of the earth. It would not surprise me to learn that there are similar remnants of psi abilities buried within our species.

If history is any guide, sometime in the next 20 years we will be regularly doing things that we now believe to be impossible. Whether those things will include controlled telepathy or clairvoyance, it's hard to say. But don't bet any large sums against it.

# Anecdotal Evidence

If there's anything a typical stick-in-the-mud scientist hates more than anecdotal evidence, I don't know what it is. *Anecdotal evidence* is unverifiable, unreliable, and unrepeatable, and it can't be used to "prove" anything. But it's the anecdotal evidence, the stories of people in the past, that makes this field so fascinating. Let's look at a couple of historical figures and the anecdotal evidence they add to this mystery.

### What Does This Mean?

**Anecdotal evidence** is what scientists call unverified stories of events by laymen. Scientists tend to be very strict as to what they accept as proof of an event or particularly of an unusual cause for that event.

## *By the Mark, Twain*

Before Mark Twain became Mark Twain, while he was still Sam Clemens, apprentice riverboat pilot on the mighty Mississippi, he was serving on the steamboat *Pennsylvania* along with his brother Henry. One night, while staying at a hotel in St Louis, Clemens had a vivid dream in which he saw Henry laid out in a metal coffin that was placed on two chairs. While he watched, he saw someone place a bouquet of flowers on his brother's chest—white flowers with a single red flower in the center.

The dream was so real that, when Sam woke, he did not at first realize that he had been dreaming. "I dressed and moved toward that door thinking that I would go in there and have a look at it," he wrote in his autobiography, "but I changed my mind. I thought I could not yet bear to meet my mother." It wasn't until some minutes later, when he was walking down the street, that he suddenly realized it had been a dream.

When the *Pennsylvania* reached New Orleans, Clemens was transferred to the riverboat *Lacy,* but his brother stayed aboard the *Pennsylvania.* A week or so later, Clemens got the news that the *Pennsylvania* had blown up (ships' boilers exploding was a common accident in those days). Many of the passengers and crew were dead, and many others were badly burned. Henry was still alive but was not expected to live for long.

Clemens joined his brother in Memphis and stayed with him until Henry died. Then he fell asleep on a bed provided by a compassionate stranger. When he woke up and went to the place where his brother's body had been taken, he found it in a room with several other victims of the *Pennsylvania* explosion. It was in a metal coffin, the only one in the room—all the others were white pine placed on two chairs. While he stood there, a lady entered the room and placed a bouquet of flowers on Henry's chest, all white except for a single red rose in the center.

## *Abraham Lincoln and Mrs. Julia Grant*

Abraham Lincoln believed that he was destined to become president but that he was also destined to die in office. In 1860, after he had been elected to his first term, he looked into a mirror in the White House and saw a duplicate of himself standing alongside him. This, in psychic lore, is known as a doppelgänger—German for "double"—and it is supposed to foretell the death of the person doubled. Lincoln also had a dream in which he heard the sound of many people crying. He went toward the noise and found himself in the East Room of the White House. He described the dream to his friend Ward H. Lamon: "There was a sickening surprise. Before me was a catafalque on which rested a corpse wrapped in funeral vestments. Around it were soldiers who were acting as guards … 'Who is dead in the White House?' I demanded of the soldiers. 'The president,' was the answer. 'He was killed by an assassin.'"

### The Mystery Deepens

There is a story that a young naval lieutenant checked into a hotel in Washington D.C. in 1865 and went to his room on the ground floor. In a short while, he came out to the room clerk and said that he couldn't stand the noise and insisted on getting another room. "What noise?" the clerk asked. "It's hard to explain," the lieutenant said. "It sounds like thousands of people crying." The clerk went to check out the room. "I don't hear anything," he said. But he gave the lieutenant another room.

Half an hour later, President Abraham Lincoln was shot by John Wilkes Booth at Ford's Theater around the corner from the hotel. He was carried into the hotel to be treated and died a short while later. The room he was taken to was the room that had been occupied by the lieutenant.

Lincoln wasn't the only one to have a premonition about his assassination. Julia Grant, the wife of General Ulysses Grant, insisted to her husband that they leave for Pennsylvania that night instead of attending the play at Ford's Theater with the president. If they didn't, she was convinced something horrible would happen to him. They left for Pennsylvania on the train, and as a result, General Grant did not sit next to Lincoln that night. Booth was unable to fire the second shot, which had been reserved for Grant.

# Morgan Robertson, the Unwitting Seer

One of the problems with assessing cases of precognition is not knowing for certain whether the prediction was really made before the event took place. There are several cases on record in which the supposed psychic or clairvoyant tried to fudge the facts and make it appear as if he or she had predicted something like an assassination or a disaster when no such prediction had been made. When the prediction is in the form of a book published 14 years before the event, however, there's no question about the integrity of the predictor. The only odd thing is that, in this case, the author of the book had no idea he was predicting anything.

It may be a case of unconscious precognition, incredible coincidence, or damn good guessing, but there is an uncanny similarity between the sinking of the steamship *Titanic* in 1912, the greatest maritime disaster of the last century, and the events described in Morgan Robertson's *Futility; or the Wreck of the Titan,* written in 1898, 14 years earlier.

## Unsinkable

The correspondences are many and eerily precise. The *Titanic* was proclaimed by its makers to be unsinkable by virtue of its modern design and construction. So, Robertson wrote 14 years earlier, was the *Titan*. The *Titanic* was the biggest ship afloat at the time, weighing 66,000 tons. Robertson had the *Titan* weighing 70,000 tons. The *Titanic* was 882.5 feet long; the *Titan* was 800. The *Titanic* set sail on its maiden voyage in April—as did the *Titan*.

### Mysterious Comments

"SHE was the largest craft afloat and the greatest of the works of men.... From the bridge, engine-room, and a dozen places on her deck the ninety-two doors of nineteen water-tight compartments could be closed in half a minute by turning a lever. These doors would also close automatically in the presence of water. With nine compartments flooded the ship would still float, and as no known accident of the sea could possibly fill this many, the steamship Titan was considered practically unsinkable....

"Unsinkable—indestructible, she carried as few boats as would satisfy the laws. These, twenty-four in number, were securely covered and lashed down to their chocks on the upper deck, and if launched would hold five hundred people.

"She carried no useless, cumbersome life-rafts; but—because the law required it—each of the three thousand berths in the passengers', officers', and crew's quarters contained a cork jacket, while about twenty circular life-buoys were strewn along the rails.... "

—Morgan Robertson, *Futility; or the Wreck of the Titan,* 1898

## Speed, Passengers, and Lifeboats

The top speed of both the *Titan* and the *Titanic* was 25 knots. Both ships could carry 3,000 passengers but were sailing on their first trip across the Atlantic with only about 2,000. Both had enough lifeboats for less than half of their passengers, not to mention the crew, but neither captain was worried about it because, after all, the *Titan/Titanic* was unsinkable.

## And So to Sink

Both ships were hit by an iceberg on the starboard (right) side, ripping open the seams below the water line. And both sank, carrying hundreds of passengers to their watery graves.

They say that truth is stranger than fiction, but in this case, fiction and truth were uncannily similar.

## And Furthermore

To compound Morgan Robertson's uncanny knack for foreseeing the unforeseeable, in 1914, the author wrote a short story called "Beyond the Spectrum" in which the Japanese carry out a sneak attack on the Hawaiian Islands in December. Twenty-seven years later, they did just that. It could have been an incredible coincidence, or Robertson could have had the strange psychic ability to foresee the future. Perhaps the Emperor of Japan read Robertson's story and thought it was a good idea.

Robertson also describes a bomb that can destroy a whole city, going off with an incredible flash of light that blinds all who look at it. Was he peering into the atomic future or just making it up as he went along?

### Here There Be Dragons

Investigators into ESP phenomena always have to be careful of the tendency of people to amplify, exaggerate, and—let's face it—lie if it will make a good story better. And after telling the story two or three times, they no longer even remember that it's a lie. People are like that. Honest.

# Doctor Rhine

Dr. Joseph Banks Rhine, a professor of botany at Duke University, became interested in ESP in the late 1920s. He invented the term "extrasensory perception" so he could discuss the phenomenon with other scientists without having to use words like "psychic" or "clairvoyant"—words associated with showmen and charlatans that would have destroyed the subject's chance at academic respectability.

## The Rhine Deck

In 1930, Dr. Rhine and a colleague, Karl Zener, devised what has become known as the Rhine deck of cards to aid them in their experiments. The Rhine deck is a deck of 25 cards, five each of five symbols: a circle, a star, a square, wavy lines, and a cross. Each is rendered very simply with a heavy line and is centered on the card.

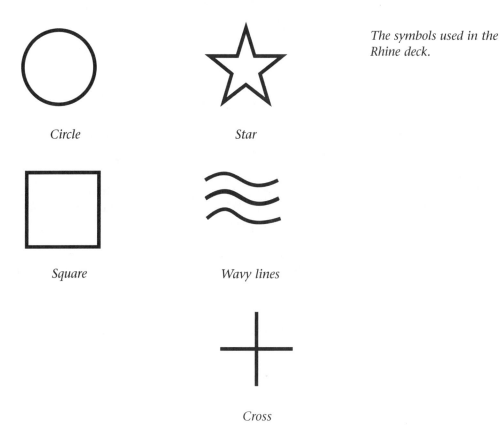

*Circle*

*Star*

*The symbols used in the Rhine deck.*

*Square*

*Wavy lines*

*Cross*

The use of the deck for testing for ESP is very simple. The deck is shuffled thoroughly and is slowly dealt out one card at a time by the tester. The subject is placed where he or she can't see the cards and tries to guess which symbol is on each card dealt. A record is kept of the hits. Pure chance would give the subject a score of 5 out of 25, or 20 percent.

## Hitting the Deck

In 1931, one subject, Adam Linzmayer, an economics student, got nine in a row correct on two different runs of cards and got a total correct of 119 out of 300 cards, or 39 percent. The odds of that happening by chance are more than two million to one.

### Mysterious Comments

"Obviously, when it comes to determining the validity of psychic phenomena, the jury is still out. The question is whether they're ever going to come back ... "

—Max Maven

In 1932, Hubert Pearce Jr., a divinity student, managed 13 hits on one test and got 261 out of 750 cards for a score of close to 35 percent.

In his book *Extra-Sensory Perception*, written in 1934, Rhine claimed that the case for ESP was now proved, but other scientists were unable to duplicate his results and claimed that his controls were too loose. When Rhine tightened up his controls, the scores went down. Although Rhine kept getting occasional impressive results testing for both telepathy and telekinesis, he was never able to devise a way to teach people to improve their scores or to consistently score above average. One might conclude, based on Dr. Rhine's experiments, that there is some sort of psi power inherent in people, but it is weak, uncontrollable, and inconsistent.

### What Does This Mean?

The **Ganzfeld** (German for "whole field") **technique** comes from gestalt psychology. It is a relaxation technique using a screen of white light to fill the visual field to encourage total relaxation of the subject/patient.

## The Ganzfeld Technique

The *Ganzfeld technique*, a means of testing for psi powers using sensory isolation of the subject, is now going on in various academic settings around this country and others.

In a Ganzfeld test for telepathy, two subjects are used: a sender and a receiver. The sender sits in a soundproof room and, for about a half-hour, concentrates on a "target"—a still picture or a video clip.

The receiver is lying down in a separate soundproof room. Ping-pong ball halves are taped over his or her eyes, and a headphone is placed over his or her ears. The room is flooded with red light, and white noise—randomly generated sounds—is played through the headphones. For the same half-hour that the sender is concentrating on the target, the receiver provides a continuous narration of his thoughts, feelings, ideas, and any images that cross his mind.

At the end of the half-hour, the receiver is shown four images and is asked to rate how close each of them comes to matching what he or she was thinking about while the ping-pong balls were taped to his or her eyes. If the image the receiver rates highest is the one the sender was staring at, it counts as a "hit."

Since there are four images, the receiver should get one out of four correct completely by chance, for a score of 25 percent. Anything substantially above that, or for that matter substantially below, is worth considering as evidence of psi ability.

According to a 1994 paper done by Daryl J. Bem of Cornell University, the score for receivers across a wide range of Ganzfeld experiments conducted in several different sites was about 35 percent. This is sufficiently enough above chance to indicate a strong case for some sort of ESP being involved.

It has also been noted that people who are considered creative or artistically gifted tend to score higher on Ganzfeld tests than the norm, even higher than the 35 percent. A group of students from the Juilliard School of Music in New York City averaged 50 percent when tested.

## You Read My Mind

We have no clever conclusion to this one, no answer to wrap up the whole problem or to explain it away. Are human beings capable of ESP?

There is no known mechanism to explain it, and nobody's ever done it consistently enough to break the bank at a Las Vegas casino—at least not that we're aware of. We'll finish with a personal story. This happened to Michael Kurland, one of the authors of this book:

> I was eating lunch with a lovely young lady named January sometime in the late 1970s at a delicatessen on 2nd Avenue in Manhattan. Suddenly, for no reason that I was aware of, I had an overwhelming desire to change tables. I was about to suggest this to January when she looked at me and, without a word, stood up and took her plate. The two of us moved to a table about three spots away from where we had been sitting and resumed our lunch.

> About two minutes after we moved, a brick came flying through the plate glass window next to where we had been sitting, showering the table and the area around it with shards of glass.

That's the story.

## The Least You Need to Know

➤ "Extrasensory perception" is a term invented by Dr. Joseph Rhine to make the study of psychic phenomena such as telepathy, clairvoyance, clairaudience, precognition, telekinesis, and dowsing respectable.

➤ Mark Twain and Abraham Lincoln had precognitive dreams—Twain about his brother's death, Lincoln about his own.

➤ Morgan Robinson's book *Futility; or the Wreck of the Titan* predicted the sinking of the *Titanic* 14 years before the disaster happened.

➤ ESP experiments continue today with the Ganzfeld technique showing some intriguing results.

# Chapter 6

# They Delved Into the Future

---

### In This Chapter

➤ Prophecy: common to many cultures throughout history

➤ The Greek oracles

➤ Early Medieval prophecy

➤ Merlin predicts

➤ Predicting the popes

---

In this chapter and the next, we'll talk about prophecy and divination from ancient times to the present. We apologize if your favorite prophet has been left out; there are so many to choose from that we had to go with the ones we found especially interesting or the best examples of the sort of divination we were talking about. And the selection is, of course, subjective.

We'll talk about *prophecy* in several other chapters such as the discussion of pyramidology and the Great Pyramid (see Chapter 9, "Monumental Mysteries"), the overview of Atlantis and the Atlantis myths (see Chapter 11, "Beneath the Waves"), and the discussion of astrology (see Chapters 13, "It's In Your Stars" and 14, "An Astrology Primer"). As foretelling the future seems to be a major preoccupation of humankind, it crops up with a great consistency in many cultures. In this chapter, we treat the pure, unalloyed version.

## What Does This Mean?

**Prophecy** is the foretelling of future events by a prophet who has been divinely selected to bring the word of the gods (or in the case of Biblical prophecy, the One God) to the people. The prophecy often involves the dire results of evil behavior. **Divination** is the act of foretelling, or attempting to foretell, the future by magical or occult means.

# Predicting the Future

Humans are perhaps the only creatures on the planet that wonder about the future with an eye toward preparing for it. Squirrels store nuts for the winter, but as far as we can tell, it's a genetically programmed habit; only in the deep primal memories of their DNA are they aware that winter is coming.

Unlike squirrels, humans consciously and continually wonder what the future holds and what we can do to improve our chances of enjoying or profiting from coming events. From the simple question of whether to carry an umbrella in the morning to more complex and momentous problems such as whether to go to law school or to accept an appointment as governess to the children of the King of Siam, we want some sort of hint as to what course to take. It would be nice to know that we could get some assistance for these difficult decisions by reading tea leaves or by inspecting the entrails of a handy goat.

When we come to a crossroads on the lonely road that is each of our lives, we want nothing more than for a wise stranger to point to each way and say, "This way lies fortune and happiness, but that way, although it looks enticing, leads to ruin and pain and a life of sorrow."

As far back as there are records, and indeed in tales brought down in ancient oral traditions going back thousands of years, we know that there have been people who made a practice of telling their neighbors what the fates had in store for them. Some of these seers became rich and influential; others were cast into prison or executed (which, we suppose, they should have foreseen).

## What Does This Mean?

An **oracle** is a person who acts as a voice for the gods to predict the future or advise on a course of action, or a place where such people give their revelations.

# The Greek Oracles

There were a variety of *oracles* scattered about ancient Greece. Around the time of Socrates, more than 400 years before the birth of Christ, some of these oracles were already ancient and respected such as the ones at Amalthea, Amphiarus, Branchidae, Delphi, Dodona, Erythrae, Phrygia, Samia, Trophonius, and Zeus Ammon, to name just a few. The oldest was at Dodona in the city-state of Epirus, south of Macedonia. There, a temple dedicated to the god Jupiter stood amid a grove of ancient oak trees, and Jupiter's voice could be heard in the wind whistling through the oaks. Or so claimed the priests of Dodona, who would interpret Jupiter's messages for people who came to seek advice.

The oracle at Dodona was mentioned in Homer's *Iliad* when the hero Achilles speaks of the Selloi, "prophets [of Dodona] with unwashed feet who sleep on the ground." Since Homer composed the *Iliad* somewhere around the tenth or eleventh century B.C., the oracle at Dodona was over 500 years old when the philosopher Plato spoke of it.

The oracles resided at sacred places, usually temples, often surrounded by groves of sacred oak or cedar trees; the association between the gods and trees was a close and ancient one. The temples were tended by priests dedicated to one or another of the ancient gods. Someone, often a priestess, would speak for the oracle who spoke for the god, and the priests would interpret.

**No Mystery Here**

Once, in ancient days, a party of Boeotians consulted the oracle at Dodona. They were advised by the priestess, Myrtile by name, to promptly go and do "the most impious thing possible." With hardly a pause, they picked up the priestess and dumped her into a pot of boiling water. It was, they explained, the best they could think of on such short notice.

Often, the spokesperson for the oracle would go into a drug-induced trance; at Delphi, it was supposedly brought about by breathing the vapors emerging from a cleft in a rock in a cavern beneath the temple. The pronouncements might be strange indeed, nonsense phrases or complex and difficult images that didn't seem to relate to the question asked, but the priests were there to interpret them. The ancient Greeks believed that madness was a sign from the gods and that temporary, drug-induced hallucinatory states enabled the gods to speak through their earthly vessel, the priestess.

What the priestesses said more often than not made little sense, and the priest's interpretations, usually issued in verse, were masterpieces of ambiguity. Take the pronouncement of the Delphic oracle when King Pyrrhus wanted advice on his upcoming battle with the Romans: "*Aio to, Aeacide, Romanos vincere posse.*"

That's all very well and good, as you Latin speakers will note, since it can be translated as either "I say unto you, Aeacide, that you can conquer the Romans," or conversely as "I say unto you, Aeacide, that the Romans can conquer you."

**The Mystery Deepens**

The Delphic oracle's mixed message to King Pyrrhus had an eerie accuracy to it. King Pyrrhus lost so many of his finest soldiers during the battle of Asculum in 279 B.C. that, when he was congratulated on winning, he replied, "One more such victory and Pyrrhus is undone." This has come down to us through the ages in the phrase "a Pyrrhic victory," meaning a victory that comes at too high a cost.

# Croesus and the Delphic Oracle

Croesus was the king of Lydia from 560 to 546 B.C. If you've ever heard the expression "as rich as Croesus," well, he was the guy. He had successfully extended his kingdom until it abutted the Persian Empire, which was the biggest and most powerful country around at the time. Its king, Cyrus II, was doing some extending and consolidating himself.

Croesus had a problem. Should he make alliances and attack Persia before Cyrus had a chance to attack him? Or should he wait and try to appease the Persians while trying to make more defensive alliances and then perhaps hope that Cyrus would turn his attentions to the east for the next few years?

## How to Pick an Oracle

When faced with a problem like this, the sensible thing to do in those years was to consult an oracle. But which one? Croesus sent messengers to six of the best oracles with a simple question: "What is King Croesus doing right now?" The exact moment at which they would ask the question was, of course, prearranged.

When the messengers returned to King Croesus and told them what the oracles had said, he found that four of them had been way off, one had it partly right, and one, the Oracle at Delphi, was right on the money: "Croesus is boiling a lamb and a tortoise together in a copper pot with a copper lid."

Now how could anyone get that by guesswork? Croesus was properly impressed. Nothing was vague or wishy-washy about that answer. It was direct and detailed, and it was right!

Croesus rewarded the temple richly and got down to the serious business. Should he, he wanted to know, go to war against King Cyrus of Persia?

## *"A Great Empire Will Be Destroyed"*

In one of the most famous prophesies of all time, the *Sibyls* (there were two of them at the time) at Delphi agreed that "If Croesus should cross the Halys, he should cause a great empire to be destroyed."

Croesus listened, but he didn't listen closely enough. Hearing what he wanted to hear, he gathered his allies and attacked Persia. A great empire was indeed destroyed—his own. Cyrus defeated him in battle and captured him. It is written that Cyrus showed Croesus mercy and did not execute him, but what did happen to him after that is not known.

### What Does This Mean?

The **Sibyls** were the priestess prophets who received messages from the gods and passed them on to the priests. They took their name from Sibyl, a great prophetess of ancient legend. The Halys was the ancient name for the river now called Kizil Irmak that flows through Turkey into the Black Sea. To cross the Halys, Croesus would have had to attack Persia.

# The Sibylline Books

Since we've mentioned the Sibyls, We'll tell you a wonderful story about them.

The Sibylline Books were a collection of ancient and mysterious predictions that were saved as oracles in Rome and were consulted by the Roman Senate whenever it was faced with emergencies or disasters. According to the Roman writer Livy, there were originally nine of these books, and they were offered for sale to Rome by Amalthaea, the Sibyl of Cumae. The Romans rejected her offer, so she burned three of the books. A year later, she returned and offered the remaining six at the same terms as the original nine. Again she was refused, so she went off and burned three more. This time, when she returned, the Romans, probably thinking that she seemed pretty sure of herself and that there just might be something to it, bought the remaining three for the same price as the original nine. Amalthaea went off and was never seen again.

The Romans kept the books in an underground vault, guarded by 15 custodians. They consulted the books until the time of Nero, when the books were burned in a great fire that swept through Rome. (Incidentally, Nero didn't fiddle while Rome burned—the fiddle hadn't been invented yet.)

**Mysterious Comments**

"If we investigate scientifically and dispassionately prophecies that have been preserved, what do we see? We find individuals, who despite personal inconvenience, having glanced at the next page of history, were appalled and gave warning to their people.

"In so-called prophecies you will find no personal designs, you will find no culpable self-gratification, you will find no slander. The symbols of the reflections are explained by the colors of distant windows."

—from a book called *Leaves of the Garden of M, or Illumination*, anonymously published in the 1920s

# Medieval Prophecy

Medieval Europe was a hotbed of prophets and prophecy, particularly religious prophecy. The expected coming of the *Antichrist*, as predicted in the New Testament, was a constant concern.

**What Does This Mean?**

The **Antichrist** is a biblical notion that shows up in four books of the New Testament: 2 Thessalonians (2:1–12),1 John (2:18, 22; 4:3), 2 John (7) and Revelation (13). He will come to deceive the faithful into thinking he is the true Christ, and his coming will signify that the final conflict between good and evil that presages the second coming of Christ is at hand.

St. Martin, Bishop of Tours, announced in the year 380 that the Antichrist had been born but was still young. In 1080, when the millenialists were convinced that the world was to end at any minute, Bishop Ranieri of Florence preached that the Antichrist was in the world. In 1412, one of the great preachers of the day, Vincens Ferrer, wrote to Pope Benedict XIII that the Antichrist was then nine years old. Many other people had seen similar visions, Ferrer explained, and therefore it must be proclaimed "so that the faithful might be prepared for the fearful battle immediately impending." (This information is from the book *The Story of Prophecy* by Henry James Forman, published by Farrar & Rinehart in 1936.)

## *Merlin Predicts*

One of the most popular prophets, seers, sorcerers, and general all-around wizards of medieval times was Merlin. He is best known as the sorcerer-seer of King

Arthur and his father King Uther Pendragon. Merlin was responsible for the sword-in-the-stone stratagem by which Arthur was able to claim his throne and also was responsible for the creation of the round table itself.

The legend of Merlin, however, which may be based on a Welsh bard who lived sometime around 500, is not merely English or Welsh. Merlin appears in folk tales in Scotland, Germany, France, and most of the other countries of Western Europe. In Geoffrey of Monmouth's *Chronicle,* written in 1152, he cites a long prediction attributed to Merlin that the dragon of the Saxons would push back the dragon of the Britons but that this would be avenged by the Normans. This may or may not be an ancient prediction, but it serves as a wonderful justification of the Norman invasion of England in 1066.

Merlin is said to have predicted that King Arthur would return in Britain's time of need. In Brittany, a province on the coast of France where the Merlin myth was also popular, King Arthur was to return in Briton's (Brittany's) time of need: a slight but significant difference.

King Louis VI of France (1081–1137), who was known as Louis the Fat, is believed to have based many of his decisions on the predictions of Merlin. If so, Louis did pretty well, subduing the French barons, repelling a German invasion in 1124, and marrying his ward Eleanor of Aquitaine, known for her intelligence and beauty, to his son, who became Louis VII.

## St. Malachy Predicts the Popes

Maelmhaedhoc O'Morgair was born in the town of Armagh in the county of Ulster in Ireland in 1094. He early on impressed his teachers with both his goodness and his intelligence, and he was ordained a priest and a deacon at the age of 25 by Celsius, Bishop of Armagh. It was then that he took on the Romanized form of his name, Malachi or Malachy. By the year 1129, he was the Archbishop of Armagh and was playing a great role in Irish ecclesiastical reform.

In 1139, he left on a trip to Rome to visit Pope Innocent II. When he reached Rome and the pope, he was visited with the gift of prophecy. The succession of the popes was a question of great interest right then since the last of a couple antipopes had just resigned and pledged holy allegiance to Innocent, ending what could have been a major schism.

Malachy prophesied who the popes would be from Innocent II on to the present and a little beyond. He didn't exactly name them—that would have been a bit much. What he did was give a two- or three-word Latin tag that, once the popes were elected, could be shown to identify them. The prophecies were, according to the story, given to Pope Innocent, who passed them on to the Vatican library where they stayed unread and forgotten for 400 years.

## The List Recovered

In 1595, a French monk named Arnold Wion from Douai found the prophecies in the library, or so he claimed, and published them in a book called *Lignum Vitae.* "It is said," Wion wrote in his preface, "that he has himself written some small works, which I have not seen, excepting only a certain prophecy concerning the sovereign pontiffs; as it is brief, and has not yet, so far as I know, been printed, and since many desire to be acquainted with it, we have reproduced it here."

There were 112 entries in St. Malachy's list—111 short phrases and one long paragraph at the end, a paragraph that describes the man (Peter the Roman by name) who will be the last pope of all and who will serve at a time when "the awful judge will then judge the peoples."

### No Mystery Here

Pope Innocent's rival, who called himself Anacletus II, occupied Rome during his lifetime. It wasn't until Anacletus's successor, Victor IV, resigned in 1138 (because of—among other things—the intercession of Abbot Bernard) and submitted to Innocent that the pope was able to reign from the Vatican in Rome.

### The Mystery Deepens

There is a very logical theory that St. Malachy's list is a forgery, probably created by Wion himself in 1590 to further the election of a Cardinal Simoncelli of Orvieto to be the next pope. The phrase in the list that would apply to the next pope was *Ex antiquitate urbus,* "from the ancient city." And Simoncelli's city was Orvieto, a contraction of the Latin words *Urbs Vetus,* "at the Ancient City." But the scheme, if there was one, didn't work. The man elected to be the next pope was Cardinal Nicholas Sfondrate, who served as Gregory XIV. Perhaps the plotters didn't have enough time to prepare. The previous pope, Urban VII, contracted malaria the day he was elected and died unexpectedly 12 days later. Gregory XIV lived up to his billing. He was a noted conservator of the Christian antiquities in Rome. And if the list didn't come into existence until 1590, its accuracy since then is still very impressive.

# The Listed Popes

I won't list all of the 111 phrases here, just some representative examples. The correspondences in some cases are eerily precise. Some others do not seem to correspond at all to the pope to which they refer, but perhaps we do not know the facts that would show the correspondence. Or perhaps St. Malachy (or Wion) was just very lucky. (The number preceding the pope's name in the following list is his number designation on St. Malachy's list.)

➤ **29** Honorious IV (1285–1287) was listed as e*x rosa leonina*, "from the leonine (lion-like) rose." The coat of arms of the Savelli family (Honorious was Giacomo Savelli) was a rose supported by two lions.

➤ **35** John XXII (1316–1334) was listed as *de sutore osseo*, "the boney shoemaker." He was a thin, boney man and was from a middle-class family of shoemakers.

➤ **61** Pius III (1503) was described as *de parvo homine*, "of the little men." Pius's family name was Piccolomini, which means "little men."

➤ **94** Clement XIII (1758–1769) was described as *rosa umbriae*, "the rose of Umbria." Before his election, he had been governor of Rieta in Umbria, whose symbol is the rose.

➤ **95** Clement XIV (1769–1774) was described as *ursus velox*, "the running bear." The man who assumed that title upon becoming pope was Lorenzo Gagnanelli, and the coat of arms of the Gagnanelli family contains a running bear.

➤ **97** Pius VII (1800–1823) was the pope against whose reign was placed the phrase *aquila rapax*, "the rapacious eagle." And yet he was held captive by Napoleon, and the pontifical territories were annexed by this rap—a-ha! It wasn't Pius who was being described as *aquila rapax* but his captor, Napoleon Bonaparte, who used an eagle as his standard and tried to take over all of Europe.

➤ **100** Gregory IV (1831–1846) fell under *de balneis hetruriae*, "from the bath of Etruria." As a priest, he was a member of the religious order of the Camaldoli founded by Saint Romuald at Balneo near Florence in Tuscany, an area that was once called Etruria.

➤ **102** Leo XIII (1878–1903) was regarded by St. Malachy's list as *lumen in coelo*, "a light in the heavens." The pope's family, the Pecci, has a large comet on its coat of arms.

➤ **103** St. Pius X (1903–1914), according to the list, was an *ignis ardent*, "ardent fire." This could refer to the ardent way he espoused conservative values on the church, which got him sanctified, or to the start of the first World War as he died, take your choice.

➤ **104** Benedict XV (1914–1922) was *religion depopulate*, and the first World War and the Russian Revolution did a good job of depopulating the religious. (The Soviet Union was officially an atheist state.)

## The Last Few

We are living in the last days of the predictions of St. Malachy, with only one or possibly two popes to go. (As of this writing, John Paul II is on the papal throne.) Starting roughly in the middle of the last century, Malachy prophesied:

➤ **107**   John XXIII (1958–1963), was *Pastor et Nauta*, "shepherd and navigator." Before his election as pope, he was patriarch of Venice, a city on the Adriatic Sea with a proud history as a maritime and naval power. At his coronation, he declared his desire to be "a good shepherd." And, for a different view, he successfully shepherded the Church through a synod, an ecumenical council, and a revision of canon law.

➤ **108**   Paul VI (1963–1978) was called *flos florum*, "flower of flowers," by St. Malachy. His personal coat of arms contained the fleur-de-lis, a heraldic picture of a three-branched lily.

➤ **109**   John Paul I (1978) was *de medietate Lunae*, "of the half of the moon." He was from the diocese of Belluno, "beautiful moon," in Italy. His reign lasted one month, from 26 August to 28 September. He came into office at the quarter moon and died on the quarter moon.

➤ **110**   John Paul II (1978–present) was *de labore Solis*, "of the sorrow (or travail) of the sun." He was born on 18 May 1920 during a solar eclipse. And next …

➤ **111**   Whoever he is, he will be *gloria olivae*, "glory of the olive." This is believed by some to suggest that he will be a Jewish pope since the olive tree is used in the Bible as a symbol for the Jewish people. Some who believe that the End of Days is near believe that, not only will the pope be Jewish, the entire Jewish people will convert to Christianity. This is to take place immediately before the final catastrophe that will lead to the second coming.

This is a lot to read into two little words: *gloria olivae*.

## The Last Bit

The final bit of writing to come from St. Malachy's list is an unnumbered paragraph at the end. Is it to refer to pope 112? Or is it an extension of the comment on pope 111? Your guess is as good as ours. In the original, it goes as follows:

> *In persecutions extrema S.R.E. sedebit Petrus Romanus, qui pascet oues in multis tribulationibus: quibus transactis ciuitas septicollis diruetur, & Iudex tremedus iudicabit populum suum. Finis.*

This translates to something like

> In the final persecution of the Holy Roman Church, there will reign Peter the Roman, who will feed his flock amid many tribulations, after which the seven-hilled city will be destroyed and the dreadful judge will judge the people. The end.

Even allowing for the fact that the lines pertaining to popes before 1590 tend to be more accurate than the ones after—even to the point of getting some specific last names right—the ones for the latter four centuries contain some impressive hits. Chance? I'd like to have St. Malachy around to pick my lottery numbers.

### No Mystery Here

Since the last paragraph of St. Malachy's list of epigrams is not numbered, it could be that *gloria olivae* is not to be the next-to-last pope right before *Petrus Romanus*. So even if the list is, by some chance, accurate, it doesn't mean the end of the world is coming just yet.

### The Least You Need to Know

➤ The desire to foretell the future is as old as humankind.

➤ The Greeks consulted oracles often, and there were a great many of them. The oracles' advice tended to be obscurely phrased and difficult to understand.

➤ The birth of the Antichrist has been predicted every few years from the death of Christ until the present.

➤ The probably mythical Merlin was the soothsayer of choice throughout much of medieval Europe.

➤ The eleventh-century St. Malachy predicted the succession of the popes to the present. These predictions may have been forged in the sixteenth century, but the record from then until now is still fairly impressive.

# Chapter 7

Jill Gates?
Wilhelm Gates?
Gil Bates?

# The Great Medieval Prophets

---

### In This Chapter

➤ Mother Shipton: prophet or myth?

➤ The predictive verses of Mother Shipton

➤ Nostradamus: doctor and prophet

➤ The predictive verses of Nostradamus

---

Over the centuries, many people have claimed the ability to prophesy. Most of them, along with their prophecies, have been forgotten, but a few have survived the ages. These are the prophets whose uncanny predictions and ability to communicate them set them apart from lesser seers. They didn't need special surroundings or hallucinogenic smoke or priests to interpret their sayings. They just looked into the future and told what they saw, and it was enough.

The facts of their lives and the record of their prophecies often become clouded as time passes. People have rewritten what they said or have altered the story of how and when the prophecies were issued. In some cases, followers did it to strengthen belief in the prophet. In other cases, they did it to support some cause or conviction of their own. In still other cases, they just wanted to make a better story.

But everyone who looks into the stories of prophets such as Mother Shipton and Nostradamus agrees that, even after the smoke has cleared away and the mirrors have been turned aside, there was something remarkable about them. If anyone could be thought to have caught a glimpse of the future and recorded it, these two are surely on that list.

# Mother Shipton

Ursula Sontheil, if there *was* an Ursula Sontheil, was born in 1488 in a cave by the river Nidd near Knaresborough, West Riding, Yorkshire, England. It was recorded by her biographer, whom we know only by the name "S. Baker," that she was "larger than common, her body crooked, her face frightful; but her understanding extraordinary."

At the age of 24, she married a carpenter named Toby Shipton and set up housekeeping in the nearby village of Skipton. Over the next few years, she developed a reputation as a prophet, and some even went so far as to consider her a witch.

## "Wolsey Shall Not Reach York"

One of the stories told about her relates that, when Cardinal Wolsey decided to move his residence to York, where Mother Shipton was living, she announced that he would never reach the city. Wolsey, taking the prophecy as a threat, sent three men, lords of his court, in disguise to find out whether she had really dared to utter those words.

They were taken to her house by a local man named Beasly, who knocked at the door. "Come in, Mr. Beasly, and the three noble lords with you," Mother Shipton called through the door. The lords accused the seer of saying that Cardinal Wolsey would never see York. "Not so," she replied. "I said he might see it but would never come to it."

"You will surely be burned as a witch," one of the lords told her.

"If this burns," she said, casting her linen handkerchief into the fire, "then so shall I."

There the handkerchief stayed, unsinged, for 15 minutes until she took it out again. The lords, properly mystified and a little frightened, left.

Cardinal Wolsey paused in his journey at a castle outside York and climbed the castle tower to gaze at the city eight miles away. He swore that, when he arrived at York, he would have Mother Shipton burned as a witch. As he descended the castle tower steps, however, a messenger from the king arrived calling Wolsey back to London. Wolsey died shortly thereafter while still on his way to London and obviously never returned to York.

### Here There Be Dragons

There is a question as to whether Mother Shipton ever really existed. The first record of her sayings, *The propheceyes of Mother Shipton ... Foretelling the Death of Cardinall Wolsey, the Lord Percy, and others, as also what should happen in insuing times,* was published in London in 1641, 90 years after her death. Whether the anonymous author (who might have been William Lilly—see Chapter 13, "It's In Your Stars") compiled existing stories about her or made them up is not known.

# The Prophetic Rhymes of Mother Shipton

The rhyming couplets attributed to Mother Shipton predict the invention of automobiles, the radio, airplanes, iron ships, submarines, and a variety of political changes that can be interpreted as the reader sees fit.

## *The Verse She Could Do*

Here is a compilation of Mother Shipton's verse as it is usually given. There are variants, but the differences are not great. For example, what I have as the second verse is often the first and may read: "A carriage without horse will go / Disaster fill the world with woe / In London, Primrose Hill shall be / In center hold a bishop's tea."

The fiery year as soon as o'er,
Peace shall then be as before;
Plenty everywhere be found,
And men with swords shall plough
   the ground.
The time shall come when seas of
   blood
Shall mingle with a greater flood.

Carriages without horses shall go.
And accidents fill the world with woe.
Around the world thoughts shall fly
In the twinkling of an eye.
Waters shall yet more wonders do,
How strange yet it shall be true.

The world upside down shall be,
And gold found at the root of a tree.
Through hills men shall ride
And no horse or ass be by their side;
Under water men shall walk,
Shall ride, shall sleep, shall talk;

In the air men shall be seen,
In white, in black, and in green.
Iron in the water shall float
As easy as a wooden boat;
Gold shall be found, and shown
In a land that's not now known.

Fire and water shall more wonders do
England shall at last admit a Jew;
The Jew that was held in scorn
Shall of a Christian be born and born.

A house of glass shall come to pass
In England, but alas!
War will follow with the work
In the land of the Pagan and Turk
And state and state in fierce strife
Will seek each other's life

But when the North shall divide the
   South
An eagle shall build in the lion's
   mouth.

An Ape shall appear in a Leap year
That shall put all womankind in fear
And Adam's make shall be disputed
And Roman faith shall like rooted,
And England will turn around.
Thunder shall shake the earth;
Lightning shall rend asunder;
Water shall fill the earth;
Fire shall do its work.

Three times shall lovely France
Be led to dance a bloody dance;
Before her people shall be free.
Three tyrant rulers shall she see;
Three times the People rule alone;
Three times the People's hope is gone;
Three rulers in succession see,
Each spring from different dynasty.
Then shall the worser fight be done,
England and France shall be as one.

Waters shall flow where corn shall
   grow
Corn shall grow where waters doth
   flow
Houses shall appear in the vales below
And covered by hail and snow;
White shall be black then turn grey
And a fair Lady be married thrice.
All England's sons that plough the
   land
Shall be seen, book in hand;
Learning shall so ebb and flow,
The poor shall most wisdom know.

## One More Paragraph

Here is an additional paragraph attributed to Mother Shipton that we found on the Mother Shipton's Cave Web site, where we also got the preceding version of the prophecies.

> The lily shall remain in a merry world; and he shall be moved against the seed of the lion, and shall stand on one side of the country with a number of ships. Then shall the Son of Man, having a fierce beast in his arms, whose Kingdom is the land of the moon, which is dreaded throughout the world. With a number shall he pass many waters, and shall come to the land of the lion, looking for help from the beast of his country, and an eagle shall come out of the east, spread with the beams of the Son of Man, and shall destroy castles of the Thames. And there shall be battles among many kingdoms. That year shall be the bloody field, and lily F.K. shall lose his crown, and therewith shall be crowned the Son of Man K.W., and the fourth year shall be preferred. And there shall be a universal peace over the whole world, and there shall be plenty of fruits; and then he shall go to the land of the Cross.

We don't know what it means, but it's pretty. As the auctioneers used to say, "Call it what you want to and use it for the same purpose."

### No Mystery Here

Mother Shipton was not the first to predict technical progress; Friar Roger Bacon who lived two centuries before her (he died in 1292), and who probably invented gunpowder, foresaw most of these things, as did Leonardo da Vinci, who was pretty much her contemporary (1452–1519).

## The Added Verse

One of the verses attributed to Mother Shipton caused a great deal of worry about 150 years ago. The verse was actually added to the Shipton verses around 1840 by Charles Hindley, who compiled a volume of her sayings. For reasons of his own, maybe to help the sales of his book, he decided to add this one:

> When the world to an end shall come
> In eighteen hundred and eighty one.

When the date passed and the world refused to end, some people decided that the date was misentered—that it should have been "nineteen hundred and ninety one."

Well now, that's come and gone also, and we're still here. They'll just have to come up with a better rhyme.

**No Mystery Here**

For more information about Mother Shipton, you can contact:

Mother Shipton's Cave Prophesy House, Knaresborough, N Yorkshire HG5 8DD England
E-mail: MotherShipton @compuserve.com

Mother Shipton actually did prophesy the end of the world with the following line:

> The world shall end when the High Bridge is thrice fallen.

Just so you'll have something to worry about, the Knaresborough High Bridge has already fallen twice.

Mother Shipton died in 1561, and it is said that a monument was erected to her between the villages of Clifton and Skipton with a plaque reading:

> Here ly's she who never ly'd
> Whose skill often has been try'd
> Her prophecies shall still survive,
> And ever keep her name alive.

# Nostradamus

He was born Michel de Nostre Dame in St. Remy-en-Provence, France, on 14 December 1503. His grand-father, Jacques de Nostre Dame, was royal physician to King René of Provence. He grew up to call himself Nostradamus, and he became the most skilled and certainly the most famous prophet outside of the Bible.

When he was 19, Michel went to the university at Montpellier, which held one of the most famous schools of medicine in Europe, the only one where they actually dissected corpses to learn anatomy. There he studied medicine and philosophy. He cut short his studies when an epidemic of the Black Plague broke out in southern France. Nostradamus traveled from town to town doing what medical science in the sixteenth century recommended for the Plague, which was not much.

Nostradamus showed great personal courage in his treatment and handling of plague victims. Most people, including doctors, avoided not only plague victims but any houses, villages, or cities containing them. Doctors who did treat plague victims wore special leather suits, soaked their clothing with oils and juices, kept a clove of garlic in their mouths, and covered their faces with goggles. The sight of them probably frightened many of their patients as much as the plague itself.

Nostradamus's approach differed from the standard medical practice of the day. He studied and analyzed the course of the disease and gained a reputation for curing his patients. One of his biographers suggests that he may have discovered antiseptic medicine three centuries before Lister. If so, he was not able to convince other doctors to take up the practice, which is not surprising since even 300 years later doctors took a lot of convincing.

Nostradamus returned to the university in 1529 to get his doctorate. The faculty was not amused by his unorthodox treatment of patients, especially because it was gaining him a great reputation as a healer. However, he passed his examinations and was granted the right to wear the four-cornered hat and ermine-trimmed velvet robe of a full-fledged doctor.

### The Mystery Deepens

A little-known fact about Nostradamus is that, in addition to books of prophecy, he also wrote dissertations on perfumes and cosmetics and on how to make quince jam with sugar, honey, and cooked wine.

## The Wanderer

For the next few years, Nostradamus wandered Europe. He settled down briefly in Agen and married a lovely, intelligent lady named Adriete de Loubejac; they had two sons. But she sickened of some disease that Nostradamus was unable to cure, and she and their sons died within a year. Nostradamus resumed his wandering.

It was during this period that his gift of prophecy revealed itself. One of its earliest manifestations was when, traveling through Italy, he met a Franciscan friar named Felix Peretti, a poor, undistinguished young monk. Nostradamus knelt before the young man. "What are you doing?" the other friars asked.

"I must kneel before His Holiness," Nostradamus explained. The friars took little notice of this strange behavior, but they remembered it years later when Felix Peretti was elected Pope Sixtus the Fifth.

## Obscure and in Verse

As we're sure you've already noticed, most of the prophecies issued in the ancient and medieval world were in verse, and many are rather obscure. The verse is easy to explain: In the days before printing and while books were still very expensive, verse made something easier to remember. People can remember thousands of lines of verse with practice. The entire *Iliad* and *Odyssey* were remembered line-for-line by ancient Greek bards, and this is how they survived for hundreds of years before writing was invented.

*Nostradamus, from an early woodcut.*

The obscureness of the prophecies, however, and the fact that their meanings often are not revealed until after the events prophesied (when they become self-evident), is not quite as easy to explain. One possibility is that a vision itself comes through obscurely—an obscure description is the best the seer can do. But that explanation is hard to accept when, in the case of Nostradamus, for example, the key word in the prophecy comes through as an *anagram* of a king's name or the name of a place. "Chiren" for "Henry" (king of France) for example, or "Rapis" for "Paris." Surely Nostradamus did not see whatever he saw in anagram form. Or when Nostrodamus says, "The young lion shall overcome the old / On the field of war in single combat" (Century I, Quatrain 35), he surely didn't have a vision in which he actually saw a young lion bounding about in battle with an older one.

We must, therefore, assume that the prophets had a clearer vision than they were telling us and that they had reasons of their own for making the prophecies obscure. One possible reason is that, if the prophecy is understood too easily or too early, it might change history and nullify the very thing it prophesies.

Nostradamus himself, in a letter to King Henry II of France that serves as his intro-duction to the second edition of the *Centuries,* explains "that the danger of the times,

O Most Serene Majesty, requires that such hidden events be not manifested save by enigmatic speech ... did I so desire, I could fix the time for every *quatrain* ... but that it might to some be disagreeable."

Another possibility is that the prophecies are vague in the hopes that something, someday, will come along that will seem to fulfill their conditions. The more enigmatic the verse, in other words, the more chances a prophet has of its coming true. Take the example of the two lions. We can all think of many ways that it could come true. A young prizefighter coming along and knocking out an old champ; an upstart company beating an established company in business. Or it could be the American Revolution, in which the brand new United States beats the old lion of Great Britain.

### What Does This Mean?

An **anagram** is a word or phrase containing all the letters of another word or phrase. Dog, for example, is an anagram of God, as harmonicas is an anagram for maraschino. Nostradamus wrote his prophecies as **quatrains** (four-line verses), which he gathered into groups of 100, each of which he called a century. There are 10 centuries and 1,000 quatrains.

## The Golden Cage

Let's see if we can interpret this one verse. It is Century I, Quatrain 35, and it reads in full:

> *Le lyon jeune le vieux surmontera*
> *En champ bellique par singulier duelle:*
> *Dans caige d'or les yeux lui crevera,*
> *Deux classes une, puis mourir, mort cruelle.*

Nostradamus's French is medieval and mixed with a hint of Latin and a whisper of Greek. Well, it would be of course, he wrote in the sixteenth century. A fair translation of this verse would be something like this:

> The young lion shall beat the old
> On the field of combat in single fight
> In a cage of gold his eyes shall be pierced
> Two wounds in one, then he dies a cruel death.

A cage of gold? Two wounds? Eyes pierced?

Well, it happened just like that and only a few years after Nostradamus wrote the prediction. On 10 July 1559, during a tournament that Henry II was holding to celebrate a pair of royal marriages, Henry jousted with Montgomery, the captain of the Scottish guard. On the third tip, they both splintered their lances, and Montgomery's lance was driven through the eyeholes in the front "cage" visor of the king's gilded helmet and into his eyes. It took Henry 10 days to die, and it was not a pleasant death.

83

### The Mystery Deepens

Some of the stories that circulated about Nostradamus during his lifetime showed the awe in which people held him even then, before many of his predictions came to pass. It is told, for example, that a royal page lost a valuable dog and came running to Nostradamus's house in the middle of the night for advice. When he knocked on the door, even before he announced who he was, Nostradamus's voice came thundering through the closed door, "What is it you want, O page of the king? You make a deal of noise for a lost dog! Go on the road toward Orleans, and you will find him being led in a leash." The page raced off, and sure enough, someone had already found the dog and was returning him on a leash.

## Ancient Egyptian Books

Nostradamus claimed that he learned his occult powers from some ancient Egyptian books he inherited from his grandfather and that he burned them after he memorized them. Since Nostradamus's family was originally Jewish, before the various rulers of Europe made all the Jews convert or leave (or die) during the fifteenth century, some biographers believe that Nostradamus may have had some original texts that Moses took with him from the secret Egyptian cults and that his family had kept hidden over the centuries. This would have made Nostradamus, we suppose, a direct descendant of Moses.

This is unlikely for so many reasons that it would take several pages just to list them. We'll cite just one: By the sixteenth century, nobody in the world could read ancient Egyptian hieroglyphics. Even the Egyptians had forgotten how.

If Nostradamus did claim knowledge based on ancient Egyptian books, it was probably just his way of shutting up nosey people.

## But What of the Quatrains?

The thousand verses (and a few extra) are not in any sort of order. The first few explain in general terms his method of divination (they're too general to help anyone else do it), and the rest predict events scattered over at least the next five hundred years. There's no way to tell what refers to what until it happens—and even then you wonder if this really was what Nostradamus was talking about. Will something else transpire that fits the imagery even better?

**Mysterious Comments**

Not everyone was a fan of Nostradamus in his own lifetime. A poet courtier named Jodelle wrote

*"Nostra damus cum falsa damus, nam fallere nostrum est. Sed cum falsa damus, nil nisi nostra damus."*

This, freely translated, starts with a pun on Nostradamus's name and reads

"We give our own in giving lies, for to deceive is our business. And measuring out the false, we give nothing but our very own."

## What Did He Say?

Let's look at a couple of the quatrains and see if we can place them.

➤ Century IX, Quatrain 90

*Un capitaine de la grand Germanie*
*Se viendra rendre par simul secours*
*Un roi des rois aide de Pannonie*
*Que sa revolte fera de sang grand cours.*

A captain of the great Germany
Will come to give false hope
A king of kings, to the aid of Pannonia
And his battles will cause a great bloodletting.

This verse is generally accepted as a prediction of the Second World War. In Nostradamus's time, Germany was split into many small states; it didn't become one Germany until 1866, when most of the states were united in a federation. It wasn't until Hitler's Grossendeutschland, "great Germany," of the Third Reich that the echo of Nostradamus's prediction began. Hitler was, in a sense, a "king of kings" since he ruled Germany, which ruled many other countries. Pannonia was a Roman province that incorporated most of modern Hungary and Czecho-slovakia—both captured and enslaved by the Nazis. And unquestionably, there was a great bloodletting with over 15 million people killed.

➤ Century II, Quatrain 57

*Avant conflict le grand tombera*
*Le grand mort, mort, trop subite & plainte,*
*Nay imparfaict: la plus part nagera,*
*Aupres du fleuve de sang la terre tainte.*

Before conflict the great will fall
The great one to death, death very sudden and sorrowful,
Born imperfect: he will go much of the way,
Near the stream of blood the ground is stained.

### No Mystery Here

During World War II, both sides used false prophecies of Nostradamus as part of their propaganda campaigns to influence the superstitious people on the enemy side.

This is a possible reference to the presidency of John Kennedy. "Before conflict" could be the war in Vietnam, which was just beginning in Kennedy's presidency. As for "death very sudden and sorrowful," there's no question that Kennedy's assassination was that. "Born imperfect?" He had Addison's disease and a bad back, but I'm not sure whether these were birth defects. And he did "go much of the way" until he was cut down. As for the last line, the war in Vietnam created a stream of blood and a stain on our national pride and sense of morality that has yet to heal.

## You're On Your Own

Here's your chance to see what you can do with the logic of divination. The following are a few of Nostradamus's quatrains that sound intriguing but for which nobody has found a historical home. Have fun!

➤ Century IV, Quatrain 47

*Le noir farouche quand aura essayé*
*Sa main sanguine par feu, fer, arcs tendus:*
*Trestout le peuple sera tant effrayé*
*Voir le plus grans par col & pieds pendus.*

The ferocious black, when he has tried
His bloody hand through fire, iron, the bent bow;
All the people will be afraid
To see the greatest hanging by their neck and feet.

## Mysterious Comments

"Everything in [Nostradamus] is ambiguous: the man, the thought, the style. We stumble at every step in the rough paths of his labyrinth. Once we enter, jeering voices seem to deride us from behind each stanza, strophe, word ... The Sphinx of France is here before us; a riddler, riddling of the fate of men: a man at once bold and timid; simple, yet who can plumb his depth?"

—Chas. A. Ward, *Oracles of Nostradamus*

➤ Century V, Quatrain 68

*Dans le Danube & du Rhin viendra boire,*
*Le grand Chameau ne s'en repentira:*
*Trembler du Rosne & plus fort ceux de Loire,*
*Et pres des Alpes coq le ruinera.*

In the Danube and the Rhine will come to drink,
The great camel, and will be glad (and will not repent),
Those of the Rhone, and even more those of the Loire will tremble,
And near the Alps the cock will ruin him.

➤ Century IX, Quatrain 47

*Les soulz signez d'indigne delivrance,*
*Et de la multe auront contre advis,*
*Change monarque mis en perille pence,*
*Serrez en caige se verront vis à vis.*

The glutted ones (you) sign from an unworthy deliverance,
And against the advice of the many,
A king changes, putting thoughts in danger,
Put in a cage, they are face to face.

Several of the words here are variant spellings and could take on different meanings. *Soulz*, for example, could be a variant of glutted, drunken, lifted up, or shoes. Take your choice.

# 124c41

Did Nostradamus foresee the future? I don't believe it for an instant. Not for an instant. And yet … some of his verses seem eerily accurate. If you ask me whether I have a better explanation of what was going on, I'll probably do my best to change the subject.

There have been many books, articles, and Web sites dedicated to Nostradamus and his prophecies, but be careful and selective when you look at them. Many people have twisted Nostradamus's predictions or have made up their own versions to fit their agendas.

---

### The Least You Need to Know

➤ Many people have claimed to be prophets, and a few have shown some apparent talent in this direction.

➤ Mother Shipton's sixteenth-century rhymes predicted automobiles, submarines, radios, and much more.

➤ Nostradamus was trained as a doctor and was talented and courageous during outbreaks of the Black Plague.

➤ Nostradamus's quatrains seem not to make much sense until after the event they foretell.

➤ Some of Nostradamus's prophecies are eerily accurate hundreds of years after his death.

---

# Chapter 8

Internet............

# Recent Prophets

---

## In This Chapter

➤ The Fatima visions: an accepted miracle

➤ The three messages of the "Lady of Light"

➤ The prophecies in Medjugorje

➤ Edgar Cayce and his prophecies

---

Modern science has established that the arrow of time goes in but one direction—at least in *this* part of the universe. This means that visiting the past in any physical way is impossible. We also recognize that leaps into the future are impossible in any way other than, perhaps, cryogenically—that is, by being quick-frozen and thawed out some time later.

And yet there have been people, as you read in Chapters 6, "They Delved Into the Future," and 7, "The Great Medieval Prophets," who seemed able to peer into the future and reveal, sometimes in confused or mystical terms but sometimes very directly, what they saw. Despite the disapproval of science, the practice of divination has not disappeared. Indeed, in some ways, it is stronger than ever, and belief in the mystical arts seems to be growing rather than shrinking. The rationality of science and the mysticism of the occult are traveling side by side these days. Many times, these two contrary notions abide in the same person.

In this chapter we'll talk about several of last century's most impressive examples of people who see more than is visible to the rest of us, and who know more of what hasn't happened yet than is allowed for in modern science.

### Mysterious Comments

"In these scientific modern times, as almost anyone will tell you, virtually no one believes in prophecy. A little closer enquiry will lead the reader, as it has led the writer, to conclude that almost everyone believes in prophecy."

—Henry James Forman, *The Story of Prophecy*

# The Events at Fatima

It was in the middle of World War I that a series of events—some say they were miracles, some say they were prime examples of mass hypnosis—happened at Cova da Iria, near the town of Fatima in Portugal. We should point out that, although mass hypnosis has become a catch-all explanation for any unusual phenomena witnessed by a group of people, there is no proof at all of the existence of the sort of mass hypnosis necessary to explain what happened at Fatima.

It began on 13 May 1917. Three children, Lucia dos Santos (whose name, incidentally, means "light of the saints") and her cousins Jacinta and Francisco Marto, spent the day tending sheep in a meadow. When they came home for dinner, they told their parents that a beautiful "Senhorita de Luz"("Lady of Light") had come to them, floating above an oak tree. She told them that she had something to say and that they should come back in exactly one month. No one believed the children's story. Although the three were known to be good children, they were, after all, children. But on 13 June, a small group of townspeople followed the children out to the meadow.

## A White Mist

Lucia, who was the oldest, began talking to someone the others could not see. As they watched, a strange white mist formed around the group, and they could all hear a faint buzzing sound. When Lucia said the lady was leaving, the branches of the oak tree were seen to bend in the direction she went.

The next month, on 13 July, several hundred people showed up, and the event proceeded as before, white mist and all. This time it ended with a loud and unexplainable bang, sharp enough to shake an arch that the townspeople had erected at the spot. Lucia claimed this time that the lady had told her three secrets.

The next month, the local governor had the children arrested and taken to the police station for questioning, trying to get them to admit they were making it all up. Meanwhile, hundreds of people gathered at the spot, which was rapidly becoming a shrine. When they heard that the children were in custody and would not be coming, they were upset, for surely now no miracle would occur.

But at the appointed time the white mist rose, and a great clap of thunder was heard followed by a bolt of lightning. Now as everyone knows, thunder follows lightning, not the other way around.

## A Glowing Globe

A month later, on 13 September, the children were back, and an estimated 25,000 people crowded around to see what would happen. Many of the observers, but not all, saw a glowing globe appear in the east and cross the sky to the oak tree. "To my great surprise," one witness affirmed, "I saw clearly and distinctly a ball of light sliding slowly and majestically through space ... Then suddenly, with the extraordinary light that it let out, this globe disappeared before my eyes, and the priest who was at my side saw it no more either."

At the same time, snow flakes that were not snow flakes "but round and brilliant" fell from the sky but dissolved upon landing.

**No Mystery Here**

In an attempt to win the confidence of the three children, the governor threatened to have them boiled in oil and told one of the girls, "Your little brother has already been fried." This, as you might guess, hardly caused them to immediately admire and trust the governor.

## The Final Proof

The Lady of Light promised the children that, at her next appearance, she would do something to prove her existence to those who doubted. On 13 October between 50,000 and 70,000 people arrived at Cova da Iria. Most expected to see a miracle, but there were enough doubters and skeptics to leaven the crowd.

Black clouds filled the sky, and it was raining heavily as the crowd assembled at ten in the morning. Photographs taken then show the assemblage peering out from under thousands of umbrellas. After an hour, Lucia asked those close to her to close their umbrellas, and gradually the umbrellas were furled as word of the request spread through the crowd.

## The Sky Cleared

At around noon, the clouds dissipated and the rain stopped. The odd white mist formed around the crowd.

Suddenly Lucia pointed to the sky and called, "Look at the sun!" Fifty thousand people turned from the oak tree they had been staring at and saw the sun, but it was not the sun they knew. As one observer—a local magistrate—described it: "It was not spherical, it looked like a flat and polished disk which had been cut from the pearl in a shell … and was clearly seen to have a ridged edge like a drawing-board." And, unlike the sun they were accustomed to, it seemed to many observers to be low in the sky, lower than the clouds.

All at once, the "sun" shimmied and shook and began to spin "at an astonishing speed." It projected rays of colored lights from its rim—green, then blue, then red. Then it seemed to fall toward the earth, fluttering like a leaf. All at once it flew off and disappeared, and once again, the crowd could see the sun they were accustomed to seeing.

The people had their miracle.

# The Three Secrets

The "Senhorita de Luz" that the children saw was, it is generally agreed by those who agree they saw anything, the Virgin Mary. She had come to deliver a message of importance to the world through these children. The message was in three parts, which the two girls were directed to keep secret at first, telling no one but their cousin Francisco, who could also see the Virgin but could not hear her. Francisco and Jacinta died during the great influenza epidemic of 1918–1919. Lucia became a nun, taking the name Sister Lucia. As of this writing, she is living in a Carmelite monastery in Portugal.

In 1941, Sister Lucia received word from the Virgin Mary, by means of an "inner vision," that she could reveal the first two parts of the message.

## A Glimpse Into Hell

Lucia related that Mary "opened her hands. The light reflecting from them seemed to penetrate into the earth, and we saw as if into a sea of fire. And immersed in that fire were devils and souls with human form, as if they were transparent black or bronze embers floating in the fire and swayed by the flames that issued from them along with clouds of smoke, falling on every side just like the falling of sparks in a great fire, without weight or equilibrium, amidst wailing and cries of pain and despair that horrified and shook us with terror. We could tell the devils by their horrible and numerous figures of baleful and unknown animals, but transparent as the black coals in a fire."

That was the girl's first vision. And then, in the second vision, Mary spoke to her, saying:

> You have seen Hell, where the souls of sinners go. To save them, God wants to establish in the world the devotion to my Immaculate Heart. If people do what I tell you, many souls will be saved and there will be peace.

## An Unknown Light

Mary continued:

> The war is going to end, but if people do not stop offending God, there will be another and more terrible war during the Pontificate of Pius XI. When you see a night illuminated by an unknown light, know that it is the great sign from God that He is about to punish the world for its crimes through war, famine, persecution of the church and of the Holy Father.

### The Mystery Deepens

On the night of 24–25 January 1938, a bright red glow suffused the sky and was particularly strong over Portugal. Thousands of people rushed from their homes, convinced that the world was on fire. Scientists said it was an unusual display of the Aurora Borealis—the Northern Lights, which are seldom seen below the Baltic Ocean. Sister Lucia believed it was the sign the Virgin told her to expect and that the first of the prophecies was about to begin: A "worse war" (than World War I) was about to break out. One month later Hitler invaded Austria.

Note, you prophesy lovers, that Benedict XV was pope when these visions occurred. Father Ambrogio D'Amiano Achille Ratti did not become pope or take the name Pius XI until 1922.

The prophecy goes on:

> To forestall this, I shall come to ask for the consecration of Russia to my Immaculate Heart and the Communion of Reparation on the First Saturdays. If my requests are heeded, Russia will be converted and there will be peace. If not, she will spread her errors throughout the world, promoting wars and the persecution of the Church; the good will be martyred, the Holy Father will suffer

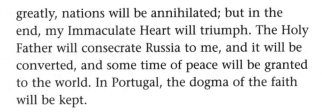

greatly, nations will be annihilated; but in the end, my Immaculate Heart will triumph. The Holy Father will consecrate Russia to me, and it will be converted, and some time of peace will be granted to the world. In Portugal, the dogma of the faith will be kept.

So far, with the first two prophecies, the Lady of Light managed to correctly predict:

➤ The end of World War I

➤ The start of World War II

➤ The spread of atheistic communism in Russia

➤ The Soviet attempt to export communism ("her errors") around the world

➤ The name of the next pope: Pius XI

But what of the third prophecy?

## No Mystery Here

The Catholic Encyclopedia says of the Immaculate Heart of Mary that it suggests "Mary's interior life, her joys and sorrows, her virtues and hidden perfections, and above all, her virginal love for her God, her maternal love for her Divine Son, and her motherly and compassionate love for her sinful and miserable children here below."

## The Third Prophecy Revealed

Sister Lucia believed the third part of the prophecy was still to be kept secret, but in 1943, when she nearly died of pleurisy, she agreed to write it down for the Bishop of Fatima. He brought it to the Vatican along with instructions from the Virgin Mother, forwarded by Sister Lucia, that it was not to be opened until 1960.

It is believed that Pope John XXIII opened and read the letter in 1960 and then resealed it and returned it to the safe without revealing what it said. It is also believed that every pope since John XXIII has similarly opened and read the letter and refused to reveal its contents.

The third prophecy was finally revealed on 13 May 2000, when Pope John Paul II visited Fatima to attend the *beatification* ceremony for "the little shepherds," Francisco and Jacinta Marto, the brother and sister who died within two years of receiving the vision.

## What Does This Mean?

**Beatification** is the next-to-last step in the lengthy process of declaring someone a saint in the Roman Catholic Church (the last, of course, is "sainthood"). This was the first time the Church had begun the sainthood process for any children who did not die as martyrs.

Before the ceremony the Pope met privately to consult with Sister Lucia de Jesus dos Santos, the 93-year-old Carmelite nun who had been the third child. The Pope had visited the shrine at Fatima twice before, once in 1982 and again in 1991, to give thanks to the Lady for saving his life after he was seriously wounded during an assassination attempt in 1981. The reason for John Paul II's interest in the shrine became clear after the ceremony, when Cardinal Angelo Sodano, Secretary of State for the Vatican, revealed the third secret. The pope did not announce it himself because of his personal involvement in the prophecy.

As paraphrased by Cardinal Sodano, the message was that "The bishop clothed in white" (the Pope) will make his way with great effort towards the cross amid the corpses of those who were martyred (bishops, priests, religious men and women, and many lay people), when he too will fall to the ground, apparently dead, under a burst of gunfire. But his life will be saved.

Surely this referred to the attempted assassination of Pope John Paul II on 13 May 1981. Or did it?

## The Doubters

Why was the message not revealed earlier? Back in 1996 Cardinal Joseph Ratzinger, the head of the Vatican's Congregation for the Doctrine of the Faith, said it was because the Vatican wanted to avoid "confusing religious prophecy with sensationalism."

But those who doubt, or perhaps it is those who would prefer sensationalism, are not yet satisfied. They don't doubt that what Cardinal Sodano said was true; the Church wouldn't lie about something like that. But is it the whole truth? Are parts of the third message still being suppressed? If so, what disaster could the message foretell that the Vatican is unwilling to reveal?

The Pope has charged Cardinal Ratzinger and his Congregation for the Doctrine of the Faith with preparing a commentary to accompany and explain the text of the actual message, after which it is to be made public. As of this writing, no date has been decided for this publication. Both the believers and the doubters wait to see what the actual text says, and just what there is that needs explanation.

# Our Lady of Medjugorje

The events at Fatima were not the last of this sort of religious miracle. We haven't heard much yet about the regular appearance of the Virgin Mary to a bunch of children in Medjugorje, a town in southern Bosnia, over the past few decades. After all, Bosnia has had enough to put it in the news lately without a minor but continuing miracle. The Medjugorje visions haven't officially been declared a miracle yet by the Vatican, but they haven't been officially discounted either. What seems to be happening is this:

Early in the evening of 2 June 1981, six children in Medjugorje saw an apparition of the Virgin Mary. Much like the one at Fatima 64 years before, it was accompanied by

strange atmospheric disturbances. The first day, the children were frightened and ran away, as might you or I. The next night, four of the original six plus two new children saw the apparition again. On the third night, they returned with holy water, which they tossed at the vision. The Lady smiled at them and revealed to them that she was the Queen of Peace.

Two months later, on 2 August, many villagers and pilgrims witnessed the same sort of sun dislocation that the crowd at Fatima had seen, and many thought they saw the word MIR ("peace" in most Slavic languages) written across the sky.

The Queen of Peace has been visiting the children of Medjugorje regularly since then, although not the same children throughout; as they grow up, they lose their ability to see her and are replaced by younger ones. Over the years, she has given some of them, gradually, 10 secrets that they are to reveal to a priest of their choosing.

> **No Mystery Here**
>
> The pope has not made any official comments on the happenings at Medjugorje, but in a letter to a Czechoslovakian bishop he wrote, "Yes, today the world has lost the sense of the supernatural. In Medjugorje, many have looked for it and found it in prayer, fasting, and confession."

The church is officially neutral on the happenings at Medjugorje to date, and that's where the matter stands. The town is getting a regular influx of pilgrims, and were it not for the Bosnian war, which has kept Medjugorje off the regular tourist route, it might have turned into a heavy-duty shrine. It may yet.

# Edgar Cayce

Edgar Cayce (pronounced "Casey") was probably the most important prophet of the twentieth century. Even though he never wrote a book himself, hundreds of books have been written about him, his life, his works, and his prophecies. A society called the Association for Research and Enlightenment (A.R.E.) was founded by Cayce to study the record of the psychic readings he gave over the years and to teach courses in self-awareness and various religious and psychic subjects.

## The Sleeping Prophet

Cayce was born in 1877 on a farm near Hopkinsville, Kentucky. As a child, it is said, he discovered that he could learn his school lessons by going to sleep with the schoolbooks under his pillow. The early newspaper reports on him used to regularly describe him as illiterate. *The New York Times,* for example, did a story on him for the 9 October 1910 Sunday magazine section, headlined "Illiterate Man Becomes a Doctor When Hypnotized." But Casey was not illiterate. He did drop out of school in the sixth grade, but he was a constant reader of all sorts of books, and he didn't read all of them by putting them under his pillow.

Cayce's technique for giving psychic readings was to lie down on a couch, make himself comfortable, and go into a self-induced trance. Then someone sitting next to him, usually his wife, Gertrude, would ask him questions about the subject. He would reply with an entirely different voice, manner of speaking, and vocabulary than he normally used. His secretary would take down everything he said in shorthand, so today there is a record of the more than 14,000 readings he gave during his lifetime.

The subject of the reading did not have to be present or even aware that the reading was happening at that time. According to the records, a reading went something like this:

Cayce would lie down on the couch and go into a state of autohypnosis, which he could apparently do almost instantly. Then his interlocutor would carefully instruct the sleeping Cayce as follows: "You will have before you the body of Frank Baum [or whoever the patient might be], who is present in this room [or who is in a hotel room at the Grand Hotel in Indianapolis, or whatever distance didn't seem to be a bar to diagnosis]. You will go over the body carefully, telling us the conditions you find there, and what may be done to correct anything which is wrong. You will speak distinctly, at a normal rate of speech, and you will answer questions which I will put to you."

After a wait, usually brief but occasionally quite a while, Cayce would clear his throat and say in a more forceful voice than the awake Cayce used, "Yes, we have the body." And then would come the diagnosis. When he was finished and had answered any questions he considered relevant, the sleeping Cayce would announce, "We are through for the present." Then a minute or so later he would wake up.

### Mysterious Comments

"Edgar Cayce's mind is amenable to suggestion, the same as all other subconscious minds, but in addition thereto it has the power to interpret to the objective mind of others what it acquired from the subconscious state of other individuals of the same kind. The subconscious mind forgets nothing.

"The conscious mind receives the impressions from without and transfers all thought to the subconscious, where it remains even though the conscious be destroyed."

—The sleeping Cayce explaining how he did what he did, as quoted in *The New York Times,* 9 October 1910

*Edgar Cayce.*

### What Does This Mean?

**Osteopathy** is a branch of medicine started in 1892 by Dr. Andrew T. Still. At first concentrating on physical manipulation of the body as a cure for all disease, it has since become respectable; a course of study at osteopathic schools is much like those in regular medical schools.

## Diagnoses and Treatments

Cayce's diagnoses would often be detailed and complex. "Along the spine, through the nervous system, through the circulation (which is perverted), through the digestive organs, there is trouble ... also inflammation in the pelvic organs, trouble with the kidneys and slight inflammation in the bladder. Seems that it starts from digestive disturbances in the stomach. The digestive organs fail to perform their function properly ..." and so on and so on.

The treatments combined *osteopathy, homeopathy, naturopathy,* patent medicines, and some would say Cayce's own psychic healing power in a manner tuned to each patient's perceived needs. Cayce was big on blaming all sorts of medical complaints on colon troubles and prescribing colonic irrigation. He was not alone; doctors at the time seemed preoccupied with the colon and prescribed colonic irrigation—an enema—for everything from depression to an earache.

Were the sleeping Cayce's modes of treatment successful? Apparently, for many of his patients they were. However (A-ha! You knew there'd be a "however," didn't you?), most people, most of the time, get well with the passage of time and the healing power of nature. Add to that the tremendous power of the placebo effect, which recent studies have shown can even work to cure problems normally treated by surgery. We are just discovering how great an ability the mind has to heal the body. So if the mind of a patient believes that a psychic healer is psychically healing the patient's body, that body just might manage to heal itself.

## On to Atlantis

As time went on, Cayce's interlocutors began asking questions that went beyond the medical problems of their patients. They asked questions that fell into the realms of astrology, religion, reincarnation, past lives, the future of mankind, and the history of Atlantis. The sleeping Cayce had answers for questions on a wide variety of subjects. He believed that he tapped into the "Akashic record," which is a sort of mystical dimension in which a record of all happenings, thoughts, and emotions from the past and the future are kept. The term was popularized by H.P. Blavatsky, the nineteenth-century founder of the Theosophical Society, a society that claims to possess and teach a variety of mystical knowledge.

The soul is androgynous, so the sleeping Cayce discovered, and can reincarnate as either male or female, taking on either the male or female polarity with the sex of the body it reincarnates into.

Cayce revealed that Atlantis had been in the Atlantic Ocean "between the Gulf of Mexico on the one hand and the Mediterranean upon the other." He gave great detail on how the Atlanteans lived and thought and behaved. Their advanced science, Cayce explained, depended on using the "Tuaoi stone," which was "in the form of a six-sided figure in which the light appeared as the means of communication between infinity and the finite; or the means whereby there were the communications with those forces from the outside."

**What Does This Mean?**

**Homeopathy**, from the Greek words *homeo* (similar) and *pathos* (suffering), is a system of medical treatment that assumes the symptoms of a disease are the body's efforts to cure the disease. Thus, if an illness is accompanied by a fever, a substance that causes a fever can cure the illness.

**What Does This Mean?**

**Naturopathy** uses natural remedies, such as sunlight supplemented with diet and massage, to cure disease.

Later, this came to mean "that from which the energies radiated, as of the center from which there were the radial activities guiding the various forms of transition or travel through those periods of activity of the Atlanteans."

Well, now we know.

So what are we to make of Mr. Edgar Cayce? From all accounts, he was a well-meaning man who almost certainly believed in his own powers. That is, the waking Cayce believed in whatever the sleeping Cayce did, although he apparently had no conscious memory of it when he was awake. Many people believed he helped them, and he probably did. He may have delayed professional diagnosis for some people

**No Mystery Here**

For more on Atlantis in fact and fiction, turn to Chapter 11, "Beneath the Waves."

with cancer or other incurable diseases, but back then when there was no real treatment, he at least had the placebo effect going for him. He gave simple and direct advice, and those who used him believed in his powers. That in itself could have cured many. As for his insights into reincarnation, Atlantis, and other occult questions, the best we can say is that there are still many people who agree with him. Of course, there are still many people who believe that the earth is flat.

The desire to know what lies ahead, and perhaps to influence it, is strong. Millions of people consult psychics and astrologers on everything from their love lives to the stock market. What these seers know that you don't is that if they are right one time in five, their customers will forget the four mistakes and remember only the success.

---

### The Least You Need to Know

➤ One of the tasks of the shaman has always been to foretell the future with the aid of hallucinogenic drugs and exhausting rituals.

➤ At Fatima in Portugal during World War I, three children may have received a message from the Virgin Mary.

➤ Children in Medjugorje, a town in southern Bosnia, have been having visions in which they receive messages from the "Queen of Peace."

➤ Edgar Cayce, the famed American psychic, diagnosed and prescribed for patients while in a trance. He also declaimed on, among other things, astrology, reincarnation, past lives, and Atlantis.

# Chapter 9

# Monumental Mysteries

**In This Chapter**

➤ The Great Pyramid

➤ A Japanese pyramid

➤ The sphinx

➤ Stonehenge

➤ Gilgal Refaim

Many thousands of years ago, in the ages of bronze, copper, and even stone, humans built giant monuments that have outlived their cultures. Ancient peoples left behind these great *megaliths*, monoliths, statuary, and structures but nothing to explain why they invested so much of their time and resources in these vast projects.

The questions that these structures have left for us are many:

➤ Who built them? In the case of the pyramids, we know which pharaohs ordered their construction, but were the workers serfs, slaves, paid artisans, or some combination of the three? In the case of Stonehenge, we don't even know who built this complex and weighty structure.

➤ How were they built? What sort of advance planning did the builders do?

➤ What tools were used to build them? How did the builders figure angles and slopes? How did they cut and shape the giant stones?

> How were the building materials, sometimes giant stone blocks weighing many tons, transported to the building site?

> What did they look like when they were new? Any wooden or brick structures or earthworks that were originally designed to be part of the edifice or the surrounding site have disappeared. The stones themselves are so worn by weather or vandals that sometimes the original shape is hard to discern.

> What were they intended to be used for? Temples? Tombs? Great calendars? Astronomical observatories? Repositories of secret knowledge? This is perhaps the greatest puzzle, and many different answers have been proposed.

### What Does This Mean?

A **megalith** is literally a huge stone. The term usually refers to ancient stone monuments like Stonehenge that are composed of groups of such stones. A **monolith** is a large single stone like an Egyptian obelisk or Mick Jagger.

In this chapter, we'll explore the pyramids, the Sphinx, and Stonehenge with an eye toward answering these and other questions.

## The Greatest Pyramid

Nobody knows for sure where the term "pyramid" comes from or what it means. We don't even know whether it's Egyptian or Greek in origin. It's been suggested that the word comes from *pyr*, the Greek word for "fire"; or from the Egyptian *pyr-em-us,* "the tall thing"; or from the Hebrew *bur-a-mit,* "the tomb." Egyptologist A. Pochan, author of *L'Enigme de la grande Pyramide* (translated into English as *The Mysteries of the Great Pyramids*), holds out for the Egyptian *pr m it,* "the abode of laments" or "the house of the dead." Some *pyramidologists* (we'll get to them shortly) found the Greek root *pyros,* "wheat," at the root of the word "pyramid," which was further confirmation for them that the pyramids were storehouses for the grain that Joseph put aside during the seven years of plenty (Genesis 41:14 onward). The fact that the pyramids are solid stone except for some narrow passages and small chambers and that very little grain could be stored in them was somehow not addressed.

### *What a Wonder*

When the ancient Greeks declared the Great Pyramid of Cheops (a ruler we now call Khufu) to be one of the Seven Wonders of the World, they were alluding to its size and grandeur. But about 150 years ago, a London mathematician and publisher named John Taylor decided it was wonderful for more reasons than that. In 1859, he published a book called *The Great Pyramid, Why was it built and Who built it?* Of course, he had answers to his questions. Taylor had determined that "the Great Pyramid was built to carry a divine revelation or prophecy."

Taylor, in speculating about the Great Pyramid, was inadvertently carrying on a long tradition of pyramidology. In the roughly 6,500 years since Khufu had the Great Pyramid built, even the Egyptian people have forgotten who built it, why it was built, and how it was built. And stories, wonderful stories, have grown up around it.

In about 1000 A.D., a native of Baghdad named Masoudi, in a manuscript he wrote called *Meadows of Gold and Mines of Gems,* related talking with an ancient *Copt* who told him the history and purpose of the pyramids:

> Surid … one of the kings of Egypt before the flood, built two great pyramids. He ordered the priests to deposit within them written accounts of their wisdom and achievements in the different arts and sciences … with the writings of the priests containing all manner of wisdom, the names and properties of medical herbs, and the sciences of arithmetic and geometry, that they might remain as records for the benefit of those who could afterwards comprehend them ….

> The king also deposited the positions of the stars and their cycles; together with the history and chronicle of time past, of that which is to come, and every future event which would take place in Egypt.

Taylor's contribution to pyramidology was to discover that the secrets of the past and the future and of all the arts and sciences were not hidden somewhere *inside* the pyramid—they were part of the pyramid itself! The Great Pyramid of Khufu was, in effect, a giant cipher waiting to be decoded by someone who could figure out the key.

### What Does This Mean?

A **pyramidologist** is someone who studies the pyramids and draws great mystical conclusions from their height, their shape, their placement, the length and shape of interior passages, and anything else relating to the pyramids that occurs to him or her.

A **Copt** is a Christian descendant of the ancient Egyptians.

*The Great Pyramid of Khufu at Giza.*

With a healthy dose of the ethnocentrism of which we are all guilty from time to time, Taylor decided that the English had been carrying pieces of the secrets of the pyramid along with them wherever they went in the form of their traditional weights and measures. A measure for wheat in England in Taylor's time was a quarter. "A quarter," Taylor wondered, "of what?"

The consensus in Taylor's time, as today, was that the pyramids are in effect giant tombs, that Khufu had the Great Pyramid built as a resting place for his body befitting his status as pharaoh and god until his *ka* (soul or spirit) could continue on its journey. There is within the Great Pyramid a large sarcophagus that would seem to support this belief, but pyramidologists have noted that it looks like it has never been used, and if it has been, the body and anything placed with it are long gone.

### The Mystery Deepens

There is a possibility that Khufu might not actually have been put in his sarcophagus in the Great Pyramid when he died. At the last minute, feeling that even a structure as mighty as the pyramid wouldn't be safe from grave robbers, he might have instructed that his body be hidden elsewhere. Perhaps even now it awaits discovery by some talented and lucky archaeologist.

But Taylor had another answer. Remember that quarter of grain? Well, Taylor decided that it must be a quarter of the volume of Khufu's sarcophagus. Therefore, it wasn't a sarcophagus at all but a master measure for wheat. Taylor also determined that the height of the pyramid was exactly 1/270,000 of the circumference of the earth. And this proved—well, what *did* it prove?

There are three problems with seeing any significance in Taylor's conclusions. First, the height of the pyramid now isn't the height of the pyramid then. The outer casing of white limestone, which early writers marveled at as it stood out brilliantly in the morning light, was removed centuries ago to make public buildings and mosques. So it's impossible to establish the original height of the pyramid. Second, even if Taylor is right, which he isn't, the pyramid's height, like any measurement smaller than the circumference of the earth, has to be *some* percentage of the circumference of the earth. Third, why would anybody build the world's largest (for many thousands of years) structure to record something that could be jotted down on a piece of papyrus?

## The Pyramid Inch

Taylor concluded that the markings along the corridors inside the Great Pyramid, whether man-made or seemingly natural, were a record of the secrets of the ancient

Egyptians. If one could but read the lines and cracks, the bends and dips, one would know everything the ancients knew about science and predictions and the workings of the universe. The decoding, Taylor thought, lay in the mathematical relationships between the different parts of the pyramid. But he was never able to work out just what these correspondences should be.

In 1864, Charles Piazzi Smyth, the Astronomer Royal of Scotland, picked up Taylor's ideas and ran with them. He found more correspondences of distance, time, location, and mathematical formulas concealed on or about the Great Pyramid than all previous seekers' discoveries put together. Here are a few:

**No Mystery Here**

The scavenging of the outer casing stones of the pyramid is a tragedy for reasons that go beyond the simple act of defacing an archaeological treasure. Early travelers reported that the sides of the pyramid were covered with hieroglyphics, which quite probably would have told us all we wanted to know about Khufu and his times and how the pyramid was built.

➤ By dividing twice the length of one side of the pyramid's base by its height you get pi. (Yes, but as we've already pointed out, we don't know the original height of the pyramid.)

➤ By multiplying the height of the pyramid by 10 billion you get the distance from the earth to the sun. (Same "Yes, but ... " as last time. Also, the distance from the earth to the sun varies at different points on the earth's elliptical orbit around the sun.)

➤ It takes exactly 365 casing stones to cross the width of the pyramid—the same number as days in a year. (Yes, but almost all the casing stones are gone, so we can't really tell how many went across.)

➤ By dividing the width of a casing stone by 25, he came up with the size of a "pyramid inch," which was the measure used to build Noah's ark and was the ancestor to the English inch. (Yes, but judging from the sizes of the few casing stones that were left, there was no standard casing stone width.)

## From Creation to the Judgment Day

The really wonderful part of Smyth's discovery is that, if the passages inside the Great Pyramid are measured off in pyramid inches, they reveal the entire history of mankind past, present, and future, from Creation to the Day of Judgment (which, Smyth reckoned, would come in either 1881 or 1911). Just how one is to read the story from the measurements is an arcane talent that has never been clear to anyone besides Smyth and his disciples.

When Judgment Day didn't come as predicted, the pyramidologists remeasured the interior and came up with a new set of dates. A British engineer named David Davidson performed a brand new analysis, which he published in 1924.

*The interior of the Great Pyramid with some of Davidson's calculations marked.*

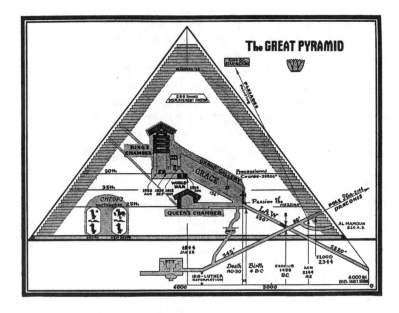

Davidson's pyramid markings correspond with dates in the Old and New Testament. When the markings approach modern times, they begin to show a bias toward history as seen from the viewpoint of Great Britain—a little odd for an Egyptian device. The Grand Gallery (the central passage inside the pyramid), for example, covers the years from 7 A.D. to "August 4–5, 1914, when Britain entered the Great War and made it world-wide."

The pyramidologists continue on to this day, combining scripture with nonsense to come up with dates for things that already have happened and predictions for an end of the world that seems to be stubbornly refusing to come when bidden.

# A Japanese Pyramid

In 1998, a pyramid was discovered submerged in the sea off the coast of the Japanese island of Yonaguni-Jima, an island in the Ryukyu chain located in the Pacific Ocean between Okinawa and Taiwan. The rectangular *ziggurat* is 75 feet underwater. Scuba divers first spotted it in 1988 but thought it was some sort of natural formation. It was 10 more years before closer examination suggested that it was artificial.

## Very Big and Very Old

The structure is 600 feet wide and 90 feet high and dates back to at least 8000 B.C. This would make it 5,000 years older than the earliest pyramid in Egypt, the Step Pyramid at Saqqara, and about contemporary with the supposed age of the Sphinx.

Robert Schoch, a professor of geology who helped date the Sphinx (more on that later in this chapter), recently undertook a scuba investigation of the site. "It basically looks like a series of huge steps, each about a meter high," he said. "Essentially, it's a cliff face like the side of a stepped pyramid. It's a very interesting structure." Schoch thought it might be possible that natural water erosion combined with a process of cracked rocks splitting apart might produce such a structure, but he said, "I haven't come across such processes creating a structure such as this."

## Smaller Steps

The probability that the structure is artificial was enhanced when divers realized that what seemed to be a road circled the pyramid and that nearby were a group of smaller step pyramids, each about 30 feet wide and 6 feet high.

"This could be evidence of a new culture," said Professor Masaki Kimura of Ryukyu University in Okinawa, "as there are no records of a people intelligent enough to have built such a monument 10,000 years ago."

## We Inherited Their Brains

Professor Kimura (or his translator) makes the usual mistake when speaking of ancient people (at least I assume he does; it might be the translater who did) —he confuses intelligence with knowledge. Considering the rate of evolution, it's almost certain that we are not perceptibly *smarter* than our ancestors of 10,000 years ago. But we do have a larger knowledge base from which to work.

Questions remain, however, as to whether these ancestors of ours had the proper tools to build such monuments, the ability to stay in one place long enough, and the necessary motivation to take on such an overwhelming project.

With the Egyptian pyramids, at least, the answer to all three questions is yes. There was a stable agricultural population that could grow the surplus grain needed and that was free to work in the winter after the crop was in. They were already settled into the area in which they built, and their motivation was a pharaoh who wanted a tomb that would impress future generations with his greatness. Well, he got it.

# The Sphinx

One of the genuine mysteries of the past is the provenance of the giant statue in Egypt called the Great Sphinx of Giza (to differentiate it from all the little sphinxes).

### What Does This Mean?

**Ziggurats** are step pyramids, which are constructed in a series of sections. Each upper section is smaller than the one below like giant square wedding cakes. They are named after the temple-towers of ancient Babylonia and Assyria.

The conventional wisdom of archeologists dates the Great Sphinx to about 2500 B.C., about the time the Great Pyramid of Khufu, which rises behind it, was built. It is attributed to Khufu (that is, he paid for it), and it is supposed to bear his face. The Great Sphinx was carved in a solid block of limestone outcropping, and it is over 240 feet long and 66 feet high.

*The Sphinx.*

## Older Than That

There is strong evidence, however, that the Great Sphinx of Giza was already ancient at the time of Khufu. Robert Schoch, a professor of geology at Boston University, studied the wind- and rain-caused erosion on the body of the Sphinx and compared it with other local statues that could be definitely dated. He found that the Sphinx was much older than originally thought, probably dating to somewhere between 5000 and 10,000 B.C.

If it is that old, it predates any known civilization in the Nile Valley, and who built it is anybody's guess. The hunter-gatherer tribes that were around 7,000 to 12,000 years ago were not supposed to have the sort of tools that would enable them to create such a statue out of solid rock. Also, they had no agriculture and therefore no access to the steady, reliable sources of food they would need to enable them to stay in one place long enough to create the great monument.

## The Stars at Night

Writer Robert Bauval and his compatriots have suggested that the Sphinx faces the direction from which the sun rose during the summer solstice approximately 10,500 years ago.

### Mysterious Comments

"In the undulating desert near Giseh rise three mighty pyramids, the tombs of three kings—Khufu, Khafre, and Menkure. At the foot of the pyramids crouches the Sphinx with talons outstretched over the city of the dead, guarding the magical secrets gathered therein."

—Kurt Seligmann, *The Mirror of Magic*, 1948

When, during recent excavations, the sand was cleared away from between the mighty paws of the sphinx, a small temple was found. The door to its interior has not been opened for, perhaps, thousands of years. Egyptologists are now trying to get permission from the Egyptian government to investigate the interior of the temple. Perhaps if they succeed, more than one riddle of the Sphinx will be answered.

### The Mystery Deepens

In Greek myth, the sphinx roamed about Thebes and challenged everyone she met to solve a riddle. If the person failed, she ate him or her. The hero Oedipus took up the challenge, and the sphinx asked him, "What animal goes on four feet in the morning, at noon on two, and in the evening upon three?" This has become known, you might not be surprised to learn, as the "riddle of the sphinx." Oedipus answered correctly: "Man, who crawls on all fours as a baby, walks upright in manhood, and uses a staff in old age." Upon hearing the right answer to her riddle, the sphinx threw herself off a cliff. As a reward, the people of Thebes appointed Oedipus their king. And then his troubles started.

# Stonehenge and All the Little Henges

On Salisbury Plain, eight miles north of the city of Salisbury in England, rests the great prehistoric monument called Stonehenge. It is constructed of two circles of giant stones, one inside the other, and recent excavations and radiocarbon dating indicate that it was built over a period of time beginning about 5,000 years ago. Until recently, it was believed to have been a Druid Temple, but the Druids came to England no more than 2,500 years ago, so Stonehenge was already ancient when they arrived.

Nonetheless, the modern Druids in England have decided that Stonehenge is a holy place, and they conduct sunrise services there in midsummer. For a while, the authorities allowed them to bury the cremated remains of their deceased parishioners inside the circle, but that has been stopped. Since Stonehenge is thousands of years older than the first Druids, and since nobody knows what sort of services the original Druids would have conducted, this is truly an example of instant tradition. But I say, as long as they don't trample the grass too badly and avoid sacrificing anyone of importance, let them have their fun!

**No Mystery Here**

One legend about the creation of Stonehenge says that it was erected by the magician Merlin, who brought the stones from the "Giant's Dance" in Killaraus, Ireland, where they had originally been transported from Africa by a race of giants who had great powers.

## Moving the Stones

The stones of the outer circle are of sarsen, a hard sandstone that was probably quarried from the Marlborough Downs, 18 miles to the north. The inner-circle stones are of a sort of spotted dolorite called bluestone, a volcanic stone quarried from the Preseli Hills of Wales, some 225 miles to the northwest. At the center of the monument is a single stone of Welsh sandstone, also from the Preselis.

One of the questions presented by Stonehenge is just how the Bronze Age farmers who constructed it managed to cart stones, each weighing several tons, as far as 225 miles. A secondary question is why constructing Stonehenge was so important to them. Why would they go to such a tremendous amount of trouble?

Although the stones look rough and unfinished, they were worked into shape, and the lintel stones (the ones on top) were fitted into the upright stones by mortise and tenon joints for stability. After 5,000 years, most of them are still standing as they were placed. How many modern structures could hope to fare as well?

# *Whatever For?*

The theories as to why Stonehenge was erected and what it was used for are numerous and range from the silly to the sublime. Of course, each of us will have a different idea of which idea is silly and which is sublime.

As stated earlier, people for centuries believed it was a Druidic temple. Here are some other theories:

> ➤ Ambrosius Aurelianus, King of the Britons, is said to have had Stonehenge erected sometime around 450 A.D. to commemorate the villainy of Hengist, a Saxon warlord, who murdered some 460 British princes during what was supposed to be a peace talk.

> ➤ Sometime around 1615 Inigo Jones, a talented architect, was asked by James I to inspect "Stoneheng" and give his opinion as to what it was. He rejected the possibility of Stonehenge having been created by either the Druids or the ancient Britons, "a savage and barbarous people ... destitute of the knowledge ... to erect stately structures, or such remarkable works as Stoneheng." Jones decided it must have been built by the Romans during their occupation of England. In reply to the objection that there is no mention of such an occupation in Roman writing, Jones said that, after all, the Romans had built so much that they couldn't be expected to list every little thing.

> ➤ In 1771, Dr. John Smith published *Choir Gaur, the Grand Orrery of the Ancient Druids*. An "orrery" is a representation of the solar system, often made with clock-works, designed to show the motion of the planets. Smith didn't mean that you could wind up Stonehenge but that all sorts of astronomical data were hidden in the stones. (He would have had fun with the pyramids.) One of the circles at Stonehenge, for example, contains 30 stones. Multiply that by the 12 signs of the Zodiac and you get 360, only five days off from the number of days in a year. Wow!

> ➤ In 1965, Gerald S. Hawkins, with the assistance of John B. White, published *Stonehenge Decoded* in which he painstakingly re-created Stonehenge (on paper and on a computer, not full-size in place) and calculated the positions of the stars at the time Stonehenge was built. He concluded that, whatever else it was for, Stonehenge could have been used to establish midwinter and midsummer sunrise and moonrise and thus to establish the seasons. Very useful for farmers in the days before calendars.

Consider, however, that the ancient builders, whoever they might have been, could have set up an array of sticks in the ground to do their calendaring much more easily. Stonehenge must have contained some great and wonderful significance for its builders, which we have yet to guess.

# Gilgal Refaim

On the Golan Heights, currently the property of Israel, sits an ancient stone monument called, in Hebrew, Gilgal Refaim—"the Circle of Refaim." It is made up of five stone rings, one outside the other, and the whole structure is about 475 feet across. The outer ring is a circle of stones 6 feet high and 10 feet thick.

There are two large entrances into the structure, one facing northeast and the other southeast. Carbon dating of *potsherds* found at the site show that it existed 5,000 years ago—a period known as the Early Bronze Age—so it is therefore older than the pyramids. Some of the stones in it weigh 20 tons, and the whole is estimated to weigh 37,000 tons. In the center of the circles is a 60-foot wide mound, probably a burial mound.

**What Does This Mean?**

A **potsherd** is a piece of broken pottery.

## The World's Largest, Heaviest Calendar

Professors Yonathan Mizrahi of Harvard and Anthony Aveni of Colgate discovered in 1968 that, 5,000 years ago, the summer solstice of each year found the first rays of the rising sun shining directly through the northeast entrance and that the star Sirius would be peering in through the southeast entrance. On the basis of this, they speculated that the structure was an astronomical observatory or a sort of calendar.

Moving 37,000 tons of stone seems like a lot of trouble to go through to spot the *summer solstice*. And why the solstice would be of such great significance to the tribes of nomadic herders who are believed to have been the inhabitants of the area is beyond speculation. But let's speculate anyway.

In the general area of Gilgal Refaim are hundreds of dolmens, megalithic (Stone Age) structures made of two upright stones with a capping stone, like a doorway with no house. Many of these are grave markers but not all. The largest of these dolmens have stones that are over 20 feet tall and weigh over 50 tons.

## It Stands Alone

One of the interesting things about the site is that it is unique in the Middle East. Whatever tribe built it did not get the idea from any other local tribes, and no other group in the area seems to have taken it up.

Both the ring structure and the dolmens are similar to ones found in northern Britain and France, but how the nomadic shepherds of the Middle East could have come into contact with a people living so immeasurably far from them, in Stone Age terms, is not known. And if the local shepherds didn't construct the great stone ring, who did?

## Did Giants Walk the Earth?

By piecing together biblical stories and myth, we can come to one possible explanation: A people called the Anakim or the Refaim lived around what is now the Golan Heights. They were a great and powerful tribe descended from the Nefilim, a race of gods who fell from the heavens. Their king, Og, of Bashan, lost a war with the tribes of Israel. His bed was captured and taken to Rabbah. It was made of iron and was 13.5 feet long and 6 feet wide.

It might be very interesting to excavate that mound in the center of the stone rings and see what lies within.

# Ancient Astronauts or Just Us?

In his 1968 best-seller *Chariots of the Gods*, Erich Von Däniken proposed that super-intelligent visitors from outer space must have aided the Egyptians in building the pyramids as well as showing up with a few words of advice at Stonehenge and other places where primitive peoples constructed great works. Other writers have proposed that the advanced culture on Atlantis (see Chapter 11, "Beneath the Waves") dispersed through the ancient world when Atlantis sank, and Atlantean master engineers did the building before they died out and the knowledge was lost.

According to Von Däniken, "If we meekly accept the neat package of knowledge that the Egyptologists serve up to us, ancient Egypt appears suddenly and without transition with a fantastic ready-made civilization. Great cities and enormous temples, colossal statues with tremendous expressive power, splendid streets flanked by magnificent sculptures, perfect drainage systems, luxurious tombs carved out of the rock, pyramids of overwhelming size—these and many other wonderful things shot out of the ground, so to speak. Genuine miracles in a country that is suddenly capable of such achievements without recognizable prehistory."

The only thing wrong with this theory is that Egypt does have an extensive, if not well-documented, history from the time before the pyramids. The luxurious tombs, colossal statues, and the rest were built over a period of several thousand years. Developing a perfect drainage system becomes a necessity in a country strung out along the banks of the Nile, which overflows and floods the lowlands with monotonous regularity year after year.

**What Does This Mean?**

The **summer solstice** is the moment when the sun appears at its furthest northern point in the sky for that year. The solstice is caused by a combination of earth's orbit of the sun and the tilted axis of the earth. At one point in earth's orbit, the North Pole leans toward the sun; at the opposite point, it leans away from the sun.

A less-than-persuasive argument for the presence of super-intelligent aliens on earth in the distant past, or advanced Atlantean know-how, is the assertion that our ancestors were too dumb to have built the pyramids, erected Stonehenge, worked out an accurate calendar, or transferred technology from one people to another. Human beings have been human beings for the past 50,000 years. There's no reason to assume that our remote ancestors weren't just as bright as we are.

### Mysterious Comments

"It is a mistake to believe that the ancients were not every bit as intelligent as we. Their technology was more primitive, but their brains were not."

—Isaac Asimov, *Extraterrestrial Civilizations*

### The Least You Need to Know

➤ A solid body of myth has grown up around the Great Pyramid of Khufu. Pyramidologists believe that in the dimensions of the Great Pyramid are concealed the secrets of the ages.

➤ The Great Sphinx at Giza might be much older than originally thought. If so, its original sculptors are lost in antiquity.

➤ In 1998, a pyramid was discovered submerged in 75 feet of water off the coast of the Japanese island of Yonaguni-Jima. It may date back 8,000 years, which would make it older than the pyramids.

➤ Stonehenge, a megalithic structure on Salisbury Plain in England, is at least 5,000 years old. Despite the modern Druid claims, it predates the original Druids, and nobody can be sure who built it.

➤ A megalith called Gilgal Refaim, "the Circle of Refaim," has sat on the Golan Heights for 5,000 years. Nobody knows who built it or why.

# Part 3
# The Big Questions

*In this section, we'll tackle the big questions. How did the universe begin? How does life begin? What happened to the dinosaurs? We'll look at the story of Atlantis, too. Is there any truth to the legend, or did Plato make the whole thing up? We'll also discuss the possibility of intelligent life on other planets.*

*Since we're talking about stars, we'll give you an overview of astrology in this section also. We'll tell you something of how it works, discuss some well-known astrologers, and something of its history. What, if anything, do the stars have to tell us?*

# Chapter 10

# Beginnings and Endings

**In This Chapter**

➤ Grappling with the mysteries of the universe

➤ What the stars tell us

➤ The Big Bang and the expanding universe

➤ The rise and fall of the dinosaurs

➤ Nemesis, our theoretical nemesis

"To every thing there is a season," the Bible tells us, "and a time to every purpose under the heaven." Scientists have spent some effort in determining the season of the universe and the times of its beginning and probable end.

There are clues: static that seems to come from all directions (called "background radiation"), the rate at which the stars burn their atomic fuel, the nature of the distribution of galaxies throughout the cosmos, the speed at which everything seems to be rushing apart from everything else, the number of supernovae exploding throughout the galaxies (at least those that are close enough for us to observe).

All of these (and a few other things) are the evidence that scientists draw upon to try to determine the age of the universe and predict its lifespan.

# How Did the Universe Begin?

"How did the universe begin?" is the sort of question philosophers love to ponder because any answer you come up with either goes against common sense or leads to more questions. Whatever answer you come up with, the next question that pops up is, "Yes, but what happened before that?"

The ancient Greeks had an answer, and in some ways, it was surprisingly modern. According to *Bulfinch's Mythology*, the Greeks believed the following:

> Before earth and sea and heaven were created, all things wore one aspect, to which we give the name of Chaos—a confused and shapeless mass, nothing but dead weight, in which, however, slumbered the seeds of things. Earth, sea, and air were all mixed up together; so the earth was not solid, the sea was not fluid, and the air was not transparent. God and Nature at last interposed, and put an end to this discord, separating earth from sea, and heaven from both. The fiery part, being the lightest, sprang up, and formed the skies; the air was next in weight and place. The earth, being heavier, sank below; and the water took the lowest place, and buoyed up the earth.

### The Mystery Deepens

The ancient Roman poet and philosopher Lucretius, who lived a little over 200 years ago, neatly posed the problem of how the human mind could hope to imagine the universe being of finite size. Picture the universe as having an end, he suggested. Then, if you could go to the end of the universe and hurl a spear outward with great force, do you think the spear would continue to fly past the end of the universe? Or do you think it would stick into the end of the universe or perhaps bounce back at you?

## The Conceptual Framework

Of course, we're assuming one thing in this discussion: that there really is a universe that extends beyond our own little solar system. You've probably never questioned this assumption since, from your childhood, you've been taught or told (or learned from watching *Star Trek* and *Star Wars*) that there is this universe beyond the Milky Way, full of stars and planets and galaxies and black holes (and Wookies and princesses that need to be rescued from the forces of the Evil Emperor).

This is a relatively recent viewpoint, however. Up through the Middle Ages, most people thought that the earth was the center of everything and that the sky was a sort of domed ceiling maybe 50 or 60 miles up. It wasn't until 1543 when the Polish astronomer Nicolaus Copernicus published *De Revolutionibus Orbium Coelestium* (Latin for *Of the Revolution of Heavenly Bodies*—if you wanted to be taken seriously back then you had to write in Latin), which suggested that the earth and the other planets revolve around the sun, that people first began to consider a universe beyond the earth.

The Catholic Church promptly put Copernicus's book on its Index (a list of books you weren't supposed to read), where it stayed until 1835. The Lutherans weren't very fond of it either. Established churches tend to be conservative, and new ideas are not easily welcomed, particularly if they're seen as rocking the boat. Copies of Copernicus's book circulated through Europe, however, and caused scientists and philosophers to rethink their ideas. The notion that the earth circled the sun led naturally to the idea that the stars might be other suns just as big as our sun but much farther away. All of a sudden, the idea of the universe as a vast space with thousands of suns came into being. Then we began to realize that it wasn't *thousands* of suns but *billions,* and we began to see that there were actually billions of galaxies, each with billions of stars.

### Here There Be Dragons

Copernicus wasn't actually the first person to suggest that the universe wasn't what it seemed. Sometime around 450 B.C. a Greek philosopher named Anaxagoras suggested that the sun was a great ball of rock. He was exiled for impiety by the horrified Athenian conservatives. A little later, about 280 B.C., another Greek, an astronomer named Aristarchus, figured out that the earth and the other planets circled the sun. His fellow Athenians didn't even bother exiling him; they just laughed at the ridiculous idea.

## Great Balls of Gas

Let's talk about the stars for a minute. It's reasonable to assume that, whether the universe as a whole is infinite or had a beginning, individual stars must have a finite lifetime. After all, the stars are giant balls of burning gas, and experience tells us that, when anything is burning, it must eventually burn out. Because our own sun is a star, determining its age and how long it might continue to burn became an obviously important question.

Determining the age of the sun and how long it might continue to burn first meant determining the process by which it burned. in the eighteenth century the best educated guess was that the sun was burning like a coal fire, and it would go out when all the coal (or whatever fuel the sun was burning) was used up. If the fuel was similar to coal and burned the way coal burns, then the sun was good for a couple hundred thousand years before it turned into a darkened cinder. But geologists believed the earth was older than that already. So that wasn't the answer.

### No Mystery Here

Consider the amount of heat our sun is constantly producing. The earth is 93 million miles from the sun (more or less, depending on where it is in its orbit), and yet a small magnifying glass can focus the sun's rays enough to set a piece of paper on fire. (Kids, this should only be done by professional magnifying-glass focusers—don't try it at home!)

### What Does This Mean?

The **spectrum** is the rainbow of colors that a beam of white light can be broken into when passed through a prism.

In 1853, a physicist named Helmholtz determined that the sun must be contracting due to the pull of gravity and that the contraction would create heat. (When you squeeze something, its molecules rub together and the friction creates heat—an oversimplification, but you get the idea.)

Helmholtz believed that the sun had originally been a ball about the size of the earth's orbit. He figured that it would have taken about 25 million years to shrink to its present size, and it would have another 10 million years or so to go before it burned out. Geologists didn't like that answer either; they already had determined that the earth must be older than 25 million years.

## It's In the Stars

Astronomers thought for a long time that certain things would remain forever unknowable, and one of those things was the composition of the stars. It was discovered, however, that different elements emit different frequencies of light when they are heated to a gaseous state. By applying this knowledge to astronomy, it was possible to analyze the *spectrum* of starlight and determine what elements were in the star.

In 1929, an American astronomer named Henry Norris Russell determined that the sun was mostly composed of hydrogen and helium—about $\frac{3}{4}$ hydrogen and $\frac{1}{4}$ helium by mass, with a sprinkling of oxygen, nitrogen, neon, and carbon. This gave physicist George Gamow the idea that the sun might be burning the hydrogen by nuclear fusion to produce helium and create a lot of heat. In 1938, physicist Hans Albrecht Bethe explained the mechanism that enabled this to happen, and he got the Nobel Prize for his troubles.

Knowing the size of the sun and how much of its hydrogen had already been converted into helium, it was possible to figure out the sun's age. It turns out that the sun is about five billion years old and has about another five billion years to burn before it enters advanced old age and starts to behave like a cranky old star. It is believed that, at that time, it will swell up in size until it encompasses the orbit of earth and therefore the earth itself.

This gives us a minimum age of five billion years for the universe since we can safely assume it is at least as old as the stars in it.

## The Redder the Shift

Early twentieth-century astronomers looking at the light from distant stars soon noticed that the spectra of most showed a shift to the red and that the farther away the star was, the more its spectrum was shifted. What could this mean? Most likely, it meant that the star was headed away from us. Just as a train whistle goes down in pitch as the train pulls away, light appears to go down in frequency if the object emitting it is receding. The fact that the more distant the star was, the more the spectrum was redshifted, suggested that the more distant the star was, the faster it was receding. (Still with me?)

So why do distant stars seem to be moving away from us in whatever direction we look? Why do they seem to be moving faster the farther away they are? We'll start with Einstein's General Theory of Relativity. Einstein says that matter "warps" space—we call that warping "gravity." Enough matter will cause space to sort of wrap around itself in four dimensions. (Some recent theories, like "String Theory" need eleven dimensions to work right, but we'll do our best to ignore those for now.) This means that, in addition to the three dimensions we're all familiar with—up and down, left and right, forward and backward—there is yet another dimension through which space can curve.

> ### No Mystery Here
>
> Some people talk about time as the fourth dimension because, in order to meet someone, you have to specify not only the three dimensions of the location (the Kickapoo building at the corner of Third and Main, fourth floor) but the time (noon). There is something to this, but time is not the fourth dimension we're talking about here. If you want to, you may think of it as a fifth dimension. Don't blame us, go talk to Einstein.

Einstein's idea of the curvature of space means that the universe can be both finite, containing a certain number of stars with a certain amount of space between them, but unbounded no matter what direction you go in. In other words, you'll never reach the "edge" of the universe because it doesn't have one.

Think of the surface of the earth, which is an unbounded but finite two-dimensional space. You can walk as far as you want (well, you'll have to swim a little) and never reach the edge of the earth. Thus, the surface has a definite size and area, yet it is simultaneously unbounded.

## *The Balloon Analogy*

Now we get to why the whole rest of the universe is retreating from us. Picture the surface of a balloon. Paint two dots on it, one representing us and the other a random star somewhere. If you start blowing up the balloon, the two dots will get farther apart. From either dot's point of view, it will look as though the other dot is racing away from it. And the farther away the two dots are on the balloon, the faster they will seem to be separating as the balloon is blown up. The two-dimensional surface of the balloon is expanding due to the three-dimensional balloon being blown up. Thus, as our three-dimensional universe expands along Einstein's fourth-dimensional curvature, its stars retreat from each other with ever-increasing speed.

# The Big Bang

It was an astronomer named Edwin Hubble who concluded in the 1930s that, based on his careful study of distant galaxies, the universe was expanding. The rate at which it is expanding is known as "Hubble's Constant." But Hubble's Constant seems to be a most inconstant constant because new values for it come along every six months or so as astronomers refine their estimates based on the latest observations. The latest figures put the age of the universe at between 15 and 20 billion years.

Since the universe is expanding, it makes sense that it was once smaller. Hubble's Constant tells us that, if you go back in time somewhere between 15 and 20 billion years, you would find the universe in its original state—shrunk to less than the size of the period at the end of this sentence. From that unbelievably small, dimensionless dot suddenly sprang the universe, and it's been growing ever since.

## *A Steady State*

British astronomer Fred Hoyle thought the Big Bang idea was ridiculous. He and his associates Hermann Bondi and Thomas Gold devised what they called "the Steady State theory," which posited a universe that had always been in existence and, presumably, always would be. To account for the expansion, they assumed that matter was continuously being created at random throughout the universe, which had to expand to make room for it. "It turns out that the required rate [of creation] is very slow," Hoyle explained, "amounting to about one atom per century for each unit of volume corresponding to that of the largest man-made building."

Hoyle's Steady State universe is logically no more or less incredible than the from-a-tiny-dot universe; whether you prefer to have your matter created all at once or gradually throughout the universe is an esthetic decision. Hoyle found the all-at-once theory displeasing and dismissively called it "the Big Bang theory" on a BBC radio show in the 1940s. The name stuck.

## *And the Winner Is ...*

Unfortunately for Hoyle and the Steady State universe, experimental evidence collected seems to favor the Big Bang. Astronomer George Gamow computed the mix of elements that would have resulted from a Big Bang, and it agreed with the mix of elements seen throughout the universe pretty well.

### The Mystery Deepens

The elements that came into being after the Big Bang were more than 99 percent hydrogen and helium, the two lightest elements. When the first-generation stars (those formed shortly after the Big Bang) aged, having converted most of their hydrogen to helium, many of them then went nova—that is, they blew up. The heat and pressure of that final death-explosion created all the heavier elements including the ones that make life possible. Life could be considered an incidental creation of the deaths of stars.

Then there is the evidence of background radiation. Background radiation was discovered in the 1960s by two scientists working for Bell Laboratories in New Jersey when they were trying to tune a 20-foot "big ear" radio antenna used to relay telephone calls to communications satellites. Whichever way they turned the antenna, they kept getting this low-pitched hum through the receiver. One by one they eliminated the possibilities, and when they were left with no answer, they called physics professor Robert Dicke at Princeton to see if he had any ideas.

It had long been thought that if the Big Bang had started the universe, there should be some sort of lingering evidence of the explosion. The hum the two scientists detected turned out to be the background radiation of the cooled-down maelstrom of fire that had been the Big Bang. It was a message from the first moments of the creation of the universe.

# The Fate of the Universe

The current evidence points to a Big Bang origin of the universe, but new discoveries are made every day. Who knows what tomorrow may bring? Even if we accept the Big Bang theory, there are still some interesting universal questions that remain to be solved.

# The Role of Gravity

The universe is getting bigger and bigger, pushed outward by the initial explosion of the Big Bang some 15 billion years ago or more. The force of gravity, however, which tries to pull everything together and has an effect even over the vast distances of the universe, should be acting on the matter in the universe to slow it down. Gravity is a weak force compared to other natural forces of attraction, but it also has literally all the time in the universe to do its job. There are three possible explanations to describe the long-term role of gravity in the universe:

➤ There isn't quite enough matter in the universe for the force of gravity to overcome the rate of expansion, so the universe is going to keep expanding for all of eternity or until something that we can't even guess at comes along to stop it.

➤ There *is* enough matter in the universe for gravity to do its job, so the expansion of the universe will eventually stop. Then the universe will start collapsing. It will eventually collapse back into the original atom it started from, the dimensionless dot. And then, who knows? Perhaps the process will start all over again. Perhaps this universe is just one in an infinite series of universes seesawing in and out of existence.

➤ The force of gravity is just enough to continually slow down the expansion of the universe until it finally is expanding so slowly that it essentially becomes akin to Hoyle's Steady State universe, never collapsing.

**What Does This Mean?**

**Quarks** are the name given to the smallest and most basic (so far) particles that make up electrons and protons and the other constituents of atoms. They were named by physicist Murray Gell-Mann, who first thought of them, after a phrase in the book *Finnegans Wake* by James Joyce.

**Metaphysical** pertains to those things that are currently beyond the scope of physics, and are best discussed by philosophers.

For a while it looked as though the collapsing universe was going to be the most likely future scenario, but measurements made within the last decade by several astronomers of the amount of matter the universe contains indicate that there isn't enough matter to supply the gravity needed. So unless we can find some more matter somewhere it looks like the ever-expanding universe is ahead on points. But the table is still accepting bets, and the winner is still unknown.

## The First Mystery

The final universal mystery is, of course, the first mystery: What happened before the Big Bang? We know or think we know what happened milliseconds after the Big Bang—all the matter and energy that would become the universe spread outward at an incredible speed. Particles called *quarks* came into being while it was still too unimaginably hot to permit the creation of such basic building blocks of matter as protons and electrons.

But what was it like in the instant before the Big Bang? We don't know, and the best guess so far is that we can't ever find out. "There is no way that one can determine what happened before the Big Bang from a knowledge of events after the Big Bang," physicist Stephen Hawking wrote. "This means that the existence or nonexistence of events before the big Bang is purely *metaphysical*."

So there's the limit. If scientists are right, there is one thing we can never know. But scientists have been wrong before. We'll just have to wait and see.

# An Incident in the Cretaceous

The end of the universe is not something we have to worry about for a while, whichever way it happens. If you need something to keep you up at night worrying, we suggest considering what happened to the dinosaurs, why it happened, and whether it might happen to us. If the extinction of the dinosaurs were a unique event, we might just pass it off as some sort of fluke, a one-of-a-kind disaster that happened 65 million years ago, and is of no concern to humans today.

## *The Geologic Eras*

Geologists who study the history of our planet and the creatures that have lived on it have divided the past into four major eras:

**Here There Be Dragons**

The extinction of the dinosaurs is just one of four major killing-off incidents we know of, and there have also been a few smaller ones. So it is definitely a good idea to learn as much as we can of what caused these disasters, and what we might need to do to prevent one in the future.

➤ The Precambrian Era, from about 4.6 billion years ago (when the earth cooled down enough to coalesce into a planet) to about 600 million years ago (when nothing more exciting than algae lived).

➤ The Paleozoic Era, from about 600 million years ago to 225 million years ago, which boasted a variety of sea creatures, mostly without backbones.

➤ The Mesozoic Era, from 225 million years ago to about 65 million years ago, which was dominated by the dinosaurs.

➤ The Cenozoic Era, from about 65 million years ago until now, which has been dominated by mammals and birds and principally, for the last 100,000 years, humans.

The Mesozoic is further divided into the Triassic Period when the dinosaurs were evolving into the dominant class of animals, the Jurassic Period when the dinosaurs ruled the land, and the Cretaceous Period when the dinosaurs suddenly vanished.

# Mass Extinctions

The first of the mass extinctions that we know about happened about 650 million years ago during the Precambrian Era when whole classes of algae became extinct. It doesn't sound like a big deal—after all, they're only algae—but algae is all that was around at the time.

The next mass extinction was in the Paleozoic Era, about 500 million years ago, when whole classes of marine life suddenly bit the mud. A third happened about 340 million years ago when whole families of fish, coral, and trilobites (little ancestors of spiders, insects, and crabs) disappeared.

About 225 million years ago, at the end of the Permian Period of the Paleozoic Era, there was a fourth of mass extinction. In this one, about 90 percent of the existing species of animals vanished in a comparatively short time. Because we know of these creatures only through the fossil record, it's impossible to judge just how short a time.

# The Age of the Dinosaur

Shortly after the Permian extinction, with the start of the Triassic Period, the dinosaurs came into their own. Whether this was because some competitors had been eliminated or because they were particularly fit it is impossible to say. But they did seem to be particularly fit, and they evolved into many different types, taking up most of the important niches in the animal world.

There were grazing dinosaurs, tree-cropping dinosaurs, carnivorous dinosaurs, dinosaurs bigger than locomotives, and dinosaurs smaller than rabbits. There were dinosaurs that lumbered about on all four legs, dinosaurs that raced about on their hind legs, and even dinosaurs that flew.

They lived long and prospered for about 150 million years. Then, about 65 million years ago, poof! No more dinosaurs. What happened to the dinosaurs has been one of the great mysteries for the past couple of centuries. Scientists have proposed a variety of explanations for the sudden disappearance.

It was seriously suggested that the larger dinosaurs regularly ran off cliffs because, by the time their pea-sized brains passed on word to the legs that a cliff was ahead, it was too late for the legs to stop. It was suggested that the carnivorous dinosaurs ate all the herbivorous dinosaurs and then starved to death. It also was suggested that the mammals that were around then—which were about the size of shrews—ate all the dinosaur eggs.

**No Mystery Here**

It is now believed by many but not all dinosaur experts that the dinosaurs were warm-blooded instead of cold-blooded (like crocodiles and other reptiles). This would mean they were even faster than we thought, had more endurance, and were better able to withstand cold weather. Birds, which may have descended from dinosaurs, are warm-blooded.

## The Crashing Asteroid

In 1980, Luis and Walter Alvarez suggested that the extinction of the dinosaurs was caused by a giant asteroid colliding with the earth 65 million years ago.

The evidence with which they supported this theory was a layer of clay separating limestone laid down at the end of the Cretaceous Period from the stone laid down after. The Cretaceous stone was rich with fossils; the stone above the clay was very poor in fossils. Perhaps the layer of clay, which must have been laid down right when the extinction happened, held a clue.

The clay contained a high percentage of the element iridium, which was not found in the rock above or below the clay deposit. Iridium is relatively rare on earth but is found in much larger amounts in certain meteorites. If a large meteorite had crashed into the earth, throwing a great dust cloud into the atmosphere, it could have cut off the sunlight for perhaps 100 or more years before it settled. This would have cooled down the surface of the earth, prevented plants from growing, and starved all the animals it didn't freeze to death. Very few life forms would have escaped. When the cloud settled, it would have deposited that layer of iridium.

## Chicxulub

It is now believed that that is indeed what happened. The meteorite that probably did the job was about six miles wide and crashed off the Yucatan peninsula in Mexico, blasting a 120-mile wide crater. The mound left by the blast and the passage of 65 million years is known as the Chicxulub structure.

Another crater in the Arabian Sea off the coast of India near Bombay is vying with Chicxulub. Called the Shiva Crater, it may have been formed by a meteor as much as 24 miles in diameter. One possibility is that both the Shiva and the Chicxulub craters, and perhaps even others, were formed at the same time when a massive asteroid that had broken into several pieces came smashing into Earth.

# Nemesis

There is an interesting correspondence to the mass extinctions that we know of: They seem to have happened roughly 150 million years apart, give or take a few million years. There have also been lesser extinctions, and when you plot them all, they seem to happen about every 30 million years (except for a couple of gaps). Coincidence? Or is something throwing giant meteors at us every 30 million years?

One possibility is that the sun has a dark, small, companion star in a great orbit that takes it about a light year and a half away and then brings it as close as the outer solar system every 30 million years. In addition, there is believed to be a great cloud of rocks somewhere outside the orbit of Pluto. This is called the Oort cloud after astronomer Jan Hendrik Oort, who worked out the theory that predicted the cloud was there.

Every 30 million years, as this dark star passes through the Oort cloud, its gravity would throw some of these rocks out of orbit and send them toward the sun. And between the Oort cloud and the sun lies the earth. Usually these incoming rocks will miss the earth, which is after all a pretty small target astronomically speaking. But once in a great while the earth might be in just the wrong place.

This hypothetical star is being called Nemesis, and astronomers are actively looking for it. If they find it, we know we have something to worry about, and we can plot its orbit so we know when to start worrying. If they don't find it—well then, something is nevertheless causing those extinctions. So we still have something to worry about—and the additional worry of not knowing what it is.

---

### The Least You Need to Know

➤ In 1543, Copernicus revolutionized the way humans viewed the universe by suggesting that the earth and the other planets revolve around the sun.

➤ Stars provide an important clue to the age and makeup of the universe and the rate at which it expands.

➤ We don't yet know whether the universe will keep expanding, start contracting, or expand to a steady state of motionless existence.

➤ The Big Bang theory is the most likely explanation for the origin of the universe, but it has been deemed impossible to know what happened even an instant before the Big Bang.

➤ The dinosaurs dominated the earth for 150 million years before becoming extinct 65 million years ago. Luis and Walter Alvarez showed that a great meteorite might have done the job.

➤ There is a possibility that a small, dark star is in a distant orbit around the sun, showering the solar system with meteors whenever it gets close and causing periodic mass extinctions of life on Earth.

---

# Chapter 11

# Beneath the Waves

---

## In This Chapter

➤ Plato: the first writer to mention Atlantis

➤ America was first thought to be Atlantis rediscovered

➤ Ignatius Donnelly thought he found the link

➤ Anghelos Galanapoulos believed Santorini blew its top

---

Everybody has heard of Atlantis, the city that sank beneath the waves thousands of years ago, drowning the lofty spires of a civilization so advanced that we have yet to catch up with it. It is believed that the civilization's refugees, after the flood, brought with them the arts of writing, pottery, and metalworking as well as fragments of their history, which have come down to us as myths that can be found among the Egyptians, the Greeks, the Mayans, and other peoples around the globe.

Oh, sorry, that isn't the way you heard it? Well, it's one of the more popular versions of the story, but there are others. Over the centuries, a single thread has been spun into a great and varied tapestry of myth, legend, and pseudo history. The Lost City (or State, or Continent, or Race) of Atlantis and the fate of the Atlanteans has figured in the writings of astrologers, cultists, occultists, mystics, past-lives researchers, Theosophists, fantasists, and science fictioneers since Plato first invoked it in about 355 B.C.

# How It Began

Aristokles, the son of Ariston who is better known to us by his nickname, "Plato," was a student of the famous Athenian philosopher Socrates. After Socrates was induced to commit suicide by the city fathers of Athens in 399 B.C. for being a bad influence on the youth of the city—he tried to get them to think for themselves—Plato wrote a series of "dialogues" that demonstrated the wisdom and humanity of his great teacher. The dialogues are re-created conversations between Socrates and his various pupils in which Socrates presents his theories of government, morality, religion, and just about everything else a philosopher is supposed to concern himself with.

## *The First Mention of Atlantis*

The earliest mentions of Atlantis that we know about are in two of Plato's dialogues, *Timaios* and *Kritias*. *Timaios* is set the day after the events described in Plato's most famous work, *The Republic,* and it begins with the four conversers (Socrates, Timaeus, Kritias, and Hermocrates) going over the points learned in that discourse. Then Kritias recalls a story told to him by his grandfather, also named Kritias, who heard it from his father, Dropides, who heard it from Solon himself, a great Athenian statesman, lawgiver, and poet who lived about 150 years before the *Timaios* dialogue took place.

Solon, the story goes, was traveling in Egypt when he got into a discussion with a priest from the temple at Sais. The priest told him that Athenians have no sense of history, that the Egyptians know more of the history of Athens than the Athenians do. For example, Egyptian records show that 9,000 years earlier there was an island in the Atlantic Ocean outside "the straits which are called by you the Pillars of *Heracles.*" And, said the priest …

> In this island of Atlantis there was a great and wonderful empire which had rule over the whole island and several others, and over parts of the continent, and, furthermore, the men of Atlantis had subjected the parts of Libya within the columns of Heracles as far as Egypt, and of Europe as far as Tyrrhenia.

Atlantis tried to conquer the rest of Europe, according to the priest of Sais, and was stopped only when Athens, leading the rest of the Greek cities, fought back. Even when the other cities deserted her, Athens stood firm and eventually won. And then Athens, showing true nobility of spirit, even freed the other cities and states that had been subjugated. Shortly after this, there were a series of mighty earthquakes and floods, and "in a single day and night of misfortune all your warlike men in a body sank into the earth, and the island of Atlantis in like manner disappeared in the depths of the sea."

## And the Next Mention

In Plato's next dialogue, *Kritias,* he goes into greater detail about the city he so casually claimed had sunk beneath the sea in the previous dialogue. He gives the place a mythical foundation involving the god Poseidon falling in lust with a lady named Kleito. Poseidon shaped this great island in the Atlantic to suit his needs and divided it up among the 10 children of his union with Kleito (five pairs of twins, all boys). Both the Atlantic Ocean and the island of Atlantis were named for his eldest son, Atlas, who was made king of one of the 10 kingdoms established on Atlantis and king-of-kings over his nine brothers.

Plato describes the geography of the island of Atlantis: the palace and temple were in the city of Atlantis, which was 11 miles in diameter, located on the south coast of the island. It was built on a hill and was protected by three consecutive canals that circled the city, creating alternating circular bands of land and water like an archery target. Another canal 300 feet wide and 100 feet deep cut straight through from the sea coast to the city, where great stone docks were constructed to hold the Atlantean fleet. Three great walls protected the city, one along each canal; the innermost was covered in brass, the second in tin, and the third in orichalcum, a metal the Atlanteans used that was almost as precious as gold. The city's buildings were quarried from red, black, and white stones that were put together "in an eye-pleasing manner."

**What Does This Mean?**

**Heracles** is the Greek hero we usually call Hercules. The Pillars of Heracles is what the Greeks called the Straits of Gibraltar, the narrow straits at the West end of the Mediterranean Sea that provide an outlet to the Atlantic Ocean and that separate Europe from Africa by a scant nine miles.

**No Mystery Here**

It is unknown which, if any, of Plato's dialogues faithfully recount the opinions of Socrates and which are Plato's own opinions put in the mouth of his teacher. It's clear, however, that the teachings of Socrates had a tremendous effect on the thinking of Plato, so a fair amount of the teacher is probably coming through in the writings of the pupil.

Plato goes into a fair amount of detail over the governing of Atlantis; governing was a subject that held his interest. Each of the 10 kings had absolute authority over his subjects, but they ruled according to the law as handed down by Poseidon at the founding of the city. But as the generations passed and the blood of the kings became less divine (their descent from Poseidon being more distant), they began to behave unseemly and "grew visibly debased." Zeus, the boss of all the gods, wanted "to inflict punishment on them, that they might be chastened and improve." He called all the gods together in their most holy habitation. "And when he had called them together, he spake as follows … "

Unfortunately, Plato stopped the manuscript there and never got around to finishing it. And that's all there is on Atlantis.

You now know all that is known for sure about Atlantis. Plato is the earliest source, and all sources that come after seem to have used him as a starting point. Nobody earlier than Plato mentions Solon's trip to Egypt, although he very well may have gone. Nobody else knows anything about the priests of Sais, although there certainly were priests in Sais, the capital of Lower Egypt.

## Straight from the Source's Mouth

There are some other sources who expanded on and amplified Plato's account. Diodorus Siculus, a historian who lived around the time of Julius Caesar, about 400 years after Plato, speaks of the island of Hesperia with Atlantean overtones. Other classical authors, such as Pliny the Elder, Cosmos Indicopleustes, and Ammianus Marcellinus, quote Plato's account, giving it varying degrees of credibility. (Pliny the Elder, for example, commented that Atlantis sank "if we are to believe Plato.") But none of them cite an earlier account, or even a different contemporary account, of Atlantis.

Let's look at some of the possible origins of Atlantis:

➤ Maybe Plato made it all up. He needed a foreign place to use as the background for his ideas, so he created Atlantis as a useful allegory and put the story in the mouth of Solon—actually in the mouth of Kritias, who heard it from Grandpa Kritias, who heard it from Dropides, who heard it from Solon, who heard it from a priest at Sais. All of this may have merely been intended to, as W.S. Gilbert put it, "add an air of verisimilitude to an otherwise bald and unconvincing narrative."

➤ Maybe someone on the chain from Solon to the young Kritias made it up—if there *was* a young Kritias. Remember that Kritias was just a character in Plato's dialogue. Who knows whether he was based on a real person? Just because Socrates was real doesn't mean his companions in the dialogues weren't fictional.

➤ Perhaps Solon really heard it from a priest at Sais, but the priest made it up. Maybe the priest was just trying to keep his distinguished visitor entertained with this story of heroic Athenians beating off invaders 9,000 years earlier.

➤ It could be that something really happened, but it got all twisted around in the telling. For one thing, it's highly unlikely that even the Egyptians kept records going back 9,000 years, so if anything did happen, it probably wasn't more than, at the extreme, 1,000 years before. But this is still enough time to garble the facts.

**No Mystery Here**

Sais was a center for worship by the Egyptians of their goddess Neith, whom the Greeks equated with Pallas Athene, the goddess of wisdom who sprang fully grown from the head of Zeus and was the guardian of Athens; this sort of made Sais and Athens sister cities. The Romans equated Neith and Pallas Athene with Minerva, who, curiously enough, sprang fully armed from Jupiter's head.

**The Mystery Deepens**

As Socrates taught Plato, so Plato in turn taught Aristotle, the other great philosopher produced by the ancient Greeks. Aristotle wrote on every field of human knowledge that existed at the time and made up some of his own. Everything we knew about biology, zoology, and logic for 1,000 years after Aristotle came from the writings of Aristotle. And yet Aristotle is only known to have made one reference to Atlantis. In a lost work quoted by the historian Strabo, Aristotle commented that "he who invented [Atlantis] also destroyed it."

**133**

And there it lay. For the next 1,500 years or so, the story of Atlantis was just another fantasy in a world full of fantasies.

*A map dated 1644 from Mundus Subterraneus by Athanasius Kircher showing Atlantis. Note that, on this map, North is down and South is up.*

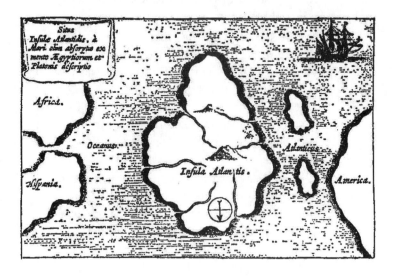

# Thank You, Columbus

Interest in Atlantis was rekindled when Columbus arrived in what eventually became America. He thought he'd arrived in the Indies, which is why, as everyone knows, the indigenous people he found here were called "Indians." It soon became clear, however, that he'd stumbled onto a continent, or at least a very large island, that lay between the west coast of Europe and the Indies.

Perhaps some learned people familiar with Plato thought that this new land was Atlantis rediscovered. The Spanish historian Francesco Lopez de Gomara wrote that Plato must have based his story on some faint knowledge of this distant land, and another historian, Guillaume de Postel, suggested that the new land should be named Atlantis whether it really was or not. Sir Francis Bacon wrote a utopian tract in 1624 called *The New Atlantis* and set it in the Americas, but he probably didn't mean for it to be taken literally. At any rate, it was clear that the intervening 1,500 years had not diminished the fascination with Atlantis.

**The Mystery Deepens**

The idea that the new continent might have been the lost Atlantis received a powerful boost when it was discovered that the Aztecs believed they had originally come from a land called Aztlan ("plain of reeds" in Aztec), which sounds an awful lot like "Atlantis" if you say it fast, downwind. The word "atl" in Aztec means "water." John Swan, in his 1644 book *Speculum Mundi (A Mirror of the World)*, wrote: "... this I may think may be supposed, that America was sometimes part of that great land which Plato calleth the Atlantick island, and that the Kings of that island had some intercourse between the people of Europe and Africa ... But when it happened that this island became a sea, time wore out the remembrance of remote countries ... "

# Ignatius T.T. Donnelly Discovers Atlantis

Ignatius Donnelly seems to have been a man who was crammed full of energy and bursting with ideas. Born in Philadelphia, he studied to become a lawyer and then, in 1856, moved to Nininger, Minnesota, and started a newspaper. He got into politics, got himself elected lieutenant governor of Minnesota when he was 28, and progressed to a seat in the United States House of Representatives in 1862. He spent a lot of his time in Washington D.C. in the reading room of the Library of Congress, indulging his eclectic intellectual interests. After an unsuccessful bid for a fifth term in the House, he retired to his home to become an author. His first book was titled *Atlantis: The Antediluvian World.*

Donnelly stated the thesis of his book on the very first page with a list of 13 assertions that he spent the rest of the book trying to prove, and which we quote for you here:

1. That there once existed in the Atlantic Ocean, opposite the mouth of the Mediterranean Sea, a large island, which was the remnant of an Atlantic continent, and known to the ancient world as Atlantis.

2. That the description of this island given by Plato is not, as has been long supposed, fable, but veritable history.

3. That Atlantis was the region where man first rose from a state of barbarism to civilization.

4. That it became, in the course of ages, a populous and mighty nation, from whose overflowings the shores of the Gulf of Mexico, the Mississippi River, the Amazon, the Pacific Coast of South America, the Mediterranean, the west coast of Europe and Africa, the Baltic, the Black Sea, and the Caspian were populated by civilized nations.

5. That it was the true Antediluvian world: the Garden of Eden; the Garden of the Hesperides where the Atlantides lived on the River Ocean in the west; the Elysian fields situated by Homer to the west of the Earth; the Gardens of Alcinous grandson of Poseidon and son of Nausithous, King of the Phaeacians of the Island of Scheria; the Mesomphalos or Navel of the Earth, a name given to the Temple at Delphi, which was situated in the crater of an extinct volcano; the Mount Olympos of the Greeks; the Asgard of the Eddas; the focus of the traditions of the ancient nations; representing a universal memory of a great land, where early mankind dwelt for ages in peace and happiness.

### Mysterious Comments

"The farther we go back in time toward the era of Atlantis, the more the evidences multiply that we are approaching the presence of a great, wise, civilized race."

—Ignatius Donnelly, *Atlantis: the Antidiluvian World*, 1882

6. That the gods and goddesses of the ancient Greeks; the Phoenicians, the Hindus, and the Scandinavians were simply the kings, queens, and heroes of Atlantis; and the acts attributed to them in mythology, a confused recollection of real historical events.

7. That the mythologies of Egypt and Peru represented the original religion of Atlantis, which was sun-worship.

8. That the oldest colony formed by the Atlanteans was probably in Egypt, whose civilization was a reproduction of that of the Atlantic island.

9. That the implements of the 'Bronze Age' of Europe were derived from Atlantis. The Atlanteans were also the first manufacturers of iron.

10. That the Phoenician alphabet, parent of all the European alphabets, was derived from an Atlantis alphabet, which was also conveyed from Atlantis to the Mayas of Central America.

11. That Atlantis was the original seat of the Aryan or Indo-European family of nations, as well as of the Semitic peoples, and possibly also of the Turanian races.

12. That Atlantis perished in a terrible convulsion of nature, in which the whole island was submerged by the ocean, with nearly all its inhabitants.

13. That a few persons escaped in ships and on rafts, and carried to the nations east and west the tidings of the appalling catastrophe, which has survived to our own time in the Flood and Deluge legends of the different nations of the Old and New worlds.

**No Mystery Here**

Donnelly's interests didn't stop with Atlantis. He also wrote *The Great Cryptogram*, which was about ciphers supposedly hidden in Shakespeare's plays that prove Francis Bacon actually wrote them (see Chapter 26, "Will the Real William Shakespeare Please Stand Up?"), and *Ragnarok, the Age of Fire and Ice*, which asserted that the last ice age was brought on by a comet hitting the earth. He also wrote several science fiction and fantasy novels that were basically vehicles for social criticism.

## No Lack of Evidence

Donnelly had a book full of evidence to back up his case. There was the matter of the legend of a great flood, which is not only in the Bible but in the Babylonian Saga of Gilgamesh, which is older than the Bible, as well as in the Satapatha Brahmana, the Mahabharata, and several other sacred texts from India. There are also deluge legends among the Aztecs, the Toltecs, and other American Indian tribes. The Indians of the Great Lakes—he doesn't specify which tribe—had the following tradition, according to Donnelly:

> In former times the father of the Indian tribes dwelt *toward the rising sun*. Having been warned in a dream that a deluge was coming upon the earth, he built a raft, on which he saved himself, with his family and all the animals. He floated thus for several months. The animals, who at that time spoke, loudly complained and murmured against him. At last a new earth appeared, on which he landed with all the animals, who from that time lost the power of speech, as a punishment for their murmurs against their deliverer. (Italics in the original.)

Surely, Donnelly reasoned, this must be a memory of the great floods that accompanied the sinking of Atlantis. Donnelly also found similarities in other legends on both sides of the Atlantic; in the alphabets of the Mayans, the Egyptians, and the Phoenicians; and in the pyramids built by the Egyptians and those built by the Mayans. There were also, he noted, many plants and animals on both sides of the Atlantic that were obviously related. He documented these similarities and relationships in great detail for more than 300 pages.

## Donnelly's Facts

Donnelly's collection of facts is fascinating; unfortunately, many of them were in accurate when Donnelly wrote about them and more have been disproved since. Donnelly quoted a French doctor who did research in Mexico as saying that one third of the Mayan language is "pure Greek." The doctor was mistaken; there is almost no similarity at all between the languages. Donnelly was also wrong when he said that the civilization of the ancient Egyptians developed suddenly and therefore must have been brought to them by the Atlantean refugees, that old world and new world cotton plants were related, that the Assyrians had pineapples, and that Hannibal (the Carthaginian general who crossed the Alps to fight the Romans) used gunpowder.

But still, he amassed a great deal of evidence which is impressive from its sheer volume, and much of it can be neither proved or disproved. From this he deduced that the Atlanteans invented the alphabet, bronze, embalming, glass, the compass, and astronomy. The biblical story of the Garden of Eden, Donnelly concluded, was a myth based on racial memories of the Golden Age of Atlantis.

Donnelly's book is entertaining and, on the first reading, very convincing. It isn't until one looks closely at the details that one realizes on what a thin support he has constructed his theory.

## The Post Donnelly Seekers

Donnelly's book sparked a new interest in the Atlantis story that has yet to subside. The hunt for the sunken island or continent has been more or less continual. Different researchers have "located" Atlantis in the mid-Atlantic Ocean (of course), in the Pacific Ocean, in the Caucasus mountains, and in southern Sweden, Algiers, the western bulge of Africa, South America, Ceylon, and Antarctica (which, apparently, was much warmer back then).

### Mysterious Comments

"There is a 'New Age' Atlantis, 'the legendary civilization of advanced sciences,' chiefly devoted to the 'science' of crystals. In a trilogy called *Crystal Enlightenment*, by Katrina Raphaell—the books mainly responsible for the crystal craze in America—Atlantean crystals read minds, transmit thoughts, are the repositories of ancient history and the model and source of the pyramids of Egypt. Nothing approximating evidence is offered to support these assertions."

—Carl Sagan, *The Demon-Haunted World*, 1996

# Helena Petrovna Blavatsky

One of the founders of the Theosophical Society and a noted mystic and spiritualist, Madame H.P. Blavatsky (1831–1891) included a version of the Atlantean myth in her complex historical-mystical-philosophical writings *Isis Unveiled* and *The Secret Doctrine.*

The story of Atlantis is part of the secret history of mankind, Blavatsky writes in *Isis Unveiled.* "Plato's guarded hints and the fact of his attributing the narrative to Solon and the Egyptian priests, were but a prudent way of imparting the fact to the world and by cleverly combining truth and fiction, to disconnect himself from a story which the obligations imposed at initiation forbade him to divulge," she explains.

In *The Secret Doctrine,* which is supposed to be a commentary and emendation of a mystical work called the *Book of Dzyan,* written by Atlantean priests in a now-forgotten language called Senzar, we learn more about Atlantis. There have been five "Root Races of Mankind":

➤ The first Root Race was a sort of astral jellyfish that lived on an Imperishable Sacred Land.

➤ The second, not quite as jelly-like, lived in Hyperboria, a mythical land of the far north.

➤ The third was the Lemurians, who looked liked four-armed apes with an extra eye in the back of their head and laid eggs. They lasted until they discovered sex, but that created conflicts, which did them in.

➤ The fourth was the Atlanteans, who were pretty human.

➤ The fifth is us.

There are two root races yet to come.

In 1904, an Austrian theosophist named Rudolf Steiner continued the Blavatsky screed with a book called *From the Akasic Records,* which detailed the progress of humanity from the ethereal plane to the material plane of existence we now inhabit. The Atlanteans ended the time of the fourth Root Race about 10,000 years ago when their greed and corruption caused them to unleash forces they couldn't control that destroyed Atlantis.

# Edgar Cayce

While delving into the past lives of a 14-year-old boy back in the 1920s (which, you will recall from Chapter 8, "Recent Prophets," he did while lying on his back in a self-induced trance), Edgar Cayce invoked Atlantis. He opined that the lad had lived in Atlantis about 12,000 years ago. Over time, Cayce added descriptive bits, locating Atlantis in the Atlantic Ocean between the Azores and the Sargasso Sea, dating the

**No Mystery Here**

You'll find more about Edgar Cayce in Chapter 8.

civilization back 200,000 years, and basing their science on a mystical "Tuaoi stone," a six-sided figure that produced energy and facilitated communication. The Atlanteans also used electricity and steam engines. They became greedy and degenerate, Cayce discovered, as had Steiner before him, and so their civilization and their island were destroyed.

Blavatsky and Cayce went far beyond Plato in their imaginings of ancient Atlantis. They also went far beyond, or perhaps to the left of, modern science. We can't argue with the Akasic Records, having never examined them, but the Root Races, as described, defy any explanation of evolution we're aware of. And Cayce's 200,000-year-old civilization based on the Tuaoi stone is the stuff of bad 1920's science fiction. But we should be grateful to anyone who adds a little excitement and humor to our lives, which their writings surely do, as long as we don't take them too seriously.

## The Santorini Connection

In the 1960s, a Greek professor named Anghelos Galanapoulos, a seismologist who for years had an abiding fascination with the Atlantis myth, realized that he might actually have the key to explaining much of the mystery of Atlantis.

It occurred to him that, if Plato's story was basically true and if Solon and the Egyptian priest had not communicated perfectly, then Solon might have mistranslated the Egyptian symbol for "100" as "1,000." In that case, all the dimensions Plato gives for Atlantis make much more sense. The events would have taken place 900 years before instead of 9,000. The great canal would be 30 feet wide and 10 feet deep instead of 300 feet wide and 100 feet deep. The city itself would shrink to a more reasonable size for a Bronze-Age culture.

If the "Pillars of Heracles" mentioned in the text referred not to the straits of Gibraltar but to a location closer to home—which might well have been the case because ships were rowed by oarsmen who hadn't yet learned to tack against the wind and seldom ventured out of sight of the coast—then he might just know where Atlantis had been located and what had happened to it.

There was reason to think that the island of Santorini (actually a small group of islands in the Aegean Sea north of Crete) had blown its top sometime around 1650 B.C. Santorini was the top of a volcano that had had major eruptions in 198 B.C., in 726 A.D., in 1573, in 1707 (that one lasted about five years), and in 1866.

*Santorini, from a 1703 copper engraving by Olfart Dapper.*

Although there are no direct records of it, the eruption of 1650 B.C. must have been a doozy. The volcanic ash from it, probably accompanied by a great tidal wave, wiped out a thriving civilization on Crete over 100 miles away. On Santorini, when layers of pumice, a form of lava left behind after the eruptions, were being mined (pumice is used to make cement), the remains of buildings were found, along with clay household utensils and some gold jewelry.

Could the buried civilization on Santorini be the lost Atlantis or at least the source of the Atlantis legend? Perhaps further excavation will give us clues—say, a giant statue of the god Poseidon. That would be an exciting end to the story. Or perhaps it would be just the beginning.

### No Mystery Here

If the legend of Atlantis has interested you enough to consider a visit to Santorini, check out the island's Web site at www. santonet.com. It's a beautiful island that does a great tourist business.

## The Least You Need to Know

➤ The legend of Atlantis began with two dialogues of Plato back around 260 B.C. Plato may have made it all up, or it may be based on old legends.

➤ Ignatius Donnelly reignited interest in Atlantis in the mid-nineteenth century. He found myths from many cultures that were similar enough to have originated in the same place, and he thought that place was Atlantis.

➤ H.P. Blavatsky and the Theosophists put an occult slant on the Atlantis story, saying the Atlanteans were the fourth Root Race. (We are the fifth.)

➤ In the 1960s, Greek professor Anghelos Galanapoulos theorized that the Atlantis legend might have originated in the destruction of the island of Santorini in a great volcanic eruption 3,500 years ago.

# Chapter 12

# We Are Not Alone

## In this Chapter

➤ Stars and their planets

➤ What's needed to support life

➤ The Fermi paradox

➤ The Drake equation

➤ The search goes on

There are, as Carl Sagan was so fond of saying, billions and billions of galaxies, and each galaxy has billions and billions of stars. That being so, it's highly unlikely that we earthlings, making up the *biosphere* of one small planet circling an undistinguished star, comprise the only life in the universe. And it's only slightly less unlikely that we humans, being—as we like to think—the most intelligent species on Earth, represent the only intelligent life in the universe.

This is the opinion of the majority of scientists who have any specialized knowledge about the possibility of life in other worlds. In this chapter, we'll explore the reasons they think so, and we'll take a look at the ongoing search for extraterrestrial life. Are we alone in the universe or not?

## They Thought They Were Alone

In the late nineteenth century, astronomers first began to seriously consider the possible existence of extraterrestrial life, but they were not very hopeful. Life, it seemed, depended on such extraordinary circumstances that the odds of finding it elsewhere were staggeringly small.

### What Does This Mean?

The **biosphere** is the totality of life on a planet from the smallest microbe to the largest whale, from the highest drifting seed pod or spore in the atmosphere to the microbes at the bottom of the deepest ocean trench.

Nineteenth-century scientists could not even conceive of getting past the most basic of these requirements: that a planet must be in orbit around a star. They knew there were plenty of stars, but life, at least life as we know it, cannot develop, or even exist, on a star. There has to be a planet circling a star, and nobody understood how stars came to have planets. One popular theory held that planets were formed as a gravitational by-product of closely passing stars. When two stars passed each other, they each, as a result of gravitational attraction, lost a little of their mass, which combined between them as the stars separated. Eventually, it cooled and coalesced into planets.

If this theory was correct, then a planet must be a truly rare occurrence throughout the universe since stars seldom pass that close to each other. And the stars would have to pass just so; otherwise, the matter ejected would either fall back or be lost in space.

Although nineteenth-century astronomers had not yet learned the true enormity of the universe, when they computed the odds, as best they could, of a planet even existing around another star and then that planet being within the star's *ecosphere* and having the right elemental makeup to generate life—well, it seemed pretty darn unlikely.

*A field of distant galaxies photographed by the Hubble Space Telescope.*

## Most Stars Are Big Mothers

As astronomers gradually discovered more about stellar processes, their view of how planets formed began to change. Today, most scientists believe that planets are created at the same time as the star they orbit and as part of the same process.

Thus, it is probable that many stars have planets. We now, in fact, have evidence that several nearby stars do have planets. More than 30 planets that circle stars other than the sun have been discovered. The evidence is indirect but powerful. It involves observing the effect of the pull of gravity a planet would exert on its star. As the planet circles in its orbit the star wobbles ever so slightly back and forth. Astronomers can observe the wobble's *Doppler effect* on the light shining from that star.

## The Dance of the Planets

When various elements are burned in the furnace of a star's interior, they give off light at specific frequencies. Astronomers keep a record of the *spectrum* of that star over a period of time. By looking at one of the characteristic lines on a *spectrograph* of the star's light—say, that of iron—to see how it was shifted by the Doppler effect, they can tell what direction the star is going. If it is shifted toward the red, the star is headed away from us. If it is shifted toward the blue, the star is approaching.

Astronomers noticed that the spectra of some stars seemed to alternate between shifting toward the red and the blue. A star's spectrum would be red-shifted for some weeks or months and then blue-shifted for the same length of time, and then red, and then blue, back and forth as if the star were dancing in place. Something had to be causing that dance.

The most logical explanation behind this dance was the pull of gravity of one or more planets circling the star. As a planet swings around a star, the star wobbles just a bit toward the planet. It was that tell-tale wobble that made the apparent spectrum swing from red to blue. Next time you jump out of an airplane reflect that, just as the Earth is pulling you toward it, you are likewise pulling the Earth. You are moving a lot further and faster toward the Earth than it is toward you, but the attraction is mutual.

### What Does This Mean?

The range of orbits around a star that get just enough energy from that star to be suitable for a life-bearing planet is known as that star's **ecosphere**.

### Here There Be Dragons

The Theory of Evolution doesn't preclude the existence of God. He might have created the Earth and all the creatures in it just last Wednesday; if He'd created our earlier memories at the same time, we'd have no way of knowing (philosophy students, particularly sophomores, love arguing that one). But if this is the case, He has left all sorts of clues that indicate that the Earth is billions of years old, that life is a few less billions of years old, and that evolution has been continual. If that's what He wants us to believe, why not go along with it?

**What Does This Mean?**

The **Doppler effect** is the name for the apparent shift in the frequency of sound or light waves when the object emitting them is coming toward or away from the observer. The usual example given to illustrate the effect is a train whistle and its relationship to a listener—the sound rises as it gets closer and falls as the train moves away.

## We Find the Big Ones

At the moment, the smallest planet that the wobble technique can detect is somewhat larger than Jupiter, which is more than 300 times the mass of the Earth. Finding more Jupiters is a fascinating prospect, but what astronomers interested in the question of extraterrestrial life really want to know is whether there are more Earths. We don't know whether life can exist on Jupiter (we think not), but we have very good evidence that life can exist on Earth!

A new instrument has been developed by astronomers at the United States Naval Observatory that should make it possible to detect Earth-size planets circling distant stars. Called the Multi-Channel Fourier Transform Spectrometer (mFTS), it uses a process called interferometry (a way of amplifying slight differences in spectra by their interference patterns) to detect small wobbles in a star, as would be produced by planets as tiny as the Earth.

As part of a project called The Exploration of Neighboring Planetary Systems (ExNPS) Study, NASA plans to launch the Terrestrial Planet Finder (TPF), which would be stationed beyond the orbit of Jupiter in the darkest part of the solar system. The TPF's job will be to search for the faintest wobbles in stars that could establish the existence of Earth-type planets.

**What Does This Mean?**

What we see as white light is actually made up of a rainbow of colors. We call those colors the **spectrum** of the light, and shining the light through a prism will cause it to break up into the band of colors that make up its spectrum. A **spectroscope** is the device that splits a beam of light into its various colors.

## Yes, But Is There Life?

It seems as though planets orbiting stars are ubiquitous, but astronomers still have to determine what percentage of them might have the necessary conditions for creating and sustaining life.

For life to come into existence on a planet, a variety of conditions must be met. The star that the planet circles can't be too big or too small. If the star is too big, then its lifetime will be too short to permit the evolution of life—really big stars burn themselves out in a billion years or so, hardly enough time for life to get beyond the stage of primitive bacteria. If the star is too small, its ecosphere, the range of orbits a planet must be within to sustain life, would be so small as to make it unlikely to contain a planet.

## The Mix Must Be Just Right

After we manage to find a star that is just the right size, one of its planets would have to be in an orbit that approximated the distance of Earth's orbit around the Sun: too much closer and the planet would fry, too much farther out and it would freeze.

If the star is the right size and the planet is the right distance from the sun, we have to see whether the ingredients for life are present. Since life evidently requires an abundance of water in its liquid form, the planet's orbit would have to be such that the surface temperature of the planet falls between the freezing and boiling points of water (from 32 degrees Fahrenheit to 212 degrees Fahrenheit) for a substantial part of the year. The planet would have to have a rocky mantle and an atmosphere made up of oxygen, hydrogen, and nitrogen. It would have to contain all the other elements that make up life: carbon, phosphorous, iodine, iron, and zinc, among others.

## Generations

For the planet to meet all these conditions, its sun has to be a second- or third-generation star.

First-generation stars are stars that were born shortly after the great expansion of the universe we call the Big Bang. These types of stars are made almost entirely of hydrogen and helium. That's all that was around in the beginning. Most of the heavier elements are created when a star ends its life by blowing up, becoming what we call a nova. That explosion, caused by the tremendous pressures developed when the dying star collapses in on itself, creates enough heat and pressure to fuse light elements into elements like carbon, oxygen, and iron, elements needed for life as we know it.

This process is still going on; stars reach the end of their lives and go nova on a regular basis, adding to the supply of heavier elements. Then the cosmic dust and hydrogen gas come together again under the pull of gravity, forming second- or third-generation stars. The areas in the universe where some part of the cosmic dust is known to be made up of these heavier elements are clearly the best bets for producing planets on which life might form.

There is no way of knowing how many second-generation stars have planets with metal cores and rocky mantles circling them, but the number must be large. After all, the amount of mass in the universe is so great that even the 1 percent of it that isn't hydrogen or helium is enough to make billions of planets. Our local Milky Way galaxy alone hosts more than 100 billion stars.

# The Fermi Paradox

If there really are a lot of planets out there in the universe that could support life, you're probably wondering why we aren't being visited right now by some curious citizens of the Milky Way. That's a good question. Nobel Prize–winning physicist Enrico Fermi asked the same question in 1943 in what has become known as the Fermi paradox.

## The Mystery Deepens

Even after the novae have done their work, 99 percent of the universe is still hydrogen and helium, and all the other elements make up the remaining 1 percent. Our sun, a second-generation star, is much richer in the heavier elements than the average star, but they still make up only 3 percent.

The paradox could be stated this way: There are tens of billions of stars right here in the Milky Way galaxy, and the galaxy and most of the stars in it are more than 10 billion years old. That provides billions of chances for an intelligent life form to develop and billions of years for it to travel about the Milky Way, colonizing millions of planets and coming into contact with any planets developing their own life. So, Fermi wondered, how come they're not here giving speeches at the United Nations, buying up waterfront property on Maui, selling us super ray guns, making fun of the primitive earthlings' artwork, or trying to convert us to the one really true faith?

Over the past half-century, a variety of reasons have been suggested as to why there is no confirmed presence of extraterrestrials on Earth. Here are a few:

### No Mystery Here

In Part 5, "Inhuman Events" (chapters 21–23), we discuss the possibility that we actually have been visited and the people who believe in this possibility.

➤ *We're it.* It could be that, despite the odds that make it seem almost certain that someone else is out there, life exists only on our tiny ball of rock circling an unimportant star. If so, the universe would seem like an awful waste of real estate.

➤ *They were here and left.* The human race is—let's be generous—5,000 years old. Earth is close to five *billion* years old. If extraterrestrials had visited Earth any time during 99.999 percent of its lifetime, they wouldn't have found anybody around worth talking to. And if they left anything behind, it's probably been buried hundreds if not thousands of feet beneath the Earth's surface as continents drifted and sheets of ice moved forward and back.

➤ *We've been taken off the list.* An advance party of aliens has been studying our radio and television signals, which after 60 years of broadcasting now reach 60 light years in all directions. By some cosmic joke, they have not been able to receive *Masterpiece Theatre* or even *60 Minutes,* just *Gilligan's Island* and *My Mother the Car.* They have decided not to bother coming.

➤ *Our timing is bad.* It could be that the life span of an intelligent species is, in cosmic terms, brief. Perhaps only a few manage to make it past 10,000 years of civilization without committing suicide through warfare or destroying the planet with pollution. If this is so, then although there might have been tens of thousands of races possessing intelligence throughout the galaxy, only a few of them would co-exist at any given time. Most of them will become extinct before being able to travel beyond their own solar system, and we may well be extinct before anyone gets around to visiting us.

➤ *The yokel effect.* The Milky Way galaxy is shaped sort of like a fried egg with a bulging center surrounded by a thinner disk. Our sun is in the thin-disk part, about three-fifths of the way out from the center. This area is not particularly rich in stars. As you head toward the galactic center, the number of stars increases, and they get much closer together. If you were captain of a space ship exploring the galaxy, charged with finding new worlds and new life, where would you go? Toward the more cluttered galactic center, where chances of finding a planet teeming with life are good? Or out to the sticks, where they don't know the latest dances and they dress funny?

➤ *We're being watched.* The Galactic Federation of Planets has sent observers to watch our development from a safe distance. As soon as we rise above our current level of savagery and show ourselves capable of not blowing ourselves or anyone else up, they'll invite us to join.

➤ *We don't know it when we see it.* Someone once pointed out that a modern jetliner flies at an altitude and a speed that would put it out of reach of the best fighters of World War II. A modern Boeing 747 could have flown over any air battle in Europe, and neither side would have known. Well, it could be that the aliens are here, but their technology is so far advanced that we can't detect them. Maybe they only want to talk to the most intelligent species and are deep in discussions with the whales, the elephants, or the ants.

➤ *Einstein was right.* In Einstein's view of the universe, the speed of light (that is 186,282 miles a second) is the absolute limiting speed anything with mass can travel. The speed of light is unbelievably fast, but the universe is unbelievably huge. It could be that no one has come to visit because it would take too long. With present technology it would take hundreds of years to travel the four light years to reach Alpha Centauri, the closest star to the sun.

### No Mystery Here

Dr. Frank Drake, professor of astronomy and astrophysics at the University of California at Santa Cruz, was interested in the possible existence of extraterrestrial intelligence for many years. He served as president of the SETI institute (discussed later in this chapter) and co-authored the book *Is Anyone Out There? The Scientific Search for Extraterrestrial Intelligence* with science writer Dava Sobel.

# Doctor Drake's Equation

Well, if aliens won't or at least haven't come here, how can we tell if they're out there? How many of the multitude of planets can we expect to support life and, more particularly, intelligent life? And how can we find out whether they do?

Back in 1961, a group of people interested in the problem gathered in Green Bank, West Virginia, for the Green Bank Conference on Extraterrestrial Intelligent Life. During this conference, astronomer Dr. Frank Drake thought about the problem of how many intelligent civilizations might be out there for us to try to find (or that might try to find us). He listed all the factors that had to be considered to resolve the problem of extraterrestrial intelligent life, and he put them together in the form of an equation.

Yes, it's an equation, but don't be nervous. This equation is easy to understand and is a really wonderful way to examine all the factors and see how they interrelate. It is usually expressed as follows:

$$N = R \times f_p \times n_e \times f_l \times f_i \times f_c \times L$$

In the preceding equation ...

N is the number of intelligent races we might find if we were to look at any given time.

R is the number of stars coming into being in an average year.

$f_p$ is the percent of these stars that form planets.

$n_e$ is the number of these planets in the star's ecosphere.

$f_l$ is the number of those planets on which life occurs.

$f_i$ is the percentage of this life that evolves into intelligent beings.

$f_c$ is the percentage of these intelligent beings that try to communicate with the rest of the universe.

All this is multiplied by L—the life span in years that a technologically advanced civilization can be expected to continue to exist. Sound complicated? Follow along and you'll see that it's actually quite simple.

## The Equation of Life

Let's plug in some reasonable approximations and see what we get. (Keep in mind that one person's reasonable approximation is another's wild-eyed fantasy, but we'll do the best we can.) We'll confine our estimates to our own galaxy, the Milky Way. What we're trying to determine is N—How many extraterrestrial intelligent species have developed a technologically advanced civilization and might be interested in communicating with us if we start looking for them?

First, we need to estimate how many stars might be possible suns for these races. We assume that biological life comes into being at a certain point in a star's lifetime, and intelligent life develops within a certain time after that. Knowing how many stars are created on average in a given year, R, should tell us how many are around the right age.

We can get this figure by dividing the number of stars estimated to make up the Milky Way with the estimated age of the Milky Way. Notice all the "estimated" hedges. The estimated age of the Milky Way, last I heard, was 10 billion years, give or take a couple of billion. The estimated number of stars is somewhere around 100 billion. This gives us 100/10 or about 10 stars being created in any given year.

**No Mystery Here**

Just to keep perspective, the Milky Way is one of billions of galaxies, each containing billions of stars.

Now we need to determine the number of these stars, as a percent, that forms with planets, $f_p$. It seems from recent evidence that the number is almost unity—that is, almost every star comes equipped with planets. But let's be cautious. Let's just say that 8 out of 10 stars have accompanying planets. So $f_p = 80$ percent.

$n_e$, the number of planets in an average star's ecosphere, is a tough one to estimate. Some of the planets that have been discovered so far seem to be gas giants, like Jupiter, that are orbiting their star at distances closer than the Earth is to the sun. That would leave little room for Earth-type planets in the ecosphere. So, purely arbitrarily, because we really don't have enough information yet, let's say that one out of every two stars with planets has one in the ecosphere. That would make $n_e$ equal to one half, or 0.5.

Judging from the fact that the amino acid precursors to life seem ridiculously easy to form here on Earth, it would seem a good bet that every planet in the right orbit that can produce life will do so. This would put $f_l$ equal to 1.

### The Mystery Deepens

There is a theory that a gas giant in a solar system—located, like Jupiter, at a comfortably great distance from the host star—would be a great aid to the future of life on the inner planets. It would serve as a mighty broom, sweeping the solar system clear of many of the meteors that would otherwise bombard the life-bearing planet. Too many hits like the one believed to have wiped out the dinosaurs would make life a chancy proposition.

## Is It Intelligent or Ain't It?

But $f_i$ is a problem. How many of these supposed extraterrestrial species would develop intelligence? If that giant meteor hadn't hit the Earth 35 million years ago and wiped out the dinosaurs, would they have developed brains larger than prunes? Let's give the utility of intelligence the benefit of the doubt and say that the leading species on any planet will get there through superior brainpower, which will eventually lead to beings as smart as we like to think we are. This puts $f_i$ also equal to 1.

We have no basis to make a decision about $f_c$ and must wildly speculate. Is curiosity a natural function of intelligence? And will that curiosity inevitably channel itself toward the stars? Perhaps the intelligent species on one planet lives under water. Would they even see the stars? Perhaps the intelligent species has seen too many movies about invaders from distant planets—wouldn't they choose not to try to communicate if only to make sure we don't know where they are? Let's assume that any species that develops intelligence is going to be curious about who else is out there and what they might have to say. Let's assign a value of 1 to $f_c$.

Now, putting an attempt to get a value for the last term in the equation (the length of time an advanced civilization can expect to stay around, L) aside for a moment, let's plug in values for what we have:

$$N = R \times f_p \times n_e \times f_l \times f_i \times f_c \times L$$

$$= 10 \times .8 \times .5 \times 1 \times 1 \times 1 \times L$$

$$= 4 L$$

This means, if our figures are right, that at any given time there are four times as many advanced civilizations out in the galaxy willing to contact us as the average length of time in years that such a civilization will last without destroying itself or dying out.

**Mysterious Comments**

"Once life has started in a relatively benign environment and billions of years of evolutionary time are available, the expectation of many of us is that intelligent beings would develop. ... The entire evolutionary record of our planet ... illustrates a progressive tendency toward intelligence. There is nothing mysterious about this: smart organisms by and large survive better and leave more offspring than stupid ones. ... Once intelligent beings achieve technology and the capacity for self-destruction of their species, the selective advantage of intelligence becomes more uncertain."

—Carl Sagan, *The Dragons of Eden*

## The L You Say

In galactic terms, the beginning of technological civilization is the advent of radio since that is the earliest technology that makes it possible to communicate with other planets. By this definition, we have been a technologically advanced civilization for less than a century, and already we're showing signs of blowing ourselves up or poisoning the Earth beyond repair. To judge by us humans, and we have nothing else to judge by, once a civilization becomes technologically adept, it quickly develops the skills necessary to destroy itself and all other life on the planet.

But let's be optimistic and assume that most advanced civilizations manage to get by the first critical couple of centuries and learn to live in peace without using up or destroying the resources of their planet. In that case, L could be a million years or longer. Let's stop at a million.

If L is equal to a million, then N equals four million. By our very cobbled-together estimate, that would mean four million advanced civilizations are out there in the Milky Way just waiting for us to communicate with them.

If these four million are parceled out at random, there should be one within 250 light years of us. Our early radio shows have been spreading out from Earth with the speed of light since the 1920s. This means that, sometime in the next 200 years, some being that looks as much like us as we look like horseshoe crabs but that could play a pretty mean game of chess if we teach it the rules, is going to be listening to *The Jack Benny Show*.

## The Truth Is Out There

Remember that many of the plugged-in numbers are ballpark estimates, and it's a very big ballpark. So let's allow for one order of magnitude in the figures each way (that's adding or removing a zero).

Therefore, let us state with absolute (un)certainty that there's a good chance that Drake's equation equals somewhere between 400,000 and 40 million intellectually aware, technologically advanced civilizations out there, trying to get in touch with us.

# Now We're Listening

Since 1960, when Dr. Drake began Project Ozma, the first attempt to detect extraterrestrial radio signals, we have been trying to listen for radio signals that might be coming from some intelligent race on another planet. For a while, Congress funded the Search for Extraterrestrial Intelligence (SETI) project run by NASA, but funding was withdrawn in 1993. Since then, several privately funded projects have taken over and are even now listening for signals from whoever may be out there.

**The Mystery Deepens**

We may already have eavesdropped on an interstellar conversation. It was at 11:16 P.M. (Eastern Standard Time) on 15 August 1977 that the "Big Ear" radio telescope at Ohio State University recorded a narrowband signal at the hydrogen frequency coming from the direction of the constellation Sagittarius. It lasted for 37 seconds and, unfortunately, was never repeated. The astronomer who first noticed it wrote "Wow!" along the side of the printout; ever since, this has been known as the "Wow!" event. Continued analysis of the signal over the past decades has ruled out most of the other possibilities, leading the scientists involved to conclude that they indeed may have recorded an extraterrestrial intelligence (ETI) event.

## Project Phoenix

In February 1995, Project Phoenix, a privately funded SETI group, began using the largest radio telescope south of the equator: the Parkes 210-foot radio telescope in New South Wales, Australia. It is now also using the 140-foot radio telescope in Green Bank, West Virginia. Phoenix plans to look at (or listen to) about 1,000 stars within

200 light years of our solar system. Phoenix is looking for signals between 1,000 and 3,000 MHz, which astronomers have concluded for a variety of reasons is a likely place to look. It has surveyed about half of its list by now and has not yet picked up the local weather report from outer space. Considering the limited number of stars and the limited frequency span it is examining, however, there's still a long way to go before getting disheartened.

## The SETI League

Another result of the cancelled funding of NASA's SETI project was the founding of the SETI League. The SETI League is composed of amateur radio and radio astronomy fans and hobbyists who search for extraterrestrial signals with backyard radio telescope dishes and a couple thousand dollars (or less) worth of equipment. Even though their equipment is nowhere near as sensitive as that of the big boys, they think that, with so much sky to cover and so many frequencies to listen to, they have as good a chance of making that once-in-a-millennium discovery as anyone else. Their search is called Project Argus, and their goal is to have 5,000 amateur radio astronomers pointing their dish antennas at the sky by the year 2001.

The International Academy of Astronautics has established rules for what to do when an extraterrestrial signal is discovered. As set forth in the "Declaration of Principles Concerning Activities Following the Detection of Extraterrestrial Intelligence," anyone finding an ETI signal should

1. Eliminate all other possibilities.
2. Notify the Central Bureau for Astronomical Telegrams of the International Astronomical Union.
3. Notify the secretary-general of the UN.
4. Make all the data regarding the signal available to scientists worldwide.

The SETI establishment would then

5. Clear any competing Earth-originating signals from around the ETI frequency.
6. Consult on when and how (and whether) to reply.

To this list we may add

7. Accept the Nobel Prize.

## SERENDIP

The University of California at Berkeley has an ongoing SETI Program called the Search for Extraterrestrial Radio Emissions from Nearby Developed Intelligent Populations (SERENDIP). The project operates as a "piggyback" SETI system on the 1,000-foot dish at Arecibo Observatory in Puerto Rico.

**155**

Without interrupting any radio astronomy observations going on, SERENDIP takes a feed of the telescope's output and passes it through the SERENDIP spectrum analyzer and looks at millions of narrowband chunks to see whether any of the signals overheard show signs of intelligence. Because we have no way of knowing from what direction an ETI signal may come, listening in whatever direction is being used for other science experiments is just as good as listening in any other direction, and this piggybacking enables the SERENDIP group to eavesdrop on the universe almost continuously. The U.C. Berkeley SERENDIP group is shortly going to add its piggyback receivers to several other radio telescopes around the world.

So the search for extraterrestrial life goes on, and until we find it we won't know for sure it's there. There are still some scientists who are convinced that life on Earth is just a lucky accident (or perhaps part of a divine plan), and that all of the remaining billions of planets circling billions of other suns are lifeless balls of rock. But most of us are convinced that someday, as we listen for radio messages from outer space, we're going to hear somebody saying hello.

---

### The Least You Need to Know

➤ Life cannot begin without the combination of a star and a planet that circles it. We now know that planets circling stars are the rule rather than the exception.

➤ A planet must be smaller than a gas giant and within the star's ecosphere to support life.

➤ The Fermi paradox raises a good question: With so many billions of chances for life to generate throughout the universe, why haven't we been contacted yet?

➤ Plugging numbers into the Drake equation indicates that there is a strong chance that intelligent life exists elsewhere.

➤ Thanks to Project Phoenix, the SETI League, SERENDIP, and other programs, we've started a methodical search for extraterrestrial intelligent life.

---

# Chapter 13

# It's In Your Stars

> ## In This Chapter
>
> ➤ Newspaper horoscopes and "cold readings"
>
> ➤ 4,500-year-old Chaldean astrology
>
> ➤ The royal astrologers
>
> ➤ Brahe, Kepler, and Lilly
>
> ➤ Modern astrology

Stop several people on the street and ask them their opinion of astrology. (I suggest you carry a clipboard so they think you're taking a survey—most people will talk to someone taking a survey.) They'll probably have one. Yet most people have only the faintest notion of what it is or how it works.

Most people who don't believe in it think of it as a slightly silly version of fortune-telling. Those who believe in it range from people who think it's probably a good omen if their new love interest is of a compatible sun sign to people who pay astrologers lots of money to find out what the stars have to say about their latest business venture.

In this chapter we'll look at the history of astrology and the powerful influence this ancient craft has had on world affairs.

# The "Science" of Astrology

It has been consistently shown by all sorts of surveys that more than half the people in the United States profess some belief in *astrology*. A third of the population thinks it's based on scientific principles, although they're aware that astrology hasn't been accepted by the mainstream scientific community. Most of astrology's practitioners find it useful and comforting and don't really care what anyone else thinks. A surprising number of people who profess not to believe in astrology still sneak a peak at their *horoscope* in the daily paper and are often amazed at the seemingly accurate advice it gives.

## *They Have It Down Cold*

Even professional astrologers agree that newspaper horoscopes are useless. What professional astrologers practice is a technique known as the "cold reading." This is a way of making general statements that could apply to just about anybody seem as though they are aimed directly at you. Fortunetellers of all types are masters of this technique, and newspaper horoscope writers practice a diluted form of it.

Here, for example, are half a dozen statements:

➤ You have a financial question that's been troubling you, and you're not quite sure how to handle it.

➤ Someone you work with doesn't appreciate your true worth.

➤ You have a really good idea that needs to be developed properly.

➤ A close personal relationship needs your attention right now.

➤ You are considering an important change in your life.

➤ Pay attention to that emotion you're trying to ignore.

### What Does This Mean?

**Astrology** is the practice of attempting to foretell or influence the outcome of an event or to assess the character, behavior, or fortune of a person by studying the interrelationship of the sun, the planets, and the stars.

### What Does This Mean?

A **horoscope** is a geocentric (earth-centered) map of the solar system at a particular moment in time. The most common are the "natal charts," which show the configuration of the heavens at the moment of a person's birth.

## *"How Did He Know?"*

Now have someone sit across the table from you, hold your hand, stare into your eyes, and recite two or three of these sentences to you. Don't be surprised if you find yourself thinking, "By gosh, that's right! How did he know?" That's the power of the cold reading.

The power of astrology goes beyond cold readings, however. Serious astrologers believe that our character and strong hints about our destiny are written in the stars for people wise enough to read them. Some noted astrologers have predicted some very specific things that have come to pass. Many other predictions have not come to pass, but astrologers would argue that scientists have been wrong a lot, too.

### Mysterious Comments

"According to all the grand masters in astrology, comets are the stars of exceptional heroes, and they visit earth only to signalize great changes; the planets preside over collective existences and modify the destinies of mankind in the aggregate; the fixed stars, more remote and more feeble in their action, attract individuals and determine their tendencies. Sometimes a group of stars may combine to influence the destinies of a single man, while often a great number of souls are drawn by the distant rays of the same sun."

—Eliphas Levi, *Transcendental Magic* (1855), Translated by A.E. Waite

# The Ancient Astrologers

In Akkad, Babylonia, Chaldea, and the other kingdoms of ancient Mesopotamia, the priests developed what we now call astrology at least 4,500 years ago. Or perhaps they adopted it from an even older civilization whose records are lost in antiquity.

The craft of astrology was based on a particular human conceit that was perfectly logical and, until recently, was not even much in dispute: the belief that Earth is at the center of the universe and that humans were put here to rule over Earth. If this were so, the reasoning went, and if the destinies of men were in the hands of the gods, then surely a celestial event—say, a comet crossing the sky—was a portent of a great and important event here on earth: perhaps the birth of a great king, a destructive earthquake, a crop failure, or a death.

The Chaldeans were considered the master astrologers, and the system they devised is still with us today in large part.

## The Astrologer-Priests

The Chaldean priests studied the heavens for portents such as comets or meteors or even strange cloud formations—the clouds were, after all, as out of reach as the stars. After a while, they discovered among the stars a harmony that was perhaps even more meaningful. As the Earth moves in its orbit around the sun, different groups of stars come into view in the night sky, and each group appears and disappears on the same date each year.

The human brain is adept at finding patterns, and the priests soon found patterns in the relative positions of the brighter stars. They superimposed on these patterns images of earthly things—a bear, a fish, a pair of scales—and the constellations came into being.

The recurring appearances of the various constellations provided the earliest way of determining the length of the year. The constellations also signaled the change of seasons. When certain constellations were visible, it was time to plant; when others appeared, it was time to harvest.

Then there were the planets. The word "planet" comes from the Greek for "wanderer." The planets were seen to wander about the sky independent of the motion of the stars. The Chaldean astronomers knew of seven planets and reckoned them to be closer to the earth than the stars. In order of their perceived distance from the earth, they were the moon, Mercury, Venus, the sun, Mars, Jupiter, and Saturn.

### No Mystery Here

Most of the world's early civilizations devised some form of astrology. The Mayans in Central America, the Chinese, and the ancient Hindus in India each developed an independent system of astrological divination. Chinese and Indian astrology, each more than 4,000 years old, are practiced to this day.

## Post Hoc Ergo What?

We no longer think of the sun or the moon as planets, and we know the earth isn't the center of the universe, but the Chaldeans were doing the best they could with the information they had. The system they devised was probably based on a kind of reasoning known as *post hoc ergo propter hoc*, which is Latin for "after this, therefore on account of this." You know the sort of thing: I wore red socks when I hit that home run; therefore, I have a better chance of hitting home runs if I wear red socks. It's the sort of fallacy that we all have to fight against because it seems so logical and right, yet is dangerously unreliable.

Let's say that a king dies just as, oh, Mars enters the constellation Taurus. Well, clearly Mars entering Taurus means hard luck for kings. If the next time Mars enters Taurus something bad happens to a king—and there are a large number of kings and many bad things that can happen to each one of them—why then, the pattern is clear.

## Chaldean Astrology

The constant correlation of the planets' positions and mundane events led Chaldean astrologers to draw certain conclusions as to which planet influenced what sort of event. Some of these conclusions were obviously powerfully influenced by the mythology surrounding the god associated with the planet.

**Samas** (the sun) was all-powerful, the bringer of light and life, the ruler of the day, yet capable of causing drought and deadly scorching heat. The position of Samas at the time of your birth was the most important determining factor in predicting your personality and your fate.

**Here There Be Dragons**

The *post hoc ergo propter hoc* fallacy is particularly popular among government officials and politicians. In California, politicians are crediting the "three-strikes" law (sentencing a criminal to mandatory life in prison for his third felony conviction) for lowering crime rates. This conveniently ignores the fact that crime rates have also gone down in all the states without this law. I'm sure you can think of your own examples.

**Nebo** (Mercury), the god of wisdom, the record keeper, was the scribe who recorded the deeds of men. Nebo was neither good nor bad, as wisdom can be used for both good and evil.

**Ishtar** (Venus) was the goddess of motherhood and love and possessed great healing power. She was good for all growing things but not so good for widows or sucking babes.

**Sin** (the moon) had a powerful but ambiguous influence. In one phase, it promoted growth and happiness; in another, she could shrivel crops and cause madness.

**Nergal** (Mars) was the evil god of the dead. He brought war and plague and was unlucky for kings. He destroyed harvests and stunted the growth of farm animals and fish. He was known as the Fiend, the Fox, or the Persian.

**Marduk** (Jupiter) was the most consistently favorable of the planets. The creator and awakener of the dead, he kept away chaos. When near the moon, he assured the birth of male children.

**Adar** (Saturn) was the god of hunting. Although often favorable to both public and private affairs, his influence could be evil. He was called the Great Misfortune.

## The Chaldean Zodiac

The Chaldean astrologers also devised the 12 signs of the Zodiac. Three have changed their designations over the centuries, but we still use nine of them just as the Chaldeans named them more than 4,000 years ago. The unchanged ones are Taurus the Bull, Gemini the Twins, Cancer the Crab, Leo the Lion, Libra the Scales, Scorpio the Scorpion, Sagittarius the Archer, Aquarius the Water Carrier, and Pisces the Fish. The one we call Capricorn the Goat was the Goat-Fish to the Chaldeans, Ares the Ram was the Day-Laborer, and Virgo the Virgin was the Earth Mother. Of course we use the Latin translations of the original names, as the Romans adopted and practiced a version of Chaldean astrology. Why there are just twelve signs is lost in antiquity.

The Chaldean astrologer-priests used the old language of Sumer in their rituals, a language no longer spoken or understood by peasants or the nonpriestly nobility at that time. This, along with the abstruse calculations needed to cast astrological charts, added a desirable aura of mystery to the procedure. Some of the predictions made by the Chaldean astrologers were very direct, such as this one, found on a tablet that dates back some 4,300 years:

> If Ishtar (Venus) appears in the East in the month Airu and the Great and Small Twins surround her, all four of them, and she is dark, then will the King of Elam fall sick and not remain alive.

Astrology, with its rigorous rules and structure, provided people in these ancient civilizations with a sense of order and control in a seemingly hostile and chaotic world. Psychologists have shown that people who believe they have some control over their lives are healthier and happier, and generally do better, then people who do not. This is true even when the control the people think they have does not exist.

# Astrology in the Medieval World

Astrology was a highly respected occupation throughout medieval Europe, and many of the finest and most prominent scholars of their day included a working knowledge of astrology among their accomplishments.

## The Royal Astrologers

Astrologers depended on the patronage of kings and nobles, and just about every king had his favorite court astrologer. Many of the popes had astrologers, and some of them were astrologers themselves including Silvester II (999–1003), John XXI (1276–1277), Julius II (1503–1513), and Clement VIII (1592–1605).

Louis XI of France (who reigned 1461–1483) invited gaggles of astrologers to his court and consulted with them regularly. Henry II of France (who reigned 1547–1559) had Nostradamus (see Chapter 7, "The Great Medieval Prophets") as his court physician; his wife Catherine de' Medici hardly made a move without consulting one astrologer or another.

**The Mystery Deepens**

In the year 1179 A.D., the Persian poet and astrologer Anwari, noting the coming conjunction (coming together) of five major planets in the sign of Libra, predicted a "great tempest" for the night of 16 September 1186 A.D., seven years off. People waited expectantly and fearfully, but the night proved to be exceptionally calm. Anwari could only shake his head in wonder. Something should have happened that night, something fearful. It wasn't until some years later that it was realized that Genghis Khan, "the Scourge of God" who swept over Europe with his Mongol hordes and created a great empire, had been born on the night of 16 September 1186.

# The Learned Astrologers

Most of the learned men in Europe during the Renaissance dabbled in astrology, and some delved deeply into the craft. Marsilio Ficino, the fifteenth-century philosopher who became head of the Platonic Academy in Florence in 1462 and who was noted for his translations of the works of Plato from their original Greek into Latin, was also astrologer to Lorenzo de' Medici, known as Lorenzo the Magnificent. Ficino predicted that Lorenzo's second son, Giovanni, would someday be made a pope. In 1513, Giovanni de' Medici was elected Pope Leo X.

Astrologers were often conflated with alchemists and magicians, and a study of the stars and the occult was considered part of the background of anyone who wished to be considered a philosopher. Noted alchemists such as Agrippa, Paracelsus, and Dr. John Dee were also known as astrologers. Indeed, Dr. Dee was Queen Elizabeth I's court astrologer. As Christopher Marlowe put it in his play *Doctor Faustus* (1589):

> He that is grounded in Astrology
> Enriched with tongues, well seen in minerals,
> Hath all the principles Magic doth require.

Many of the early astronomers were also astrologers, some because a king who would not support them to merely gaze at the stars would reward them handsomely if they also cast horoscopes. Others apparently believed in the predictive power of astrology and had no problem combining the two disciplines.

## Tycho Brahe

Tycho Brahe (1546–1601), the Danish astronomer who wore a shiny silver nose after his own was cut off in a duel, prepared the first accurate star maps and performed the

**163**

earliest intensive study of a supernova. He also taught mathematics as applied to astrology at the University of Copenhagen and cast horoscopes for King Frederik II.

### Mysterious Comments

In Tycho Brahe's book on the supernova, *De nova stella* ("On the new star"), he recorded the supernova's astrological portent: "The star was at first like Venus and Jupiter and its immediate effect will therefore be pleasant, but since it became like Mars, there will next come a period of wars, seditions, captivity, death of princes, and destruction of cities, together with dryness and fiery meteors in the air, pestilence and venomous snakes."

## Johannes Kepler

Johannes Kepler (1571–1630) devised the basic laws of planetary motion, which prepared the way for Isaac Newton's formulation of the law of gravity. He was also a noted astrologer; his predictions for the year 1619 included what became known as the prophecy of the six M's: "Magnus Monarcha Mathias Mense Martis Morietur" ("The great monarch Matthias will die in the month of March"). On 20 March 1619, Emperor Matthias of the Holy Roman Empire did decidedly and definitely die.

## William Lilly

The Englishman William Lilly (1602–1681) was one of the first to publish an astrological almanac. The first, issued in 1641, was called *Merlinus Anglicanus Junior,* in which he prophesied the important events of the coming year. After assuring Oliver Cromwell that the art of astrology did not go against Biblical scripture, and after predicting that Cromwell would win his war against the Cavaliers, Lilly became a favorite of Cromwell and his army.

When Cromwell did win and several of Lilly's other predictions had come true (or at least Lilly claimed they had), he made a good living issuing predictive pamphlets and almanacs.

In Lilly's *Astrological Predictions* for 1648, he wrote the following:

> In the year 1656 the Aphelium of Mars, who is the general signification of England, will be in Virgo, which is assuredly the ascendant of the English monarchy, but Aries of the Kingdom. When this absis therefore, of mars, shall appear in Virgo, who shall expect less than a strange catastrophe of human affairs in the commonwealth, monarchy, and Kingdom of England? There will

then, either in or about these times, or near that year, or within ten years more or less of that time, appear in this kingdom so strange a revolution of fate, so grand a catastrophe and great mutation unto this monarchy and government, as never yet appeared; of which as the times now stand, I have no liberty or encouragement to deliver my opinion, only, it will be ominous to London, unto her merchants at sea, to her traffique on land, to her poor, to all sorts of people inhabiting in her or her liberties, by reason of sundry fires and a consuming plague.

Having predicted this fire, Lilly, in a pamphlet entitled "Monarchy or no Monarchy," published in 1651, provided an illustration of a great field of corpses being buried, backed by an illustration of Gemini suspended above a great fire. (Gemini is the sign for the city of London.)

When the great fire of London burned down most of the city in 1666, someone in the House of Commons remembered the predictions, and Lilly was called before a committee of parliament in October 1666, a month after the embers had died down, to explain himself. Was his foreknowledge based on astrological calculations? Or did he have some guilty knowledge of a plot to burn down the city?

*William Lilly.*

### Mysterious Comments

"Mr. Lillie in all these dreadful Eclipses and malignant Aspects, finds much matter of bad, dismal and disastrous concernement, to Princes, Lawyers, Husbandmen, Graziers, etc. but none at all ever to Wizards, Witches, Conjurers, Fortune-tellers, Sorcerers, Stargazers, Astrologers, etc. No malignity of any Aspect belike is able to reach them."

—Thomas Gataker, *Against the Scurrilous Aspersions of that grand Imposter, Mr. William Lillie* (1653)

When Charles I had been executed, or so Lilly explained, Lilly drew up astrological charts to find out what was going to happen thenceforth to the parliament and to the nation. "Having found, Sir, that the City of London should be sadly afflicted with a great plague, and not long after with an exorbitant fire, I framed these two hieroglyphics ...." He had, he explained, put his findings in the form of pictures accompanied by mystical hieroglyphic symbols so that the true meaning might be concealed from "the vulgar" but might be understood by the wise.

One of the members asked him, "Did you foresee the year of the fire?"

"Of that I made no scrutiny," Lilly replied.

That evidently satisfied the committee, and Lilly was sent away without further comment. Lilly and his contemporary astrologers had quite a following among the nobility and, with the publication of the cheap astrological almanacs, among the common people. Astrology gradually fell out of favor, however, being classed with witchcraft and fortunetelling. Astrologers began treating astrology as a branch of occult science, coequal with numerology and palmistry.

As a result of the conflating of astrology with fortunetelling and the occult, the Vagrancy Act of 1824 added astrologers to fortunetellers and various other "rogues and vagabonds" who were forbidden to practice their knavish skills in Britain.

It was still legal to sell astrological almanacs, however, and Richard James Morrison, under the pen-name Zadkiel, began publishing his annual astrological almanac in the year 1830. It sold about 60,000 copies a year for many years. It was known for its positive, precise, and confident tone. Zadkiel didn't hedge. Of a certain Sunday, he wrote: "This day is evil till after one o'clock, when you may write letters, commence short journeys, and ask favours." When Morrison quit the business, other Zadkiels took over, and the almanac continued to do very well for many years.

# The New Astrology

From the discovery of the planet Uranus by William Herschel in 1781, astrology has been busy adding to and revising the traditional influences, confluences, and conflicts to adapt to the changing view of the solar system. When Neptune was added to the list of known planets in 1846 and when Pluto raised the total of known planets to nine in 1930, astrology was further expanded and inflated to give the new planets a place in the affairs of humans.

Uranus became the planet of revolution, violence, magic, alchemy, and other occult things. To Neptune was ascribed the traits of mysticism, fantasy, and imagination; it was the planet of untrustworthy people and confidence tricksters. Pluto oversaw invisible forces and was the planet influencing the masses and those who would themselves influence the masses: actors and politicians as well as advertisers and propagandists. Could the negative aspects attributed to these planets at least partly reflect the astrologers' resentment at having three new planets thrust upon them?

# Hitler's Astrologers

There is a persistent myth that Adolf Hitler made strategy decisions during World War II with the aid of his private astrologers and that British intelligence had a team of astrologers working to find out what Hitler's astrologers were going to tell him.

In his book *Urania's Children: The Strange World of the Astrologers*, Ellic Howe investigated this myth and determined that there is little if any foundation for the story. He quotes Fräulein Schröder, who was Hitler's private secretary before and during the war years (1933–1945): "I must confess that I never noticed anything of the kind and the subject was never mentioned in conversation. On the contrary, Hitler refuted this by his firmly held conviction that people born on the same day, at the same place and at the same hour, in no way had the same fate."

The Nazis did create horoscopes foretelling victory for distribution in Germany. Since astrology had been very popular in Germany before the war, they found it a useful propaganda tool. By the same token, the British created their own horoscopes foretelling Hitler's defeat and clandestinely distributed those.

**No Mystery Here**

A noted French occultist named Eliphas Levi wrote *Histoire de la Magie (A History of Magic)* in 1860, in which he includes astrology along with the Kabbalah, necromancy, charms and philtres, the philosophers' stone, and other wonders as coequal branches of what he called the "Astral Light." He quotes someone called Ballanche as saying, "Astrology is a synthesis because the Tree of Life is a single tree and because its branches spread through heaven and bearing flowers of stars are in correspondence with its roots, which are hidden in earth."

Although there is no scientific basis for astrology, and no logical reason to assume that the position in the night sky of great balls of mud or gas millions of miles away from us has any effect on human affairs, the enthusiasm for astrology continues unabated around the world. What's your sign?

## The Least You Need to Know

➤ Newspaper horoscope columns are worthless and are based on "cold readings," which can be very convincing.

➤ Astrology was practiced 4,500 years ago by the Chaldeans, who named many of the constellations.

➤ Many medieval and renaissance astronomers practiced astrology. Kings and popes consulted astrologers, and some popes were astrologers themselves       .

➤ In 1648, astrologer William Lilly, one of the first astrologers to write and publish an astrological almanac that did very well, predicted the Great Fire of London, which took place in 1666.

➤ Contrary to persistent myth, Hitler probably didn't believe in astrology or consult astrologers.

# Chapter 14

# An Astrology Primer

## In This Chapter

➤ Dixon's predictions

➤ The "Jeane Dixon effect"

➤ Same birthday—same life?

➤ The character traits attributed to the sun signs

➤ How a horoscope works

Astrology is alive and well today and has more adherents than ever, if the polls and surveys are to be trusted. It is estimated that there are more than 10,000 professional astrologers in the United States and probably 10 times that number throughout the world.

Many movie stars are known to consult astrologers regularly for career advice. Industrialists have consulted astrologers to determine what corporations to buy next. There are columns of astrological advice in every major newspaper. Former president Ronald Reagan consulted Jeane Dixon (or at least his wife Nancy did for him), a noted astrologer, to help with the weighty decision-making necessary for the chief executive.

In this chapter, you'll get an overview of how astrology works (or at least, how it professes to work) and what astrologers are looking at when they produce those complicated charts with the mysterious signs and squiggles all over them.

# Jeane Dixon

Jeane Dixon (1918–1997) was one of the leading American astrologers of the twentieth century. She sprang onto the national scene when, in 1956, she predicted that a tall young man with blue eyes and brown hair would win the next presidential election and would die in office. When John Kennedy in 1961 became the youngest man ever to become president (he was 43) and then was assassinated in 1963, her prediction was remembered. In 1965, Ruth Montgomery wrote a book about Dixon called *A Gift of Prophecy: The Phenomenal Jeane Dixon.* The book sold more than 3 million copies and created a demand for Dixon's services as an astrological columnist and as a speaker.

Dixon made many bold and outrageous predictions over the years, most of which failed to come true. She predicted, for example, that the Soviets would land a man on the moon ahead of the United States and that World War III would start in 1958.

## The Jeane Dixon Effect

Dixon realized that people remembered predictions that came true and tended to forget or discount predictions that did not. Among those who study such things, this has become known as the "Jeane Dixon effect." Many seers of all stripes have taken advantage of this human foible to enhance their careers; they know that one outrageous prediction coming true (and the more outrageous the better) more than makes up for a dozen that fall flat. This is why as every New Year approaches you see predictions in the tabloids like "Flying Saucer Will Land On White House Lawn" or "Lost Continent to Rise In Pacific While California Sinks!" If it doesn't come true, all will be forgotten; if by some chance it should happen, however, some mystic's fortune is made.

## An Astrologer for the FBI

It is now known, courtesy of papers released by the FBI in a Freedom of Information Act request, that in the 1960s Jeane Dixon was a secret spokesperson for the FBI, using her reputation as a seer to discredit left-wing groups and the antiwar movement. Using information supplied by the FBI to enhance her predictions, she declared in her speeches that the Soviet Union was masterminding the peace movement and the civil rights movement.

Sometimes she added extra spice to her predictions on her own. In a 1969 article in the *National Enquirer,* she stated that Soviet leaders were instigating, financing, and controlling student uprisings and race riots in the United States. An internal FBI memo noted that there was no proof of any such thing, but on the bottom of the file copy of the memo, FBI Director J. Edgar Hoover hand-wrote a defense of Dixon's conclusions as basically true, even if not accurate in detail.

### The Mystery Deepens

In May 1999, 45-year-old money manager Martin Frankel disappeared from his million-dollar Connecticut home, taking with him somewhere between $218 million and $3 billion of other people's money. In his home, along with close to 100 computers and wide-screen televisions tuned to the financial news channels, searchers found numerous personalized horoscopes cast to answer such questions as "Should I leave?" "Will I be safe?" and "Will I go to prison?" As of this writing, Frankel is in Germany awaiting extradition to the United States to face charges of fraud and embezzlement. It would be interesting to see what advice his horoscopes gave.

# An Amazing Parallel

If astrology has any predictive value, it would follow that people born at the same time in the same place would pretty much have the same fates. There has been some fascinating research that shows that some identical twins, even when raised apart, lead parallel lives. Tim and Tom, for example (not their real names), were separated at birth. One was raised in Indiana and the other in Ohio, and they did not meet until they were 36 years old. Yet both had become firemen. Both had married dark-haired women three years their junior—one named Joan and the other named Joanne. And both had dogs named Sparky.

Spooky? I'll say. Was it their time of birth, genetics (identical twins have identical DNA), or pure chance? In his book *Astrology: The Space Age Science*, Joseph Goodavage relates several cases of what he calls "parallelism." Let's look at two of them.

The housekeeper of a Tucson, Arizona, doctor and his wife found the couple's five-year-old adopted daughter Tina tied up, beaten, and half-starved, cowering in a basement room behind the furnace where the couple kept her. The housekeeper notified the police, and the couple was arrested. On 30 March 1964, they were sentenced to two years in prison.

### No Mystery Here

Joseph Goodavage began studying astrology in the 1960s so that he could debunk it, but he soon found himself fascinated by the coincidences, parallels, and correlations he found. Soon he was writing books and articles and lecturing on astrology, particularly on its possible use in forecasting the weather.

In another state at about the same time, a dentist and his wife were arrested and sentenced for beating and starving their five-year-old adopted daughter, whom they kept tied up in the basement.

Tina and the other five-year-old were twin sisters who had been separated in infancy. "Was this coincidence or Law?" Goodavage asks. "And if it is the result of a Law, what kind of Law?"

For our second example, let's go further back in history. King George III and a commoner named Samuel Hemmings were born within a minute of each other on 4 June 1738 in the English parish of St. Martin's-in-the-field.

In October 1760, King George III was coronated, and Sam Hemmings opened his ironmongery business. On 8 September 1761, both King George III and Sam Hemmings got married. Their lives' successes and failures, illnesses and accidents, all mirrored each other (allowing for the difference in their rank) until King George died on 29 January 1820. Samuel Hemmings, ironmonger, also died on 29 January 1820.

### Mysterious Comments

"Ignoring, for the moment, astrology's mantic side, I am willing to admit that its symbolism, considered as a whole, represents a marvelously constructed collection of analogies representing a wealth of ideas relating to the cyclical nature of human life (birth, growth and death), human typology, psychology and so on."

—Ellic Howe, *Urania's Children*

# The Basic Rules

All the basic rules, customs, and procedures of casting a horoscope are empirically derived; that is, they're based on the observations and experiences of astrologers who have come before. The process is divided into two separate parts: casting (creating) the horoscope chart and interpreting what it means.

To cast a horoscope, it's necessary to know the time and location of the subject's birth (if it is a natal [birth] horoscope), the more precisely the better. Horoscopes can be cast for people; for countries; for businesses; for any sort of launching, creation, or happening; or for a tragedy such as an assassination, an earthquake, or a serious accident of some sort.

Astrologers have divided the heavens into 12 arbitrary sections, each representing a 30-degree swath of sky ($12 \times 30 = 360$ degrees, a full circle). Each of these 30-degree sections is represented by a constellation that at one time was found within that section. These are known as the signs of the Zodiac. As we saw in the preceding chapter, many of these constellations are of ancient origin, some of them more than 4,000 years old. As the earth has slowly shifted its location in relation to the background stars over the centuries, the sky of today is not the sky of 4,000 years ago, and the constellations have shifted their apparent seasonal locations. Astrologers, however, still treat the sky as it appeared thousands of years ago.

Knowing the time and location of the subject's birth, the astrologer can determine exactly what point in the Zodiac was overhead at the time, and exactly where the planets were in relation to the signs of the Zodiac. This is the information needed to create the subject's horoscope.

## The Signs of the Zodiac

The astrological year begins on March 21 and ends on the following March 20. The following table shows the signs of the Zodiac and their associated dates. The signs represent the area of the sky that the sun enters on these dates.

**What Does This Mean?**

If you draw an imaginary line from the center of the sun to the center of the earth and then keep the line tight as the earth circles the sun, you will have created a flat surface in space called the plain of the ecliptic. The orbits of all the planets except Pluto lie on or fairly close to this plane (if you extend it far enough). The Zodiac is the imaginary belt in the heavens that contains the plain of the ecliptic; along it lie the 12 signs of the Zodiac.

## The Signs of the Zodiac

| Sign | Associated Dates |
| --- | --- |
| Aries (the Ram) | March 21 through April 19 |
| Taurus (the Bull) | April 20 through May 19 |
| Gemini (the Twins) | May 20 through June 20 |
| Cancer (the Crab) | June 21 through July 22 |
| Leo (the Lion) | July 23 through August 21 |
| Virgo (the Virgin) | August 22 through September 22 |
| Libra (the Scales) | September 23 through October 22 |
| Scorpio (the Scorpion) | October 23 through November 21 |
| Sagittarius (the Archer) | November 22 through December 21 |
| Capricorn (the Goat) | December 22 through January 20 |
| Aquarius (the Water Carrier) | January 21 through February 19 |
| Pisces (the Fish) | February 20 through March 20 |

I doubt there are many people, regardless of whether they believe in astrology, who don't know what their Zodiac sign is. Students of astrology believe that each sign influences the personality of the people born under it. The basic character traits of each sign are fairly well agreed upon, but of course they may be modified by other factors such as planetary positions at birth or childhood experiences.

## Character Traits

Here is a brief guide to the generally agreed-upon attributes of each astrological sign. We have compiled it from several references, listing those qualities on which there was agreement. Notice that the bad or undesirable qualities of a sign generally are the sign's good qualities exaggerated. Someone who is a Taurus, for example, is steadfast—a good quality. But when steadfastness is exaggerated, it becomes stubbornness, which is not always so good.

➤ **Aries (the Ram).** People who are Aries are impetuous, quick-witted, and energetic as well as creative and quick to adapt to new situations. They anger easily but don't stay angry. They must fight a tendency to egoism and narcissism. They do better when self-employed but will work well with a Taurus partner. For romance, they should seek a Gemini, Libra, Leo, Sagittarius, or another Aries. Marlon Brando and Louis Armstrong are both Aries, as was Thomas Jefferson.

➤ **Taurus (the Bull).** Like the sign, Taurines are strong and steadfast. Their emotions often are in control; reason takes a back seat. They have an unfortunate tendency to be stubborn—one might say "bull-headed." Taurines are good engineers and builders. Their best romantic partners are Scorpios, Capricorns, and Virgos, and they may do well with Libras but that's riskier. Both President Harry Truman and Karl Marx were Taurines, as was Adolf Hitler.

➤ **Gemini (the Twins).** Geminis are quick and adaptable and are able to grasp new situations quickly. The flip side of this is that they may neglect what's available in going after what's new or different. They may have dual natures, although actual split personalities are rare. Geminis partner well with Aquarians and Libras as well as Aries, and they should do very well with Leos or Sagittarians. Richard Wagner and Arthur Conan Doyle were both Gemini, as was President John F. Kennedy.

➤ **Cancer (the Crab).** Cancers are traditionalists by nature and are noted for their tenacity. They are affectionate and sensitive and are easily hurt by adverse criticism. They are good scientists and teachers and make good actors if they can take the constant rejection that is the actor's bane. Cancers are good business partners for Aquarians and Capricorns. Romantically, they go well with Capricorns, Pisceans, Scorpios, and Libras. Rembrandt was a Cancer, as was Salvador Dali (and yet none of my reference books list "artist" as a very high possibility for Cancers).

➤ **Leo (the Lion).** Leos have the exuberance, the idealism, and the strength of character that make them born leaders. They have a tendency to believe they are right, no matter the number of critics or the strength of the evidence against them. They are easily flattered and must beware of false friends. They team up well with all other signs in business and are romantically best fit with other Leos, as well as people born under Aries, Sagittarius, Cancer, and Virgo. Napoleon and Mussolini were both born under Leo.

### Mysterious Comments

"Many valid criticisms of astrology can be formulated in a few sentences: for example, its acceptance of precession of the equinoxes in announcing an 'Age of Aquarius' and its rejection of precession of the equinoxes in casting horoscopes; its neglect of atmospheric refraction; its list of supposedly significant celestial objects that is mainly limited to naked eye objects known to Ptolemy in the second century, and that ignores an enormous variety of new astronomical objects discovered since (where is the astrology of near-Earth asteroids?); ... the failure of astrology to pass the identical-twin test; the major differences in horoscopes cast from the same birth information by different astrologers; and the absence of demonstrated correlation between horoscopes and such psychological tests as the Minnesota Multiphasic Personality Inventory."

—Carl Sagan, *The Demon-Haunted World*, 1996

➤ **Virgo (the Virgin).** Virgos are equipped with keen intelligence and common sense, although they are worriers. They are good at gathering and arranging information (or flowers for that matter). Virgo is the patron sign of Paris and of cats. Virgos tend to be what psychologists call "anal compulsive," which makes them hoard things and causes them to be good with small details. Virgos get along well with any of the other signs in business but must be careful lest they find that they are giving more than they get. Romantically, Virgos go best with other Virgos, but Pisces will do fine, and Aries and Taurus are not wholly incompatible. Virgos and Libras should be cautious about coming together; it might work well if they can get over trying to dominate each other. The authors Tolstoy and Goethe were both Virgos.

➤ **Libra (the Scales).** Libras are very intuitive and have an innate love of balance and harmony. They are sympathetic and understanding and are quick to support a worthwhile charity or a worthy cause. Libras move well in society and are excellent mediators, perhaps because they can see both sides of a question. Libras can succeed in many of the arts and tend to excel in either acting or singing (or both). Libras do well in business with Gemini, Virgo, or Scorpio, provided they are *primus inter pares*—the first among equals. In love matters, Libra and Sagittarius are natural partners, Libra and Aries are a fine combination, and Libra and Leo could do well together. Aquarius, Gemini, and Scorpio can also produce suitable mates for a Libra. Eleanor Roosevelt was a Libra, as was Gandhi.

➤ **Scorpio (the Scorpion).** Bold and fearless, Scorpios have an innate sense of precision that makes them skillful at whatever they attempt. They are usually quiet observers of life until they are impelled to action. They are known for quick tempers and aggressive behavior when provoked and for their erotic tendencies when aroused or sufficiently interested. Scorpios make good partners for Libras in business; the boldness of the former is balanced by the careful judgment of the latter. Cancer, Pisces, and Taurus are Scorpios' best choices for romance. President Theodore Roosevelt was a Scorpio, as was French (actually Dutch) exotic dancer Mata Hari, who was executed as a spy during World War I although she was probably innocent.

➤ **Sagittarius (the Archer).** Sagittarians are energetic and happy. Sagittarius is usually represented by a centaur (half horse, half man) with a bow and arrow. As such, the Sagittarian is a combination of the steadiness of the horse—all four feet on the ground—and the high aim of the archer. Sagittarians accomplish a lot while others are still wondering what to do. What a Sagittarius has to watch out for is aiming too low. Sagittarians love to travel and make good ships' captains, commercial pilots, and prospectors. A Sagittarius in partnership with a Capricorn is a good combination. Sagittarians love best with others of their own sign or Geminis, Aries, or Leos. Libra is also a good potential mate for Sagittarius. Winston Churchill and James Thurber were both Sagittarians, as was John F. Kennedy Jr.

**No Mystery Here**

When John F. Kennedy Jr. died in a plane crash in July 1999, the tabloid weekly the *Globe* wrote that he could have "averted tragedy" if he had read and followed his horoscope for July 16, which warned Sagittarians to "remain close to home." Lynne Palmer, the *Globe's* astrologer, reported that "His headstrong Sagittarian nature refused to bow to the laws of the universe."

➤ **Capricorn (the Goat).** Capricorns are calm, deliberate, and intellectual. Although they can be quite witty, they tend toward melancholy. They are good at reasoning and at organizing. Capricorns have a tendency to love solitude, but this must be tempered because, combined with their tendency toward melancholy, it can be unhealthy. They make good diplomats and philosophers. In business, they do well as accountants or lawyers, and they are natural teachers. Capricorns do well in business with Taurines or Virgos. When in business with Aquarians, the Capricorn must lead. Romantically, Capricorns team up well with Virgos, Taurines, and Aries. Louis Pasteur, Woodrow Wilson, and Joseph Stalin were all Capricorns.

➤ **Aquarius (the Water Carrier).** Aquarians have an unassuming disposition and make friends easily. They seek out knowledge and spend much of their time in study. They are helpful when necessary but can be tactless. Aquarians may rebel against convention more easily than other signs, but they are interested in humanity and the common good. They make good scientists, musicians, and explorers. As business people, they are good buyers and dealmakers. Aquarians work well with just about any other sign. Romantically also, they are adaptable and understanding and do well with any other sign, but they might do just a bit better with a Gemini, Leo, or Libra. Franklin Roosevelt and Abraham Lincoln were Aquarians, as were actor James Dean and scientists Darwin, Francis Bacon, and Galileo.

➤ **Pisces (the Fish).** Pisceans are very knowledgeable but rarely show it off; it doesn't occur to them that others don't know as much as they do. They are modest and not very aggressive and have to be careful that others do not take advantage of their unselfishness. Pisceans are good friends to have, being both loveable and loving, and will stick with you when others have run away. They succeed in science and engineering and fit nicely into bureaucracies. Pisces works well with Aries and does well in business with Taurus, Virgo, or Capricorn. Pisceans will enjoy romance with Cancers, Virgos, and Scorpios. George Washington was a Pisces, as were pianist and composer Frederic Chopin and dancer Nijinsky.

## Cusps

People born on a "cusp"—that is, within a few days on either side of the intersection of two signs—are said to partake of influences from both signs, and these modifications of their characters make them different from either. The Libra-Scorpio cusp, roughly from October 21 to 29, for example, produces a person who combines the intuitiveness of a Libra with the skillfulness of a Scorpio, making the person quick to assess a situation and handle it appropriately.

**The Mystery Deepens**

Each period of time represented by a sign of the Zodiac can be subdivided into three "decans" that further define the character of the person born therein. A first decan Libra (September 23–October 2), for example, is overly sensitive and has a strong sense of justice. A second decan Libra (October 3–12) is fair minded and a natural leader. A third decan Libra (October 13–22) is fonder of luxury and is more generous.

# Casting a Horoscope

The sort of horoscope we're talking about here, also known as a natal (birth) chart, is a chart of the location of the planets in the Zodiac at a given moment—usually the moment of birth of the subject. For these purposes, the astrologers class the sun and the moon as planets. The constellations are regarded as the "fixed stars" among which the planets move.

An in-depth discussion of the technique of putting together natal charts is beyond the scope of this book, so you should consider this more of a general outline of how the system works. For a deeper discussion, we recommend *The Complete Idiot's Guide to Astrology*.

Creating a horoscope is a purely arithmetical task, and any two people drawing up horoscopes based on the same data should arrive at identical charts. The interpretations of the pattern revealed by the horoscope, however, vary according to the training and the life-experience of the astrologer.

To cast the horoscope, you need an *ephemeris* for the year in question, which will enable you to figure out the exact location of the planets across the Zodiac at the moment of birth (or at whatever moment for which you are casting the horoscope). You will also have to correct for the actual birth time down to the nearest minute, if you have that information exactly.

**What Does This Mean?**

An **ephemeris** (plural ephemerides; it's Greek) is a yearly table of the location of the different planets in the heavens. To compile a horoscope, it is necessary to have an ephemeris of the birth year of the subject. There are now computer programs that do this automatically.

### The Mystery Deepens

Unfortunately, there isn't enough room in this book to reproduce the tables of houses or the ephemeris necessary for the calculations to make your own horoscopes. There are, however, several excellent programs you can buy for your PC (or Mac) to do the horoscopical calculations for you. There are even several that you can download free from the Internet, although they are usually simplified versions of more complex programs that their creators would like to entice you to buy. We don't want to name any specific one because their price and quality change with each revision, but they are easily found.

SIMPLIFIED SCIENTIFIC
EPHEMERIS OF THE PLANETS' PLACES
Calculated for Mean Noon at Greenwich
August, 1909
New Moon August 15th in ♌ 21° 59′
Longitude of the Planets

| D | ☉ ° ♌ ′ | ♀ ° ♍ ′ | ☿ ° ♌ ′ | ☽ ° ≈ ′ | ♄ ° ♈ ′ | ♃ ° ♍ ′ | ♂ ° ♈ ′ | ♅ ° ♑ ′ | ♆ ° ♋ ′ | ☊ ° ♊ ′ |
|---|---|---|---|---|---|---|---|---|---|---|
| 1 | 8 33 | 3 56 | 5 12 | 3 22 | 23 13 | 14 58 | 3 40 | 18ʀ18 | 17 40 | 13 50 |
| 2 | 9 31 | 5 9 | 7 17 | 17 55 | 13 | 15 10 | 57 | 15 | 42 | 47 |
| 3 | 10 28 | 6 21 | 9 22 | 2 ✕39 | 14 | 21 | 4 12 | 13 | 44 | 44 |
| 4 | 11 25 | 7 34 | 11 27 | 17 28 | 14 | 33 | 27 | 11 | 46 | 41 |
| 5 | 12 23 | 8 47 | 13 30 | 2 ♈14 | 14 | 45 | 41 | 9 | 48 | 38 |
| 6 | 13 20 | 10 0 | 15 33 | 16 48 | ʀ14 | 56 | 55 | 7 | 50 | 34 |
| 7 | 14 18 | 11 13 | 17 35 | 1 ♉ 8 | 23 14 | 16 8 | 5 8 | 18 5 | 17 52 | 13 31 |
| 8 | 15 15 | 12 26 | 19 35 | 15 11 | 13 | 20 | 20 | 3 | 54 | 28 |
| 9 | 16 13 | 13 38 | 21 34 | 28 55 | 13 | 32 | 31 | 1 | 56 | 25 |
| 10 | 17 10 | 14 51 | 23 32 | 12♊22 | 13 | 44 | 42 | 17 59 | 58 | 22 |
| 11 | 18 8 | 16 4 | 25 28 | 25 35 | 12 | 56 | 52 | 57 | 18 0 | 19 |
| 12 | 19 6 | 17 17 | 27 23 | 8 ♋33 | 11 | 17 8 | 6 1 | 55 | 2 | 15 |
| 13 | 20 3 | 18 29 | 29 16 | 21 20 | 10 | 20 | 9 | 53 | 4 | 12 |
| 14 | 21 1 | 19 42 | 1 ♍ 8 | 3 ♌56 | 23 10 | 17 33 | 6 17 | 17 51 | 18 6 | 13 9 |
| 15 | 21 59 | 20 55 | 2 59 | 16 21 | 9 | 45 | 24 | 49 | 8 | 6 |
| 16 | 22 56 | 22 7 | 4 48 | 28 35 | 7 | 57 | 30 | 47 | 10 | 3 |
| 17 | 23 54 | 23 20 | 6 35 | 1♍45 | 6 | 18 10 | 35 | 45 | 12 | 0 |
| 18 | 24 52 | 24 33 | 8 22 | 22 45 | 5 | 22 | 39 | 44 | 14 | 12 56 |
| 19 | 25 50 | 25 45 | 10 6 | 4 ♎39 | 4 | 34 | 42 | 42 | 16 | 53 |
| 20 | 26 47 | 26 58 | 11 50 | 16 29 | 2 | 47 | 45 | 40 | 18 | 50 |
| 21 | 27 45 | 28 10 | 13 32 | 28 19 | 23 0 | 18 59 | 6 47 | 17 39 | 18 19 | 12 47 |
| 22 | 28 43 | 29 23 | 15 12 | 10♏12 | 22 59 | 19 12 | 48 | 37 | 21 | 44 |
| 23 | 29 41 | 0♎35 | 16 51 | 22 14 | 57 | 24 | 48 | 35 | 23 | 41 |
| 24 | 0♍39 | 1 47 | 18 29 | 4 ♐29 | 55 | 37 | ʀ47 | 34 | 25 | 37 |
| 25 | 1 37 | 3 0 | 20 6 | 17 2 | 53 | 49 | 45 | 32 | 26 | 34 |
| 26 | 2 35 | 4 12 | 21 41 | 29 59 | 51 | 20 2 | 43 | 31 | 28 | 31 |
| 27 | 3 32 | 5 25 | 23 15 | 13♑23 | 49 | 15 | 40 | 29 | 30 | 28 |
| 28 | 4 30 | 6 37 | 24 47 | 27 17 | 22 47 | 20 27 | 6 36 | 17 28 | 18 32 | 12 25 |
| 29 | 5 28 | 7 49 | 26 18 | 11≈38 | 44 | 40 | 31 | 27 | 33 | 22 |
| 30 | 6 26 | 9 1 | 27 48 | 26 25 | 42 | 53 | 25 | 25 | 35 | 18 |
| 31 | 7 24 | 10 13 | 29 17 | 11✕28 | 22 39 | 21 6 | 6 19 | 17 24 | 18 36 | 12 15 |

*A page from an old ephemeris.*

# The 12 Houses

It's also necessary to know the position of the planets relative to the *houses*, of which there are 12. These are related not to the Zodiac but to the Midheaven, which is the point above the birth place at noon on the birth day. Figuring the location and boundaries of the houses is complex and varies according to the system used. The easy way to handle this is to use a table of houses; the Placidus tables are probably the most widely used. Tables of houses can be bought wherever astrological books and supplies are sold.

The houses are said to control various aspects of life and the human condition. (As astrologer Steven Forrest puts it, "We *are* our signs, and we *do* our houses.") Although there are some differences among astrologers about just what the different houses represent, here are some common themes:

➤ First house: Childhood, personality, physical condition.

➤ Second house: Money and things material, gain or loss.

➤ Third house: Family, communications, writing and documents.

➤ Fourth house: The home, birthplace, mines and underground places. In a man's chart, his mother; in a woman's, her father.

➤ Fifth house: Sex, especially nonmarital; pleasure, education, gambling.

➤ Sixth house: Health, servants, food, clothing, small animals.

➤ Seventh house: Partnership, marriage, agreements, open enemies. In a woman's chart, the husband; in a man's chart, the wife.

➤ Eighth house: Death, inheritances, wills, loss, accidents; a partner's wealth.

➤ Ninth house: Spirituality and philosophy, sea voyages and other travel, foreign countries, religion.

➤ Tenth house: Vocation or job, profession, employer, superior, business, government.

➤ Eleventh house: Wishes or hopes, society, friends, companions, counselors, the wealth of employers.

➤ Twelfth house: Secret enemies, prisons, hospitals, plots, unseen difficulties, large animals.

## *Drawing the Lines*

Once the planets are placed on the horoscope chart, lines may be drawn (or imagined) between them to demonstrate their *aspects*. An aspect means that two planets are related to each other by one of a set of geometric angles. Some of the angles are beneficial; some indicate challenges.

There are five major aspects: Conjunctions, Squares, Oppositions, Trines, and Sextiles. Additionally, two planets with the same degree of inclination are Parallel.

The Opposition and the Square are believed to indicate evil influences or at least bad luck, while the Sextile and the Trine are both favorable. The Conjunction and the Parallel are indeterminate, their value being decided by which planets are involved and how those planets "get along."

It is in the interpretation of the horoscope or natal chart (based on the birthday of the subject) that the true skill of the astrologer comes into play. A good astrologer combines knowledge of the subject with knowledge of the patterns created by the planets to come up with a possibly meaningful analysis of the subject's needs, desires, and possibilities.

# Digging Deeper into Astrology

Many other factors can be involved in creating and interpreting the horoscope; this has barely scratched the surface. It might be a good idea to consult someone knowledgeable on the subject before digging deeper because many of the so-called astrology texts are more deeply into numerology and other occult aspects that classical astrologers decry. *The Complete Idiot's Guide to Astrology* is, as you might expect, a dependable and useful primer on the subject.

**No Mystery Here**

The work of the astrologer, and the interested amateur, has been made easier by the number of computer programs and online services available for casting a horoscope. No longer is it necessary to spend hours of drudgery poring over ephemerides and doing the complex math, but it is still a good idea to understand what is happening and how it works.

**What Does This Mean?**

The **aspects** of the planets on a horoscope chart are their distance apart and the angles formed by connecting them. An aspect means that two planets are related to each other by one of a set of geometric angles. Some of the angles are beneficial; some indicate challenges.

### Mysterious Comments

"It is the stars, the stars above us govern our condition."

—Shakespeare, *King Lear*

I am, I admit, somewhat skeptical about the relationship of the planets' positions to the lives of people. I don't think we're important enough in the great scheme of things to rate such personal attention from the cosmos.

But I have a good friend who is a professional astrologer, and I have seen her cast and interpret horoscopes for people I know whom she had never met before. They have been eerily on the money. I prefer to think of her as an astute natural psychologist who is able to read small body language signs and, perhaps unconsciously, meld them into her interpretations. But she thinks it's the planets. Who knows? Perhaps she's right.

### The Least You Need to Know

➤ Jeane Dixon gained notoriety for predicting that the next president would die in office, and John Kennedy fulfilled her prediction.

➤ The "Jeane Dixon effect" is another way of saying that people forget bad predictions and remember good ones.

➤ There have been many documented cases of people born at approximately the same time and place, including identical twins raised separately, who lead parallel lives.

➤ There are 12 astrological signs under which it is possible to be born, and each is associated with certain psychological characteristics.

➤ Casting a horoscope is done by following precise and complex rules and consulting ephemerides and other charts.

➤ The interpretation of the chart requires the most talent and knowledge on the part of the astrologer.

# Part 4

# Human Events

*We'll start this section by giving you a history of spiritualism, its precursors, where it came from, who practiced it, and what they did or claimed to do. Then we'll take a little diversion into crime. We'll look at the kidnapping of the Lindbergh baby and its aftermath. Was Bruno Richard Hauptmann really the killer? Lizzie Borden is in this section too. You know the rhyme, how she took an axe and gave her mother forty whacks. Did you know that she was found innocent? Who was the real killer? And we've got the case of Mata Hari, the exotic dancer who was executed as a German spy during World War I. But who was the real Mata Hari?*

# Chapter 15

# Well Done, Rare Old Medium

**In This Chapter**

➤ The Fox sisters' rap

➤ The first seances

➤ Emanuel Swedenborg

➤ Friedrich Anton Mesmer

➤ Andrew Jackson Davis, "The Poughkeepsie Seer"

➤ Daniel Dunglas Home

Death is one of the eternal mysteries and is of consummate interest to all of us who walk this planet and who have been granted the mixed blessing of the ability to reason. Who wouldn't like to know what happens when we die?

Can we communicate with the dead? Would they have anything interesting to say? Would they be interested in anything we have to say? Or have they left this life entirely behind in going on to whatever it is they go on to?

A variety of beliefs are offered by the various religions or philosophies of humankind. Some people believe that one life is all we get. Some believe in reincarnation. Some believe in a heaven and a hell and perhaps a purgatory or a limbo where we can work out problems or work off sins. Some believe in a sort of eternal universal mind that we are all part of and that, in death, we rejoin.

### Mysterious Comments

"FAUST: Then where is hell, and how came you out of it?

MEPHISTOPHELES: Why this is hell, nor am I out of it.
Thinkst thou that I who saw the face of God,
And tasted the eternal joys of heaven,
Am not tormented with ten thousand hells
In being deprived of everlasting bliss!"

—Christopher Marlowe, *The Tragical History of Doctor Faustus*

Few people would disagree that it would be nice to know something about the after-life for certain. No matter how strong our faith is in a particular religion, there are times when we would like concrete assurances—perhaps from someone who's been there and can advise us on what preparations to make. Some people have claimed to be able to converse with the other side. In this chapter, we'll examine a few of these individuals.

## The Hydesville Sisters

The set of beliefs and practices we know as *spiritualism* sprouted from a seed planted by two young sisters in Hydesville, New York, in 1848.

### What Does This Mean?

**Spiritualism** is the belief in the ability to communicate with the spirits of the dead. The religion founded on that belief is also known as spiritualism.

Ever since 15-year-old Maggie Fox, her 12-year-old sister Katie, and their parents, John and Margaret, had moved into their Hydesville house in December 1847, they had been plagued by strange rapping sounds that came in the night and kept the family awake. After investigating the more rational possibilities, such as loose shutters and a neighboring shoemaker who assured them he didn't do any hammering after ten at night, Margaret, a devout churchgoer, was just about convinced that the strange raps were the work of the devil.

On the night of Friday, 31 March 1848, Maggie attempted to communicate with whatever was making the rapping sounds. "Count to four," she suggested. "Rap, rap, rap, rap."

Margaret Fox, frightened but game, asked the rapper to count to 10. It obliged. She then asked the ages of her children. The rapper rapped them out correctly.

"Is it a human being making the noise?" she asked. No rap.

"Is it a spirit? If it is, make two raps." Two raps.

"Is it an injured spirit?" Two raps.

"Were you injured in this house?" Two raps.

After a laborious couple hours of yes-or-no questioning, Mrs. Fox was able to evolve the story. The rapper was the spirit of a man who had been murdered in the house and buried in the cellar. Margaret called the neighbors in as witnesses to what was happening. In their presence, the spirit continued his story. He had been murdered by one John Bell, a tenant of the house from five years before. Bell had slit the rapper's throat while he slept to rob him of $500.

The rapper communicated more details—his background and that of his family as well as the location of his body. The victim was a peddler named Charles Rosna who had living relatives in Orleans County. He said that the murder had taken place on a Thursday night, and that his body was buried in the center of the cellar.

At this point, the questioning was halted for the night, and the group of questioners split up. The Foxes spent the night with neighbors. Who can blame them?

## Dig We Must

Word of the extraordinary happenings at the Foxes' house spread rapidly, and the next evening, curious neighbors filled the house and yard. The rapping commenced at dusk to the awe and delight of those in the house. Those consigned to the yard strained to hear. After a while, John Fox cleared the house except for a few stalwart friends, and they commenced digging in the center of the cellar where the rapping spirit directed. They got about two feet down when the hole started filling with water faster than they could bail, and they called a halt.

A couple days later, the Foxes' son David supplied a pump to try to drain the hole, but the water outpaced the pump, and they got no further with the digging. They never got much deeper, and never found a body. Although some reports have them discovering bits of burned bones, those reports are at best third hand and are certainly attempts to enhance an already provocative narrative.

The fame of the "Ghost of Hydesville" spread, and the curiosity-seekers kept coming. It was soon noticed that the ghost did not confine itself to the house but seemed to follow the two sisters about. Margaret Fox sent her daughters to stay in Rochester with their older sister, Leah, in hopes that the ghost would remain closer to home.

### The Mystery Deepens

On 24 November 1904, 56 years after the rapping commenced, some children playing in the cellar of the Hydesville house were startled to find a human skeleton protruding from a crumbling cellar wall. It was that of a middle-aged man, and it had evidently been in its hiding place for at least 50 years. It's doubtful that it was the peddler Charles Rosna since his corporal existence was never established, but just whose it was and how it came to be closed up in the wall rather than buried has never been established.

## Leah Holds a Lecture

The rapping spirit followed the two girls. The gawking citizens of Rochester who gathered below Leah's window frightened away her pupils (she was a piano teacher), so to make a little money, Leah arranged for some meetings—they were not called *seances* yet—in private homes. The private meetings, needless to say, were a success. In addition to the rapping, some of the guests reported feeling a ghostly presence, and several reported the physical sensation of being touched when there was nobody who could have been touching them.

### What Does This Mean?

A **seance** is an attempt to contact the spirits of the dead. The word comes from the French for a "sitting," since the participants sit around a table, usually holding hands, while the event proceeds.

The next step was a public lecture in Corinthian Hall, Rochester's largest auditorium. Admission was 25 cents, 50 cents for a gentleman accompanied by two ladies—either way a lot of money in those days. At the end of the lecture, during which some raps were heard and some possible explanations ruled out (although no explanations as to just what it could be were offered), the audience appointed a committee to investigate the phenomenon more closely and to report back at the next lecture.

The report was favorable. Within a couple of months, the Fox sisters were giving seances, and their (or the spirit's) ability to contact the "dear departed" relatives of their guests was well established.

**The Mystery Deepens**

On 21 October 1888, 40 years after the rapping began, Maggie Fox gave a public lecture and demonstration at the Academy of Music in New York City. She insisted that the whole thing had been a hoax begun by the sisters as a prank on their mother and that it had gotten out of hand. She stood on a table in her stocking feet and demonstrated how the raps had been made by snapping the joint of her big toe. The rapping was heard clearly all over the hall. "That I have been mainly instrumental in perpetrating the fraud of spiritualism you already know," she told the audience. "It is the greatest sorrow of my life. I began the deception when I was too young to know right from wrong." But those who had embraced spiritualism refused to believe her, choosing instead to believe she had been bribed by the churches or the newspapers into making a false confession.

# An Early Seance

In 1915, Dr. Augustus H. Strong gave a talk before the Rochester Historical Society describing a seance that was held in the house of his father, Deacon Strong, back in 1850 when he was 15 years old (as related in the book *The Spirit Rappers* by Herbert G. Jackson Jr. [Doubleday, 1972]):

> That was a memorable evening for me. It began very solemnly, with the wheeling out of a heavy mahogany center table into the middle of the parlor. Then the company gathered tremblingly around it, and formed a closed circle by clasping hands around its edge. Then we waited in silence. Katy Fox was opposite me. I thought I observed a slight smile upon her face. I was less observant of the proprieties at that time than I have been since, and I ventured, alas, to wink at Katy Fox. And I thought that Katy did something like winking in return. She was a pretty girl, and why shouldn't she? But she soon composed her countenance. The seance proceeded solemnly to the end. But for me there was no more solemnity or mystery. All the rest of the performance seemed a farce.

> There was no manner of doubt about the rappings. These began under the table. Then they seemed to proceed from the floor. At last they came from the doors of the room, and even from the ceiling. Questions were proposed to the so-called spirits, and ambiguous or commonplace answers were spelled out. I do not remember a single communication that gave knowledge of any value, or beyond what the questioners already possessed. But the effect upon our two guests

was great. That courtly gentleman got down on his knees and peered under the table, to discover the source of the sounds. It was all in vain. He was deeply impressed, concluded that these rappings were veritable messages from beyond the grave, went away a believer. Some weeks after, my father learned that his guests left the Presbyterian Church, and had joined the Spiritualists. He never forgave himself for leading those two innocents into temptation.

**Mysterious Comments**

"In eternal twilight I move, but I know that in the world there is day and night, seedtime and harvest, and red sunset must follow apple-green dawn. Every year spring throws her green veil over the world and anon the red autumn glory comes to mock the yellow moon."

—the shade of Oscar Wilde, as taken by automatic writing by Werner Laurie

# Swedenborg, Mesmer, and Davis

The seed of spiritualism, to reuse our earlier metaphor, fell upon fertile ground. Sometimes a movement or idea seems to come from nowhere and sweep the country, such as the Atkins diet, pyramid power, crystals, or Est therapy. Spiritualism was like that; in no time at all seances were being held in all sorts of homes, by all sorts of people, and the dead were becoming much more communicative than they ever had been before.

## Conversing with the Dead

But movements that seem to spring from nowhere usually have precursors that prepare people's minds to accept these wonderful new ideas. One of these antecedents, coming about a century before the Fox sisters began rapping, was Emanuel Swedenborg. Born in 1688 in Sweden, he traveled widely about Europe before settling down at the University of Upsala to write highly regarded books about astronomy, algebra, navigation, and chemistry. In 1714, Swedenborg resigned from the university to devote himself to religious and philosophical studies. He began to converse with the dead and they with him. "I was speaking only the other day with the Apostle Paul about this ... " he would say to make a point in a discussion. We would assume he made his point; it is hard to argue convincingly with a man who can ask and get the advice of the apostles.

Swedenborg also spoke with visitors from the moon and most of the planets. He had a reputation as what we would now call a psychic, once bringing the Queen of Sweden a message from her dead brother—a message that, it was said, made her faint. He also knew of a great fire that was burning in Stockholm in July 1759, even though he was in Gothenburg about 300 miles away and there was no means of communication at the time that could have transmitted the information. When the widow of the Dutch ambassador needed to locate a missing document, Swedenborg told her it was in a secret drawer in the ambassador's desk—which is where it proved to be.

When John Wesley, the founder of Methodism, wrote to Swedenborg proposing that the two of them meet, Swedenborg replied that he could not take engagements that far in advance as he was scheduled to die on 29 March 1772. Which he did—it was a natural death as far as we know.

Swedenborg was an amazing melange—part scientist, part occultist, part seer. If intelligent beings ever lived on the moon or Mars or Saturn, they have long since moved on. But how do we explain others of his messages and predictions? His followers, called Swedenborgians, are still around today. They publish books and tracts about their guru's life. A church based on his principles, called the Church of the New Jerusalem, is still active.

## Animal Magnetism

Dr. Friedrich Anton Mesmer arrived in Paris in 1778 and quickly became a great success with demonstrations of his new system of healing, which he called *animal magnetism* (but which became popularly known as *mesmerism*). The technique could reportedly relieve pain, cure illnesses, and serve as an anaesthetic to allow for painless operations.

Mesmer's salon was crowded with all sorts of patients who were eager to be cured of their diseases by the great Dr. Mesmer. Many of them apparently were cured, at least for the moment. Yet there were also those who doubted him, who called him a quack and a fool. One prelate, the Abbe Fiard, was convinced that Mesmer had sold his soul to the devil.

**What Does This Mean?**

**Animal magnetism** is the name originated by Franz Mesmer for the invisible "force" he used to cure his patients. It became popularly known as **mesmerism.** We now call it hypnotism.

People following in the path of Mesmer quickly claimed that mesmerized subjects showed strong evidence of *clairvoyance* and that some were able to converse with the dead. Soon hundreds of stage performers were touring Europe and the Americas giving demonstrations of mesmerism's amazing powers.

### No Mystery Here

Mesmer began by using magnets fastened to various parts of the body to cure diseases, a technique that was in vogue at the time and that is coming back into fashion today. He quickly noted that it was the relationship of the doctor, not of the magnets, to the patient that seemed to do the healing. Thus, his theory of "animal magnetism."

### What Does This Mean?

**Clairvoyance** is the ability to see something separated by time or space from the observer.

The mesmerism craze not only primed people to accept the possibility of direct conversations with the dead, it also trained a group of performers in the basic skills they would need to give demonstrations of spiritualism when that persuasion caught the public eye.

## The Poughkeepsie Seer

In 1843, young Andrew Jackson Davis of Poughkeepsie, New York, went to a lecture on mesmerism and discovered that he was a good subject. He had been hearing voices since he was a child, and he could hear them much better when he was in a trance. While entranced, he wandered off into the mountains and was visited by the spirits of Swedenborg and Galen, an early Greek physician.

With the aid of his spirit friends, Davis began teaching various spiritual subjects, often while in a trance. It was while in a trance that he dictated a book to his amanuenses, Reverend William Fishbough and Dr. Lyon. It was called *The Principles of Nature, Her Divine Revelations, and a Voice to Mankind.* Published in 1847, a year before the Fox sisters heard the rapping of the peddler, it was an immediate success. You can easily see why from the opening paragraph of a chapter in which Davis describes how the universe began:

> In the beginning the Univercoelumm was one boundless, indefinable, and unimaginable ocean of Liquid Fire. The most vigorous and ambitious imagination is not capable of forming an adequate conception of the height and depth and length and breadth thereof. There was one vast expanse of liquid substance. It was without bounds— inconceivable—and with qualities and essences incomprehensible. This was the original condition of Matter. It was without forms, for it was but one Form. It had no motions, but it was an eternity of Motion. It was without parts, for it was a Whole. Particles did not exist, but the Whole was as one Particle. There were not suns, but it was one eternal Sun. It had no beginning and it was without end. It had not length, for it was a Vortex of one Eternity. It had not circles, for it was one infinite Circle. It had not disconnected power, but it was the very essence of all Power. Its inconceivable magnitude and constitution were such as not to develop forces, but Omnipotent Power.

It could be said that he predicted the imminent birth of the Spiritualist movement with the following paragraph:

> It is a truth that spirits commune with one another while one is in the body and the other in the higher spheres—and this, too, when the person in the body is unconscious of the influx, and hence cannot be convinced of the fact; and this truth will ere long present itself in the form of a living demonstration. And the world will hail with delight the ushering in of that era when the interiors of men will be opened, and the spiritual communion will be established.

Davis is considered by Spiritualists to be the "John the Baptist" of the movement, coming before and preparing the way.

## The Physical Medium

The half-century after the birth of spiritualism saw the rise of *mediums* of all types and spirit phenomena of all descriptions. The spirits wrote on slates, appeared in ghostly photographs, left their handprints in wax, and levitated thousands of tables.

The royalty among mediums during this period were the so-called physical mediums—people who produced phenomena that could be seen, heard, and sometimes even smelled. The prince of physical mediumship was Daniel Dunglas Home.

### Daniel Dunglas Home

Home (pronounced "Hume") was born in 1833 in Scotland. When he was nine, he moved to the United States with his aunt, who had adopted him as a baby from her sister for reasons that are unclear. Home had his first psychic experience at the age of 13 when he saw a friend who had died three days before in a town 300 miles away. When he was 17, mysterious raps began occurring in his presence, much like the raps the Fox sisters had been experiencing for the past two years. His aunt called ministers in to

**Here There Be Dragons**

Seeing ghosts can be a sign of impending doom. James IV of Scotland was warned by a ghost not to take his army into England. He did so anyway and was killed at Flodden Field. Queen Elizabeth I of England was warned of her death by her own ghostly double. Mozart was ordered to compose a Requiem by a mysterious stranger who visited several times to make sure Mozart was doing so. The Requiem was done just in time to be played at Mozart's own funeral.

**What Does This Mean?**

A **medium** is a person who claims the ability to communicate with the spirits of the dead or to act as a channel for the spirits to communicate directly with the rest of us.

pray over him, but the rapping increased. This seems to have convinced the aunt that Home was possessed by the devil, and she kicked him out of her house.

*D.D. Home levitating for some of his friends, a contemporary print.*

What Home seems to have learned during these early years on his own was how to entertain friends and acquaintances well enough to be invited to stay with them for extended periods of time. As he developed his ability to amuse and mystify audiences, he never ran out of friends. As time went on, his friends became wealthier and hailed from more exalted social circles.

## The Levitating Man

Home gave demonstrations of psychic ability that went way beyond the attempts of ordinary mediums. He was renowned for his ability to levitate, for example. Usually Home himself levitated, but occasionally he would levitate one of the guests at the seance. Since seances are conducted in darkness, it isn't clear what his audience saw or thought they saw, but they were always suitably impressed. In Home's presence, musical instruments played by themselves. On one occasion, as recorded by Sir William Crookes, who was investigating Home in England at the time, Home was holding an accordion that was seemingly playing itself. It continued to play as he passed the instrument to the person sitting next to him and then placed it on the table.

Why levitation became one of the accepted manifestations of spiritualism we don't know. Perhaps the spirits were thought to be uplifting.

Crookes then produced a cage in which to put the accordion. Homes placed the accordion in the cage and closed the door—and the instrument kept playing. Crookes subjected Homes to a series of laboratory tests, with Homes' permission and cooperation, and was unable to detect any sort of fraud. However it should be pointed out that scientists are notoriously unable to detect fraudulent mediums, mystics and psychics. The physical universe, which they are used to asking questions of to get their results, may be obscure but it does not deliberately lie to them. Professional magicians are much better at catching frauds than the untrained observer, and even they can be fooled. The other possibility, of course, is that Home could levitate.

One of Home's better effects was plucking large, red-hot coals from a fire and cupping them in his hands for extended periods without getting burned. His most famous single feat of physical mediumship was indeed astounding. Whether he did it as described in the following or merely made his audience think that's what happened hasn't been established. At any rate, it hasn't been repeated or even attempted by any medium or magician since.

**No Mystery Here**

Sir William Crookes (1832–1919) was a noted chemist and physicist. He discovered the metallic element thallium, improved vacuum tubes, and founded the technical journal *Chemical News*.

It was in London on 16 December 1868 that the event, which came to be known as the Ashley Place Levitation, occurred. In a pair of adjoining small rooms, in the presence of three young men—Viscount Adare, Lord Lindsay, and Adare's cousin, Captain Charles Wynne—Home levitated himself out one window and in through another. Here is how Lord Lindsay described it in a letter written two years later:

> I was sitting [conducting a séance] with Mr. Home and Lord Adare and a cousin of his. During the sitting Mr. Home went into a trance, and in that state was carried out of the window in the room next to where we were, and was brought in at our window. The distance between the windows was about seven feet six inches, and there was not the slightest foothold between them, nor was there more than a twelve-inch projection to each window, which served as a ledge to put flowers on. We heard the window in the next room lifted up, and almost immediately after we saw Home floating in the air outside our window. The moon was shining full into the room; my back was to the light, and I saw the shadow on the wall of the windowsill, and Home's feet about six inches above it. He remained in this position for a few seconds, then raised the window and glided into the room feet foremost and sat down.

# To Cheat or Not to Cheat

Many mediums, including some of the most famous, have been caught cheating. Perhaps their ectoplasm turned out to be sheets of gauze, their manifestations nothing but stage magicians' tricks, or their voices from beyond merely the voice of an assistant hidden in the cabinet. Most defenders of spiritualism admit such tricks, but they say that just because *some* are tricksters doesn't mean *all* are tricksters. And because a noted medium resorted to tricks once doesn't mean that all her effects are fraudulent. Mediums are under heavy pressure to perform, they explain, and if the spirits don't perform on a certain night, well, the mediums don't want to disappoint their audiences.

Maybe so, but my doubts center on what the spirits do when they return from the great beyond. Except for an occasional poor soul who needs to avenge his murder and subsequent burial in the basement, most people probably would have better things to do in the beyond than come back to rap on tables, rattle tambourines, blow horns, and tap out childish messages on a ouija board. Unless, of course, there is a purgatory, and this is it.

---

### The Least You Need to Know

➤ Maggie and Katie Fox started the Spiritualist movement as teenage girls when mysterious rapping sounds began following them around.

➤ Emanuel Swedenborg was speaking with the dead early in the eighteenth century.

➤ Dr. Friedrich Anton Mesmer developed animal magnetism, which evolved into hypnotism.

➤ Andrew Jackson Davis, "The Poughkeepsie Seer," is regarded by spiritualists as the "John the Baptist" of the spiritualism movement.

➤ Daniel Dunglas Home was the prince of physical apparition-producing mediums.

➤ Many mediums have been caught cheating. This doesn't prove that all mediums cheat, but it does raise questions.

---

# Chapter 16

# Gurus or Charlatans?

---

**In This Chapter**

➤ The Count de Saint-Germain

➤ Count Cagliostro

➤ Rasputin

---

One person's guru is another's charlatan, and often no amount of debate or analysis can persuade either side that they're mistaken. There are people who, by their very presence, inspire us to climb higher, and there are people who shout, "Onward!" and urge us higher up the hill of fallacy toward the peaks of error and folly.

Sorry, we couldn't resist that little excursion into the land of metaphor. When the train of irony pulls out—Oops! Almost did it again. What we're trying to say about idols is simply that, at the time, the false look so much like the real that it's hard to tell them apart. In this chapter, we'll take a look at a few of the more interesting examples.

## The Count de Saint-Germain

Everything about the life of the Count de Saint-Germain is a mystery except for the part that is merely an enigma. Apparently from Germany, he first appeared in France in the 1760s when he was apparently in his 40s. He had a habit of casually speaking about things that had happened in the distant past as though he had actually seen them happen.

For example, he described long conversations he had had with Francis I of France (1494–1547), Henry VIII (1491–1547), and Richard I of England (1157–1199) as well as the Queen of Sheba (10th century B.C.). Saint-Germain was an immediate hit at the court of Louis XV, and soon he was associating with the royalty and nobility of the court.

When he first arrived in Paris, he was introduced to the Countess de Gergy, who asked him if, perhaps, his father had been in Vienna in 1710 because she remembered talking to him when she was ambassadress to Austria. Saint-Germain told her that his father had died long before that but that he himself *had* lived there at that time. He reminded her of a few things they had done together.

"Impossible," she said. "The Count de Saint-Germain that I knew at that time was at least 45 years old, and you are barely that age now." Saint-Germain shook his head. "I am very old," he told her.

**Here There Be Dragons**

A skeptic tried to get some hint of Saint-Germain's real age by interviewing his butler, Roger. "I can't help you," Roger told the man, "I've only been with the Count for the past hundred years."

## The Mystery Grows

His real name, where he came from, and how old he was remain mysteries 200 years after his (we assume) death. The facts that are known make him a truly remarkable man, and the legends surrounding him raise him to the level of a superman, a master of the occult, and a repository of ancient wisdom.

Saint-Germain appeared to be in his early 40s during the entire 25 or so years that he was among the French. He was of middle height, which for that time would have been around 5'4", and was not particularly handsome. He seemed to be extremely rich, and his clothing was expensive but tasteful. It is said that his clothes were covered with precious gems, but rich men of the time dressed that way; it was the sort of excess that led to the French Revolution.

Saint-Germain spoke and wrote French, English, German, Spanish, and Portuguese as well as Greek, Latin, Sanskrit, Arabic, and Chinese. He was an accomplished painter in oils, achieving colors of a brilliance that impressed professional artists who begged to know the secret. He played both the harpsichord and the violin with virtuoso proficiency, impressing musicians with his ability to improvise. He composed operas. He was a master chemist and mechanic, claiming invention of the steamboat.

But wait, there's more. He was already a master hypnotist when Mesmer (see Chapter 15, "Well Done, Rare Old Medium") was just developing his theories. He claimed to possess the ability to make himself invisible whenever he chose. He could make diamonds or, according to one report, remove the flaws from existing diamonds; perhaps he could do both. There is some dispute as to whether he could transmute base metals into gold.

Saint-Germain was believed to be a member of the Freemasons, the Rosicrucians, or both. At the time, both were mystical secret organizations deeply involved in politics. He may have been involved in secret plots, but against whom or to what end is not known.

He gave, or possibly sold, an elixir of youth to women of nobility, but he couldn't have made much money at it: He told anyone who would listen that the true secret of long life was to eat sparingly and abstain from liquor. One time, when he was in Holland, he was invited to dine with Casanova. He refused, commenting that he never ate with people he didn't know and that, at any rate, he only ate pills, bread, and cereal.

**No Mystery Here**

In 1743, composer Jean Philippe Rameau said he remembered having seen Saint-Germain back in 1701, when he looked to be about 50. He seemed, Rameau remarked, to have somehow become about 10 years younger than he had been 40 years before.

**Mysterious Comments**

"Sometimes [Saint-Germain] fell into a trance, and when he again recovered, he said he had passed the time while he lay unconscious in far-off lands; sometimes he disappeared for a considerable time, then suddenly reappeared, and let it be understood that he had been in another world in communication with the dead. Moreover, he prided himself on being able to tame bees, and to make snakes listen to music."

—J. van Sypesteyn, *Historische Herinneringen* (quoted in Isabel Cooper-Oakley's *The Count of Saint-Germain*)

## Life After Death

When he had been in Paris for many years, after Louis XVI had ascended the throne, Saint-Germain fell out of favor at the court. One story is that he tried to warn Louis and his Queen, Marie Antoinette, that if they didn't reform their policies there would be a revolution. He accepted the offer of the Landgrave (prince) of Hesse Cassel, whom he had apparently known previously, to come live with him. He died peacefully at Sleswig in 1784. Or did he?

In 1789, Madame d'Adhemar, a confidant of Marie Antoinette, went to a chapel to meet with a stranger who had sent letters of advice to the queen. The stranger turned out to be Saint-Germain. He is said to have appeared in Paris many times during the Terror, as the period immediately after the revolution is called, and he was seen amidst the crowd that filled the Place de la Grève, watching the aristocrats being guillotined. He has been reported in various places since then. If you turn to the bibliography at the back of this book, you will find the following entry:

Saint-Germain, Comte C. de. *Practical Astrology*. Chicago: Laird & Lee, 1901.

# Alessandro, Conte di Cagliostro

Giuseppe Balsamo was born in 1743 in Palermo, Sicily, the son of a shopkeeper. His early life showed no signs of latent greatness or even competence. He became a novice in the monastery of the Benfratelli when he was 13, and he was assigned to work with the monk who made up and dispensed salves, potions, and herb remedies. He learned his herbs, but he found the life of a monk too confining; the brothers found him intractable and unteachable. He soon left the monastery.

For the next few years, "he abandoned himself to a life of riot and debauchery," as Charles Mackay put it in *Extraordinary Popular Delusions* (London: Harrap, 1852). Mackay continues, "The first way in which he distinguished himself was by forging orders of admission to the theatres. He afterward robbed his uncle, and counterfeited a will. For acts like these, he paid frequent compulsory visits to the prisons of Palermo."

Somewhere along the way, Balsamo acquired the trappings of a sorcerer and alchemist, and the story spread that he had sold his soul to the devil in return for the secret of making gold. A silversmith named Marano offered him 60 ounces of gold to show him the secret. Balsamo took the silversmith to an out-of-the-way spot one midnight, drew a magic circle on the ground, and proceeded to call up the devil. Suddenly, several imps with pitchforks (or several friends of Balsamo in devil costumes with pitchforks) appeared and beat the poor silversmith until he fell unconscious. When he awoke, his 60 ounces of gold were gone.

Marano returned to town, too embarrassed by his own cupidity and gullibility to tell the authorities what had happened. He vowed to take true Sicilian revenge and murder Balsamo the first chance he got.

## Balsamo Becomes Cagliostro

When Balsamo heard about this, he left Sicily in haste. A short while later, he showed up in Medina, Arabia, as Count Cagliostro. There, the new count hooked up with a Greek alchemist named Altotas; Altotas hadn't discovered the *philosopher's stone* yet, but he had developed a method of softening and conditioning flax fiber into a superior linen cloth. Cagliostro convinced Altotas that the flax process could be more lucrative than transmuting lead to gold, and the two of them went around the Near East processing flax and making money.

The two ended up in Malta as guests of the Knights of Malta. Altotas and Pinto, the Grand Master of the Knights, were soon ensconced in their alchemical laboratory trying to change a pewter platter into a silver one.

Cagliostro wished Altotas luck and went on to Rome. It was in Rome that Cagliostro declared himself a secret master of the ancient order of Rosicrucians, claiming the ability to transmute base metals into gold. He began selling patent medicine nostrums to cure all diseases and to restore youth and vitality.

It was in Rome that Cagliostro met Lorenza Feliciani, a beautiful young lady whose social status was much higher than his own but whose purse was much lighter. In addition to her beauty, she had a quick intelligence, a ready wit, an engaging manner, and a moral sense on a par with Cagliostro's own. It was, as you might guess, a match made in .... Well, at any rate, they soon fell in love and were married.

Cagliostro taught his new bride everything he knew about alchemy, wizardry, and fleecing the unwary, and she proved to be an apt pupil. Cagliostro grew whiskers, put on the uniform of a colonel in the Prussian Guard, and changed his wife's name to the Countess Seraphina Cagliostro; they set off on their travels to perfect their skills and to build their reputation.

**What Does This Mean?**

The **philosopher's stone** was a substance that was believed to have the power of transmuting base metal into gold.

**No Mystery Here**

Balsamo tested a series of names before settling on Count Cagliostro. He was, variously, the Marquis de Melissa, the Baron de Belmonte, the Baron de Pelligrini, the Baron d'Anna, the Baron de Fenix, the Baron de Harat, and my personal favorite, the Chevalier de Fischio.

They traveled through Poland, Germany, and Russia, selling miraculous potions, telling fortunes, and transmuting metals. While they were in Russia, Catherine the Great's doctor had some of the potions they were peddling analyzed and decided they were useless. The two were expelled from the country.

## The Fleecer Fleeced

In 1776, they arrived in London and set up shop. They rented an apartment on Whitcombe Street and worked hard at appearing so ordinary that everyone would be convinced they were hiding some great secret. Unfortunately, the first people

**201**

to become convinced that he had supernatural powers were a gang of swindlers named Vitellini and "Lord" Scot and a Miss Fry who was posing as Lady Scot. They demanded Cagliostro's help in picking numbers for the lottery. Cagliostro gave them a couple of numbers, and the numbers won.

### The Mystery Deepens

The first place Count and Countess Cagliostro went was to Sleswig to introduce themselves to the aging (or possibly the eternally young) Count de Saint-Germain. He took them in, and they spent some time with him. Presumably, Saint-Germain recognized in the young couple kindred spirits. It would be interesting to know in just what way he found them kindred.

### No Mystery Here

Pastor Johann Kaspar Lavater of Zurich, a highly regarded and learned man, requested an audience with Cagliostro while he was in Strasbourg in 1780, but Cagliostro refused to see him. The pastor sent Cagliostro a letter asking, "In what precisely does your knowledge reside?" Cagliostro replied, "*In verbis, herbis et lapidibus*" (Latin for, "In words, herbs and stones"). This shows he was well aware of the part that the power of suggestion played in his miracle cures.

When he refused to give them any more numbers, the trio had him arrested on trumped-up charges; it was weeks before Cagliostro could arrange bail. He might understand the enigmas of the universe, but the mysteries of the British legal system baffled him. Vitellini and Scot managed to get a judgment against him for 200 pounds. Disgusted, the Cagliostros left England, traveled the continent practicing their various crafts, and ended up in Strasbourg in 1780.

Cagliostro and Madame Cagliostro practiced healing the diseased in Strasbourg, and soon they had lines of people waiting to see them. They gave alms to the poor and solace to the sick, and they became known for their philanthropy as well as for their healing powers. Madame Cagliostro, who was about 25 and a striking beauty, made casual references to her "eldest son, now 28 years old, who is serving as an officer in the Dutch navy." This soon had rich and foolish elderly men and women purchasing Cagliostro's elixir of youth.

It was in Strasbourg that Cagliostro made friends with Cardinal Prince Louis René Edouard de Rohan. He impressed the cardinal by apparently manufacturing a diamond while the cardinal watched and then handing it to him as a gift. The cardinal took it to his jeweler, who pronounced it real and quite valuable. After that, Cardinal de Rohan regarded Cagliostro as a fellow philosopher and introduced him to important people in Paris when they traveled there together.

*Cagliostro.*

Cagliostro at first had no interest in moving to Paris, but bad luck seemed to be plaguing him. The Strasbourgers—both the rich to whom he had been selling eternal life and the poor to whom he had been liberally giving away money—turned against him and for all the wrong reasons. The poor accused him of being the Antichrist, of being in league with the devil, of being a demon in human shape, of being the wandering Jew. The wealthy decided he was the agent of a foreign government, a police spy, a degenerate. Soon the Cagliostros felt it would be a good idea to leave Strasbourg and try their luck in a more cosmopolitan center. For a while they settled in Bordeaux, but it proved to be another Strasbourg with people welcoming them at first and then turning against them (although wherever he went, there were as many who remained faithful to him as turned against him). So they moved on to Paris.

## Paris

In Paris, he took out all the stops. The peasants had accused him of being a magician? Very well, he would be a magician. The influential Parisians he had met through Cardinal de Rohan were astounded; they had never seen the like of Count and Countess di Cagliostro. He called up the spirits of the dead from the netherworld and conversed with them. He transmuted metals.

He spoke to angels. His occult powers enabled him to foretell the future. He had the power to extend the span of a human life to 5,557 years. In Paris, Cagliostro founded the "Egyptian Lodge" of the Freemasons, attracting members from other lodges as well as new members. He called himself the Grand Kophta and created a whole new set of initiation rites for his Egyptian Lodge. He accepted anyone as a member; the only condition was that members must believe in the immortality of the soul.

Lorenza headed a women's branch of the Egyptian Lodge as Grand Master with the title of the Queen of Sheba. The lodges did very well and had hundreds of members.

Cagliostro was regarded as a superior being and was held in awe by many people who knew him. Although he did soak the rich to get most of his wealth, he gave it away readily enough to the poor and those in need.

### The Mystery Deepens

In *The Mirror of Magic,* Kurt Seligmann describes an evening at the Egyptian Lodge: "During the séances, magical ceremonies were performed with the intention of communicating with the seven 'pure spirits.' An innocent girl, the 'Dove,' was led to a table where a glass bottle was flanked by two torches. The girl had to stare into the bottle, in which absent persons, future happenings, or angels would appear; or she was led behind a screen where she would experience a mystical union with an angel."

After being framed by the Countess de La Motte in an improbable scheme to charge an expensive necklace to Marie Antoinette, Cagliostro and his wife were arrested by the Paris police and thrown into the Bastille, where they languished for six months until the trial began.

When Cagliostro was finally allowed to speak in open court, he absolutely denied having anything to do with stealing the necklace, and called de La Motte names in Latin, asking her lawyer to translate for him as it would be impolite to call her these things in French. Cagliostro was found innocent and released.

Despite having been found innocent, Cagliostro was urged to leave Paris. He and his wife spent the next four years traveling around Europe. In 1789, they were arrested by the Papal government in Rome. The charges were that he was a freemason, a heretic, and a sorcerer. For this he was condemned to death, although his wife was allowed to join a nunnery rather than stand trial. His death sentence was commuted to life imprisonment, and he died a year later in the Castle of St. Angelo.

The mystery in Cagliostro's case is not whether he was a true sorcerer—he probably was not. The mystery is what sort of personal chemistry did he possess that enabled him to convince so many people for so long that he could do the things he claimed he could do?

# Rasputin

Grigory Yefimovich Novykh was born somewhere between 1865 and 1872 in the village of Pokrovskoye in Siberia. His father, Efim Novykh, was a drunken peasant, and Gregory showed every sign of following in his father's bootsteps. He was dirty, unkempt, ragged, and into wine and women. His nickname, which stayed with him, was Rasputin—"debaucher."

Then, when he was about 30, he met a holy man and spent the day talking with him. It transformed his life. He put aside his pitchfork and traveled into the world, crossing Siberia to visit the holy places. The next time the people of Pokrovskoye saw him, a couple of years later, he had a holy light in his eyes and he preached. He possessed the ability to heal and to prophesy—or so the people began to say.

It was reported to Tsar Nicholas II that there was a "pious Grigory" in the village of Pokrovskoye who could make it rain or stop raining and who had the power to heal. The Tsar would have given a good chunk of his kingdom right then for someone who truly possessed the power to heal. His only son, the Tsarevich Alexei, had been born a hemophiliac, something he had inherited from his great-grandmother, Queen Victoria.

Alexei's mother, the Tsaritsa Alexandra Feodorovna, granddaughter of Queen Victoria, was in agony every time her son hurt himself. She also was in an agony of suspense in between times, knowing that the next injury, however slight, might be fatal. She prayed constantly for a miracle to help her son.

Rasputin was that miracle. The Tsaritsa, who would have tried anything, introduced Rasputin to the court and to her son. This simple Russian peasant proved able to do with prayer what none of the court physicians, or the priests for that matter, had been able to do: He relieved Alexei of his pain and pulled the boy back, time after time, from the edge of death.

**No Mystery Here**

Hemophilia, a genetic disease in which the blood fails to clot, is carried in the female line, but normally women do not get it, only their male children. If a mother is a carrier, each of her children has a 50 percent chance of inheriting the disease; the girls who inherit the defective gene will be carriers, the boys will have hemophilia. For a hemophiliac the slightest bruise can mean days of agony as the blood collects at the site but fails to clot; the slightest cut causes the danger of bleeding to death.

## The Miracles of Rasputin

The stories of Rasputin's miracles are legion, and they are recorded in the diaries and journals of the time. Alexei was in great pain and could not sleep. Alexandra called for Rasputin. He came and held the child's hand. "Nothing hurts you any more," he told Alexei. "Listen to me! Sleep!" The pain went away, and the lad fell asleep.

While traveling during World War I, Alexei got a cold and blew his nose, but even that was dangerous: The blood vessels in his nostrils burst, and the bleeding could not be stopped. The Tsaritsa sent Rasputin a telegram. The doctors shook their heads; this was it, the boy would die.

Suddenly, after hours of bleeding, the blood stopped flowing just in time to save the boy. The doctors rushed to tell his mother. "I know," she told them calmly. "What time?"

"Six thirty," the doctors replied.

Alexandra showed them Rasputin's reply telegram: "GOD WILL HELP YOU. BE HEALTHY." The time stamp showed that it had been sent at six-thirty that morning.

The Tsaritsa saw Rasputin as a miracle worker, and he proved it time after time. The Tsar saw him as a man of the people, and the royal family had been isolated from the people for too long. Maybe the Tsar had something to learn from the peasant holy man.

Gradually, as his power over the royal family grew, Rasputin reverted into the character of the drunken, lecherous peasant. He took young women of dubious virtue with him to restaurants and cavorted with them in drunken semi-orgies. He told filthy and certainly untrue stories about his relationship with the Tsaritsa and her young nieces, who also lived at the palace. He was said to have a strange and unholy influence over the royal family. His nickname outside the palace had been "the Mad Monk"; now it was "the Holy Devil."

During World War I, when the Tsar went off to the front to lead his troops, the Tsaritsa practically ran the country, and Rasputin practically ran the Tsaritsa. How could she refuse anything to the man who was keeping her son alive? How could such a holy man, who surely had the ear of God, be ignored when he gave advice? Rasputin combined debauchery with mysticism and practiced both on a grand scale. He had taken to issuing prophecies, some on the conduct of the war and some on internal matters. He predicted, for example, that a certain major battle would be lost if the commander were not replaced. The commander was not replaced, and the battle was lost.

With the Tsar away, Rasputin set about replacing the strong, effectual ministers of state he didn't like—the ones who might have tried to get rid of him—with weak, ineffectual ones more to his liking. This was not what the country needed in a time of crisis.

By 1916, the Russian people increasingly hated and feared Rasputin, whom they saw as controlling the Tsar with his mystical powers. In this state, and with the war going badly, the country was ripe for revolution. The conservative members of the government, mostly members of the Tsar's own family and other high nobles, increasingly saw the death of Rasputin as necessary to save the country.

**The Mystery Deepens**

The Tsaritsa was told of Rasputin's escapades, but the people who told such stories soon found that they were no longer welcome at the palace. Besides, Alexandra had been reading about Russian holy men, and the reading showed her that they were all an earthy lot. She rationalized, with the aid of her reading, that there was an obvious reason for his actions: Rasputin was taking the sins of the world on his shoulders by committing them.

## The Final Miracles

Rasputin made a will and gave it to the Tsaritsa. "… know that if your relatives commit murder," the will said, "then not one of your family, your relatives and children, will live more than two years. The Russian people will kill them …. They will kill me. I am no longer among the living. Pray."

On 17 December 1916, Prince Yousoupov, Grand Duke Dmitri Pavlovich, and a right-wing politician named Pourishkevich set out to assassinate Rasputin in the prince's house. First they attempted to poison him with cyanide, but the poison had no effect. Then they shot Rasputin at point-blank range with an army revolver. Rasputin fell but then staggered to his feet again, leapt at his attacker, and tried to strangle him. Then he ran out into the yard where they shot him again. As they were loading his body into the back seat of a car to get rid of it, Rasputin opened his eyes once again and glared at them. Imagine the superstitious horror they must have felt by this time. But finally he died.

On 16 July 1918, seven months after the assassination of Rasputin, the Tsar and his entire family were murdered by the Bolshevik revolutionaries, fulfilling the Mad Monk's final prophesy.

As long as there are impossible dreams that we all dream—of long life, of cures to fatal diseases, of great riches, of being irresistible to the opposite sex—there will be charlatans with convincing stories and overwhelming personalities to take advantage of the rest of us. But of course we are too wise to fall for such foolishness, aren't we?

**The Least You Need to Know**

➤ The Count de Saint-Germain was said to be hundreds of years old, and he never denied it. A hypnotist, artist, musician, alchemist, and linguist, he impressed all he came into contact with.

➤ Cagliostro trod a similar path to Saint-Germain, but unexpected obstacles kept blocking his way. He was imprisoned by the Vatican for being a freemason, a heretic, and a sorcerer, and he died in prison.

➤ Rasputin, the mad monk, had an uncanny ability (probably hypnotic in nature) to alleviate the suffering of Alexei, the hemophiliac son of Tsar Nicholas II.

➤ Rasputin left a will shortly before he was murdered. In it, he predicted that the royal family would not outlive him by more than two years. They were murdered seven months later.

# Chapter 17

# The Lindbergh Baby Kidnapping

---

### In This Chapter

➤ The kidnapping of the "Little Eaglet"

➤ A poorly handled case from the beginning

➤ The "help" of a man named Jafsie

➤ Bruno Richard Hauptmann—guilty or innocent?

➤ Is the Lindbergh baby alive today?

---

Charles "Lucky Lindy" Lindbergh had been a national hero since he became the first person to fly solo across the Atlantic Ocean, taking off from Mineola, New York, in the Spirit of St. Louis on 20 May 1927 and landing in Paris, France, the next day. This earned the "Lone Eagle" a level of public adoration that was not seen again until the Beatles came to New York. His marriage two years later to Anne Spencer Morrow, a poet and the daughter of Dwight W. Morrow, then Ambassador to Mexico and reputed to be one of the richest men in America, was the closest thing to a royal wedding this country had ever seen. When their child was born, common people rejoiced.

On 1 March 1932, Charles Augustus Lindbergh Jr., the 20-month-old son of Charles Lindbergh and his wife Anne Morrow Lindbergh, was kidnapped from his crib in his upstairs bedroom in the Lindbergh home in the Sourland Hills of Hunterdon County, New Jersey, outside of Hopewell and northwest of Princeton.

Although a carpenter named Bruno Richard Hauptmann was convicted and executed for the crime, the trial was conducted in such an atmosphere of hysteria, the prosecution was so determined to get a guilty verdict, the defense was so inept, and the case against Hauptmann was actually so weak, that, on looking back on the events with the detachment of seven decades, it seems doubtful that Hauptmann was the kidnapper.

# The Kidnapping

On the evening of the kidnapping, Charles Jr., called "Little It" by his parents, was put to bed by Anne Lindbergh and the child's nurse, Betty Gow, at about eight o'clock. The nurse stayed with him until he fell asleep. When Anne came to look in on her baby at nine o'clock, he was peacefully sleeping. When Betty Gow checked at ten to ten, the baby was gone.

Lindbergh told the butler to call the police and then grabbed a loaded rifle and searched the grounds. A wooden ladder was lying on the ground outside the nursery window. There was a note in an envelope on the windowsill. Lindbergh wouldn't let anyone open the envelope until the police arrived and it could be dusted for fingerprints.

**Mysterious Comments**

"... bend your glance backward to the opening chapter of the Lindbergh case. Do you remember—could anyone ever forget—the foaming and senseless cataract of gorgeously uniformed state troopers that descended on the Lindbergh home in motorcycles, roared up and down the road trampling every available clue into the March mud, systematically covering with impenetrable layers of stupidity every fingerprint, footprint, dust trace on the estate?"

—Henry Morton Robinson, *Science Versus Crime*, 1935

## *The Ransom Note*

Sometime after midnight, a fingerprint expert arrived and dusted the ransom envelope for prints. Nothing useful was found. He opened the envelope and examined the letter within. It, too, had no prints. It read as follows:

Have fifty thousand dollars ready, 25,000 in twenty-dollar bills 15,000 in ten-dollar bills, and 10,000 in five-dollar bills. In 4-5 days we will inform you where to deliver the money. We warn you for making anyding public or for notify the police. The child is in gute care Indication for all letters are signature and three holes.

Unfortunately, the police were already there, and as for making anything public—well, there hadn't been anything so public since P.T. Barnum added the third ring to the American circus. Newscasters had already spread the word of the kidnapping all over the world.

## The Evidence

The ladder and a chisel found on the ground nearby were examined. It was assumed that the chisel had been used to pry open the nursery window. The ladder was a three-section, noncommercial product that had been made by a not-particularly-skilled carpenter. One of the rungs near the top was broken, presumably having given way during the kidnapping.

Police reported finding two sets of footprints at the base of the ladder, but many people had walked there since the kidnapping was discovered. The nursery was dusted for fingerprints—walls, furniture, crib, windowsill, doors, and doorknobs—and no prints were found, none at all. It was as though someone had wiped the entire room clean. This fact suggested the possibility of an inside job, although it is just as possible that the housekeeping staff was very efficient, and the kidnapper wore gloves.

# The Colonels

There in the night, a quartet of colonels assembled to decide what to do next. Of the four, only one had any police background—Colonel H. Norman Schwarzkopf, a West Point graduate who was now the superintendent of the New Jersey State Police. The other three were Colonel William Joseph "Wild Bill" Donovan, a World War I hero who was preparing to run for governor of New York (he would lose but go on to head the OSS during World War II); Colonel Henry Breckinridge, a very social Wall Street lawyer; and Colonel Lindbergh himself.

### No Mystery Here

From the beginning, the investigation was fragmented, was mishandled, and suffered from the triple liabilities of the Lone Eagle's fame, his ego, and his tendency to manage everything himself. Everyone who dealt with Lindbergh deferred to his opinions, and Lindbergh had a very high opinion of himself. He tended to give orders when it would have been more profitable to listen to advice.

The four colonels decided that the "snatch" was probably a gangland job. They decided to ask the aid of Mickey Rosner, a Broadway character who was believed to have underworld connections. He put them in touch with Salvatore "Salvy" Spitale and Irving Bitz, a pair of New Yorkers who ran speakeasies.

Lindbergh, at Rosner's suggestion, appointed Spitale and Bitz as the official intermediaries in dealing with the kidnappers. Spitale's contribution was to call a press conference in his New York apartment and announce to the assembled reporters, "I been in touch all around, and I come to the conclusion that this one was pulled by an independent."

### The Mystery Deepens

Legally, the government could take no action in the case because there was no federal antikidnapping law, but where Lindbergh was concerned exceptions would be made. Attorney General James Mitchell announced that, "Although there is no development to suggest that the case is one within Federal jurisdiction," the full law-enforcement machinery of the government was being mobilized. This would include the cooperation of the Justice Department's Bureau of Investigation (not yet called the FBI), headed by a young J. Edgar Hoover; the services of the U.S. Post Office Department's investigators; and the assistance of the Coast Guard, the Customs and Immigration Services, and as many of the 563 Prohibition Bureau agents as required.

## More Notes

The first of a series of follow-up ransom letters arrived for Lindbergh, identified as genuine by a pair of red and blue circles punctuated by three holes. The police wanted to examine it, but Lindbergh gave it to Rosner, who rushed it to New York to show it to his gangster connections. Somebody took a photograph and peddled copies of it all over town at five bucks each.

When the second note arrived, the police observed that it had been mailed from the same area of Brooklyn as the first note. New York City Police Commissioner Ed Mulrooney came up with the idea of staking out the mailboxes in that area. A special device would be installed in each box to isolate the letters as they were put in, and the mailer of any letter to Lindbergh or anyone connected to him would be tailed.

Lindbergh forbade the scheme, feeling that any such attempt might endanger the life of his son. Mulrooney argued for his idea, assuring Lindbergh that his men were professional, that the subject would never know he was being tailed, and that they would drop the tail rather than risk being found out. He also pointed out that, if they knew where the boy was being held, they could attempt to rescue him.

Lindbergh put his foot down. He assured Mulrooney that, if the chief went ahead with the scheme, he would use all his influence to see that Mulrooney was broken. Mulrooney had no choice but to acquiesce. The next day, a third ransom note was dropped into one of the boxes that would have been being watched.

# Jafsie to the Rescue

At this time, a strange character came into the scene—Dr. John F. Condon, a 72-year-old schoolteacher who was principal of a public school in the Bronx. Condon had some eccentric extra-curricular activities. He wrote letters to the newspapers, usually the *Bronx Home News,* on topics of current interest. The letters, which took the form of articles, poems, essays, and calls-to-arms, were not signed Dr. John F. Condon. He took his model from an earlier time and signed his pieces P.A. Triot, L.O. Nestar, L.O. Nehand, or J.U. Stice.

Condon had the *Home News* print a story saying that he was offering his services as an intermediary. He offered an award of $1,000 for information leading to the safe return of the "Little Eaglet," as the newspapers were calling the missing baby. This was certainly an impressive gesture, probably representing a larger percentage of his net worth than the Lindbergh's $50,000 reward represented of theirs. With the state of New Jersey's offer of a $25,000 reward, this brought the total to $76,000, a fairly hefty amount for 1932.

## Condon Is Accepted

Condon's article in the *Home News* actually brought a response—a letter with the red-and-blue rings and the three punched holes. The kidnappers would accept Condon as an intermediary (if indeed it was the kidnappers who sent the letter). Condon rushed to the Lindbergh estate. Lindbergh, noting the circles and holes, promptly accepted the letter as genuine. Neither Lindbergh nor Condon knew that copies of the first letter were being retailed throughout the country at $5 a print.

Condon replied as the letter instructed—three words in the agony column (as the personal classified ads column used to be called) of the *New York American* with his new signature, formed from the three initials of his name:

"Money is ready. Jafsie"

**Mysterious Comments**

In explaining his qualifications as an intermediary to Anne Morrow Lindbergh, Condon said he had once won a $20 prize by submitting the following New Year's resolution to the *Home News*: "That I shall, to the best of my ability, and at all times, help anyone in distress."

# The Kidnappers Communicate

A telephone call to Jafsie directed him to the Woodlawn Cemetery in the Bronx, where he had a conversation with a man who claimed to be one of the kidnappers. The man told Jafsie that his name was John, that he was a Scandinavian sailor, and that there were five other members of the gang: three men and two women. The Little Eaglet, John claimed, was being held on a boat. As proof, John promised to supply the baby's sleeping suit, the one without the flap in back.

**The Mystery Deepens**

Jafsie did try to verify that John was one of the kidnappers. Where, he asked, had the original note been left?

"In crib," John told him.

Jafsie waved two safety pins that he had taken from the baby's blanket. "What are these?"

"Safety pins."

"Where are they from?"

"The crib."

Jafsie was satisfied, deciding that only the kidnapper could know that.

Jafsie received a package in the mail containing a baby's sleeping suit, which Lindbergh identified as his son's. On what basis he made this identification is not known since the garment contained no laundry mark or other means of distinguishing it from the thousands of identical others sold in stores. It is hard to believe, especially considering that the baby had a mother and a nurse, that Colonel Lindbergh had an intimate knowledge of his son's sleeping garments.

## Jafsie Grows Restless

Jafsie by now was growing bored with his anonymity. What was the fun in being the go-between if nobody knew about it? He put an ad in the *Home News:*

> Money is ready. No cops. No secret service. I come alone, like last time. Jafsie

**Here There Be Dragons**

At Lindbergh's insistence, Commissioner Mulrooney was not told of the meeting between Jafsie and John. Therefore "John" was not shadowed when he left the cemetery. The best chance to apprehend the gang was thus lost.

He took to going around in fancy costume, one time dressing as a woman with his pants legs rolled up and his mustache hidden behind a drawn-up collar. He begged to be recognized. He *worked* at being recognized, but the newspapermen, who had spotted the Jafsie ads and were wondering who he was, somehow didn't recognize him. It was very frustrating. The New York police also wanted to know who "Jafsie" was, but Lindbergh wouldn't tell them.

# The Drop

On Friday, April 1—a portent nobody wanted to think about—Jafsie got a letter telling him to prepare to pay the ransom. The agreed-upon amount was now $70,000. Little It had now been missing for one month. The ransom was packaged—$50,000 in a wooden box, carefully constructed out of several different woods for later identification, and the remaining $20,000 wrapped in brown paper. The serial numbers of all the bills had been noted, and $20,000 of it was in gold notes—gold-backed currency that was just then going out of circulation and therefore would be that much more noticeable.

The next night, a man in the Bronx hailed a taxi. He gave the driver a letter to deliver to Jafsie. It was the final ransom note, telling Jafsie to proceed immediately to a flower shop and look under a stone in front of the door. By chance, Lindbergh was with Jafsie when the taxi driver delivered the letter, and he drove the schoolteacher to the flower shop.

They found the note under the stone. It directed Jafsie to nearby St. Raymond's Cemetery. There, Jafsie met a man he thought was the same John he had met before. The man asked for the $70,000. Jafsie told him they couldn't raise that much and that they only had $50,000. The man agreed to settle for the smaller amount; after all, they were in the middle of a depression. Jafsie went back to Lindbergh's car to get the box, smugly satisfied with himself at having saved Lindbergh $20,000. He gave John the money, and John gave him a note and faded away over the tombstones. Again the police had not been notified, and the man was not followed.

The note said the baby was being held on a boat called the *Nelly* off Martha's Vineyard, a resort town on an island off Cape Cod, Massachusetts. Lindbergh flew to Martha's Vineyard and spent two days buzzing every boat in the area before he was willing to admit that they had been hoaxed.

# The Body

Seventy-two days after the Little Eaglet vanished, William Allen, a truck driver, parked his truck on a road near the Lindbergh house and trotted into the woods to relieve himself. Before he had a chance to do so, he found the unclothed corpse of a small child lying in the underbrush. He notified the police, and the body was taken to the morgue in Trenton about 12 miles away.

Lindbergh and Betty Gow, the nurse, came to the morgue to identify the body. After examining it for something less than three minutes, they agreed that it was the missing baby. Little It had been found.

The body was promptly cremated at Lindbergh's instruction. This is a pity because there is strong presumptive evidence indicating that the identification was wrong and that the body was not that of the Lindbergh baby. The corpse was badly decomposed, to such a state that it was impossible to tell even the sex of the child by looking at it. The left leg was missing from the knee down, and the right foot was missing, so Lindbergh couldn't have depended on a slight physical deformity of the baby's toes for identification.

**Mysterious Comments**

Dr. Philip Van Ingen, a New York physician who was Little It's doctor, examined the corpse carefully. He had examined Charles Jr. only a couple of weeks before the kidnapping. "If someone were to come in here and offer me ten million dollars," he told the coroner, "I simply wouldn't be able to identify these remains."

## The Old Fox

One of the most famous detectives of the day, a shrewd, self-taught catcher of murderers named Ellis Parker, lived in nearby Burlington County, New Jersey. In his 30 years as a detective, he had had a hand in the conviction of more than 100 murderers, a cumulative feat that had earned him the nickname "the Old Fox."

Parker thought the finding of the body was very odd. He knew the area had been gone over before by the state police, and it was unlikely that they would have missed a body just lying there on the ground. He looked at pictures of the corpse and realized that it was overly decomposed for the length of time it was supposed to have been there. He checked the mean temperatures over the months in question and found that it had indeed been too cool for the decomposition to reach such an advanced state.

Parker checked the physical records. The missing baby had been 29 inches long. The dead child, allowing for the missing foot, had been 33 inches long. Parker concluded that it was not the Lindbergh baby. After some thought, he evolved the theory that bootleggers, who had been seriously inconvenienced by all the police interest in stopping and examining cars and searching remote areas for the baby, had provided the authorities with the corpse they were looking for. Perhaps they had known of the deformed toes, and that's why the corpse's feet were missing.

## The Old Fox Rebuffed

Neither Lindbergh nor the police were interested in Parker's theories. The police went back to harassing the Lindberghs' household staff. The maid at the New Jersey house, a British girl named Violet Sharp, had originally lied about where she had been the night of the kidnapping because she was out with a young man who was not her regular boyfriend. The police decided to probe deeper into this and questioned Violet severely, letting her know in the strongest possible terms that they did not believe her story. These were the same police who had beaten up a suspect in the Lindbergh basement only a few weeks before, and Violet must have known about that. Violet, a neurotic, sensitive girl, committed suicide.

**No Mystery Here**

Congress, which had before it a bill to make kidnapping a federal offense, had been holding off on passing it so as not to endanger the Little Eaglet. Now that the baby had been found dead, Congress passed what immediately became known as the Lindbergh law. This legitimized allowing J. Edgar Hoover's Bureau of Investigation to join the New Jersey State Police and the New York City Police in tramping around the Lindberghs' estate and searching for clues.

As time passed and nothing more was discovered, the police focused on the ransom money. Copies of the list of numbers on the bills were sent to every bank and many businesses. One bill—a $20 gold certificate—turned up in New Castle, Pennsylvania, two months after the ransom drop. Nobody saw who spent it. For a year, that's where the case sat. And then, a year after the kidnapping, the country went off the gold standard.

People were required to turn in their gold-backed money by a certain date or it no longer would be honored. Shortly before the May 1 deadline, a man entered the Federal Reserve Bank in Manhattan and plumped down $2,990 of the ransom money goldbacks for exchange. Unfortunately, the bank was so busy that nobody remembered what the man looked like. The deposit slip he filled out gave his name as J.J. Faulkner of 537 West 159th Street. Experts couldn't decide whether it was or was not the same as the handwriting on the ransom notes. There was no Faulkner living at 537 West 159th, and one had not been in the memory of the postman who had been delivering mail to that apartment house for 18 years. The lead petered out.

## Jafsie Rejected

During the following months, as nothing more was discovered, Jafsie began suffering from rejection syndrome. He took to visiting police stations and announcing, "I am Jafsie. Let me look at your prisoners. Cemetery John may be among them." One day, while he was riding a city bus, he suddenly yelled, "Stop this bus! I am Jafsie. I see the Lindbergh kidnapper—there across the street!" By the time Jafsie ran across the street, the suspect had disappeared.

The police compiled Jafsie's various descriptions of Cemetery John and found that they were looking for a five-foot eight-inch-tall man who was six feet tall, both small-framed and barrel-chested, with a square chin that came to a point, eyes that were both large brown and small blue, and a nose that was both small and large.

### No Mystery Here

Even though most gold-backed bills had been turned in, and they were no longer legal tender, the small number remaining were still accepted by banks, which then withdrew them from circulation.

## A Few Bills Turn Up

A small number of the ransom bills began turning up in circulation in the Bronx, but they were always identified too late to trace back to their source. A five-dollar bill was used to buy a ticket to the movie *Broadway Through a Keyhole* at the Loew's Sheridan Square Theater in Greenwich Village in November 1933. The ticket seller, Mrs. Cecilia Barr, thought the purchaser looked "furtive." She examined the bill after he left her window, thinking it might be a counterfeit, and found that it was a Lindbergh bill. By the time the police arrived, the man was nowhere to be found.

# Bruno Richard Hauptmann

Ten months later, two-and-a-half years after the kidnapping, a gas-station attendant in the Bronx received a ransom bill from a man who bought gas at his station. He had taken the license number of the man's car because of what he described as the man's "furtive behavior."

The next day, a German carpenter named Bruno Hauptmann was placed under arrest at his home in the Bronx. A search of his garage turned up almost $15,000 in ransom bills. Hauptmann, who was married and had a son who was born around the time of the kidnapping, claimed he had no knowledge of the crime. According to Hauptmann, the money had been turned over to him by a friend named Isadore Fisch, who asked him to hold it while he went back to Germany. Hauptmann said he had spent some of it because Fisch owed him money.

**No Mystery Here**

The police verified that there *was* an Isadore Fisch, but Fisch had died in Germany and was thus unavailable to confirm Hauptmann's story. They could have looked into the Fisch connection further, but for some reason they didn't seem that interested in confirming Hauptmann's story.

Mrs. Barr, the cashier at the Loew's Sheridan Square Theater, identified Hauptmann as the man who had passed her the ransom bill a year before. The cab driver who had taken a ransom note to Jafsie's house picked Hauptmann out of a lineup—consisting of Hauptmann and two uniformed officers. Jafsie was brought in to look at Hauptmann. "That is not the man," he told the investigators. "Cemetery John was much heavier."

The New Jersey State Police were determined to convict someone for the Lindbergh baby snatch, and here was someone who, with a little care, they could convict. They came up with two witnesses who placed Hauptmann near the crime scene at the time of the crime: Millard Whited and Amandus Hockmuth. Both had previously been questioned and had denied seeing anyone. Now both suddenly changed their stories. It was never brought out at the trial—at which they both testified—that Whited had been in trouble with the police and might be buying his way out with his testimony and that Hockmuth suffered from cataracts and was legally blind.

# The Trial

Hauptmann was put on trial for kidnapping and murder in the courthouse in Flemington, New Jersey. The trial was destined to be a carnival, and Flemington made the most of it. Every bed in town and most of the pool tables were rented for the duration. The tabloid *New York Daily Mirror* supplied Hauptmann with an attorney: a flamboyant, incompetent drunk named Edward J. Reilly.

Called "The Old Lion" in public and "Death House Reilly" behind his back, Reilly had a prodigious reputation for creating a large and newsworthy fuss as his clients in capital cases were convicted and executed. He had two local lawyers as co-counsels, but Reilly was the man in charge.

### The Mystery Deepens

The police had Hauptmann write a series of letters to compare them with the ransom notes. Hauptmann later maintained that they had dictated the letters—including misspellings—to him, and he had put down what they told him. Several handwriting experts were called to make the comparison. The results were mixed: some were convinced that Hauptmann had written the notes; some were convinced that he hadn't. The police thanked the experts who said he hadn't written the notes and sent them home, retaining the ones who said he had.

### Here There Be Dragons

In the years since Hauptmann's execution several other prime suspects have been unearthed including a con man and ex-spy named Jacob Nosovitsky, Anne Lindbergh's older sister Elisabeth, and Charles Lindbergh himself. The evidence against each is as circumstantial and incomplete as the evidence against Hauptmann was, and the question of what happened to the Lindbergh baby is still an open one.

## The Evidence Is Presented

A wood expert employed by the New Jersey State Police testified that one of the pieces of wood in the kidnap ladder was sawed from a plank that was part of the floor in Hauptmann's attic. Jafsie's phone number was found written in pencil on a closet door in Hauptmann's house. When the state cautiously introduced evidence about the corpse in the woods, Reilly stood up, weaving slightly, and announced, "We concede that the corpse that was found was that of the Lindbergh baby." Both his co-counsels and the state's attorneys were astounded at this giveaway.

Jafsie positively identified Hauptmann as Cemetery John. This was despite his earlier statement that Hauptmann *couldn't* have been Cemetery John. The legally blind Hockmuth testified to seeing Hauptmann around the Lindbergh house. Reilly didn't question either of them.

## *The Conviction*

Hauptmann was convicted and was sentenced to death. On 3 April 1936, four years, one month, and two days after the kidnapping, Bruno Richard Hauptmann was electrocuted in the prison in Trenton, New Jersey. He went to his death maintaining his innocence. It later came out that the pencilled phone number on his closet door, one of the strong points against him, had been forged after his arrest by a reporter who was trying to strengthen the story he was writing.

# Are You the Lindbergh Baby?

The only thing we can be sure Hauptmann was guilty of was possession of some of the ransom money. (The rest of the money, incidentally, has never turned up.) To an unbiased observer, it was never established that Hauptmann was Cemetery John, it was never established that Cemetery John was connected to the kidnapping and not just the agent of an extortion attempt, and it was never established that the body in the woods was that of the Lindbergh baby.

**No Mystery Here**

If you have a lot of spare time, and find yourself fascinated by the Lindbergh kidnapping, you can research the case at the Lindbergh Archives at the New Jersey State Police Museum in West Trenton, which is open to the public, or make an appointment to review the more than 45,000 pages of documents on the case at the FBI Headquarters in Washington, D.C. Many of the documents are now reproduced on the FBI's Freedom of Information Act Web site: http://foia.fbi.gov/.

Several men have come forward over the years claiming to be the Lindbergh baby grown up, but they've all been disqualified one way or another. If the body found in the woods was not Charles Augustus Lindbergh Jr., then he'd be in his 70s now. He'd almost certainly have no memory of his abduction or his life before it. It would be possible today to establish his identity with DNA testing. Perhaps, sometime this decade or the next, a new ending will be written to the story of the Lindbergh baby kidnapping.

---

### The Least You Need to Know

➤ Charles Lindbergh's son, Charles Jr., was kidnapped from the family's New Jersey home on 1 March 1932.

➤ Through their deference to Lindbergh and their general inefficiency, the police failed to develop any clues they might have had.

➤ Instead of depending on the police, Lindbergh sought the help of gangsters and a strange retired school principal named Dr. John F. "Jafsie" Condon.

➤ Jafsie delivered the ransom money to someone in a graveyard; the person may or may not have been the kidnapper, and Charles Jr. was not returned.

➤ An infant's body, which may or may not have been that of Lindbergh's son, was found in the woods 10 weeks after the kidnapping.

➤ Bruno Richard Hauptmann was arrested two-and-a-half years after the kidnapping based on his possession of some of the ransom money. Hauptmann maintained his innocence but was executed for the crime.

# Chapter 18

WANTED

The New
Orleans
AXEMAN

# It's a Crime

## In This Chapter

➤ Sacco and Vanzetti were tried for robbery and murder

➤ The New Orleans axeman

➤ The trial of Dr. Sam Sheppard

Luckily for society, most criminals are impulsive, slapdash, and inattentive to detail. There's the well-known story of the would-be bank robber who wrote his hold-up note on the back of his own withdrawal slip. He couldn't understand how the police were waiting for him when he got home with the loot.

Most crimes, in fact, are easily solved—either because of ineptitude on the part of the criminal or because the crime fits into a particular pattern. There is generally a certain pattern and order to different types of crimes, and investigators look for the usual pattern when they investigate. For example, most murders are committed by someone the victim knows. Most of the time, investigating from this standpoint proves to be the right approach.

But what if the pattern is lacking? Investigators may unconsciously supply it themselves. The husband is the usual suspect when a wife is murdered. Knowing this, homicide detectives may concentrate on searching for evidence to prove the husband guilty, ignoring evidence that points in another direction.

Many police forces are simply not very good at solving complex or unusual crimes. It is a combination of unusual circumstances and mistaken preconceptions, in large part, that result in innocent people being convicted of crimes and sometimes even executed. In this chapter, we'll look at three crimes that were anything but open-and-shut cases—crimes that haunt us for one disturbing reason or another to this day.

### The Mystery Deepens

It has been established with reasonable certainty that, during the twentieth century, at least 72 men executed in the United States were innocent. There may have been many more, since the investigation of a crime usually ends with the execution of the person convicted.

# Death to the Anarchists

On 15 April 1920, a five-man gang held up a shoe factory in South Braintree, Massachusetts, and got away with the $15,776.51 payroll, killing the paymaster and a guard in the process. Two Italian *anarchists*, factory worker Nicola Sacco and fish peddler Bartolomeo Vanzetti, were tried for the crime.

The only possible connection the two had with the events in South Braintree was that they both had pistols, and one of them—Sacco—looked something like one of the robbers. But neither anarchism nor Italian immigrants were popular in Massachusetts in the 1920s, and Sacco and Vanzetti were brought to trial. The courtroom was ringed with armed plainclothes guards to ward off the feared attack of gangs of violent anarchists.

### What Does This Mean?

Anarchists believe that the best government is no government. In the past, some of them have tried to bring down governments by means of assassinations and other acts of terror.

## The "Expert" Witnesses

The prosecution based its case on two expert witnesses, ballistics experts who testified that the murder bullets came from the anarchists' guns. The first, Charles Van Amburgh, was later shown to have a habit of doctoring his testimony to fit the needs of the prosecution. In one later case, it was established that he gave false evidence to convict a man who was eventually proven to be innocent. The second expert witness, police Captain William Proctor, later admitted in an affidavit that his statement that one of the murder bullets had markings "consistent with being fired by that pistol" merely meant that the bullet *could* have come from Sacco's gun—or from many others—and that he personally didn't believe it had been fired by Sacco's gun. He further admitted that he had been heavily coached by the prosecution. When he attempted to take Sacco's pistol apart on the stand to demonstrate something, it soon became apparent that he didn't know how.

The fact that a gang of Mafia hoodlums led by the Morelli brothers was going around robbing payrolls, that this robbery was consistent with others, and that it could be demonstrated that neither Sacco nor Vanzetti could be members of this gang, was ignored by the judge and the jury. Judge Webster Thayer believed he was supposed to convict, and he did everything in his power to convey that belief to the jury. Out of court, he called the defendants "dago sons of bitches."

On 14 July 1921, the jury found the two defendants guilty, and Judge Thayer sentenced them to death.

**Mysterious Comments**

"Did you see what I did to those anarchist bastards?"

—Judge Webster Thayer to a friend after the Sacco-Vanzetti trial

## A Review of the Case

Governor Alvin Tufts Fuller of Massachusetts, not understanding the worldwide fuss about the trial, appointed a commission headed by Abbot Lawrence Lowell, the president of Harvard University, to look into it. The Lowell Commission found everything to be in order, although it did comment on Judge Thayer's "grave breach of official decorum." They seemed to be more concerned with whether courtroom proprieties had been observed than whether the defendants had been innocent or guilty.

On 23 August 1927, Nicola Sacco and Bartolomeo Vanzetti were executed.

Years later, Mafia informant Vincent Teresa claimed he had been told by Butsey Morelli that Morelli and his brothers had in fact committed the crime for which the two anarchists had been executed. "These two suckers took it on the chin for us," Butsey said. "That shows you how much justice there really is."

### No Mystery Here

Harvard Law School professor Felix Frankfurter, who later became a justice of the Supreme Court and a founder of the American Civil Liberties Union, wrote a book bitterly denouncing the Sacco-Vanzetti trial as a travesty of justice.

### What Does This Mean?

The **Black Hand** was an extortion and terror organization that preyed on Sicilian immigrants. Members would send a demand for money to shopkeepers, threatening to burn down the store, destroy merchandise, or kidnap the victim's wife or children if they were not paid. The note would be signed with the device of a crudely drawn black hand.

Whether the Morelli brothers really committed the robbery-murder is not provable so long after the event, but it seems fairly clear that neither Nicola Sacco nor Bartolomeo Vanzetti were involved.

# The New Orleans Axeman

In New Orleans in 1911, three Italian grocers named Rosetti, Crui, and Schiambra were axed to death. In two of the cases, Rosetti and Schiambra, their wives had been killed also. No one was prosecuted for the crimes, and it was generally thought to have been the work of the *Black Hand*.

## The Axeman Cometh

The axeman remained dormant for seven years, but on 24 May 1918, he returned. He chiseled through a panel of the back door to the apartment of Joseph Maggio, an Italian grocer, and attacked Maggio and his wife as they slept.

Maggio's two brothers, Jake and Andrew, lived across the hall. Jake heard what he described as "groaning noises" at about five in the morning and woke up Andrew. They ran across to Joseph's apartment and found Joseph half out of bed and his wife sprawled on the floor. They had each been hit once with an axe, and their throats had been slit with a straight razor. The razor lay on the floor; the axe—Maggio's own—was found on the rear steps. Neither Mrs. Maggio's jewelry on the dresser nor the $100 in cash under the pillow had been taken. The wall safe was open and empty, but the brothers thought there had been nothing in it. The brothers immediately called the police.

The police arrived, looked the scene over, and arrested the two brothers. A neighbor had seen Andrew coming home between one and two in the morning. What that had to do with Joseph Maggio and his wife being axed to death three hours later is not recorded.

On the sidewalk about a block away, someone had chalked, "Mrs Maggio is going to sit up tonight just like Mrs Toney." Somebody remembered that one of the 1911 axe victims had been named Tony Schiambra. Was his wife, who also had been killed, the "Mrs Toney?" Was this another Black Hand killing?

## Polish Grocer or Spy?

On the morning of June 28, a Polish grocer named Louis Besumer and a woman thought to be Mrs. Besumer were attacked in Besumer's apartment behind his grocery store. It was the arrival of John Zanca, a baker making his morning bread deliveries, that probably saved their lives. The store was closed, so Zanca went around to the back. He noticed that a panel had been chiseled out of the rear door. The door was still locked. Zanca pounded on the door. A bloody Besumer opened the door, moaning "My God! My God!" Through the door, Zanca could see the woman on the bed, her head in a pool of blood. She was rushed to Charity Hospital where she remained unconscious for several days.

The police found a bloody axe—Besumer's own—in the bathroom. They found letters written in Russian, German, and Yiddish in a trunk. They learned that Besumer was new to New Orleans, having come from South America by way of Jacksonville, Florida, a scant three months before. The whole country was in the middle of a great, albeit unwarranted, spy scare, so the newspapers jumped to the obvious conclusion. The next morning the *New Orleans Times-Picayune* headline read "Spy Nest Suspected!"

Besumer's story was published the next day. He was not a German spy, he explained, he was not even German. He was a Pole. The injured woman was not his wife but Mrs. Harriet Lowe, who had come from Jacksonville with him. His wife was ill and was staying with relatives in Cincinnati. He had been hit while asleep and didn't know who hit him or why. When he came to, he had found Mrs. Lowe lying on the floor and carried her to the bed. He was about to go for help when Zanca arrived.

## Broad-Jumping to Conclusions

Government agents decided to look into the suspicious case of this Pole who had been hit by an axe while in possession of letters written in foreign languages. When Besumer went to the hospital to see Mrs. Lowe the next day, they refused to let him in. A bathrobe he had brought for her was taken and ripped apart to see what lay concealed within. The next day, Besumer's grocery and apartment were searched. Nothing incriminating was found.

On July 5, Louis Besumer was arrested. It was given out to the press that Mrs. Lowe had awakened, and the first thing she said was, "I have long suspected that Mr. Besumer was a German spy."

When she was interviewed the next day, Mrs. Lowe, in a vain effort to protect her reputation, said she was, indeed, married to Besumer. "I did not say Mr. Besumer was a German spy," she added. "That is perfectly ridiculous." Besumer was released.

Mrs. Lowe said she had been knocked unconscious by someone she didn't see. When she awoke, a tall, heavy-set man with an axe was standing over her. She screamed and "the next thing I remember is lying out on the gallery with my face in a pool of blood."

Mrs. Lowe changed the details of her story several times, which the police found suspicious. On August 5 she died, murmuring something like "Besumer hit me with the axe " with her last breath—or that's what it sounded like to the policeman writing it down. The police arrested Besumer again.

## One Victim Is Saved

That night, Edward Schneider, a young man who had been working late at the office, came home to find his pregnant wife lying in a pool of blood. He rushed her to Charity Hospital in time to save her life. She remembered only that she had awakened to see a man with a raised axe standing over her and that she had screamed as he brought it down. For a change, the axe was not found at the scene. She recovered and had a healthy baby a week later.

## A Dark, Tall, Heavy-Set Man

The day after that, the nieces of Joseph Romano, 18-year-old Pauline and 13-year-old Mary, heard noises in their uncle's bedroom. They burst in, and Pauline saw a "dark, tall, heavy-set [man] wearing a dark suit and a black slouch hat" standing by her uncle's bed and hitting him with an axe. When they came in, the dark man disappeared with frightening suddenness. They rushed their uncle to the hospital where he died two days later. (In a break with tradition, the police didn't arrest the two girls.)

Axeman hysteria swept New Orleans after this incident. The police were inundated with calls from people who saw mysterious strangers chiseling panels from doors, leaping over back fences, or creeping through the streets with axes in their hands. The growing paranoia was understandable.

**Mysterious Comments**

"Armed men are keeping watch over their sleeping families while the police are seeking to solve the mysteries of the axe attacks. Five victims have fallen under the dreadful blows of this weapon within the last few months. Extra police are being put to work daily."

—*The New Orleans States*, 14 August 1918

Then, on 10 March 1919, nine months after the last attack, the axeman struck again. In the town of Gretna, just across the river south of New Orleans, Charles Cortimiglia and his wife, Rosie, and infant daughter, Mary, were attacked in their home with the Cortimiglias' own axe. Sixty-nine-year-old Iorlando Jordano and his 18-year-old son Frank, who lived across the street, heard screaming and rushed over to help. They bandaged up the Cortimiglias and called the ambulance, but it was too late for little Mary, who was dead in her mother's arms.

## Rosie Changes Her Story

Now here's a strange twist to the narrative: Rosie Cortimiglia, who had told of waking to find a tall, dark man over her, changed her story. It was the Jordanos, she now insisted, who had attacked her and her husband and had killed her baby. The motive, she said, was jealousy because the Cortimiglia grocery store and the Jordano grocery store were across the street from each other. Her husband refuted her story, expressing bewilderment that she should claim such a thing, but she stuck to her guns.

The police experimented and discovered that hefty Frank Jordano couldn't have wedged himself through the hole in the door where the panel had been removed. They also admitted that the modus operandi was exactly that of the axe killer. But, nonetheless, they arrested the Jordanos and scheduled a trial for May.

## The Jazz Lover

A few days later, the *Times-Picayune* received a letter:

Hell, March 13, 1919
Editor of the *Times-Picayune*
New Orleans, Louisiana

Esteemed Mortal:

They have never caught me and they never will. They have never seen me, for I am invisible, even as the ether that surrounds your earth. I am not a human being, but a spirit and a fell demon from the hottest hell. I am what you Orleanians and your foolish police call the Axeman.

When I see fit, I shall come again and claim other victims. I alone know who they shall be. I shall leave no clue except my bloody axe, besmeared with the blood and brains of him whom I have sent below to keep me company.

If you wish you may tell the police not to rile me. Of course I am a reasonable spirit. I take no offense at the way they have conducted their investigations in the past.

In fact, they have been so utterly stupid as to amuse not only me, but His Satanic Majesty, Francis Josef, etc. But tell them to beware. Let them not try to discover what I am, for it were better that they were never born than to incur the wrath of the Axeman. I don't think there is any need of such a warning, for I feel sure the police will always dodge me, as they have in the past. They are wise and know how to keep away from all harm.

Undoubtedly, you Orleanians think of me as a most horrible murderer, which I am, but I could be very much worse if I wanted to. If I wished, I could pay a visit to your city every night. At will I could slay thousands of your best citizens, for I am in close relationship to the Angel of Death.

Now, to be exact, at 12:15 (earthly time) on next Tuesday night, I am going to visit New Orleans again. In my infinite mercy, I am going to make a proposition to you people. Here it is:

I am very fond of jazz music, and I swear by all the devils in the nether regions that every person shall be spared in whose home a jazz band is in full swing at the time I have mentioned. If everyone has a jazz band going, well, then, so much the better for you people. One thing is certain and that is that some of the people who do not jazz it on Tuesday night (if there be any) will get the axe.

Well, as I am cold and crave the warmth of my native Tartarus, and as it is about time that I leave your earthly home, I will cease my discourse. Hoping that thou wilt publish this, that it may go well with thee, I have been, am and will be the worst spirit that ever existed either in fact or realm of fancy.

THE AXEMAN

It could, of course, have been a fraud. But on Tuesday, March 19, St. Joseph's Night, the sounds of jazz permeated the city. One of the most popular piano pieces that night was the recently published "The Mysterious Axeman's Jazz." The axeman stayed home.

On May 21, Iorlando Jordano and his son Frank were put on trial. Rosie and Charles Cortimiglia sat apart and didn't speak or look at each other; they had separated after her accusation of the Jordanos. Each of them took to the stand, Rosie testifying against and Charles for the Jordanos. The defense called a parade of character witnesses along with a reporter for the *New Orleans States*, Andrew Ojeda, who had interviewed Rosie shortly after she regained consciousness in the hospital. He testified that she had said, "I don't know who killed Mary. I believe my husband did it!" At this revelation, the courtroom went wild, and it took the judge some time to regain order.

After three more days of competing witnesses, the case went to the jury. They were out for less than an hour, and when they returned, they found the Jordanos, father and son, guilty. The judge sentenced Frank Jordano to be hanged, his father to spend the rest of his life in prison.

## The Next Few Chops

On the morning of August 10, Frank Genusa answered a knocking at his door, and his friend Steve Boca fell into his arms. Boca, a grocer who lived down the alley, was covered with blood; a deep axe blow had split his head open. Genusa called an ambulance, and Boca was taken to Charity Hospital where he recovered. But he remembered nothing useful; a dark man had stood over him with an axe, he had seen the blow coming, and then nothing. The police, over Boca's protests, arrested Genusa. They eventually let him go.

### No Mystery Here

On April 30, the long-delayed trial of Louis Besumer began. With the war hysteria over and nobody seriously believing that Besumer had been a German spy, the weakness of the prosecution's case was evident. The jury stayed out for only 10 minutes before returning with a verdict of not guilty.

William Carson, a druggist, was up late reading on September 2 when he heard noises at his back door. He asked who was there and, when he got no reply, fired several shots from his revolver through the door. The next morning, the police found chisel marks on one of the panels of the door.

The next day, neighbors of 19-year-old Sarah Laumann broke into her house when she failed to answer the bell. They found her in bed with minor head wounds and a concussion. A bloody axe was found outside one of her windows. The axeman had not entered through a door panel for a change. It is possible that the ringing bell frightened him off before he had time to complete his bloody task. The girl recovered but remembered nothing at all.

On October 27, a grocer named Mike Pepitone was attacked in bed and killed. His wife, who (luckily for her) was sleeping in the next room, was awakened by the noise and opened the door to her husband's room just in time to see a black figure fleeing out the other door. When questioned, she stated that she did not recognize him, that it was too dark and her glimpse was too fleeting.

## The Murder of Mumfre

Mike Pepitone was, as far as is known, the axeman's last victim. But the story has several sequels. On 2 December 1920, a woman dressed in black and heavily veiled stepped from a doorway in Los Angeles and shot and killed a man named Joseph Mumfre. She was taken into custody and told the police only that her name was Mrs. Esther Albano. Several days later, she told all. Esther Albano was really Mrs. Mike

Pepitone, wife of the New Orleans Axeman's last victim. She claimed that Mumfre was the Axeman, that she had seen him running from her husband's room. "I believe that he killed all those people," she said.

Although both the Los Angeles and the New Orleans police forces were dubious at first, her story checked out to the extent that it could be checked. Mumfre had been released from prison in 1911, just in time to have killed the first five victims. Then he had gone back to prison for an unrelated offense and was released again less than a month before the attack on the Maggios. Between August 1918 and March 1919, when the axeman was strangely inactive, Mumfre had been in prison for burglary. The facts fit perfectly, but it was all coincidental with no proof but Mrs. Pepitone's word.

On 7 December 1920, Rosie Cortimiglia went to the city room of the *Times-Picayune* and asked to speak to a reporter. When several appeared, she fell to her knees and burst out crying. "I lied! I lied!" she shrieked. "God forgive me, I lied! It was not the Jordanos who killed my baby. I did not know the man who attacked us."

Rosie, thin, pale, and ill-looking, was led to a chair. "Look at me," she told the reporters. "I have had smallpox. I have suffered for my lie. I hated the Jordanos, but they did not kill Mary. St. Joseph told me I must tell the truth no matter what it cost me. You mustn't let them hang Frank!"

She was taken to the Gretna jail, where she threw herself to the floor. "Forgive me! Forgive me!" she screamed at Frank Jordano. "You are innocent. God has punished me more than you. Look at my face! I have lost everything—my baby is dead, my husband has left me, I have had smallpox. God has punished me until I have suffered more than you!" The Jordanos were released.

### The Mystery Deepens

In April, Mrs. Pepitone stood trial. Her attorney tried for justifiable homicide but, although the court was sympathetic, that wouldn't wash. She was sentenced to 10 years. She was out in three and disappeared from history.

Whether Joseph Mumfre was the man with an axe and a grudge against (mostly) Italian grocers or whether it was the Black Hand after all or some third party, we'll never know for sure. But the axe attacks stopped with Mumfre's death. The final toll was 11 dead, six wounded, and a city scared out of its wits for almost two years.

# The Sam Sheppard Case

In the early morning hours of 4 July 1954, Bay Village police were called to the home of Dr. Samuel Sheppard, a wealthy and popular osteopathic surgeon. They found an apparently battered and barely coherent Dr. Sheppard downstairs being tended by the mayor of Bay Village, who was his next-door neighbor. Upstairs in the bedroom was the body of Marilyn Sheppard, Dr. Sheppard's wife, who had been beaten to death.

## *The Bushy-Haired Man*

Nothing like this had ever happened in Bay Village, an exclusive suburb of Cleveland, Ohio, and the murder quickly became a subject of passionate interest. Dr. Sheppard's story was that he had been sleeping on the living room couch when he was awakened by the sound of Marilyn screaming upstairs. He rushed upstairs but was knocked down—and out—by a "white figure" on the staircase. The next thing he remembered was waking up on the beach (his house bordered Lake Erie) sometime later. He rushed home and ran upstairs to find Marilyn dead in the bedroom. He came back downstairs and called his next-door neighbor, Mayor John Spencer Houk, and then collapsed on the living room couch. Houk and his wife hurriedly dressed—it was around 5 A.M.—and rushed over. Houk tried to rouse a confused Sheppard while Houk's wife went upstairs and found Marilyn Sheppard's mutilated body. Sheppard was able to describe his attacker only as "a bushy-haired man."

**The Mystery Deepens**

Dr. Sheppard was taken to the hospital by his brother, a doctor who feared that Sheppard's spine had been injured. The police who came to question him found this fact suspicious, as they did the fact that his story remained vague; he couldn't improve on his description of the "white figure." Why they found his trip to the hospital, where he was immediately accessible as soon as authorities wanted him, or his inability to describe an assailant that he saw only in the dark to be suspicious is not known.

# The "Surgical Instrument"

The coroner found a bloodstain on the pillowcase under Marilyn's body that seemed to him to have the shape of "a surgical instrument." The specific instrument could not be identified, but the term "surgical instrument" seemed to have hypnotized the police. They settled on Sheppard—a surgeon—as the murderer of his wife Marilyn. The people of Bay Village turned against Dr. Sheppard when they learned that he had a mistress. Although Sam and Marilyn were known to have a happy marriage despite possible infidelities on both sides, and no other reason was ever alleged as to why he would want to beat his wife to death, Dr. Sheppard was tried and convicted for the murder of Marilyn Sheppard.

*Dr. Sam Sheppard in custody.*

It was not until after Sheppard's conviction that people from his defense team were allowed to enter the house where the murder had been committed; it had been under police seal by order of the coroner. Sheppard's lawyer, William J. Corrigan, asked Dr. Paul Leland Kirk, professor of criminalistics at the University of California at Berkeley and one of the most respected forensic scientists in the world, to do a complete analysis of the forensic material in the case.

# Dr. Kirk's Version

Kirk went over the prosecution's exhibits: the pillowcase with the strange bloodstain, Dr. Sheppard's trousers, and the wristwatch Sheppard had been wearing, which had a bloodstain on it. Why the watch had been an exhibit is not clear since Dr. Sheppard had testified that he had felt for Marilyn's pulse when he found her upstairs; it should have been no surprise that the watch was bloodstained.

By the time Kirk was allowed to look at the evidence, the crime was eight months old. He was still able to arrive at a closely reasoned and intensely detailed conclusion, however, and it was quite different from the conclusion reached by the police, the district attorney, and the jury.

Kirk was able to re-create the crime from the blood splatters in the bedroom. The blood spots on two of the walls were caused by the direct battering of Marilyn's head, and the spots on a third wall were from the swinging of the weapon. Kirk found that a heavy flashlight would have produced wounds like the ones inflicted on Marilyn, and there was no sign that anything like a "surgical instrument" had been used. The strange design on the pillowcase, which had so attracted the coroner, was just the result of the pillowcase having been folded over while it was damp with blood.

### No Mystery Here

Dr. Kirk was able to determine that the murder weapon had been held in the assailant's left hand, which would have been an interesting fact for the jury to hear. Dr. Sheppard was right-handed.

An area on one side of the bed that was bare of blood showed where the killer must have stood, and its very bareness testified to the tremendous amount of blood that must have fallen on the killer. There was no shower of blood found on Dr. Sheppard or his clothing that would correspond to what the killer must have received.

Kirk also concluded that, in defending herself, Marilyn must have severely bitten her assailant. There were no bite marks on Dr. Sheppard. All the blood stains in the room tested as type O, which was the type of both Marilyn and Sam, but there was one large spot on the door that had an entirely different rate of agglutination than that of either of the Sheppards. "These differences," he reported, "are considered to constitute confirmatory evidence that the blood on the large spot had a different origin from most of the blood in the bedroom."

Unfortunately, the blood stains were now so old that Kirk could go no further in that direction.

### No Mystery Here

The Sam Sheppard case was the inspiration for the television series *The Fugitive*, in which protagonist Richard Kimble was in a perpetual search for the "one-armed man" who had committed the crime of which Kimble was convicted.

## The Ohio Courts Vacillate

Despite Kirk's evidence, the Ohio courts were wary of granting the defense's request for another trial based on new evidence. Why wasn't this evidence produced at the first trial? The fact that the defense had been barred from the murder scene was, apparently, irrelevant. Dr. Samuel Sheppard spent nine years in prison before his new attorney, a young F. Lee Bailey, finally succeeded in getting a new trial. The basis of this appeal was that, given the climate of anger in the Cleveland area after the murder, it had been impossible for Sheppard to get a fair trial. In 1966, Dr. Samuel Sheppard was retried and found innocent of the murder of his wife. The guilty party was never caught. Sheppard died of liver failure in 1970.

In 1998, a revisiting of the blood samples collected by Dr. Kirk, using new DNA techniques, established the blood of a third person at the crime scene. Suspicion unofficially (officially the case was closed) focused on a man named Richard Eberling who had been at the Sheppard home as a window washer. Eberling, who was serving life in prison for an entirely different murder, died in 1998 without admitting his guilt in the Sheppard case.

The Ohio Supreme Court recently agreed to allow Dr. Sheppard's son, Sam Reese Sheppard, to file a lawsuit against the state of Ohio for wrongful imprisonment. In this suit Sheppard had to prove actual innocence—a stronger standard than a "not guilty" acquittal. Despite overwhelming forensic evidence that there was a third person present in the house on the night of the murder, and that the person was convicted murderer Richard Eberling, the Cuyahoga County, Ohio jury found that Sam Reese Sheppard "failed to meet the burdon of proof" to establish his father's innocence. Perhaps they were influenced by the amount of money the State of Ohio might have had to put out if they had found for Sheppard. Perhaps they were influenced by the Cuyahoga County Prosecutor's unfounded claim that the DNA evidence had been "tainted," a claim that worked so well for the O.J. Simpson defense team. Sam Reese Sheppard plans to appeal.

### The Least You Need to Know

➤ Police understand the ordinary circumstances of crimes, but the unusual may confound them.

➤ In 1920, Italian anarchists Nicola Sacco and Bartolomeo Vanzetti were arrested and tried for a payroll robbery and murder in Massachusetts. They were executed despite a large popular outcry and a more than reasonable doubt of their guilt.

➤ From 1918 to 1920, an axe murderer terrorized New Orleans. He killed 11 people and injured six. The axeman may have been murdered himself; he was never officially caught.

➤ Dr. Samuel Sheppard was arrested and tried for the 1954 murder of his wife Marilyn. He was found guilty and was sentenced to life in prison.

➤ Sheppard served nine years before he was granted a new trial. This time he was acquitted.

# Chapter 19

# Did Lizzie Borden Take an Axe?

**In This Chapter**

➤ The most famous unsolved American murder

➤ The events of that fateful day

➤ The strongest suspect: Andrew's daughter Lizzie

➤ The trial of Lizzie Borden

One of the most famous women in American crime—and the subject of what is certainly the most famous stanza in American crime verse—Lizzie Borden was indicted and tried for the murder of her father and stepmother in Fall River, Massachusetts, in 1892. She was acquitted. The murder has never officially been solved. If you look at the case one way, there's strong reason to think Lizzie must have done it. If you look at it another way, it seems just about impossible for Lizzie to be guilty. But if she didn't do it, who did? It seems just as impossible for anyone else to have committed the double axe murder.

## The Borden Family

Andrew Jackson Borden was one of the leading citizens of Fall River, a mill town and seaport that had been important in the Commonwealth of Massachusetts since the Revolution. The Borden clan had been among the most influential citizens of Fall River for even longer than that. In the past 20 years prior to 1892, with the success of the cotton mills, the population of the town had more than doubled, growing from under 50,000 to over 100,000. The town's leading citizens, Andrew Borden among them, had prospered.

Andrew lived with his second wife, nee Abby Durfee Gray, and the two surviving daughters of his first marriage, Emma and Lizzie, in a two-and-a-half-story frame house at 92 Second Street. The house was ill-planned and ill-favored, and the neighborhood was shabby genteel. Both daughters thought their home was below their station in life and had urged their father to move to a nicer house in a better neighborhood. Andrew, being a frugal man unconcerned with appearances, refused to consider it.

# The Crime

As nearly as can be reconstructed, the events of the tragedy of Thursday, 4 August 1892 unfolded as follows:

Sister Emma was not home that day, having left a few days before to visit friends in Fairhaven, a nearby seaside town. The girls' Uncle John had arrived the day before, Wednesday, for an unannounced visit. John Vinnicum Morse, the 60-year-old brother of Andrew Borden's first wife, was a regular guest at the Borden house. He came from his home in Dartmouth, Massachusetts, several times a year to visit relatives, to conduct bits of business, and to gossip with the Bordens.

The first person awake in the Borden household on that Thursday morning, as on most mornings, was Bridget Sullivan, the maid. Bridget was a respectable Irish girl whom Emma and Lizzie persisted in calling "Maggie," after a previous servant. She came down from her attic room at about six o'clock to build the fire in the kitchen stove and to start preparing breakfast. At about seven o'clock, the older Bordens and Mr. Morse came down and chatted around the breakfast table. Lizzie slept late and did not join them.

At about a quarter to eight, Mr. Morse left the house to visit a niece and nephew, and Mr. Borden locked the screen door behind him. (It was the custom in the Borden house to keep most of the doors locked. Even the doors between certain rooms upstairs were usually locked.) Lizzie came down a short while later but said she wasn't hungry. She had coffee and a cookie or two. There was perhaps a mild touch of some stomach disorder going around, and Bridget felt the need to go out in the backyard and throw up sometime after breakfast. Two days before, the elder Bordens had been quite ill during the night, both of them having fits of vomiting. Presumably it was not food poisoning since nobody else in the house was similarly affected. It might have been the onset of the stomach illness or something more sinister.

**No Mystery Here**

Over the past century, the Borden murders have been the subject of innumerable magazine articles and books as well as a couple of plays, an opera, a ballet, several movies and television shows, and a musical comedy sketch that included the memorable song, "You Can't Chop Your Poppa Up in Massachusetts."

## The Mystery Deepens

The breakfast itself has attracted most students of the Borden murders. Uncle John remembered that, on this hot August morning, he sat down to mutton, bread, "sugar cakes," bananas, and coffee. Bridget denied the bananas. Her recollection was mutton-broth, mutton, johnnycakes, coffee, and cookies. It is the mutton and mutton broth that seems to have fascinated observers. Edmund Pearson, a noted student of murder, says in his commentary on the Borden case (in *Studies in Murder*, Macmillan, 1924) that "for a hot morning in midsummer, it was a breakfast well adopted to set the stage for a tragedy."

Andrew Borden left to go downtown at quarter past nine, and Abby Borden went upstairs to make the bed in the guest bedroom where Uncle John was staying. She asked Bridget to wash the windows. At about nine thirty, she came downstairs briefly and then went back up, remarking that she had to put pillow cases on the pillows in the guest bedroom.

### No Mystery Here

On Thursday, 4 August 1892, the date of the "Fall River Tragedy," Andrew Borden was 70 years old. His wife, Abby, was 64; Emma was 41; Lizzie was 32.

Bridget went about her chores: collecting the necessary window-washing paraphernalia from about the house and pails of water from the barn, pausing to talk to the hired girl next door over the fence, and washing the windows. She had finished the outside at about ten thirty and began on the inside. Fifteen minutes later, Mr. Borden returned home. Bridget let him in, and Lizzie came downstairs. "Mrs. Borden has gone out—she had a note from somebody who was sick," she told her father. She always called her stepmother "Mrs. Borden" these days; the relations between Abby and the two girls, especially Lizzie, were rather strained.

Mr. Borden took the key to his bedroom off a shelf and went up the back stairs. The access to his bedroom was by the back stairs only; there was no hallway, and the front stairs gave access to only Lizzie's room and the guest bedroom. (Sister Emma's bedroom was reached through Lizzie's room.) There were connecting doors between Lizzie's room and her parent's bedroom, but they were usually kept locked.

Mr. Borden stayed upstairs for only a few moments before coming back down and settling in the sitting room. Lizzie began to heat up an iron to iron some handkerchiefs. "Are you going out this afternoon, Maggie?" she asked Bridget. "There is a cheap sale of dress goods at Sargent's this afternoon, at eight cents a yard." But Bridget, overcome by her work in the heat of the day and her recent illness, resisted this tempting suggestion and went up the back stairs to her room in the attic to take a nap. This was shortly before eleven o'clock.

## *"Father is dead."*

At about a quarter past eleven, Lizzie, from the foot of the stairs, yelled upstairs to Bridget, "Maggie, come down!" "What is the matter?" Bridget called. "Come down quick!" was Lizzie's response. "Father is dead. Somebody came in and killed him!"

Bridget rushed downstairs. Lizzie stopped her from going into the sitting room and sent her running for the doctor. Dr. Bowen, a family friend, lived across the street. Bridget ran across and gave Mrs. Bowen the message. The doctor was out, so Bridget ran back home. "Where were you when this thing happened?" she asked Lizzie.

"I was out in the yard, and I heard a groan and came in, and the screen door was wide open."

By now, the neighbors were starting to assemble, and somebody called for the police. Mrs. Churchill, a next-door neighbor, came over and held Lizzie's arm. "Oh Lizzie!" she said. "Where is your father?"

"In the sitting room."

"Where were you when it happened?"

"I went to the barn to get a piece of iron."

"Where is your mother?"

### No Mystery Here

The quotes used in this section, and throughout the chapter, are taken from the trial testimony, as reported in the *Boston Globe* at the time.

"I don't know. She had a note to go see someone who is sick, but I don't know but that she is killed, too, for I thought I heard her come in …. Father must have an enemy, for we have all been sick, and we think the milk has been poisoned."

Dr. Bowen had returned by this time, and he hurried to the house and entered the sitting room. Andrew Borden was lying on the sofa. He had been attacked with a sharp object, presumably an axe, and so much damage had been done to his head and face that Dr. Bowen, his medical advisor and friend, could not at first positively identify him. "Physician that I am," Bowen testified, "and accustomed to all kinds of horrible sights, it sickened me to look upon the dead man's face." Because there were no signs of a struggle, Dr. Bowen concluded that Borden had been killed in his sleep, probably by the first of the many blows that had struck him.

## There Is Another

It was 10 or 15 minutes before anyone thought of going upstairs to see if Abby Borden had come home. Bridget was afraid to go alone, so Mrs. Churchill went up with her. They went up the front stairs. Mrs. Churchill was the first to see the body.

> "As I went upstairs," she said later, "I turned my head to the left, and as I got up so that my eyes were on the level with the front hall, I could see across the front hall and across the floor of the spare room. At the far side on the north side of the room, I saw something that looked like the form of a person."

Bridget went into the guestroom for an instant to take a look, and then they both ran back downstairs. There was something about Mrs. Churchill's appearance that told the story. "Is there another?" a neighbor asked.

"Yes," Mrs. Churchill said. "She is up there." Abby Borden was lying on the floor on the far side of the bed in the guestroom, in a pool of blood.

In one of the little ironies that fate is so fond of sprinkling in life's path, on the day that put Fall River on the map of American crime, the Fall River Police Department was off to Rocky Point on its yearly picnic. The only policeman sent to answer the initial call was Officer Allen, the committing officer at the police station. He immediately ran back to the station house to inform the city marshal of the events, leaving nobody in charge at the crime scene. In his absence, neighbors overran the house, comforting Lizzie, peering at the horrible sights, and trampling on and destroying any clues that might have been present. There is no way to know what memento some curious onlooker might have walked off with during the next few hours.

### The Mystery Deepens

Abby Borden was killed at least an hour, and possibly as much as two hours, before her husband. The killer, if it was anyone but Lizzie or Bridget, must have concealed him- or herself in the house for that length of time, waiting patiently for Andrew Borden's return, risking one of the two women residents glancing into the guestroom and seeing Abby's body at any moment.

A county medical examiner named Dr. Dolan passed the house by chance at quarter to twelve. He looked in and was pressed into service by Dr. Bowen. He examined the bodies and the condition and contents of their clothing. Andrew Borden had his wallet and watch and $81.56 in cash. Hearing that the family had been sick two days before and that Lizzie suspected the milk, he took samples of it. Later that afternoon he had the bodies photographed and then removed the stomachs and sent them, along with the milk, to Harvard Medical School for analysis.

# The Investigation

The police were reluctant to suspect Lizzie of the double murder. Indeed, it went against the perceived social understanding of the later Victorian era to even consider the possibility that a proper lady of the upper middle class (and a Sunday school teacher and secretary of the Christian Endeavor Society) could commit such a heinous crime; to further consider that she could have done it to her own parents was impossible. But as other solutions were advanced, they had to be discarded as even more impossible. At first, Uncle John was a suspect, but his alibi checked out in every detail. Was it the work of an outside killer?

## Clues and Suspects Galore

On the day after the crime, the Borden sisters put the following advertisement in the newspapers:

FIVE THOUSAND DOLLARS REWARD

The above reward will be paid to any one who may secure the arrest and conviction of the person or persons, who occasioned the death of Andrew J. Borden and his wife.

Signed,

Emma L. Borden and Lizzie A. Borden

There were a profusion of clues discovered in the next couple of days, all of which went nowhere. A boy reported seeing a man jump over the back fence of the Borden property. Two policemen found a man matching the boy's description. His name was Bearsley S. Cooper, and he was chief of a nomadic horse-dealers' camp. But unfortunately, he had an unbreakable alibi for the time in question. A bloody hatchet was found on the Sylvia farm in South Somerset, and the police raced out to make an arrest. It proved to be chicken blood, however, and they went away empty-handed.

For a while, the police concentrated on Bridget. But her good character and complete lack of motive, combined with Lizzie's account of her movements, which put Bridget in the wrong place to have committed the crimes, caused them to lose interest in her as a suspect.

**Mysterious Comments**

"The usual crop of 'strange,' 'wild' and 'crazy' men, of tramps and vagrants, of 'foreigners,' and other guilty-looking persons was more prolific than ever. There was a suspected Portuguese, who was called a Portuguese because he was a Swede; and there were miscreants who turned up in lonely places, days and weeks after the murders, still brandishing axes or hatchets dripping with gore ... "

—Edmund Pearson, *Studies in Murder*, 1926

## Just the Facts

There was a six-day hearing to go over the facts, after which an indictment was issued against Lizzie Borden for the murder of her father. (For some reason, Mrs. Borden was not mentioned on the indictment. Perhaps they felt the murder of one parent was enough.) Lizzie was arraigned and pled not guilty.

The evidence, all circumstantial, was weighty. First of all, the history: Lizzie and her father and stepmother had been living what one observer called "an armed truce" for some time. The condition had gotten worse when Andrew Borden gave his wife some bank stock in 1887. The daughters protested, feeling that they should get a gift of equal value. The witnesses, relatives and friends, indicated politely that it was Lizzie who did most of the protesting. It was then that Lizzie ceased calling her stepmother "mother" and began calling her "Mrs. Borden."

To keep peace in his family, Andrew deeded his daughters a rental property, "the homestead on Ferry Street, an estate of 120 rods of land, with a house and a barn, all valued at $3,000." The girls didn't think that was enough, so he added 10 shares of stock for each of them. It was in the Crystal Spring Bleachery Company, and Andrew had paid $100 a share for them. They sold the stock soon after for less than $40 a share. Andrew gave his daughters other shares of stock and gifts of money over the years, but they remained unsatisfied and the scrabbling continued.

Lizzie's actions and statements in the days immediately preceding the crime had also attracted the attention of the investigators. She had told her friend Alice Russell that "I feel as if something were hanging over me that I cannot throw off." She added that her father had enemies, and she was afraid something was going to happen to the family. She was not clear as to what or who the enemies were. She had attempted to purchase some prussic acid from a local drug store for the purpose of "killing moths in a seal skin coat." The druggist had refused to sell it to her.

## The Borden Burglary

The story of the burglary of the Borden household, which took place a year before the murders, was used by both Lizzie's supporters and her detractors to support their cases.

It happened in June 1891. In response to Andrew Borden's complaint that his residence had been burglarized, a police captain inspected the premises. He found that Mr. Borden's desk in a small room on the second floor had been broken into. Over $100 had been taken along with Andrew Borden's watch and chain, some assorted small items, and a stack of street-car tickets.

The puzzle was how a stranger could have gotten into and out of the house unseen, and it was never satisfactorily answered, although Lizzie offered the fact that the cellar door was open. Neighbors on both sides of the street were questioned, and none of them had noticed a stranger at the time. According to the police captain, Andrew Borden several times said to him, "I am afraid the police will not be able to find the real thief." Exactly what he meant by that will never be known.

### The Mystery Deepens

On October 10, Henry G. Tricky, a reporter for the *Boston Globe,* wrote an article detailing the prosecution's case. One witness testified to seeing Lizzie in her stepmother's room while passing in the street below; another witness, also in the street, had heard a scream and seen a woman wearing some sort of rubber hood inside the Borden house. Other witnesses testified to several incriminating conversations between Lizzie and her father. Two days later, the *Globe* printed a full retraction, admitting that it had been "grievously misled" and that the whole story was a hoax. The aptly named Tricky was indicted by a grand jury for his part in the affair and fled to Canada, where he was killed in a railroad accident that November.

## The Trial

The trial of Lizzie Andrew Borden for the murder of her father, Andrew Borden, and her stepmother, Abby Durfee Borden (who had since been added to the indictment by the grand jury), began in the New Bedford Court House on 5 June 1893. News of the trial filled the front pages of every major newspaper in the country, and between 30 and 40 reporters from the Boston and New York papers and the wire services were in the courtroom every day.

The Commonwealth, represented by district attorneys Hosea M. Knowlton, who had been with the case since the beginning, and William H. Moody, who had been appointed to aid Knowlton in his disagreeable task, slowly and painstakingly built its case. It was not an easy thing to bring a capital charge against a sober, middle-class, church-going lady known for her charity work, but they did their best.

To convict someone of a crime in the absence of a believable confession or credible eyewitnesses, it is necessary to show some combination of motive or intent, means, capacity, and opportunity. Perhaps not all five will apply in every case, but the prosecutor should come as close to this ideal as possible. It is also helpful to show guilty knowledge. The Commonwealth had to show that Lizzie had a reason to kill her parents or that she desired to kill her parents, was capable of obtaining and wielding the axe, and was in the right place at the right time.

They attempted to show guilty knowledge by means of her words and actions both before and after the crime. Motive was established with a gaggle of witnesses who testified to Lizzie's dislike of her stepmother and her animosity toward her father. Means and opportunity were shown by the defendant's presence in the house during both murders—in the barn during her father's death, if she was to be believed, getting lead for sinkers. But the barn loft was the hottest place on the property on that hot day, and she had shown no interest in fishing for many years. Her statements as to her exact location were contradictory and evolved over the three days after the murders. Indisputably, she was there, and she could have committed the murders. And, the prosecutors maintained, it was hard to see how anyone else could have.

## A Burning Question

Lizzie's friend Alice Russell testified that she had seen Lizzie standing with Emma, burning a dress in the stove three days after the crime. When Emma asked what she was doing, Lizzie had replied, "I am going to burn this old thing up, it is covered with paint." Neither Emma nor Miss Russell had attempted to stop her at the time, although Alice had commented, according to her testimony, "I wouldn't let anybody see me do that, Lizzie."

This offered a possible answer to one of the questions that had been plaguing the prosecution. If Lizzie had committed the murders, why was there no trace of blood on her or her clothing? It would be unlikely to hit someone repeatedly in the head with an axe and not get heavily splattered with blood; it would be even more highly improbable

**No Mystery Here**

The specific means—the murder weapon—was never positively located. There was an axe head without a handle in the cellar that could have been the weapon. No trace of blood was found on it, but it could have been wiped clean, presumably at the same time that the handle was removed.

to do it twice, and it would be impossible to plan on doing it. A couple of theories had been advanced to explain Lizzie's lack of blood stains: the smock-worn-over-other-garments theory and the naked-Lizzie theory. But the smock would have been badly bloodstained itself, and she would have had to hide it somewhere. And the mores of the Victorian age were such that, although it is conceivable that Lizzie took an axe to her father, it is inconceivable that she would have appeared before him naked, even to kill him.

The burned dress, however, offered an explanation: Lizzie simply changed her dress. Against this was the fact that Alice Russell testified that she had seen no blood on the dress being burned. Lizzie claimed that the dress was paint stained, and perhaps this was so. It was customary in the Borden household to burn worn, stained, and useless clothing; if it were blood instead of paint, it would have been odd for Lizzie to keep the garment for three days after the murders. Also, the murders were at least an hour apart. Had she worn the blood-spattered dress between the two killings? Surely Bridget would have noticed. Had she changed into it twice? This shows a level of rationality not consistent with the obviously frenzied attack on the two elder Bordens.

## The Lawyers Fight It Out

On the seventh day of the trial, Moody attempted to offer Lizzie's own testimony at the inquest as evidence. Lizzie's defense team, headed by George D. Robinson, a man known for his intelligence and probity who had once been governor of Massachusetts, objected strenuously, and the jury was withdrawn so the lawyers could fight it out in their absence. Moody averred that, while a confession might not be admissible, Miss Borden's statements were all denials, and it was in the nature and inconsistency of those denials that evidence of guilt was to be found. Robinson claimed that, because Lizzie had been the prime suspect at the time and a warrant for her arrest had been drawn up but not executed, she should have been advised of her rights. Since she had not been and had not had the advice of counsel, any statements she made at the time could not be used against her. He ended his oration, "If that is freedom, God save the Commonwealth of Massachusetts!"

Moody pointed out that it was not common to have counsel at a hearing but that she had had counsel before the hearing, who was free to have told her whatever he thought she should know. The three-judge panel went off to confer. When they returned, they excluded the testimony and called back the jury. The defense won that round, as it had won earlier when it had excluded the testimony of the druggist identifying Lizzie as the woman who had tried to buy prussic acid.

Several medical witnesses, including Dr. Dolan, who had been at the scene, were called by the prosecution. A macabre note was added when one of them produced the skull of Andrew Borden to demonstrate how the blows were struck. The defense took advantage of the prosecution's medical witnesses to establish one of the strongest points in Lizzie's favor: That, as previously mentioned, whoever committed the murder would have to have been splattered with blood.

When the prosecution rested, the defense put on witnesses offering a variety of corroboration and alternate possibilities. An ice cream peddler had seen a woman, presumably Lizzie, coming out of the barn, thus bolstering her story that she had been there. A pair of neighbors had heard a loud thump the night before. Two children claimed to have been playing in the barn loft that afternoon and found it cool and comfortable. A passerby had seen a "wild-eyed man."

The defense did not feel the need to demolish the prosecution's case. The most damaging bits of evidence had been excluded, and popular sentiment was clearly on the side of the defendant. They just needed to introduce enough reasonable doubt to give the jury an excuse to acquit. Lizzie chose not to testify in her own defense.

The trial lasted 13 days, and the jury was out for little more than an hour. They found Lizzie not guilty. Public opinion, by that time, was unanimously of the sentiment that Lizzie had been persecuted by the police and the courts quite enough.

Emma and Lizzie, who henceforth called herself "Lizbeth," moved into a large house about a mile and a half from their old home. Some years later, Emma separated from her sister and moved to Fairhaven, and the two ceased talking to each other. Rumors about sensational revelations regarding the murders persisted for years, but no such revelations were ever forthcoming. Lizbeth died in June 1927, one week before her sister. They were both buried in the family plot in Fall River, next to their father, mother, and stepmother. In Lizzie's will, she left $500 for the perpetual care of her father's grave.

**Here There Be Dragons**

In many trials there is some testimony that must be looked at with deep suspicion, and the Borden trial was no exception. Mr. Joseph Lemay testified that he had been walking in a deep wood some miles from the city 12 days after the murders when he heard someone saying, "Poor Mrs. Borden! Poor Mrs. Borden! Poor Mrs. Borden!" He looked over a conveniently placed wall and spied a man sitting on the ground. The man, who had blood spots on his shirt, picked up a hatchet, shook it at him, and then leaped over the wall and disappeared into the woods.

## The Unanswered Questions

Over 100 years have passed since that fateful day in Fall River, but still we can't be sure of what we think we know. If Lizzie didn't do it, that means someone snuck into the Borden house on a day when many of the neighbors were on their porches to catch what breeze they could, murdered Abby Borden, and took the chance that she'd scream and bring Lizzie and Bridget and most of the neighbors running. Then he or she waited around for an hour for Andrew and killed him downstairs where anybody could have walked in. Then he or she took the bloody axe and departed with nobody seeing him or her leave.

### No Mystery Here

If you find yourself fascinated by the Borden case, you're not alone. There is a *Lizzie Borden Quarterly* published by Bristol Community College, 777 Elsbree St., Fall River, MA 02720-7391 ($14 a year) as well as more than a dozen Web sites dedicated to continuing research on the Borden mystery. The Lizzie Borden Bed and Breakfast Museum is at 92 Second Street, Fall River, MA (Phone: 508-675-7333, Web site: www.lizzie-borden.com/).

On the other hand, if Lizzie Borden did give her mother 40 whacks, what happened to the axe? Could one of the people who tramped through the house before the police arrived walked off with it? And how did Lizzie manage to butcher two people without getting massive amounts of blood on her? If the dress she burned had had blood on it, would she have burned it in front of her sister and her friend? And wouldn't they have noticed the blood?

There are other suspects. Some would have sister Emma sneaking back to commit the murders, but it's hard to see how she could have done it successfully. A favorite candidate is the maid, Bridget Sullivan, but if she did it, it's hard to see why she would have spared Lizzie.

Andrew Borden supposedly had an illegitimate son who committed suicide some years after the murders. Did he carry a guilty secret to his grave?

The papers from the Lizzie Borden defense are still unreleased; they're locked up in the offices of the Springfield, Massachusetts, law firm that descended from the one that defended Lizzie. The firm has no intention of releasing the documents, protecting Lizzie's right to privacy in death as they defended her liberty in life.

---

### The Least You Need to Know

➤ In August 1892, Andrew and Abby Borden were hacked to death in their home in Fall River, Massachusetts.

➤ Lizzie was tried for the crime and was acquitted.

➤ It's hard to see how anyone could have committed the crime and gotten away clean, but somebody did.

➤ The file on the case held by Lizzie's defense lawyers has never been released.

# Chapter 20

# The Mysterious Mata Hari

---

### In This Chapter

➤ The Dutch girl with the Indonesian name

➤ Behind the veils

➤ "For love and pleasure"

➤ Spying for the Germans and the French—sort of

➤ The trial and execution of Mata Hari

➤ The myths of Mata Hari

---

Mata Hari is undoubtedly the world's most well-known female spy. She has been dead for three-quarters of a century, and her name is still a synonym for the seductive woman agent. But …

➤ Her name was not really Mata Hari.

➤ She was almost certainly not a spy.

➤ Most of the stories told about her are not true.

In this chapter, we'll look at the life of this mysterious woman and attempt to separate fact from fiction. The information about Mata Hari's life comes from a variety of sources, and we've listed in the bibliography at the end of this book three of the best books devoted to her.

# Mata Hari's Story

Mata Hari herself described her early life thus: Born in Java of a rich Dutch father and a famous Javanese beauty who died giving birth to her, Mata Hari was taken to India at the age of 14 and was placed in the temple of the mystic cult called Kanda Swandi. It was the priests who named her Mata Hari, "eye of the morning," for her beauty, and they dedicated her to Siva. They began training her to dance and to perform the other rites needed by a Temple Virgin.

When she was 16, she was stolen from the temple by Sir Campbell MacLeod, an officer in the British Army who had seen her dance and had fallen in love with her. Sir Campbell and Mata Hari MacLeod lived well in India, where she gave birth to a son and daughter. The native gardener poisoned the boy, so Mata Hari killed him with her husband's revolver. She and her husband and her little daughter had to flee to Europe. Once there, her husband died of a sudden relapse of fever. The daughter went to a convent, and Mata Hari had to do something to support herself.

"I finally decided," she related, "by means of the dance, to interpret the soul of the Orient to the rest of the world." And so she did.

That part is true. She danced. But the rest of her story is more fiction than fact.

# Margaretha's Story

The woman who became Mata Hari was born 7 August 1876 as Margaretha Gertrude Zelle, the daughter of Adam and Antje Zelle, in the town of Leeuwarden, Holland. Adam owned a hat store and, in a time when all men wore hats, did well.

Margaretha attended a convent school but didn't seem to like it much. She was a tall girl—five foot nine in a day when the average man was five foot seven—and she was almost flat-chested. Yet there was something provocatively sensuous about her.

### The Mystery Deepens

In Medan, the MacLeods' children were hospitalized for food poisoning, possibly from a gravy poured over their rice at dinner. On the second day at the hospital, Norman died. Non, who had eaten less of the dinner, survived. It was believed but never proved that the poisoning was done intentionally by the children's *ayah* (nurse) out of spite because MacLeod had ordered the nurse's lover out of the kitchen.

When Margaretha was 18, she married a 39-year-old captain in the Dutch Colonial Forces by the name of John MacLeod, probably to escape home and school. MacLeod took his young wife to Java, first to Ambarawa in central Java and then to Toempoeng in the east near Bali, where they stayed for a while. The MacLeods had two children, Norman and Juana-Luisa, who was called Non.

Captain MacLeod was next posted to Medan, where he was put in charge of a colonial army reserve regiment.

MacLeod was an alcoholic and was a mean drunk. When drunk, he would beat his wife and wave his loaded revolver in her face. When he was sober, he would send her to his fellow officers to borrow money. He never asked her what the terms of the loan were.

People who knew her in those days said she enjoyed the attention she got from the young officers and the unmarried planters, but they had no reason to believe the relationships thus formed went beyond the bonds of propriety. On the other hand, if they had, neither party would have advertised the fact.

# The Dance Begins

In 1901, the MacLeods returned to Europe with Non and separated. The child stayed with her father, and Margaretha went to Paris. With no marketable skills beyond a certain lithe beauty and a willingness to share it with wealthy men, she was able to get along, though not as well as she would have liked. She decided that, since Orientalia was in vogue in Paris at the time, she would educate the Europeans in the art of Hindu temple dancing.

The fact that the Hindus don't indulge in temple dancing was beside the point. Wealthy Parisians didn't know that. Her performance of a temple dance to the Hindu god Siva was an instant success because of her innate grace, her sensuous movements, and an innovation that she introduced: dancing almost nude.

At the beginning of her dance she was swathed in veils, but as the dance progressed, the veils came off, progressively revealing more and more of her charms to Siva and to the audience until, at the end, as she lay prostrate before her god with almost all revealed. Then she was chastely covered with a robe before she rose and accepted her applause. It was certainly an educational experience.

**What Does This Mean?**

Margaretha took a name that she had discovered and liked in Indonesia: **Mata Hari,** which means "eye of the day" in a local language and would usually be translated as "eye of the dawn." She chose to translate it as "eye of the morning."

### Mysterious Comments

"It was on the purple granit altar of the Kanda Swany that, at the age of thirteen, I danced for the first time, completely nude."

—Mata Hari

And so, this Dutch girl with the Indonesian name danced an erotic dance to an Indian Hindu god—and was a Parisian sensation.

By 1909, she was a European sensation. Many clubs vied for her act, and many rich men vied for the chance to be her "protector," as it was then called. It was around this time that a Dutch woman named Anna Lintjens came to work for her as a maid. Anna would stay with Mata Hari for the rest of her life.

## The Lovers

By the beginning of World War I, Mata Hari had been a successful dancer and courtesan for 10 years and hadn't saved a soul. The war, which had encompassed all of Europe and was slowly creeping over the rest of the world, was a bore and a nuisance to her. She had been forced to go to Holland by way of Spain, and now she wanted to return to Paris. She renewed her Dutch passport—it is dated 15 May 1916—and applied for a British pass. Since Belgium was occupied by the German Army, the easiest way to Paris from Holland was by ship to Britain and then to France.

But the British refused her a pass. The Home Office, for reasons of its own, considered her "undesirable." After all, she danced (almost) nude. Besides, they had heard she was a German spy.

## The Offer

As it happens, she had received an offer to work for the *Nachrichtendienst.* The German consul in Amsterdam, a man named Kroemer, had visited her at her house unexpectedly one night. He did not want what most of her male visitors wanted; he wanted her to gather information for Germany. He was authorized, he said, to offer her 20,000 francs. "That's not much," she said.

### What Does This Mean?

**Nachrichtendienst,** literally translated as "information service," was the name of the German military secret service during World War I.

"Prove yourself to us," he told her, "and you can have all you want." A couple days later, he returned and gave her the money along with three vials of invisible ink—the first to wet the paper, the second to write the message, and the third to go over the paper and render the message invisible. He told her that her agent number would be H-21.

Mata Hari convinced herself that the Germans owed her the money (something about some furs that had been taken away from her on a train and for which she had never been recompensed). She had no intention of spying for the Germans, but she took the money anyway.

## To Spy or Not to Spy

Mata Hari returned to Paris by way of Madrid. On the boat to Madrid, she threw the three vials out the window and promptly put the affair out of her mind.

When she reached Paris and checked into the Grand Hotel, the French police took to watching her. She, they admitted, did not behave like a spy—no mysterious meetings, no furtive behavior. She was completely open with everything, even her amours. But was that not in itself suspicious?

In August 1916, she applied for a pass to visit the town of Vittel where her current lover, a 21-year-old Russian captain named Vadim Maslov, was lying wounded in a hospital and in danger of losing his sight. She seems to have been serious about Maslov. But was Vittel not near the location where a military flying field was being established? When there last, she had made friends with the pilots. What for Mata Hari was as natural as breathing—making friends with men—the *Deuxieme Bureau* thought suspicious.

> **What Does This Mean?**
>
> The **Deuxeime Bureau,** the Second Bureau of the French Army, was the French spy and counterspy service.

When she couldn't get permission to go to Vittel, Mata Hari went in to talk to Captain Georges Ladoux of the Deuxieme Bureau. He told her that they suspected her of German loyalties. She protested her innocence. She told them she had German lovers, but after all, she had had lovers of all nationalities. And her soul was French. They hinted that perhaps she should spy for France. She thought that over. She agreed, if they would have her. They pretended to believe her protestations and gave her a pass to Vittel, but they continued to watch her.

Mata Hari spent most of September in Vittel with her young lover. When she returned to Paris, she told Captain Ladoux that she was willing to work for the Deuxieme Bureau if they would pay her well. She needed the money to marry Captain Maslov and take care of him if he was blinded by his wounds. "I want to be rich enough not to have to deceive Vadim with others," she told Ladoux.

Ladoux agreed to use her as an agent and said he would pay her according to the value of the information she acquired. She offered to get back in touch with the crown prince and seduce him again. She had no doubts about her ability to do it. If France would pay her a million gold francs, she would make the attempt. Ladoux sent her to Holland by way of Spain to spy for France, but he still suspected that she was actually a German agent. She went through Madrid to the port of Vigo and caught the *Hollandia* for Holland. French agents followed her every move until she boarded the ship.

### The Mystery Deepens

In the first decade of the twentieth century, public nudity was rare enough to be a powerful aphrodisiac, and Mata Hari had a variety of rich and powerful lovers—none of them for very long, it seems. As she moved about Europe from one capital city to the next, however, they sufficed. Among her lovers were an official of the Berlin Police named Griebl and briefly, so it is believed, Crown Prince Wilhelm of Germany. But her interests were never political. She was interested in men and in money, not in countries or politics.

# Mistaken Identity

The *Hollandia* stopped at the British port of Falmouth, and British officials came on board to check out the passengers. Then came one of those little twists of fate that separate fact from fiction. No fiction writer would dare include such a transparent device. A British policeman named George Reid Grant thought he recognized in passenger Madame Zelle MacLeod a known German spy, one Clara Benedix, who was supposedly living in Spain disguised as a flamenco dancer. He compared her to a photograph he carried and decided they were the same person. Acting on this misidentification, he had Mata Hari taken off the ship, and he and his wife Janet (a British policeman was not permitted to escort a female prisoner without a chaperon) took her to London on the night train.

For the next three days, she was interrogated by the British police, who grudgingly conceded that she was not Clara Benedix. Sir Basil Thomson, who was then an assistant commissioner and head of the Special Branch, had a long talk with her. She might not be Benedix, but the British had long suspected she was a German spy known as AF 44.

Mata Hari decided to tell Sir Basil her secret. She was a spy, she admitted to him, but for the French. Sir Basil telegraphed Captain Ladoux to verify her story. Naturally, he did not mention that the British had arrested Mata Hari by mistake, thinking her to be Clara Benedix. He just said he had arrested Mata Hari on suspicion of being a German spy. Ladoux, still thinking she *was* a German spy, came to the logical but mistaken conclusion that the British knew what they were doing; they must have some sort of proof that she was indeed a German spy. Ladoux suggested that they send Mata Hari back to Spain.

## In Madrid On Her Own

On 11 December 1916, she was back in Madrid. She cabled to Ladoux for instructions and received no answer, so she decided to get to work on her own. She obtained a list of diplomats then in Madrid and noted that a Captain Kalle was the German military attaché. She wrote to Kalle and asked for an appointment.

At three the next afternoon, she went to see Kalle at his house. He welcomed her, according to her later testimony, offered her a cigarette, and asked her what she wanted. "I am not in the habit of receiving ladies who could have been sent by our enemies," he told her, "but I am sure that with you this is not the case." She laughed and asked him how he could be sure.

"Because I am now a major," he told her. "I was promoted 10 months ago. I'm sure any French agent would know that and would not have written to me as 'Captain'."

Mata Hari told the major that she had lived in Berlin for three years (an exaggeration), that she had been the mistress of a rich German industrialist (true—his name was Alfred Kiepert), and that she had just been arrested in Britain as a German spy. "Who," she asked innocently, "is Clara Benedix?"

Kalle told her he didn't know and that, anyway, German intelligence was not conducted from their embassy in Madrid. He said they had made a deal with the King of Spain that they would only conduct espionage out of their Barcelona consulate. "Right now," he told her, "I'm busy arranging for a U-boat to transfer some German and Turkish officers to the French zone of Morocco. It takes up all my time."

## A German Conquest

Mata Hari said that, before she left Major Kalle, she had "made a conquest of him." Presumably, she meant she had taken him to bed and felt he would now do what she wished. It was her vanity speaking. The U-boat story is a good sign he was using her and was perhaps already aware that she was a French agent. Or maybe he was just trying to impress her to get her into bed. The Germans knew well that the French were aware of their efforts in Morocco.

She wrote Ladoux of her "conquest" and passed on the information about the U-boat. "I await your instructions," she wrote.

# A Chance Meeting

Colonel Joseph Denvignes was in charge of French espionage in Madrid. He met Mata Hari by chance at her hotel the next day, being introduced by two Dutch consuls, and was quickly smitten with her. He was even more smitten when she informed him that she was one of his agents.

The next morning, he went back to her hotel and told her that she should go back to Kalle and get more information about the U-boat operation. This was not wise, as even Mata Hari realized, for it was bound to make Kalle suspicious if he wasn't already. But for the smitten Denvignes, it was probably an excuse to have breakfast with his seductive new spy.

**No Mystery Here**

Kalle probably knew she had been seeing Denvignes. The lovesick French colonel, breaking every rule of espionage, had shown up at the Ritz at every mealtime for three days before he left and had dinner with her.

A few days later, after asking Mata Hari to come live with him and "brighten up my apartment," Denvignes left for Paris. That afternoon she went to have three o'clock tea with Major Kalle. His attitude toward her had suddenly changed. "You have certainly passed on what I told you [about the U-boats]," he told her. "The French are sending messages all over the place to find out where those officers landed."

"It wasn't me," she told him. "How do you know what the French are telegraphing?"

"We have the key to their radio cipher."

Now that would have been worth knowing except it almost certainly wasn't true. Picture an intelligence chief telling a (presumed) enemy spy that he has broken the cipher. Even in those easy and innocent times, that one wouldn't have washed.

"If it was known that I told you about the U-boat," Kalle told her, "I would be in trouble in Berlin." Kalle then took her to bed and proceeded to get into even more trouble in Berlin. He told her that the Germans knew the French were dropping spies behind German lines by airplane—a novelty in 1916—and that German spies carried invisible ink crystals under their fingernails. It was all what today would be called disinformation. The Germans already knew that the French knew that the Germans knew about the French airplane spies, so that information was useless. And the bit about the invisible ink was made up, perhaps to see if French counterintelligence would start examining the fingernails of suspected spies.

Mata Hari thought it was her subtle wiles in the bedroom that had caused the major to spill all. To keep up her pretense of wanting to help the German cause, she told Kalle whatever she could think of. She didn't have any military information, but she did have the latest Paris gossip. She told him that there was antagonism between the French and British soldiers, that there were food shortages in certain areas, and that

Princess George of Greece was having an affair with Aristide Briand, the Prime Minister of France. The princess was trying to get her lover to help her husband claim the Greek throne or so gossip had it. Kalle listened patiently to the gossip and gave her 3,500 pesetas in cash (worth about $650, which was about six months' salary for an average working man back then).

## Back to Paris and Disaster

Having acquired several bits of what she thought was important military information, Mata Hari now decided it was time to go back to Paris.

On her return to Paris, Colonel Denvignes promptly left for Madrid, and Captain Ladoux was never in when she called. She tried desperately to get in touch with Vadim Maslov, her Russian lover, and to raise money to pay her hotel bill. She spent a lonely Christmas in Paris, but in late January 1917, Maslov was able to leave the front for a while and spend some time with her. On January 15, having found in her movements no indiscretions of the sort that would interest counterintelligence, the French police stopped following her. If she was aware of it, she might have thought they were finally beginning to believe she was on their side. She would have been mistaken.

## Arrested

On February 13, two policemen came to her room at the Hotel Elyse-Palace and arrested Mata Hari for "espionage, attempted espionage, complicity in espionage, and intelligence with the enemy to further his enterprises."

After a preliminary interrogation by Captain Pierre Bouchardon, an army examining magistrate, she was taken to the Saint-Lazare women's prison and was put in a padded cell, a normal precaution for new prisoners to discourage suicide attempts. Several days later, she was transferred to cell number 12, which had previously housed Mme. Caillaux, who had shot the editor of *le Figaro*; Mme. Steinheil, who had murdered a president of the Republic; and Marguerette Francillard, who had been executed as a spy.

## The Intercepts

Why had she been arrested? Three days before, someone in the war ministry had prepared a report for the military governor of Paris. The report, which is unsigned, claimed that "the woman Zelle" belonged "to the Cologne intelligence center, where she is listed under the designation of H-21."

On 13 December 1916, when Mata Hari was in Madrid, her German friend Kalle sent a message to Berlin that was intercepted by the French:

> H-21 informs us: Princess George of Greece, Marie Bonaparte, is using her "intimate relations" with Briand [the French prime minister] to get French support for her husband's access to the Greek throne. She says Briand's enemies would

welcome further defeats in the war to overthrow him. Britain has political and military control of France. French are afraid to speak up. General offensive planned for next spring.

### The Mystery Deepens

In 1916, there was a radio intercept station on top of the Eiffel Tower. From there, the French intercepted the German radio traffic between Madrid and Berlin, and they could read much of the coded traffic. The British had obtained the German diplomatic code book in Persia in 1915 and had shared their find with the French. In 1916, the Germans discovered that their code was compromised and changed it. But the French decryption experts soon broke the new code and were able to resume reading the German messages.

H-21 must be a German agent. But who? Two weeks later, on Christmas Day, they received another intercept:

Give H-21 3,000 francs and say that:

(1) The results obtained are not satisfactory;

(2) The ink which H-21 received cannot be developed by the French if the correspondence paper is treated in conformity with instructions before and after the use of invisible ink;

(3) If, in spite of that, H-21 does not want to work with invisible ink, the agent should come to Switzerland and, from there, communicate his [or her, it's the same in French] address to A.

A further message tells Berlin that he (Kalle) has given H-21 3,500 pesetas. More messages followed, culminating with one saying that H-21 was going to Paris and that her servant, Anna Lintjens, should be given 5,000 francs to get to her.

That certainly pinned down whom they were talking about. Anna Lintjens had been Mata Hari's maid since 1909.

There are two problems with the conclusion that Mata Hari was indeed a German agent. The first is that it seems a bit strange to carefully refer to an agent as only H-21 through a series of messages and then carelessly give the real name of the agent's maid. The second is that all the H-21 messages were sent in the old code, the code that the Germans knew the French could read. You can almost hear Captain Kalle laughing as he thought of the trouble he was going to get that amateur spy Mata Hari in when the French decoded those messages.

For six months, Mata Hari was confined in a cold, damp, rat-infested cell while Bouchardon, the examining magistrate, talked to her and about her and tried to decide what to do with her. Her attorney, Edouard Clunet, a 74-year-old ex-lover who had been her attorney for 11 years, was an expert in corporate law, but he hadn't tried a criminal case in 20 years. He tried to get her released or at least transferred to a hospital, but he was ignored. At first, Bouchardon was not told of the existence of the intercepted messages, which were the shaky foundation of the charges against Mata Hari. Then, when he was told, he was not told the most important fact—that they had been sent in the old code.

### No Mystery Here

Why did the Germans reveal H–21's identity when they knew it would certainly get Mata Hari a stiff prison sentence if not the firing squad? Perhaps it was in revenge for the 20,000 francs she had taken from Kroemer and done nothing for. The *Nachrichtendienst* disliked being cheated.

Bouchardon kept coming back to the 20,000 francs she had been given by Kroemer. (She told them about this sometime during her months of interrogation.) Was that not a lot of money for someone who had done nothing? "Not for me," she told him, surprised that he would question a man giving her the modern equivalent of about $10,000.

She defended her befriending of soldiers, saying she did it sometimes out of sympathy, sometimes for money. With Kalle, she admitted telling him some gossip but insisted it was merely that—gossip. After all, if she was to become a French spy, she would have to do something.

Then why did he give her 3,500 pesetas? "We were intimate," she said. "He offered me a ring. I don't like that sort of jewelry and declined it. I assumed the money was a sort of replacement." She said that all her actions were to deceive the Germans. Bouchardon suggested they could equally be interpreted as deceiving the French. She was not a trained spy, she reminded him, adding: "I had never done spying before. I have always lived for love and pleasure."

On 24 July 1917, Mata Hari was tried by court-martial for being a German spy. The texts of the German diplomatic messages, incriminating enough if one did not know of the two-code situation, were rewritten by one or more of her accusers to be even more damning. There is no doubt that the sentence was certain before the trial began.

The three judges were convinced of her guilt. The presenting of evidence was a mere formality to taking her out and shooting her. Clunet firmly believed her to be innocent and did his best, but he was banging his head against the stone wall of Gallic intransigence. The judges *knew* her to be guilty, and they were not about to be swayed by contrary evidence.

"I am not French," she told the court. "I have the right to cultivate any relations that may please me. The war is not a sufficient reason to stop me from being a cosmopolitan." The court did not agree. France, at the time, was suffering from mutinies in the ranks and defeatism at home. Examples had to be made. Mata Hari was an example. Maitre Clunet's attempts to get her clemency were ignored. There was an appeal by the Dutch government, in the name of their queen, on behalf of this Dutch subject who didn't really seem to have done anything serious enough to be shot for. It was denied.

On October 15 at 5 A.M., Margaretha Zelle MacLeod was taken to the rifle range at Vincennes where the sentence of execution was read aloud. Witnesses relate that she was resigned and unafraid. She was loosely tied to a tree. She declined a blindfold. At 5:47 A.M., she was shot by a 12-man firing squad.

The story of Mata Hari's life is one of almost continual romance and mystery. But was she really a spy? If so, for whom did she spy? Nothing in the secret records that have been released has positively answered either question. But it seems clear that the reason so many people were willing to believe such bad things about her was that she had many lovers and she took her clothes off in public.

# Mata Hari—the Myths

Everyone who had anything to do with espionage in World War I was said by someone to have been Mata Hari's lover, her boss, her antagonist, or all three. Admiral

Canaris, head of the Abwehr (German Military Intelligence) in World War II, spent a few days in Madrid. He is supposed to have been Mata Hari's lover while there. The problem is that, when he was there, she wasn't. Some writers even have Canaris as the man who sent her to her doom in France, although at the time he was merely a young naval officer, and it was 20 years before he would be running agents.

A surprising number of people claimed to have been present at her death. According to A.E.W. Mason, a popular novelist of the time, he returned to England in October 1916, stopping for a few days in Paris. There he claims to have witnessed the execution of Mata Hari, the famous spy, and a few weeks later he was back again in Spain, this time on Lord Abinger's yacht. One wonders if he noticed there was a war on.

Mata Hari supposedly was responsible for the torpedoing of somewhere between three and a couple of dozen ships in the Atlantic by passing on their position to an agent waiting for the information in Madrid. How she could possibly have obtained such information is not told. The names of the ships are not recorded anywhere. Kurt Singer, a populizer of espionage subjects, writes that there was a plot by one of her lovers to put blank cartridges in the firing squad rifles, and that was why Mata Hari "faced death so bravely." How the examining doctor would have avoided noticing that she was not dead is not mentioned.

The final myth was that Mata Hari's daughter Banda was executed for espionage many years later. One story has her spying for the Americans against the Japanese in Indonesia during World War II; another has her spying for the Americans against the Chinese during the Korean War. Both stories end with her getting shot. The problem with these romances is that Non, Margaretha Zelle MacLeod's only daughter, died suddenly at the age of 21, probably of an embolism.

Regardless of truth, Mata Hari has come into the language and into the universal myth that is our past. She is now one with Casanova, Cleopatra, and Joan of Arc.

---

### The Least You Need to Know

➤ Mata Hari was born Margaretha Gertrude Zelle in Holland.

➤ She adapted the name Mata Hari and, to make a living, took up exotic dancing with few clothes on.

➤ Part of her legend—that she was very successful at dancing and had a succession of rich and powerful lovers—is true.

➤ The other part of her legend is exaggerated. She got involved in World War I espionage only by accident and was never really a spy.

➤ The French authorities, after going through the motions of a trial, executed her as a spy.

---

# Part 5

# Inhuman Events

*The present fascination with what we call "flying saucers" began in 1947, when a formation of strange craft was seen flying among the Cascade Mountains in Washington State. Since then the number of sightings has grown into the thousands, with more being reported practically every week. Are they scout craft, forbidden to make contact with the local natives? Are they from another dimension, unable to interact with this planet in any meaningful way (although we can see them)? Do they land every night, kidnap hundreds of people, and subject them to tests? Are the tales of abduction true?*

# Chapter 21

# Saucers That Fly

**In This Chapter**

➤ UFO references throughout history

➤ Flying cigars and flying saucers

➤ Project Sign, Project Grudge, Project Blue Book

➤ A pilot is killed chasing a UFO

➤ The Robertson Panel and the Condon Report

People have reported seeing mysterious flying objects at least as far back as there are written records. They have seen angels, dragons, fiery wheels, chariots, many-headed monsters, sailing ships, great pearls, whirling disks, giants, children, frogs, and islands. Many *UFOlogists* consider these ancient accounts to be indications that our ancestors saw and attempted to describe mysterious flying objects that may well have been what we today would call *UFOs*.

It was after World War II that the unidentifiable sightings began to be described as UFOs by the Air Force, and the term "flying saucers" became common parlance. It was only then that the occupants of these mysterious craft came to be seen not as products of earthly origin but as possible visitors from other worlds.

### No Mystery Here

The popular image of the "flying saucer"—round with a dome on top—is only one of the shapes commonly reported by observers. UFOs have also been described as egg-shaped, cigar-shaped, pencil-shaped, boomerang-shaped, and triangular. Triangular craft seem to be the most commonly sighted these days.

### What Does This Mean?

The term **UFO,** an acronym for unidentified flying object, was coined by the Air Force in 1947 to give it something more official-sounding to call the objects than "flying saucers." A **UFOlogist** is a person who studies reports of UFOs to try to determine just what was seen.

# What the Ancients Saw

Spotting strange objects in the sky is an ancient pastime dating back at least as far as biblical days. Several passages of the Bible have been interpreted by UFOlogists as possible descriptions of ancient alien astronauts or their vehicles.

## *Ezekiel*

A particular favorite is the book of Ezekiel. Here, for example, are a few verses from chapter 1 (verses 4 through 9) that could be read as an attempt to describe a visitation by an alien being:

> And I looked and behold, a whirlwind came out of the north, a great cloud, and a fire infolding itself, and a brightness was about it, and out of the midst thereof, as the color of amber, out of the midst of the fire.

> Also out of the midst thereof came the likeness of four living creatures. And this was their appearance; they had the likeness of a man.

> And every one had four faces and every one had four wings.

> And their feet were straight feet; and the sole of their feet was like the sole of a calf's foot: and they sparkled like the color of burnished brass.

> And they had the hands of a man under their wings on their four sides; and the four had their faces and their wings.

> Their wings were joined one to another; they turned not when they went; they went every one straight forward.

This could be a description of extraterrestrial scout craft or aliens in space suits, or it could be a hallucination, or it might just be an allegory for we know not what.

## The Pharaoh Sees a Circle of Fire

The Royal Annals of Egyptian Pharaoh Thuthmosis III (quoted in *Flying Saucers Have Landed* by Desmond Leslie and George Adamski, translated by Boris Rachewiltz) record that:

> In the year 22 [1479 B.C.], third month of winter, sixth hour of the day ... the scribes of the House of Life found it was a circle of fire that was coming in the sky. (Though) it had no head, the breath of its mouth (had) a foul odor. Its body one rod long and one rod large. It had no voice ... Now, after some days had passed over these things, Lo! They were more numerous than anything. They were shining in the sky more than the sun ... Powerful was the position of the fire circles. The army of the king looked on and His Majesty was in the midst of it. It was after supper. Thereupon, they went up higher directed toward the South.

A foul-smelling circle of fire ... not your usual description of a UFO, but we can't think of any *identified* flying object that fits the description.

## The Great Pearl

Sometime around the year 1060, an object described as "a great pearl" was seen rising from several lakes or swamps in southern China. These sightings went on for a period of several weeks. One observer reported that, as the pearl hovered over a lake, a door in the pearl opened and a bright light shone from inside. Then the door closed and the pearl flew away.

## The Prefect

In 1619, Christopher Scherer, the prefect (like a governor) of a canton in Switzerland, wrote to a friend that he had seen ...

> ... a fiery shining dragon rise from one of the caves on Mount Pilatus and direct himself rapidly toward Flu[um]elen to the other end of the lake. Enormous in size, his tail was longer and his neck stretched out ... in flying he emitted on his way numerous sparks.

Around the same time, other people reported seeing a long cylinder-shaped device flying around Flüelen. Similar craft were seen that year flying over an Italian monastery and a small town in Scotland.

In all probability, these stories were not deliberate falsehoods, as we assume some of the more outrageous modern UFO stories to be. A made-up story would probably be more circumstantial, more terrifying, and more closely related to existing myth.

A great three-headed dragon lands nearby and eats up two or three townspeople—that sort of thing. These people saw events they could not understand and related them in terms they were familiar with. Were they sightings of what we call flying saucers? We'll never know for sure, but that's as good a guess as any.

### The Mystery Deepens

A 2,000-year-old Hindu religious poem called the "Mahabharata" describes the destruction caused by a flying disk called a *vimana*: "Varanasi burned, with all its princes and their followers, its inhabitants, horses, elephants, treasures and granaries, houses, palaces, and markets. The whole of a city that was inaccessible to the gods was thus wrapped in flames by the vimanas and was totally destroyed."

### What Does This Mean?

The **dirigible** is a lighter-than-air craft with a rigid, usually cigar-shaped frame filled with hydrogen or helium gas and a passenger compartment called a gondola suspended beneath it. The Goodyear blimp looks like a dirigible (though technically it isn't because it doesn't have a rigid frame).

# Flying Silver Cigars

The last half of the nineteenth century was full of reports of flying cigars, flying sausages, and other flying phalluses that Freud would have found fit fruit for his fanciful philosophizing. But I digress.

It is true that people interpret what they see in terms of what they know, so it isn't surprising that in the 1890s, when someone saw or thought he saw a strange object flitting across the sky, he described it as a *dirigible*. After all, the newspapers and magazines were regularly printing stories about inventors who had almost perfected their lighter-than-air craft and were going to demonstrate them any day now.

People not only saw these flying cigar shapes at a time before any dirigibles were actually flying, they watched them land and had conversations with the pilots and crew.

The year 1897 was a particularly good one for airship sightings. Visitations from these impossible craft were seen in almost every state, and one or two of them apparently crisscrossed the country. Sightings of what were often described as "flying silver cigars" were reported sequentially in town after town.

## Alex Hamilton Loses a Cow

It was Monday, 19 April 1897, when Kansas farmer Alex Hamilton had a run-in with an airship. He and his son Wallace and a tenant named Gid Heslip heard "a noise among the cattle" at about ten thirty that night. They went to look and Hamilton found "that an airship was slowly descending upon my cow lot, about 40 rods (600 feet) from the house." They approached and got a good look:

> It consisted of a great cigar-shaped portion, possibly 300 feet long, with a carriage underneath. The carriage was made of glass or some other transparent substance alternating with a narrow strip of some material. It was brightly lighted within and everything was plainly visible—it was occupied by six of the strangest beings I ever saw. They were jabbering together, but we could not understand a word they said.

According to Hamilton, the airship lassoed a two-year-old heifer and flew off with the animal dangling beneath. A farmer some miles away found the hide, legs, and head of the unfortunate cow lying in his field the next day.

An account of Hamilton's adventure, along with a notarized statement by some of the town's leading citizens to the effect that Hamilton was known for "truth and veracity," appeared in the weekly *Yates Center Farmer's Advocate* and was picked up and reprinted by newspapers all over the country.

### No Mystery Here

Among the observers of a great "cigar-shaped" object in the skies over Europe in 1882 were E. Walter Maunder, an astronomer at the Royal Observatory in Greenwich, England, and Pieter Zeeman of Holland, who would win the Nobel Prize for physics 20 years later.

### Here There Be Dragons

It has been suggested that Alex Hamilton was a member of a local liars club. A fixture of nineteenth-century America, these clubs fostered the telling of tall tales in as realistic a manner as possible.

## Space Ship Hits Windmill

On 19 April 1897, the *Dallas Morning News* reported that an airship had hit a windmill near Aurora, Texas. The pilot of the ship was killed, and his body was buried in the town cemetery. Further …

> Mr. T.J. Weems, the U.S. Signal Service officer at this place and an authority on astronomy, gives it as his opinion that [the defunct pilot] was a native of the planet Mars. Papers found on his person—evidently the records of his travels—are written in some unknown hieroglyphics and cannot be deciphered.

**269**

How Mr. Weems knew what Martian pilots look like is not recorded. Neither the body nor an appropriate headstone can be found in the Aurora cemetery, and the pilot's papers are nowhere to be found. Nobody in town remembered there ever being a windmill in the vicinity when they were interviewed by UFOlogists in the 1970s. There is now no way to tell whether the *Dallas Morning News* was hoaxed or whether an alien spaceship indeed crashed and traces of it were subsequently removed.

# The Very First Flying Saucers

For the next half-century, things were pretty quiet in the realm of mysterious flying objects, but after World War II, a new class of UFOs flew into view. Whereas previous sightings had usually been explained as earthly inventors testing their inventions, these new craft were almost immediately regarded as being from another world. Some researchers decided they were the products of a sort of mass hysteria brought on by the dropping of the atomic bomb and fears of a coming atomic war. Others thought the "visitors" were real and were here to investigate a planet just entering the atomic age.

## Kenneth Arnold Sees Skipping Saucers

The first sighting of what became known as "flying saucers" happened on Tuesday, 24 June 1947. Kenneth Arnold, a 32-year-old private pilot, was flying through the Cascade mountain range in Washington State, when he saw "a chain of nine peculiar looking aircraft flying from north to south at approximately 9,500 feet elevation." Arnold timed the craft with his wristwatch and estimated they were traveling at about 1,660 miles an hour.

Arnold told his story to Nolan Skiff, an editor at the *East Oregonian* newspaper. He described the craft he saw as being 45 to 50 feet long, not quite that wide, about three feet thick, sort of boomerang-shaped, and "mirror-bright." He said they flew "like a saucer would if you skipped it across the water."

The story was put out on the AP news wire, and the "flying saucer" was born. Here is that first story as it went out over the wire. Note the details it gets wrong:

> PENDLETON, Ore. June 25 (AP)—Nine bright saucer-like objects flying at "incredible speed" at 10,000 feet altitude were reported here today by Kenneth Arnold, a Boise, Idaho pilot who said he could not hazard a guess as to what they were.
>
> Arnold, a United States Forest Service employee engaged in searching for a missing plane, said he sighted the mysterious objects yesterday at three P.M. They were flying between Mount Rainier and Mount Adams, in Washington State, he said, and appeared to weave in and out of formation. Arnold said that he clocked and estimated their speed at 1,200 miles an hour.

On the same day Arnold saw his boomerang-shaped craft, there were more than a dozen other reported sightings of strange objects in the skies of Oregon and Washington. Within the next week, there were more than 25 sightings.

**The Mystery Deepens**

During World War II, American and British pilots often reported seeing mysterious objects that came to be called "Foo Fighters" accompanying them on missions. They were described as small disks, no more than a couple feet in diameter, that would fly alongside the plane for a while and then either zoom off or disappear. At night, small balls of fire might be seen. There was fear that these might be some sort of enemy secret weapon, but after the war, it was discovered that enemy pilots reported seeing similar objects. Nobody on either side had any explanation for them.

# The Mysterious Death of Captain Thomas Mantell

At about one in the afternoon on Wednesday, 7 January 1948, the Kentucky State Highway Patrol began getting reports of a strange saucer-shaped object about 200 or 300 feet in diameter crossing the state. The Highway Patrol called Godman Air Force Base just outside of Louisville, Kentucky, to see if the military knew anything about this.

The officers in the control tower at Godman had no idea what the object might be, but they didn't doubt the patrol's story. They could see the thing for themselves right out the tower window. They called over the base commander, Colonel Hix, to take a look. There it sat—floated, flew, whatever—in the distance, round, high, and bright silver.

At 1:45 P.M., a flight of four Air National Guard F-51 Mustang fighter planes was close to arriving at Godman. Colonel Hix called the flight leader, Captain Thomas Mantell, and asked him if he and his flight would fly over to the object and see if they could figure out what it was before they landed. One of the pilots begged off; he didn't have enough fuel left. The other three planes climbed to an altitude of 10,000 feet and searched for the silver saucer. At first they couldn't spot it, but then Mantell called in: "I see something above and ahead of me and I'm still climbing." At this point, the other two pilots broke off the chase since they weren't equipped with oxygen. (It's dangerous to go much over 12,000 feet without oxygen.)

### No Mystery Here

"The planet Venus" would become a common explanation for UFO sightings by people who didn't want to believe there was anything mysterious to be seen. "Swamp gas" (methane gas produced by rotting vegetation and possibly ignited by spontaneous combustion) and "mass hysteria" were also offered as explanations.

Moments later Mantell radioed, "It's above me and I'm gaining on it. I'm going to 20,000 feet." That was Captain Mantell's last transmission. Two hours later, word came in that his plane had crashed. The investigation of the crash revealed that the canopy lock on Mantell's cockpit was still in place, showing that he had not tried to parachute from the plane during its more than three-mile fall to the ground.

The official explanation was that Mantell had been chasing the planet Venus, which was very bright at that time. Well, it may have been bright, but it almost certainly wasn't visible at one in the afternoon. Next guess?

The one plausible explanation, which didn't come out until four years later, was that Captain Mantell had been chasing a Navy skyhook balloon. The balloons, part of a then-classified research project, flew—or perhaps drifted is a better description—at an altitude of about 60,000 feet. In the thin air at that altitude, they expanded into a silvery globe several hundred feet across. The lack of any perspective might have made a balloon appear much closer than it actually was.

The only thing wrong with this theory is that there is no record of a skyhook balloon being released on 7 January 1948. Some of the records have been lost, however, and it's possible that there *was* such a launch. On the other hand, perhaps Captain Mantell lost his life chasing a true UFO.

### The Mystery Deepens

About a year later, another National Guard pilot, Second Lieutenant George Gorman, gave chase to a UFO that he spotted when he was attempting to land his F–51 Mustang at the Fargo, North Dakota, airport. He closed in on it and later reported that "it was from six to eight inches in diameter, clear white, and completely round, with a sort of fuzz at the edges. It was blinking on and off. As I approached, however, the light suddenly became steady and pulled into a sharp left bank." The official report concluded that Gorman had been chasing a lighted weather balloon. The only balloon in the area, however, was too far away and was headed in the wrong direction. And balloons seldom pull into sharp left banks.

# The UFO Blitz

At 2:45 A.M. on Saturday, 24 July 1948, Captain Clarence S. Chiles and his copilot, John B. Whitted, were flying their Eastern Airlines DC-3 near Montgomery, Alabama, when they saw "a bright glow" and watched as a "long rocket-like ship" flew past them. It was "a wingless aircraft, 100 feet long, cigar-shaped, and about twice the diameter of a B-29, with no protruding surfaces, and two rows of square windows ... From the sides of the craft came an intense, fairly dark blue glow ... like a fluorescent factory light." The ship "pulled up with a tremendous burst of flame from the rear and zoomed into the clouds at about 800 miles an hour." A passenger who happened to be awake also saw the strange craft. Investigators also turned up a ground maintenance crewman at Robins Air Force Base in Georgia who had seen the same thing an hour earlier.

This was only one of a few thousand reports that came in over the next few years—many of them from pilots, aircrew, or other observers who could be trusted to tell the difference between an airplane's landing lights and a UFO. When trained observers start turning in reports like that, the Air Force has to take notice. The crafts reported might be mass hysteria or swamp gas or sightings of the planet Venus, but they might also be secret weapons from some other country, or even extraterrestrial visitors.

## *The Air Force Investigates*

In late 1947, the Air Force began Project Sign, a serious attempt to evaluate the wave of flying saucer reports it was getting. One of the first things it did was invent the term UFO (unidentified flying object) as a more respectable name for the sightings it was investigating. The Technical Intelligence Division of Air Material Command at Wright Patterson Air Force Base in Dayton, Ohio, collected and analyzed the reports.

**Mysterious Comments**

"The phenomenon reported is something real and not visionary or fictitious ... It is recommended that ... Headquarters, Army Air Forces issue a directive assigning a priority, security classification, and Code Name for a detailed study of this matter."

—General Nathan F. Twining
Commanding Officer
Air Material Command, 1947

The officers assigned to Project Sign created a standard questionnaire on which the sightings could be reported (see Appendix C). It's a lot easier to compare and evaluate reports when they're all written on the same form.

At the end of 1948, Project Sign issued a Top Secret Estimate that said there were good reasons for believing we were being visited by extraterrestrial beings. The Chief of Staff of the Air Force, General Hoyt S. Vandenberg, said it was nonsense. He said no tangible proof had been recovered, and he refused to accept the findings. He ordered all copies of the report destroyed. He was the boss, and all copies of the report are believed to have been destroyed. The information we have about it comes second hand from people who claim to have read it before it was burned.

After Project Sign became defunct, the Air Force initiated Project Grudge. Who had the grudge against whom was not specified, but my guess is that the Air Force was investigating all the continuing civilian—and worse, Air Force—sightings only grudgingly. It was tacitly understood by the officers of Project Grudge that bringing in any reports that couldn't be explained by the planet Venus or some sort of optical illusion would not be a good career move.

## Flying Saucers Over the Capital

On Saturday, 19 July 1952 at 11:40 P.M., seven blips appeared on the radar screen in the traffic control tower at Washington National Airport. Controller Edward Nugent called over his supervisor, Harry G. Barnes, and together they watched as the blips approached Washington D.C. from the south-southwest at about 100 miles an hour. Barnes called Tower Central, the final approach radar center, and was told that they, also, had the objects on their screen. One of the objects, "a bright orange light," was visible from the tower window.

These were the first of what became a full night of UFO sightings over the capital. Thousands of people saw the objects, which included orange balls, bright blue-white balls, and shiny white craft that moved and turned at incredible speeds. The evening came to an impressive close when hundreds of people watched seven white disks pass over the White House and the Capitol building.

The runways at Andrews Air Force Base, the closest military field, were closed for repairs, so no chase craft could take off from there. By the time intercept fighters arrived from Newcastle Air Force Base in Delaware at around 3 A.M., the strange intruders were gone.

### What Does This Mean?

A **temperature inversion** is a condition where warm air doesn't rise because it is trapped near the ground by a layer of heavy colder air above it. Droplets of moisture caught in the air can cause a lensing effect that creates mirages—distorted images of things that are actually many miles away. Temperature inversions can also be responsible for bad smog conditions.

One week later, the UFOs came back for a repeat performance. This time, F-94 Interceptor jets came up to meet them. The pilot of one of the interceptors reported that four "white glows" circled his plane for a few moments before shooting away at a speed so great he was unable to follow.

The Air Force held a press conference on Tuesday, 29 July, and attributed the whole thing to *"temperature inversions."* Why these particular temperature inversions should bring sightings of objects never seen before was not explained.

# Project Blue Book

In 1952 Project Grudge was replaced by Project Blue Book, headed by Captain Edward J. Ruppelt, who was determined to get at the truth of the UFO phenomena. For a while, UFO sightings were taken seriously and were investigated in earnest. But this spirit of investigative earnestness didn't last.

## The Robertson Committee

On Wednesday, 14 January 1953, a five-man panel of scientists was assembled by the CIA to consider the UFO question. The panel was headed by H.P. Robertson, head of the Weapon System Evaluation Group at the Defense Department. Naturally, this became known as the Robertson Panel. The scientists decided that some 95 percent of the sightings were hoaxes, cases of mistaken identity, or natural phenomena. It therefore concluded that the unexplained 5 percent, no matter how good the sighting or how trustworthy the informant, must also be unworthy of study.

Thereafter, Project Blue Book became more of a vehicle for debunking UFO reports rather than investigating them with an open mind, which the Robertson Panel judged to be a waste of time and resources.

### Here There Be Dragons

The Robertson Panel's conclusion was, to say the least, bad science. It's on a par with the eighteenth-century scientists who decided that, because none of them had ever seen stones falling from the sky, all reports of meteorites must be hoaxes.

But the persistent 5 percent of the sightings that defied easy explanation caused the Chairman of the Department of Astronomy at Northwestern University, J. Allen Hynek, who was the scientific consultant to Project Blue Book, to complain that the Air Force was trying to disparage or ignore the evidence that some of the UFO sightings were actually worth investigating.

The Air Force responded to the criticism from Hynek and others by appointing a committee formed at the University of Colorado and headed by Dr. Edward Condon, the former director of the National Bureau of Standards, to do a thorough investigation. For starters, Dr. Condon pinned down just what they were talking about:

> An unidentified flying object (UFO, pronounced OOFO) is here defined as the stimulus for a report made by one or more individuals of something seen in the sky (or an object thought to be capable of flight but seen when landed on the earth) which the observer could not identify as having an ordinary natural origin, and which seemed to him sufficiently puzzling that he undertook to make a report of it to the police, to government officials, to the press, or perhaps to a representative of a private organization devoted to the study of such objects.

### Mysterious Comments

*"By far the most usual way of handling phenomena so novel that they make for a serious rearrangement of our preconceptions is to ignore them altogether, or to abuse those who bear witness to them."*

—William James, *Pragmatism* (1907)

The Condon Report, as the committee's massive (1,485 pages in the government Printing Office edition) report came to be called, examined UFOs from every angle and found no persuasive evidence of extraterrestrials.

**Mysterious Comments**

"During the years that I have been its consultant, the Air Force has consistently argued that the UFO's were either hoaxes, hallucinations, or misinterpretations of natural phenomena. For the most part I would agree with the Air Force. As a professional astronomer ... I have had no trouble explaining the vast majority of the reported sightings.

"But I cannot explain them all. Of the 15,000 cases that have come to my attention, several hundred are puzzling, and some of the puzzling incidents, perhaps one in 25, are bewildering. I have wanted to learn much more about these cases than I have been able to get from either the reports or the witnesses.

—J. Allen Hynek, "Are Flying Saucers Real?" *The Saturday Evening Post*, 17 December 1966

# Bye-Bye, Blue Book

In 1969, Project Blue Book was officially disbanded, agreeing with the Condon Report that there was no point in continuing to hunt for UFOs because there was nothing to find. The following conclusions were made:

1. No UFO has ever posed a threat to national security.
2. No evidence has been submitted to indicate that UFO sightings represent technological developments beyond the range of our scientific knowledge.
3. There is no evidence that sighted objects are of an extraterrestrial nature.

What didn't become known for some years, however, was that the Condon Committee was irredeemably biased from the get-go. As one of the organizers wrote in a private memo as the project got underway ...

> Our study would be conducted almost exclusively by nonbelievers who, although they couldn't possibly *prove* a negative result, could and probably would add an impressive body of evidence that there is no reality to the observations. The trick would be, I think, to describe the project so that, to the public, it would appear a totally objective study but, to the scientific community, would present the image of a group of non-believers trying their best to be objective but having an almost zero expectation of finding a saucer.
>
> —University of Colorado Assistant Dean Robert J. Low

The Condon Report, of course, ended neither the sightings of UFOs nor the search for explanations of their existence, purpose, and origin. In the next two chapters we'll take a closer look at where the continuing story of UFO sightings and "close encounters" has taken us in the recent past.

---

### The Least You Need to Know

➤ Some UFOlogists believe that some biblical descriptions refer to ancient astronauts.

➤ In the late nineteenth century, many people saw "silver cigars" flying about the sky.

➤ In 1947, private pilot Kenneth Arnold became the first person to see what later became known as "flying saucers."

➤ The United States Air Force investigation of the sightings quickly turned into an attempt to explain them away as either bogus or of natural origin.

➤ The Condon Report was written with a built-in bias against UFO reports being true.

---

# Chapter 22

# The Roswell Incident

## In This Chapter

➤ The Roswell Incident

➤ Roswell rediscovered

➤ Area 51

➤ Majestic-12

Probably the most famous incident in UFO history occurred at Roswell, New Mexico, beginning on 13 June 1947. William W. "Mac" Brazel, foreman of the J.B. Foster ranch, found bits of debris from something that had crashed about seven miles from the ranch house. The debris was spread over an area about 100 yards wide and maybe 1,000 yards long, and it seemed to be made up of "rubber strips, tinfoil, a rather tough paper, and sticks."

Brazel told his wife about the debris, and a couple weeks later they went to the spot to collect samples to bring into the nearby small town of Corona to see whether anybody knew what it was or where it had come from. Nobody did. It wasn't from a conventional weather balloon. Weather balloons were regularly lofted from the nearby Air Force base, and Brazel had previously seen the debris from several of them on the ranch property. This was different.

It was 24 June 1947, 10 days after Brazel's initial spotting of the debris field, that Kenneth Arnold saw his skipping saucers over the Cascade Mountains. Flying saucers were, you might say, in the air. There had been dozens of sightings of mysterious flying objects from all over the country, and the newspapers were full of flying saucer reports. Brazel thought that maybe what he had found was debris from one of these flying saucers. The next Monday, 7 July, when he was in Roswell, he told Sheriff George Wilcox about it.

# The Air Force Takes a Look

Sheriff Wilcox called the nearby Army Air Field, and they sent two officers to investigate. Wilcox also told a reporter for the local Roswell paper about the "flying disk," and the paper's headlines the next day read: "RAAF Captures Flying Saucer on Ranch in Roswell Region."

The two investigating officers, Major Jesse A. Marcel, intelligence officer of the 509th Bomb Group, and Captain Sheridan Cavitt, the group's counterintelligence officer, arrived at the ranch too late in the evening to see anything, so they stayed overnight and went out the next morning. Brazel showed them the debris field, and they collected what objects they could find and took them back to their base.

### The Mystery Deepens

The morning after the investigating officers looked at the debris field the base public relations officer issued a press release that probably seemed like a good idea at the time. In part it said ...

> "The many rumors regarding the flying disc became a reality yesterday when the intelligence office of the 509th Bomb Group ... was fortunate enough to gain possession of a disc through the cooperation of one of the local ranchers and the sheriff's office of Chaves County."

## *Meanwhile, Back at Headquarters ...*

The collection of crash debris was transferred to Eighth Army Air Force Headquarters at Carswell Air Force Base near Fort Worth. There, Warrant Officer Irving Newton examined it and decided it was from a large radar reflector attached to some of the weather balloons to follow their flight from the ground.

Brigadier General Roger M. Ramey, the commanding officer of the Eighth, held a press conference on the evening of Tuesday, 8 July, to refute the earlier press release. "The wreckage is in my office now," he explained, "and as far as I can see there is nothing to get excited about." He explained Warrant Officer Newton's identification of the debris as from a radar reflector, posed for pictures holding pieces of something-or-other, and the reporters present were mollified. The story of the crashed flying saucer disappeared from the papers, and that seemed to be the end of it.

The rash of flying saucer sightings seemed to taper off around then, at least for a while. As *Newsweek* magazine put it in its 21 July 1947 issue …

> Where the flying saucers had gone, no one knew last week and few cared. Saucer-eyed scientists blamed the whirling phenomena on (1) optical illusions followed by (2) mass suggestions. As quickly as they had arrived, the saucers disappeared into the limbo of all good hot-weather headlines.

### Mysterious Comments

"Some of the supposed meteor explosions in our atmosphere might be saucers from Venus or other planets, driven by intelligent creatures. I think it is very stupid for human beings to think no one else in the universe is as intelligent as we are."

—Rear Admiral George Dufek, U.S.N. (as quoted in *Flying Saucers: Top Secret* by Donald Keyhoe)

# Roswell Rekindled

In 1980, William Moore and Charles Berlitz rediscovered the Roswell story and decided there was more to it than a crashed weather balloon. After interviewing Jesse Marcel, the Air Force intelligence officer who had gathered up the detritus from the Foster ranch, and everyone else they could find who had been around at the time, they came up with a strange and fascinating scenario, which they detailed in their book, *The Roswell Incident*.

Here is a précis of the story they tell:

> Shortly after passing over the town of Roswell, New Mexico, during the night of Wednesday, July 2, 1947, a UFO was hit by lightning, causing some bits of the craft to fall off over the Foster ranch. The saucer finally crashed 150 miles to the west, in an area of New Mexico called the Plains of San Agustin.

### No Mystery Here

Mr. and Mrs. Dan Wilmot reported seeing a UFO "shaped like two inverted saucers facing mouth to mouth" passing over their house in Roswell headed northwest during the evening of Wednesday, 2 July 1947. Their account appeared in the same edition of the *Roswell Daily Record* that ran the story of the crash on the Foster ranch.

On Thursday morning after the crash, according to Moore and Berlitz, a soil conservation engineer named Grady L. Barnett found the crash site and was shortly joined by a couple of archeologists who were in the area. There they saw the wreckage of a saucer-shaped ship as well as the bodies of some humanoid extraterrestrials about four feet tall.

A short while later, soldiers arrived from White Sands Missile Test Range and strongly suggested that the civilians vacate the site. The military authorities sealed off the area and suppressed the story so well that the saucer crash soon became a weather balloon, and no hint at all came out about the bodies of the little aliens.

Jesse Marcel remembered that the thin bits of metal he collected at the ranch crash site were so strong that they couldn't be dented with a sledgehammer and that the debris "was nothing that came from earth." Why he decided to take a sledgehammer to the thin bits of metal, he didn't say.

In addition to the super-strong metal, the military also collected some light slender I-beams with strange hieroglyphic symbols written in what appeared to be an alien language.

That's the story they told, and it sold a lot of books.

# The Plot Thickens

*The Roswell Incident* was the first of a torrent of books about whatever it was that happened in the New Mexico desert that evening. Each book presented new and even more amazing facts about the Roswell happening, and they soon took on all the qualities of a modern myth.

## Articles of Faith

It is now an article of faith among many UFOlogists that something strange and wonderful happened in the sky over Roswell, New Mexico, on that June night in 1947. Many people believe one or more of the following:

➤ That the military had something to hide regarding the incident

➤ That the truth includes a crashed flying saucer and the bodies of several little aliens

➤ That the saucer bits and the bodies were taken away to an Air Force Base, or possibly to the fabled *Area 51,* for study

➤ That one or more of the aliens might still have been alive

➤ That the military is actively *back-engineering* the mechanisms found on the downed saucer

➤ That the government is secretly in touch with the saucer-people and is making some sort of deal with them that will have a great effect on our lives when it is revealed

## A Different Truth

There is some truth to this. The Air Force now admits that it was hiding something about the Roswell crash, but the truth the Air Force admits to is not the truth UFO believers want to hear.

At the time of the incident at Roswell, the Air Force was conducting a top-secret program code-named Project Mogul. Under this program, they were lofting large weather balloons carrying specialized instruments to detect pollutants that would be carried through the upper atmosphere as a result of Soviet nuclear weapons testing. It was one of these secret balloons, the Air Force believes, that crashed on the Foster ranch outside of Roswell, New Mexico.

The Roswell research crowd has had various reactions to the Air Force's explanation. Some maintain it is just another cover-up. Some believe it's probably true but has nothing to do with what happened at Roswell. At least a couple of writers now maintain that the saucer hit the Mogul balloon, and that's why they *both* crashed.

### What Does This Mean?

**Area 51,** also known as Groom Lake, is alleged to be a secret Air Force base about 90 miles north of Las Vegas. It is supposedly where top-secret military aircraft, from the U-2 to the Stealth fighter, were test flown.

**Back-engineering** is a technician's term for taking something apart to see how it works and how to make more.

Personally, I'm doubtful. I think that finding real aliens in a crashed alien spaceship would be the most important story of the past 2,000 years. The number of people who would have known about it—from base guards, to civilians, to scientists—would have been too large to keep such a secret all these years. Instead of one or two people with dubious claims, we would have had a dozen people with detailed stories—some probably with photographs. After the first dozen, with the secret out, 100 more would have come forward. A story like this is just too exciting to keep from your spouse, your mother, your best friends, and after all these years, your children and grandchildren.

## Roswell Reading

Many books have appeared since Moore and Berlitz wrote *The Roswell Incident,* some with pro-alien leanings and some with anti-alien leanings, and all based on ever-newer and more deeply probing research. Here are a few:

**Pro-Alien**

*Crash at Corona: The U.S. Military Retrieval and Cover-Up of a Ufo,* by Don Berliner and Stanton T. Friedman

*The Truth About the Ufo Crash at Roswell,* by Kevin D. Randle & Donald R. Schmitt

*Beyond Roswell: The Alien Autopsy Film, Area 51, & the U.S. Government Coverup of Ufos,* by Michael Hesemann & Philip Mantle

*The Roswell Ufo Crash: What They Don't Want You to Know,* by Kal K. Korff

*The Roswell Message: 50 Years On—The Aliens Speak,* by Rene Coudris

**Anti-Alien**

*The Real Roswell Crashed-Saucer Coverup,* by Philip J. Klass

*Ufo Crash at Roswell: The Genesis of a Modern Myth,* by Benson Saler, Charles A. Ziegler, and Charles B. Moore

# The Body Is the Evidence

In 1995, 48 years after the whatever-it-was crashed at Roswell, a film appeared from nowhere that once again set the Roswell pot to boiling. It supposedly was shot by an Air Force cameraman back in 1947 to record the autopsy of one of the alien casualties of the crashed Roswell saucer.

The Fox TV network aired a documentary called *Alien Autopsy* to show the footage. At first viewing, it is very convincing. But then the *Star Wars* films are very convincing to some people, and the techniques of fooling people with film get better and cheaper every day.

The owners of the film have refused to allow it to be examined and dated by experts at Kodak, which puts its authenticity in serious doubt. It's hard to imagine that anyone holding such a film would hesitate to have it authenticated if they believed it to be real.

# Majestic-12

The government conspiracy theory has been popular among UFOlogists since the first serious UFO books began to appear in the early 1950s. In May 1987, a document appeared that springboarded the concept of government conspiracy to stranger and more vast proportions than anything dreamed of in previous philosophies.

The document that "surfaced" was related to the Roswell incident and was on a roll of 35mm film sent anonymously to television producer Jaime H. Shandera. Dated 18 November 1952, the document was supposedly a preliminary briefing for president-elect Eisenhower about a top-secret operation code-named Majestic-12. As the document explained:

> OPERATION MAJESTIC-12 is a TOP SECRET Research and Development/ Intelligence operation responsible directly and only to the President of the United States. Operations of the project are carried out under control of the Majestic-12 (Majic-12) Group which was established by special classified executive order of President Truman on 24 September 1947, upon recommendation by Dr. Vannevar Bush and Secretary [of Defense] James Forrestal.

TOP SECRET / MAJIC

EYES ONLY

* TOP SECRET *
* * * * * * * * * * * * *

0 0 3

EYES ONLY

COPY ONE OF ONE.

On 24 June, 1947, a civilian pilot flying over the Cascade
Mountains in the State of Washington observed nine flying
disc-shaped aircraft traveling in formation at a high rate
of speed. Although this was not the first known sighting
of such objects, it was the first to gain widespread attention
in the public media. Hundreds of reports of sightings of
similar objects followed. Many of these came from highly
credible military and civilian sources. These reports resulted in independent efforts by several different elements
of the military to ascertain the nature and purpose of these
objects in the interests of national defense. A number of
witnesses were interviewed and there were several unsuccessful
attempts to utilize aircraft in efforts to pursue reported
discs in flight. Public reaction bordered on near hysteria
at times.

In spite of these efforts, little of substance was learned
about the objects until a local rancher reported that one
had crashed in a remote region of New Mexico located approximately seventy-five miles northwest of Roswell Army Air
Base (now Walker Field).

On 07 July, 1947, a secret operation was begun to assure
recovery of the wreckage of this object for scientific study.
During the course of this operation, aerial reconnaissance
discovered that four small human-like beings had apparently
ejected from the craft at some point before it exploded.
These had fallen to earth about two miles east of the wreckage
site. All four were dead and badly decomposed due to action
by predators and exposure to the elements during the approximately one week time period which had elapsed before their
discovery. A special scientific team took charge of removing
these bodies for study. (See Attachment "C".) The wreckage
of the craft was also removed to several different locations.
(See Attachment "B".) Civilian and military witnesses in
the area were debriefed, and news reporters were given the
effective cover story that the object had been a misguided
weather research balloon.

* * * * * * * * * * * * * *
* TOP SECRET *
* * * * * * * * * * * * * *

EYES ONLY TOP SECRET / MAJIC

EYES ONLY

T52-EXEMPT (E)

0 0 3

*A photocopy of pages 3, 4, and 5 of the original six-page Majestic-12 document.*

TOP SECRET / MAJIC

EYES ONLY
••••••••••••••
• TOP SECRET •
••••••••••••••

<u>EYES ONLY</u>                                           COPY <u>ONE</u> OF <u>ONE</u>.

A covert analytical effort organised by Gen. Twining and
Dr. Bush acting on the direct orders of the President, resulted in a preliminary concensus (19 September, 1947) that
the disc was most likely a short range reconnaissance craft.
This conclusion was based for the most part on the craft's
size and the apparent lack of any identifiable provisioning.
(See Attachment "D".) A similar analysis of the four dead
occupants was arranged by Dr. Bronk. It was the tentative
conclusion of this group (30 November, 1947) that although
these creatures are human-like in appearance, the biological
and evolutionary processes responsible for their development
has apparently been quite different from those observed or
postulated in homo-sapiens. Dr. Bronk's team has suggested
the term "Extra-terrestrial Biological Entities", or "EBEs",
be adopted as the standard term of reference for these
creatures until such time as a more definitive designation
can be agreed upon.

Since it is virtually certain that these craft do not origin-
ate in any country on earth, considerable speculation has
centered around what their point of origin might be and how
they get here. Mars was and remains a possibility, although
some scientists, most notably Dr. Menzel, consider it more
likely that we are dealing with beings from another solar
system entirely.

Numerous examples of what appear to be a form of writing
were found in the wreckage. Efforts to decipher these have
remained largely unsuccessful. (See Attachment "E".)
Equally unsuccessful have been efforts to determine the
method of propulsion or the nature or method of transmission
of the power source involved. Research along these lines
has been complicated by the complete absence of identifiable
wings, propellers, jets, or other conventional methods of
propulsion and guidance, as well as a total lack of metallic
wiring, vacuum tubes, or similar recognizable electronic
components. (See Attachment "F".) It is assumed that the
propulsion unit was completely destroyed by the explosion
which caused the crash.

••••••••••••••
• TOP SECRET •
••••••••••••••

<u>EYES ONLY</u> TOP SECRET / MAJIC          T52-EXEMPT (E)

EYES ONLY

004

TOP SECRET / MAJIC
EYES ONLY

005

••••••••••••••
* TOP SECRET *
••••••••••••••

COPY <u>ONE</u> OF <u>ONE</u>.

A need for as much additional information as possible about
these craft, their performance characteristics and their
purpose led to the undertaking known as U.S. Air Force Project
SIGN in December, 1947.  In order to preserve security, liason
between SIGN and Majestic-12 was limited to two individuals
within the Intelligence Division of Air Materiel Command whose
role was to pass along certain types of information through
channels.  SIGN evolved into Project GRUDGE in December, 1948.
The operation is currently being conducted under the code name
BLUE BOOK, with liason maintained through the Air Force officer
who is head of the project.

On 06 December, 1950, a second object, probably of similar
origin, impacted the earth at high speed in the El Indio -
Guerrero area of the Texas - Mexican boder after following
a long trajectory through the atmosphere.  By the time a
search team arrived, what remained of the object had been almost
totally incinerated.  Such material as could be recovered was
transported to the A.E.C. facility at Sandia, New Mexico, for
study.

Implications for the National Security are of continuing importance in that the motives and ultimate intentions of these
visitors remain completely unknown.  In addition, a significant
upsurge in the surveillance activity of these craft beginning
in May and continuing through the autumn of this year has caused
considerable concern that new developments may be imminent.
It is for these reasons, as well as the obvious international
and technological considerations and the ultimate need to
avoid a public panic at all costs, that the Majestic-12 Group
remains of the unanimous opinion that imposition of the
strictest security precautions should continue without inter-
ruption into the new administration.  At the same time, con-
tingency plan MJ-1949-04P/78 (Top Secret - Eyes Only) should
be held in continued readiness should the need to make a
public announcement present itself.  (See Attachment "G".)

••••••••••••••
* TOP SECRET *

TOP SECRET MAJIC
EYES ONLY                          T52-EXEMPT (E)

005

It told of the creation of the 12-member Majestic-12 (also known variously as Majic 12 and MJ-12) Group to control the operation, and it discussed the replacement of Secretary Forrestal, who died suddenly in 1949, with General Walter B. Smith. All the people listed are real and held posts in the government or in civilian life that would qualify them for inclusion in such a committee.

## A Closer Look

The document explained that a UFO had crashed in "a remote region of New Mexico" and that, along with the wreckage, the bodies of four small, human-like beings had been recovered. Secrecy was maintained by telling reporters that the object had been "a misguided weather research balloon."

So far so good. Although it's doubtful whether the military—or any other basically bureaucratic organization—could have been prepared and able to act so promptly and efficiently in response to a completely unexpected event, it is at least within the realm of possibility.

Here's where the plot thickens. The scientists could not determine what the method of propulsion for the crashed craft had been. "Research along these lines has been complicated by the complete absence of identifiable wings, propellers, jets, or other conventional methods of propulsion and guidance, as well as a total lack of metallic wiring, vacuum tubes, or similar recognizable electronic components."

Some alien writing was found among the wreckage, but "Efforts to decipher these have remained largely unsuccessful." The word "largely" would seem to imply that some bits of writing were, indeed, deciphered. If so, the deciphering of even a small sample of a truly alien language, written in an unknown alphabet, would rank as a truly great achievement.

## Other Questions

On 6 December 1950, this document would have us believe, "a second object, probably of similar origin, impacted the earth at high speed in the El Indio–Guerrero area of the Texas–Mexican border after following a long trajectory through the atmosphere." It burned up when it hit, leaving little evidence for investigators.

Now accidents do happen, but consider a civilization advanced enough to cross interstellar space and traverse our skies without detection—or at least interception—for an extended period of time. To crash two vehicles within four years seems a bit careless.

Someone in Salt Lake City turned a copy of the MJ-12 documents over to the FBI. After a hasty investigation, the FBI concluded that the documents were phony, wrote BOGUS across the face of its copy, and filed and forgot the whole thing.

Some UFOlogists, who presumably were inclined to believe the story, examined the letter included as Appendix A of the Majestic-12 documents, which was purported to be from President Truman to Secretary Forrestal. In an example of open-minded scrutiny that government officials would do well to emulate, they determined that the president's signature was a forgery—a tracing of the signature from another document.

Nonetheless, some people continue to believe the documents are true; others believe that, whether MJ-12 is true or not, the idea of governmental conspiracy that inspired it is anything but a hoax.

### No Mystery Here

The UFOs/Aliens section of About.com, an Internet news and information service, ran a poll asking this question: "Do you believe that the U.S. recovered an extraterrestrial craft at Roswell, NM in 1947?" Of the more than 300 respondents, 75 percent answered "Yes." Of course, this might have been biased by the predisposition of the people who would check out that Web site.

---

IUP SECRET
EYES ONLY
THE WHITE HOUSE
WASHINGTON

September 24, 1947.

MEMORANDUM FOR THE SECRETARY OF DEFENSE

Dear Secretary Forrestal:

As per our recent conversation on this matter, you are hereby authorized to proceed with all due speed and caution upon your undertaking. Hereafter this matter shall be referred to only as Operation Majestic Twelve.

It continues to be my feeling that any future considerations relative to the ultimate disposition of this matter should rest solely with the Office of the President following appropriate discussions with yourself, Dr. Bush and the Director of Central Intelligence.

*The Majestic-12 letter with President Truman's forged signature.*

# The Continuing Story

In 1998 and 1999, a barge load of new documents relating to the Majestic-12 saga have come to light—letters from President Franklin Roosevelt to important government and military figures, more letters from President Truman, letters from President Eisenhower, and a variety of briefing and technical documents. All in all, more than 2,000 new pages of material have come into the hands of UFO researchers. Some of them are obvious fakes—wrong dates, wrong information—but some of them might be genuine. Time, we all hope, will tell.

---

### The Least You Need to Know

➤ The crash of what the Air Force claimed was a weather balloon near Roswell, New Mexico, started a UFO cottage industry that is still growing.

➤ The Roswell story has grown to include crashed flying saucers and alien bodies and a complex government conspiracy.

➤ Papers were discovered in 1987 that told of a secret operation called Majestic-12 initiated after the 1947 Roswell crash.

➤ The FBI determined that the Majestic-12 documents, which related the finding of the bodies of four aliens, were bogus.

---

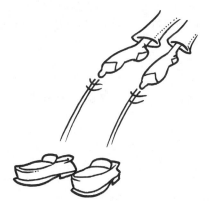

# Chapter 23

# Those Who Got Carried Away

## In This Chapter

➤ The close encounter of Betty and Barney Hill

➤ The abduction phenomenon

➤ Hypnosis vs. the truth

➤ The final answer

In the world of UFOs, there is no more controversial subject than the question of actual alien encounters—people who claim to have spoken with aliens, or gone for rides with them in space ships, or been abducted from their cars or living rooms. In this chapter we'll look at the full range of these encounters, from the ones that seem so plausible that it's hard not to believe them to the ones that seem so bizarre that it's hard to believe anyone would dare make up such a story.

## The Interrupted Journey of Betty and Barney Hill

On the night of Tuesday, 19 September 1961, Betty and Barney Hill were driving to their home in New Hampshire after spending a holiday in Canada. They were on Route 3 somewhere south of Lancaster when they noticed a very bright star near the moon—a star that seemed to be getting bigger and brighter as they watched. It was probably a satellite crossing the sky, Barney decided, and they stopped the car to watch it through a pair of binoculars.

### Here There Be Dragons

One of the great problems with UFO research has always been the wide range of encounters, from sightings to multiple abductions, claimed by contactees. Some of them may be true, some are surely false, and the UFOlogist has only his or her common sense backed by experience as a guide. But everyone's experience is different, and one person's common sense is another's folly. It is important to remember that some people will go to great lengths to fool you just for the sheer pleasure of success.

### No Mystery Here

For the story about scientific search for intelligent life elsewhere in the universe, how it is being done, and what we hope to find, see Chapter 10, "Beginnings and Endings."

Whatever it was, it didn't move in a straight line, so it couldn't be a satellite. Barney decided it must be an airplane. Betty wasn't so sure, but she couldn't think of anything else it might be. After a minute, they drove on.

## Close Encounters of the Fourth Kind

The object seemed to be keeping up with them as they drove. Whether it was actually following them or they just happened to be going in the same direction was impossible to tell. But now the object was close enough to see in some detail. It was a circular disk "as wide in diameter as the distance between three telephone poles," as Barney later described it. A row of windows went around it, and two fins with red lights stuck out of the rear.

The disk halted over a field by the road. Barney stopped the car to get a better look. He walked toward the immense craft, which seemed to be hovering about 50 feet off the ground, and he could make out figures at the windows gazing out at him. When he was about 75 feet away, a door in the craft opened. Barney became convinced that they were going to try to capture him, so he ran back to his car and drove off.

A short while later, the Hills heard a strange beeping noise and found that they were enveloped in some sort of haze. When they emerged from the haze, to the continued sounds of the beeping noise, they realized that an indefinite amount of time had passed, but the car was still moving and Barney was still driving it.

## Enter the Air Force

The next day Betty called the local Air Force base to tell them about their experience. Barney didn't want to talk about it, but he agreed to go over it with the Air Force officer by phone.

The Hills' story was written up for Project Blue Book (see Chapter 21. "Saucers That Fly"), but the Air Force classed it with the "insufficient data" group since the

Hills couldn't provide information about the craft's location or maneuverability. Barney, who was sensitive about the subject and didn't want to be laughed at, didn't tell the Air Force investigators about the beings he had seen in the giant disk.

### The Mystery Deepens

The earliest known alien abduction claim occurred in Brazil on 16 October 1957. Twenty-six-year-old Antonio Villas-Boas was driving his tractor on his father's farm when a red glowing saucer landed in a nearby field on three spindly legs. Villas-Boas's tractor stalled. Several human-looking beings emerged in white protective clothing and helmets with eye slits and took him inside. They undressed him and sponged him down with a thick, odorless liquid. Later, a short female with blonde hair, large slanted eyes, and a conspicuous lack of clothing entered the room. She said nothing but began to caress him, and he responded. Afterward, the woman pointed to her stomach and then to the ceiling, indicating that their baby would be born elsewhere. Then they kicked him off the ship and departed. Villas-Boras said he felt he had been used like a good stallion to improve their breed.

## Two of Our Hours Are Missing

When the Hills thought it over and discussed the experience with a few UFO investigators, they came to realize that they could not account for two hours of that evening's experience. They retraced their route several times but couldn't reconstruct just where they had gone. Several landmarks, including a diner they believed they had pulled up to, were nowhere to be found.

### No Mystery Here

At approximately the same time as the Hills were interacting with their UFO, the radar operator at nearby Pease Air Force Base reported a brief contact with an unidentified object.

Because of the missing hours, because Betty had been suffering from vivid nightmares involving alien abduction, and because Barney had developed a severe case of persistent insomnia, the Hills sought out a sympathetic psychiatrist. After visiting several, they settled on Dr. Benjamin Simon of Boston. Simon gave each of them separately a course of hypnotic therapy during which they separately came to remember having been kidnapped by aliens and taken aboard the alien ship.

### No Mystery Here

*The Interrupted Journey,* the Hills' story, was made into a movie in 1975 called *The UFO Incident.* James Earl Jones played Barney.

Since the Hills' experience, analysts have searched for repressed memories of alien encounters in their patients—a controversial practice we'll discuss later in this chapter—but Dr. Simon was not particularly interested in UFOs. He was most interested in simply helping his patients, and he felt that the objective reality of their claims was not relevant to his clients' successful treatment. His job was to draw the details of the experience out of the Hills' memory and help them deal with it.

Over a six-month period, he drew from each of his patients a story of what occurred during the missing two hours. He instructed them to forget the details after each session; they would remember the whole story only when the therapy ended. If his hypnotic instructions "took," they could not compare stories during the six months of their therapy. And yet the stories told by Betty and Barney Hill were almost identical.

After a distorted version of their story appeared in a local newspaper, the Hills decided that it might be better if they told the story themselves. With the help of author John G. Fuller, they did. The book, *The Interrupted Journey,* sold very well and opened the door for others who realized that they, too, had been abducted by aliens.

## Examined by Aliens

The story that the Hills came to believe as a result of their hypnotic therapy sessions is a frightening one and can well explain Betty's nightmares and Barney's insomnia. We should point out that Dr. Simon at no time accepted the Hills' recovered memories as true. He believed they were a sort of *folie á deux,* with Barney picking up on his wife's nightmares and subconsciously joining her in creating an alien abduction fantasy.

### What Does This Mean?

**Folie á deux** (French for "madness of two") is a term used in clinical psychology to describe a common delusion shared by two people when one of them seems to have influenced the other.

As put together from the tapes of the Hills' sessions with Dr. Simon (which were passed on to Fuller with the Hills' permission), what happened to them—or what they believed happened to them on that September night—was this:

Barney, acting on some compulsion he didn't understand, left Route 3 and took a side road that led deep into the woods. He stopped when six men stepped in front of the car. It wasn't until later that he realized they weren't human. Three of them removed him from the car, and three went to get Betty. Barney felt a compulsion to keep his eyes closed during most of the rest of what happened; it seemed less scary with his eyes closed.

They were taken inside the aliens' ship, and each was examined in a different room. Betty didn't feel Barney's compulsion to keep her eyes closed, and she talked with her captors, who answered her with some sort of mental telepathy. They put her on a table and examined her carefully, head to foot. At one point, they stuck a needle in her navel. When she cried out in pain, the alien she described as the leader put his hands over her eyes and told her that it would stop hurting, and it did. She was told that the needle was a "pregnancy test."

**The Mystery Deepens**

There are 10 signs said to indicate that a person may have had a close encounter of the fourth kind:

Missing periods of time

Frequent nightmares about aliens and/or UFOs

Sleep disorders

Unusual body sensation upon waking

Unexplained marks or scars on the body

A feeling of being watched

Repeated sightings of UFOs

Partial memory of an alien encounter

Sudden spontaneous healing of a long-term illness or affliction

Phobic reaction to discussions about UFOs or extraterrestrials

While she was waiting for them to finish examining Barney, she asked the leader where the ship had come from. He reached into a drawer and pulled out a star map.

"… there were all these dots on it," she described. "And they were scattered all over it. Some were little, just pin points. And others were as big as a nickel. And there were lines, they were on some of the dots, there were curved lines going from one dot to another. And there was one big circle, and it had a lot of lines coming out from it. A lot of lines going to another circle quite close, but not as big."

Betty said the heavy lines on the map showed the trade routes among the stars, the solid lines were places the aliens went occasionally, and the broken lines represented expeditions, according to the leader. Betty later drew what she could remember of the map, and her drawing was reproduced in Fuller's book.

The Hills' story of their experience, however bizarre it may seem to those outside the UFO field, has a ring of truth to it. For one thing, although later abductees had the Hills' story to use as a basis for their own (assuming they either consciously or unconsciously made it up), the Hills had no earlier story to copy. And each of their stories, independently told, agreed substantially with the other's. And their obvious honest reluctance to tell the story at all adds to their veracity. It may not have happened as they told it. They may have imagined the whole thing. But we think that, whatever actually happened, they believed their story as they told it.

### The Mystery Deepens

In 1968, an Ohio schoolteacher named Marjorie Fish created a three-dimensional map of the stars within 50 light years of the sun, concentrating on stars that were like our sun and that might be presumed to have accompanying planets. She was able to find a correspondence between her map and the map Betty Hill had drawn from memory. If Fish's map is right, the stars Zeta 1 Reticuli and Zeta 2 Reticuli are the centers of an interstellar trading empire. When the story and the maps were published in an article in *Astronomy* magazine and comments from astronomers were solicited, some thought the correspondence between the two maps was interesting. Others, including Carl Sagan, thought it was no better than pure chance.

## The Abductee Parade

Ever since the Hills discovered that they had been abducted and examined by aliens, a wave of abduction experiences has engulfed the country. The number of people who believe, or profess to believe, that they have been abducted has climbed well into the thousands. And those are just the ones willing to talk about it. By extrapolation from the results of polls conducted by professional organizations (Gallup, Roper), some UFOlogists have estimated the number of abductees in the United States to be somewhere between a couple hundred thousand and a few million. That isn't a very high percentage considering the population of the country (300 million), but it certainly suggests a lot of very busy aliens out there.

In 1994, Dr. John E. Mack, a professor of psychiatry at Harvard Medical School, published a book called *Abduction: Human Encounters with Aliens*. The careful, scholarly presentation of material, along with the professional credentials of the author, imbued the subject with a certain measure of respectability. Mack advanced the startling notion that, not only are people being abducted by aliens, some are being abducted repeatedly. As he put it:

> Although some abductees may recall only a single dramatic experience, when a case is carefully investigated it generally turns out that encounters have been occurring from early childhood and even infancy. Indications of childhood abductions include the memory of a 'presence' or 'little men' or other small beings in the bedroom; recollections of unexplained intense light in the bedroom or other rooms... instances of being floated down the hall or out of the house; close-up sightings of UFOs; vivid dreams of being taken into a strange room or enclosure where intrusive procedures were done ...

Mack's findings, which gave an air of scholarly respectability to the UFO abduction phenomenon, are very popular with UFOlogists. But we think there is a very real possibility that Mack's use of hypnotic regression (see below) has created the phenomena that he has discovered.

### Mysterious Comments

"There is a tendency, sometimes called role expectancy, on the part of many hypnotic subjects to comply with what they perceive as the expectations of the hypnotist. This can occur even when the hypnotist has no conscious investment in the outcome, and is of course even more likely to occur when the hypnotist does have such an investment. This is more the rule than the exception in hypnosis."

—Michael B. Conant, Ph.D., Director of The Institute for Bioenergetics and Gestalt in Berkeley, California

## At the Sound of My Voice

The aliens seem to practice democracy. In his book *Secret Life,* David M. Jacobs describes over 325 hypnosis sessions conducted on more than 60 abductees. His subjects were "by and large, average citizens who were not trying to commit a hoax, and who, with one exception, were not mentally disturbed. They were Protestant, Catholic, Jewish, white, black, male, female, younger, older, professional, nonprofessional, married, single, divorced, employed, unemployed, articulate, and inarticulate."

## What Does This Mean?

A **hypnotic trance** is a suggestible state induced in a subject by a hypnotist in which the hypnotist can verbally impose an artificial view of reality on the subject. The subject will see what the hypnotist tells him (or her) is there, hear what the hypnotist directs him to hear, and remember what he is instructed to remember.

A **hypnotic regression** is an attempt to take the subject back in time to an earlier period in his life while under hypnosis.

## Here There Be Dragons

Writer Larry Janifer, in drawing up a list of benefits for joining the Galactic Union, concluded that the most important was the right not to be considered food by any other member.

Some people claim to have remembered the abduction experience spontaneously; whatever mental block the aliens used to suppress the memory didn't work. But most of what we might call the reputable ones—the abductees whose stories are somewhat convincing (if you accept the idea of aliens who communicate telepathically, levitate, and walk through walls)—have come to the memory of their abduction unwillingly through the help of a hypnotherapist. They seek therapy for a variety of reasons: depression (one of the most common), agitation, insomnia, anxiety, or a variety of phobias. The therapist puts the subject in as deep a *hypnotic trance* as he or she can manage and *regresses* the person back in time to look for the source of the problem. What the therapists often find is an alien abduction experience paralleling that of the Hills—even from people who claim to have never read or even heard of the Hills' story.

Whatever one thinks of their stories, one cannot doubt the sincerity of most of these people. They are remembering, in great detail, what to them are truly horrifying experiences. In some cases, they remember being abducted repeatedly since childhood, with the aliens sometimes emerging through walls to get them and taking them out the same way.

## *Try to Remember*

There is some question about the validity of recovering such memories through hypnosis. The problem starts with the hypnotic process itself. A subject under hypnosis wants to please the hypnotist. Objective truth is the first casualty of this desire. A hypnotized subject will tell you what he or she thinks you want to hear and will even remember what he or she thinks you want him or her to remember. This memory will be, to the subject, a real one. Even when the hypnotist is trying as hard as possible to be objective in guiding patients hypnotically, subjects can pick up on the most subtle, unintentional cues of the therapist.

Many therapists, let it be said, are far from objective. They believe they are going to get a certain type of response; they probe unintentionally or otherwise for this response, and that is the response they, more often than not, get. Therapists who believe in alien abduction must guard against leading their subjects to similar beliefs—just as therapists who were molested as children must guard against helping their subjects "remember" similar experiences. It's no secret that "false" memories of therapy patients have been on the rise in recent years. This should serve as a warning to consider, along with an abductee's memories, the therapist's preexisting world view.

# The True UFO

The case for UFOs is based almost entirely on eyewitness evidence. And eyewitness evidence, as any trial lawyer will tell you, is the worst kind.

The fact that we have no empirical proof of the existence of UFOs doesn't mean they don't exist, however. There are a variety of possible explanations as to what UFOs actually are, although each one comes with a pretty strong caveat:

➤ UFO sightings might indicate visitors from other planets (the most popular contender for the answer). BUT, as far as we know, there is no way to cross interstellar distances without expending an extraordinary amount of time and energy. Still, there might be a way to do it that our science hasn't uncovered yet.

**Mysterious Comments**

Scientist and writer Isaac Asimov was asked whether there might be scientific laws we haven't yet discovered. "Of course there might be," he replied. "But if so, we haven't discovered them yet."

➤ Aliens might be crossing over from another dimension to visit us in this one. BUT, although several current theories of cosmology and physics allow for the possibility of alternate coexisting universes, no theories allow for how one might go about crossing from one to another.

➤ UFO sightings might be secret military experiments from some earth country. BUT, if the technology is as advanced as the reports indicate, where did it come from?

➤ They might be some sort of recurring mass hallucination. BUT, if so, how can people in different areas with no known connection report seeing the same object at the same time?

➤ They might all be hoaxes. The fact that some of them are *certainly* hoaxes tars the rest in the popular mind. BUT why would reputable people with more to lose than to gain by reporting a UFO contact nonetheless claim to have seen— or even been taken aboard—flying saucers?

So the final answer to the UFO question still remains to be written. There have been hoaxes, there have been mistaken reports of weather balloons and the planet Venus, and there have been hypnotically induced tales of contact that just aren't credible, even if the person telling the story obviously believes it. There remain, however, some stories that defy all explanations. Some sightings by pilots and others refuse easy answer; some close contact experiences make one shiver as though one has briefly touched the unknown.

---

### The Least You Need to Know

➤ Betty and Barney Hill saw a UFO in New Hampshire in 1961. Their experience, recalled through hypnosis, was later paralleled by other abductees.

➤ Events recalled under hypnotism are not always trustworthy, though for many abductees this is often the only means of remembering.

➤ The final answer to the UFO question remains to be written.

---

# Part 6
# Unanswered Questions

*Vampires and werewolves and ghouls. Are the legends based on fact, or do they stem from the fears of uneducated peasants? Did you know that some vampire stories from the mid-eighteenth century are well authenticated? Likewise there have been some unimpeachable reports of werewolves. As for ghouls[md]well, some of our modern-day murderers come awfully close.*

*We'll also look at animals that might or might not exist, like the Loch Ness monster and Bigfoot. Finally, for a change of pace, we'll ask the question, "Who really wrote Shakespeare's plays?" We'll bet you thought it was a guy named William Shakespeare, didn't you? Well, it might have been. But maybe[md]just maybe[md]it was someone else.*

# Chapter 24

# The Undead and the Inhuman

**In This Chapter**

➤ The legend of the vampire

➤ The lamia: the first vamp

➤ Lycanthropy legends

➤ Ed Gein and Jeffrey Dahmer

All those frightening beings in horror movies and scary books, all those grotesque creatures that lurked under the bed or peered at you from behind the closet door when you were a child—they're all imaginary, right? There are no ghosts, no ghouls, no zombies, no vampires, no creatures of the night—nothing to fear except fear itself. Right?

The legends of these creatures aren't new; they're hundreds, some of them even thousands, of years old. They may have their roots in the fears of peasants, crouched behind doors closed against the horrors of the night, trembling as the muffled hoofbeats of an unknown night rider pass their cottage on a mysterious errand. Or perhaps there is some truth to them. Perhaps they're distorted memories of ancient practices better forgotten, of unspeakable acts that had best remain unspoken.

These creatures come from somewhere, and the descriptions given of them and their foul practices are eerily consistent among eras and cultures. So bolt the doors, draw the curtains, and let's examine what truth there may be behind the stories of the undead and the inhuman …

# Vampires

Occasionally in Eastern Europe, when workmen are widening a road or digging the foundation for a new building, they come across a body that might be hundreds of years old, buried far from the nearest cemetery. If the burial site is near an old cross-roads, they know the body is probably that of a criminal. In the old days, a criminal couldn't be buried in hallowed ground, and burying him by a crossroads was sup-posed to confuse his ghost and prevent it from returning to the village from whence it came. (In fact, the *gibbets* themselves were erected by crossroads.) With a few rough jokes, the workmen wrap the remains in a bit of can-vas and turn it over to local authorities to be disposed of however they see fit.

**What Does This Mean?**

A **gibbet** is a gallows, particu-larly one in which the hanged man is left to dangle for some time after the execution as a visi-ble warning to others who might be tempted into a life of crime.

But what if the newly unearthed corpse has an aspen stake driven through its chest? And what if it is unusu-ally well preserved? Why, then all jokes stop. The workmen cross themselves, mutter a prayer to St. Dismas or St. Martin, and hastily cover it up again. If the corpse absolutely *must* be moved, they move it gingerly, being careful not to disturb the stake.

For everyone in this part of the world knows that's the way the undead are buried—with a stake driven clear through them to prevent them from rising from the grave at midnight and attacking fowl or swine or small children or, on certain nights when they are most powerful, adults in their beds.

## By Their Names Shall You Know Them

In English, we have adopted the Magyar word for such creatures, *vampir,* which is a cognate with the Bulgarian *vapir* and the Russian *upuir*. The Greeks have their *vryko-lakas* (which may alternately mean werewolf in some areas of Greece), while the Italians and Spanish make do with *vampiro*. The root may come from the Turkish *uber,* which means "witch." The description of the creature and its abilities varies slightly from place to place, but the basic traits are the same.

**What Does This Mean?**

A **vampire** is a reanimated corpse that needs human blood to sustain itself.

The *vampire* is usually regarded as one of the undead—that is, a reanimated corpse. The vampire is not inter-ested in any of the things it cared about in life; it only wants to lure victims to their death and suck their blood—perpetuating the curse that befell it in life, when it too was killed by a vampire that drained it of its blood. It possesses supernatural strength and the hypnotic ability to will people to come to it. It may be able to turn itself into a bat or a wolf or a dog or a cat to approach its prey unnoticed.

It returns to its grave with the daylight. Contrary to common belief, although it shuns daylight, it does not dissolve or shrivel up when the rays of the sun strike it; that is a modern variation that traditionalists will have none of. It does, however, cower in the presence of a cross, and touching it with a cross will cause the point of contact to blister and burn.

A vampire is afraid of fire because it can burn (but then so are we and for the same reason), and it cannot cross running water unless it is closed away from it, as in a ship's cabin or in a closed coffin. Garlic offers protection from a vampire as does putting mustard seeds in front of the door. The vampire, for some reason, is irresistibly drawn to counting spilled mustard seeds, and if enough are scattered about, it will be transfixed in its counting until daylight.

### Here There Be Dragons

Vampire hunters had best wear a cross at all times and equip themselves with garlic and holy water. A circle of holy water will protect the hunter or, if the hunters are clever and lucky, can be used to trap the vampire. The vampire can be kept in its coffin by putting a holy wafer on its chest. It can be killed by driving a stake through it somewhere around the heart; aspen, hawthorn, whitehorn, or maple are the best woods. Beheading the vampire with a sexton's spade will also end its reign of terror.

## The Lamia

An early version of the vampire, complete with the sexual overtones that the modern era has reintroduced to the legend, was the ancient Roman lamia. Described as a supernatural creature that looked like a woman but had unnatural lusts, the lamia would steal children and suck their blood. Its favorite recreation, however, was seducing men and, after a night of wild abandon, sucking their blood as they slept.

Legend has it that the first-century sage and prophet Apollonius of Tyana encountered a lamia while traveling through Corinth. A young man named Menippus, who was a student of Apollonius, fell in love with a beautiful and rich Phoenician lady, and she apparently with him, although he was possessed of nothing save his looks and the cloak on his back. Menippus asked Apollonius to be the guest of honor at his wedding breakfast. The sage agreed, although he normally ate no more than a handful of grain and drank no more than a cup of water. When he arrived at the feast, Apollonius looked around and asked Menippus to whom all the gold and silver goblets and other fine decorations in the hall belonged. "To the lady," Menippus told him. "This cloak is all I possess."

Apollonius lifted a goblet, which was light as gossamer, and perceived the truth. "All this adornment is not reality but a semblance, and thy fine and dainty bride is not a mortal but a vampire, a lamia. These beings are devoted to the delights of Aphrodite, but still more to devouring human flesh."

### Mysterious Comments

"[The lamia] are wont to lust not for love but for flesh; and they particularly seek human flesh and by arousing sexual desire they seek to devour whom they wish."

—Philostratus, *The Life of Apollonius of Tyana*

The lady laughed at him, commenting that philosophers were always spoiling the pleasures of honest people, and asked him to leave. But Apollonius waved his hand and murmured a spell; the goblets disappeared, the plates disappeared, the trappings in the hall fell away, and the cooks and servants turned to dust before their eyes. The lady begged the sage to torment her no more and confessed that she had intended to fatten Menippus before eating him, "for it was her habit to feed upon young and beautiful bodies, because their blood is pure and strong."

This misogynistic view of women as having a hypnotic effect on men akin to that of the vampire resurfaced in the 20th century. In the 1920s, a "vampire," soon shortened to a "vamp," was the slang expression for the type of woman who could use sexual allure to cause a man to do her bidding.

# Welcome, Vampire

The term "vampire," or its equivalent in the various European languages previously mentioned, came into use in the first half of the eighteenth century when a wave of vampire sightings swept Europe accompanied by bouts of mass hysteria. A typical story from the time, as related by Montague Summers in his book, *The Vampire in Europe,* is the account of Arnold Paole.

## Arnold's Story

In 1727, Arnold Paole returned from the Middle East to his hometown of Meduegna, near Belgrade, and bought a farmhouse and two acres of land. He became engaged to a young girl named Nina, the daughter of the farmer next door. Nina saw that Arnold seemed to be constantly depressed and asked him why. He told her that he believed he was fated to die young because of something that had happened to him while he was in the Army.

He was stationed in Kostarta, Greece, he said, and while there was attacked by a vampire. He had managed to subdue the creature, however, after which he found the vampire's grave and killed it. But the experience so unnerved him that he had quit the army as soon as he could and returned to Meduegna. He hoped that he had suffered no ill effects from his adventure with the vampire, but the possibility was preying on his mind.

Arnold's fears, unfortunately, proved true. At the next harvest, he fell from the top of a hay-wagon and was knocked unconscious. They carried him home, where he died shortly thereafter. His body was buried in the local churchyard.

## Arnold Wanders in Death

About a month after he was buried, people reported seeing Arnold wandering around the village at night. Several people claimed he had visited them in the night and that, after he left, they had felt weak and tired. Within a few weeks, several of the people he had visited died mysteriously. The villagers were in a state of panic.

Winter was coming on, and the villagers were glad to stay home at night and lock their doors. But the story spread that Arnold could pass through locked doors and barred windows, and the panic increased.

Finally, it was decided that Arnold Paole's body had to be disinterred and inspected for signs of vampirism. Digging up a body was a serious matter, and an official committee was formed of two Army officers from Belgrade, two Army surgeons, and a drummer boy to carry the surgeons' instruments. The mayor of the village and other notables, along with the church sexton and his assistants, were also present.

## Buried Secrets

When Arnold's coffin was opened, they found the corpse leaning to one side, the mouth agape, the lips covered in blood. "So you have not wiped your mouth since last night's work!" the sexton cried. He straightened the body, and the group scattered garlic over it and drove a stake through it—upon which warm blood spurted from the wound.

The investigators then exhumed the bodies of four people who had died since Arnold and drove whitehorn stakes through them, just to be sure. To be doubly sure, the bodies were removed from the graveyard and were cremated, after which the ashes were replaced in the graves. But that wasn't the end.

### Mysterious Comments

"About half a dozen years after the body of Arnold Paole had been cremated, the infection seems to have broken out afresh, and several persons died apparently through loss of blood, their bodies being in a terribly anaemic and attenuated condition. This time the officials did not hesitate immediately to come with the danger, and they determined to make a complete examination of all the graves in the cemetery to which any suspicion attached."

—Montague Summers, *The Vampire in Europe*

A Commission of Enquiry was set up, and the graves were opened. Some showed the normal stages of decay, but others did not. In the coffin of a 20-year-old woman named Stanya who had died three months before, they found a body untouched by decay, the chest full of fresh blood, and new skin and nails growing on both hands and feet.

Several others were found in this same condition. The necessary measures were once again taken, and this time the outbreaks of vampirism ended in the village.

What are we to think of a legend so well documented, and yet so alien to modern scientific thought? Possibly that the image of the vampire—a superhuman creature that lives on human blood, the very stuff of life, and can compel obedience—is a powerful symbol, what psychiatrist Carl Jung might have called a universal archetype, that fills some need in the human psyche. Fear of death is universal, and here is a creature that rises from the dead and kills the living. But it's just a myth—right?

### No Mystery Here

The surgeons signed the official Commission of Enquiry report, which is dated 1732. Their names were Isaac Siedel, Johannes Flickinger, and Johann Baumgartner. The report presumably still exists in the files of the Belgrade bureaucracy.

# Werewolves? Here Wolves!

The *lycanthropy* legends are truly ancient; accounts of humans being changed into wolves can be found in Greek and Roman mythology. It was one or another of the gods, offended by some slight the human had offered, who did the transforming. The gods took offense easily and many of them took this nasty, shape-changing sort of revenge. Humans were changed not only into wolves but into pigs, cows, sheep, dogs, cats, bears, hyenas, and whatever other creatures might amuse the offended god.

Werewolves, or at least stories about them, were endemic in the middle ages, giving the poor peasant yet one more thing to worry about. The Bohemians called their werewolves *vilkodlak,* according to a lexicon compiled in 1212, while the Slovak name was *vrkolak,* close to the Serbian *vlkoslak* and the Russian *wawkalak.* The Russians also worried about the *oborot,* or shape-changer, another sort of werewolf. The German for werewolf is, strangely enough, *werewolf,* while the Italian is *licantropo* and the French *loup-garou.*

Werewolves, the story goes, can only be killed by burning, by decapitation, or by being fatally stabbed by a silver knife. When guns were invented, it was allowed that a silver bullet would do as well. (Could that be why the Lone Ranger used silver bullets? Was the Old West infested with werewolves?) In the middle ages, there were many reports of men and women running about in the forests as wolves, killing sheep and children and terrorizing the countryside. When caught and tortured, which was how the authorities obtained confessions and was but one more example of the "good old days" that we miss so much, they inevitably confessed and told detailed stories of their crimes.

**What Does This Mean?**

**Lycanthropy** is the power of a human to turn into a wolf. It is also the name for the belief that one can turn oneself into a wolf. There is also kuanthropy, the ability to turn into a dog, and boanthropy, the ability to turn into a cow (which I can't imagine is overly popular).

## The Miraculous Salve

The stories all had a certain uniformity, which makes one suspect that the questioners tortured until they heard what they wanted to hear. A typical werewolf story went something like this:

> I met a stranger in the woods who gave me a salve and a wolf skin. Then he told me that he was the Lord of the Forest (read: "the devil") and that I should take my clothes off and rub the salve all over me. When I did that, I found that I could run through the forest with the speed of the wind and that I had an insatiable hunger for human flesh.

> I found a young girl playing in the woods, and I killed her and ate part of her and threw the rest to the wolves. I don't know where, or who, she was. When I looked down at my body, I saw that my hands and feet had changed into the paws of a wolf. In the morning, I changed back into a man and put my clothes back on.

# A Horrible Illness

Toward the end of the sixteenth century, a minor epidemic of lycanthropy broke out in France. Between one and two dozen cases appeared throughout the country in 20 or 30 years, and the people infected believed they were werewolves without any prompting from the rack or hot pincers.

### Here There Be Dragons

Another 1598 case involved a tailor from Châlons who lured children into his shop or attacked them in the woods, killed them by ripping their throats open with his teeth, and then prepared, cooked, and ate their flesh. A cask full of bones was found at his house, and it proved impossible to determine how many children he had murdered. He was found guilty of lycanthropy and was burned at the stake.

In 1598, some farmers working a field heard screaming in a wood nearby and went to investigate. They discovered two wolves feasting on the mutilated body of a young boy. The farmers were chasing the wolves away when they came upon a half-naked man crouched in the bushes. His hair was long, his beard was matted, and his hands were covered with blood. His fingernails were as long as claws and had shreds of human flesh caked beneath them.

The man, a beggar named Roulet, confessed that he had killed the boy and was eating the corpse when the peasants found him. He claimed that he was able to turn himself into a wolf with the aid of a salve his parents had given him. The two wolves the farmers had seen leaving the corpse were his brother Jean and his cousin Julian, who joined him in his lycanthropic endeavors.

When questioned by the magistrate he repeated that he had killed and eaten the child and that he had become a wolf. "Were you dressed as a wolf?" the magistrate asked. "I was dressed as I am now. I had my hands and my face bloody because I had been eating the flesh of the child."

"Do your hands and feet become the paws of a wolf?"

"Yes, they do."

"Does your head become like that of a wolf—your mouth become larger?"

"I don't know."

Luckily for Jean and Julian, they were able to produce firm alibis for the time in question, and they were not charged. Roulet was taken to a madhouse (a just and fair decision for that time—we often do not do as wisely today).

The werewolf, and to a lesser extent other shape changers, are such common myths, cutting across many cultures and staying with us through the centuries, that it's clear that there is some deep truth in them. Not, perhaps, in reality, but somewhere deep in the human subconscious. In reality, as we know too well, there are human monsters, but they do not do us the favor of changing their shape so that we can easily recognize them.

**310**

# Real Live Ghouls

A *ghoul,* says the *Dictionary of Satanism,* is an evil being that robs graves and feeds on corpses. The name comes from Arabic and describes a demon that lurks in dark places to grab unsuspecting passers-by. If other creatures of the night—vampires, werewolves—are most likely apocryphal (no matter what the vampire lovers say), ghouls—human beings who eat the flesh of their fellows—have been all too real. Here are a few of their stories.

**What Does This Mean?**

A **ghoul** is an evil being that robs graves and feeds on corpses.

## *Ed Gein*

Ed Gein (rhymes with "mean") was born in 1906 and grew up with his brother, Henry, on the family farm outside of Plainfield, Wisconsin. His mother was a strict disciplinarian with a distaste for sex, which may have been intensified by the fact that her husband, Gein's father, was an abusive alcoholic. She warned her children often about the dangers of premarital sex. Gein's father died in 1940, and his brother was killed fighting a fire in 1944.

The following year his mother died of a stroke, leaving Gein alone on a primitive farm with no electricity in a desolate area. After his beloved mother died, he boarded up her bedroom and sitting room, leaving them in a sort of shrine-like state. The rest of the house slowly filled with debris and garbage—and the macabre mementos of his ghoulish experiments.

In 1952, Gein read of the sex-change operation performed on Christine Jorgensen, one of the first such procedures. The operation fascinated him. He studied textbooks on anatomy. He began to visit the local graveyard and dig up female corpses to dissect. He believed he could turn himself into a female by clothing himself in female body parts, which he wore as he danced under the moon at night. He made a belt of nipples and a vest of a human torso, complete with breasts. By this time he was, by any standard, completely mad.

**No Mystery Here**

The name of the star Algol, the second brightest star in the constellation Perseus, comes from the Arabic for "the ghoul" for its mysterious habit of dimming and brightening almost as you watch. The reason for this curious behavior, discovered by John Goodricke in 1783, is that Algol is actually a double star. When the fainter star passes in front of the brighter star, it appears to dim.

Sometime during this period, he began killing local women and taking the bodies home. It is not known how many he killed. He admitted to the two murders of which he was eventually found guilty, but the total may have been much higher. On 16 November 1957, he found 58-year-old Bernice Worden alone in her Plainfield hardware store and killed her. He took her body and the store's cash register with him when he left. The investigators found a half-written receipt for antifreeze on the counter, and Mrs. Worden's son remembered that Gein had mentioned needing anti-freeze the day before.

When officers went to Gein's house to investigate, they were confronted with a scene that has seldom been equaled for grotesque horror. The house was festooned with skulls and shrunken heads. Some of the skulls had been fashioned into bowls and drinking cups. There were pieces of furniture upholstered in human skin and articles of clothing and bracelets created from human skin.

A human heart was resting in a skillet on the stove. In a shed to the side of the house they found the missing Mrs. Warden. As Judge Robert H. Gollmar described in *Edward Gein: America's Most Bizarre Murderer* (1981):

**No Mystery Here**

Gein was the inspiration for the ghoulish villains in the 1959 novel *Psycho* by Robert Bloch, made into a movie by Alfred Hitchcock, and the 1990 novel *Silence of the Lambs,* by Thomas Harris, adapted for the screen by Ted Tally and directed by Jonathan Demme.

… Mrs. Warden had been completely dressed out like a deer with her head cut off at the shoulders. Gein had slit the skin on the back of her ankles and inserted a wooden rod, 3 feet long, and about 4 inches in diameter, and sharpened to a point at both ends, through the cut tendons on the back of her ankles. Both hands were tied to her side with binder twine. The center of the rod was attached to a pulley on a block and tackle. The body was pulled up so that the feet were near the ceiling.

One of the heads found in the house was identified as that of Mary Hogan, who had disappeared from the tavern she managed in Pine Grove, Wisconsin, on 8 December 1954. The others were not identified or were not shown to have been alive when Gein acquired them. The body parts indicated that at least 15 people, living or dead, had been dismembered, disemboweled, and otherwise disfigured at the hands of Ed Gein. He confessed to killing Mary Hogan and Bernice Worden and to stealing bodies from the cemetery. The authorities suspected him of at least three other murders but couldn't prove anything.

The two they could prove were evidence enough to get Gein committed to the Central State Hospital at Waupun, Wisconsin, where he spent the rest of his life. He died in 1984.

# Jeffrey Dahmer

At 11:25 P.M. on 22 July 1991, Tracy Edwards, a slender black man who looked younger than his 31 years, ran out onto a Milwaukee street, a pair of handcuffs dangling from his left wrist, and hysterically flagged down a passing police car. What he told the two policemen, Robert Rauth and Rolf Mueller, sounded like part of the plot of a particularly unbelievable horror novel. But it was their job to check it out, and check it they did.

Edwards had gone to the apartment of Jeffrey Dahmer, a man he had met in a bar with a bunch of his friends, believing that the friends were following behind in another car. The friends never showed up, however, and after a couple of beers, Dahmer suddenly snapped a handcuff on Edwards' left wrist. Edwards immediately started struggling, which prevented Dahmer from fastening his other wrist. "His face was completely changed," Edwards said. "I wouldn't have recognized him." Dahmer pushed the tip of a large butcher knife against Edwards' chest and said, "You die if you don't do what I say." After a couple of agonizing hours during which Edwards was afraid for his life at every second, he took a desperate chance and lashed out at Dahmer, knocking the wind out of him. Then he raced for the door and made it outside, where he stopped the police car.

When the two officers knocked at the door of apartment 213 of the Oxford Apartments, a calm and rational Dahmer answered. It was all a misunderstanding, he assured the officers. Merely a lovers' quarrel. The police ordered him to produce the handcuff key, but he balked. He was afraid to leave the door and let the police see inside. The officers insisted. Dahmer refused. He resisted the officers, who subdued him and put him in handcuffs. Then they looked around the apartment.

## The Mystery Deepens

A truly shocking story came to light when police found that, two months before Dahmer's arrest, a 14-year-old Laotian boy named Konerak Sinthasomphone had escaped from Dahmer's clutches and staggered bleeding into the street. But because he was drugged and acted incoherent and because he didn't speak English very well, the policemen who investigated believed Dahmer when he told them it was just a lovers' quarrel. They didn't want to get involved in a homosexual lovers spat and gave the boy back to Dahmer. Parts of Sinthasomphone's body were later found in Dahmer's apartment.

It was worse than even Edwards had imagined—much worse. There were photographs of naked men on the walls. Upon closer look, it was clear that some of them were dead. Some of the bodies were missing parts. A foul stench permeated the apartment. One of the officers opened the refrigerator door, and a severed human head stared back at him from inside.

The subsequent investigation revealed a trail of murders going back to 1978, when Dahmer was 18. The apartment itself revealed the heads or skulls of 11 people. There were body parts in the refrigerator, in a large barrel in the bedroom, in a kettle in the closet, and in a filing cabinet. A human heart was in the freezer.

Dahmer was found guilty of 15 murders and was sentenced to life imprisonment. In November 1992, the building Dahmer had lived in was razed to the ground so the neighbors could begin to forget. In November 1994 Dahmer was killed in prison by Christopher Scarver, a psychopathic murderer who believed he was Christ.

---

### The Least You Need to Know

➤ A vampire is a reanimated corpse that needs human blood to sustain itself. Contrary to popular belief, it cannot be killed by sunlight, though it does prefer to avoid the sun.

➤ The lamia is an unnatural creature that looks like a woman but eats babies and sucks the blood from men after making love to them.

➤ The 1727 case of Arnold Paole becoming a vampire was documented by a Commission of Enquiry made up of three Army surgeons.

➤ Lycanthropy is the power to turn yourself into a wolf or the belief that you possess this power. There were many cases of lycanthropy reported in Europe during the late Middle Ages.

➤ Ghouls, evil beings who rob graves and eat the dead, are, unfortunately, very real. Ed Gein and Jeffrey Dahmer are two examples.

---

# Chapter 25

# The Crypto-Zoo

---

### In This Chapter

➤ Cryptids defined

➤ The Loch Ness monster

➤ A few more lake monsters

➤ The Tasmanian tiger

➤ Yeti

➤ Sasquatch

---

There seems to be a trait in human nature that makes us hope there are discoveries still to be made, that Alexander the Great's lament 2,300 years ago that there are no new worlds to conquer was premature. Combine this with the yen we all share for the supernatural, and you can begin to understand the tales of strange animals, missing links, and giant sea creatures that have persisted through the centuries.

Some legends turn out to be hoaxes that make us skeptical of those that remain. But our fantasies are continually fed by the discoveries of new species, some in unlikely places. The coelacanth, an ancient fish believed extinct for 70 million years until one was caught by a fisherman in the 1930s, is one example. Another is the kraken, the legendary giant squid—legendary, that is, until 1997, when a fishing boat netted three off Tasmania and brought them back for biologists to study. Such discoveries make us wonder whether other creatures that once existed, but that are generally believed to be extinct, may yet be found—for example, dinosaurs, giant sharks, and the thylacine, or Tasmanian tiger.

Then there are the phantom creatures that exist only in the stories of people who claim to have seen them. There may also be the tantalizing but inconclusive evidence of mysterious bite marks, footprints, tufts of fur, or the occasional blurry photograph. The existence of creatures such as Bigfoot and the chupacabra does not seem to correspond to any other creature living or extinct, and they have not been scientifically proven. Yet the creatures persist in the as-yet-undiscovered world of the unknown.

## No Mystery Here

In Vietnam in the past quarter century, several previously uncatalogued animals have been discovered including a deer, an antelope-like animal called *Pseudoryx nghetinhensis*, and a pheasant. It's not difficult to see that there are other regions in the world that are even less accessible than the highlands of Vietnam. Who knows what other finds may yet be made?

## Cryptids

The widespread interest in *cryptids* has spawned a branch of study called, appropriately, *cryptozoology.* Serious cryptozoologists examine the evidence for animals whose existence is not scientifically established, and they sometimes organize field studies to try to find actual specimens or more definitive evidence of their existence.

## Leviathans in the Lakes

Okay, everyone knows about the Loch Ness monster. But what about the serpents of Loch Morar, Loch Shiel, and Loch Arkaig? The Bunyip? The Beast of Vorota? The Flathead Monster? The skrimsel?

Every country with deep, cold lakes seems to have had sightings of a serpent-like creature in at least one of them, and descriptions of the creatures tend to be surprisingly alike. Some of the sightings could have been inspired by people reading or hearing about "Nessie" or tales of sea serpents or dinosaurs. But some of them, such as the Skrimsels, which have been sighted since the Middle Ages in Iceland, don't lend themselves to such an easy explanation. The following are some stories of lake monsters. You be the judge.

## What Does This Mean?

**Cryptid** is the term for an animal whose existence has not been proven but that might exist. **Cryptozoology** is the study of such creatures.

### The Loch Ness Monster

Tales of sea serpents have tended to be dismissed as the wild imaginings of superstitious (or drunken) sailors, but lake serpents are another story. Maybe it's because lakes are smaller and the monsters that inhabit them tend to be seen again and again that lake creatures seem to be taken more seriously. By far the most famous of them is "Nessie," the Loch Ness monster.

Sightings of a strange creature in Loch Ness have been chronicled since the sixth century, when St. Columba is said to have chased the creature away from a man swimming in the lake by invoking the name of God. But Nessie wasn't much known outside the villages around the loch until a new road opened up the area to tourism in the 1930s. Then, one summer evening in 1933, a Mr. and Mrs. Spicer were driving down the new road when a huge animal crossed in front of them and disappeared into the bushes in the direction of the loch.

The Spicers described the creature as having a long neck in a number of arches and a huge, lumbering body. The Spicers had started something. The idea of a monster in the lake caught the public's imagination. Dozens of sightings of it were reported. Rewards were offered for its capture, and search parties were organized to find it.

### No Mystery Here

The reasons for Nessie's unusual fame aren't all that clear. Location probably had something to do with it. Loch Ness has a certain claim to fame of its own as the deepest lake in Scotland, reaching a depth of 754 feet at its deepest part. The city of Inverness sits at one end of it, and the loch has been a popular vacation spot for many years.

Someone took a snapshot of it. Hoaxes surfaced almost immediately, one of the earliest a set of fake tracks made by a stuffed hippopotamus foot.

On 19 April 1934, a London surgeon, Colonel Robert Wilson, took perhaps the most famous photograph of Nessie. It shows a long neck and head curving gracefully out of the water. The authenticity of that photo was hotly debated. After Col. Wilson's death, his son said the photo was a fake, and in 1994, another man, Christian Spurling, said that he had built the model of the serpent used in the photograph. Spurling's confession has had little effect on the Nessie legend. Some people have even disputed its truth, citing analyses that concluded that the photograph was real.

Meanwhile, sightings of Nessie have continued, and other pictures, less clear but intriguing nonetheless, have been made showing strange phenomena on the loch. In the 1970s, a team of scientists took sonar and flash pictures with underwater cameras and caught fuzzy images of long-necked creatures 20 to 30 feet long.

Perhaps the most recent find of interest is a large cavern at the bottom of the loch; some believers in the monster have already nicknamed it "Nessie's lair." Whether it turns out to hold any further clues about the elusive Nessie, or Nessies, remains to be seen. But regardless of whether anything is found, it's clear that there will be no shortage of enthusiastic searchers.

*Colonel Wilson's photo-graph of the monster in Loch Ness.*

### The Mystery Deepens

Loch Morar, southwest of Loch Ness in Scotland, is the second-deepest lake (after Loch Ness itself) in Great Britain. Recorded sightings of a creature, much like Nessie, in the loch go back to 1907. In 1969, the creature (nicknamed "Morag" by locals) collided with a fishing boat—perhaps the closest encounter anyone has had with a lake serpent. The two fishermen on the boat tried to push it away with an oar and finally scared it off with a rifle shot. The animal they saw so closely was about 25 to 30 feet long with rough brown skin and a snake-like head.

## Lake Serpents of North America

The lakes of North America are not to be left out of the mysterious creature hunt. There have been sightings of curious creatures in most of the big lakes, and some of them have attained the status of local legend. None have achieved the fame of Nessie, but we're a young country. Give us a few hundred years.

### "Champ": The Serpent of Lake Champlain

Lake Champlain is a large lake that borders New York, Vermont, and Canada. Before white settlers moved to the region, the Native American tribes had their own legends of a creature in the lake. Since the early nineteenth century, there have been more than 130 sightings of the creature or creatures. One group of people who saw it in 1871 described a long neck above the water and said it left a large wake behind it. In 1873, P.T. Barnum offered a reward of $50,000 for its capture. A century later, a group of schoolchildren described it as having humps. At some point, it (or they) acquired the nickname "Champ."

### Ogopogo

This poor serpent, which allegedly lives in Lake Okanagan in British Columbia, Canada, got its name from a silly song from the 1920s that went something like this: "His mother was an insect, his father was a whale, a little bit of head and hardly any tail, and Ogopogo was his name." People have claimed sightings of it just about every year, and one woman reported being bumped on the legs by it while swimming.

### The Flathead Monster

Another North American serpent allegedly lives in Flathead Lake in Montana. The first reported evidence of it came in the 1920s when fishermen reported that something was tearing their nets to shreds. In 1960, a couple saw a huge black creature with a head like a horse, rubbing against a pier like an animal scratching its back. Other people have reported it as having three humps and swimming very fast.

## Lake Monsters in Scandinavia

Scandinavia has more than its share of serpent sightings. In Norway, sightings of a lake serpent (affectionately known as "Rommie") have been recorded since the eighteenth century in Lake Rommen in the southern part of the country. In the 1930s, a man walking home through the woods at night claimed to have seen something like a giant slug, 10 or 12 feet long, pulling itself along from a small lake to Lake Rommen. Sweden has over a dozen known lake monsters in lakes with names such as Storsjon, Bullaren, Salstern, Vastjutten, Svarttjarn, Malgomaj, Stensjon, Amanningen, Tavelsjon, Lickasjon, Fegen, Mjorn, and Tingstade Trask. Most descriptions of them are familiar: dark in color, huge size, snake-like head, and long neck.

**Here There Be Dragons**

The monsters of one Swedish lake, Lake Regnaren, are different. They have been described as enormous "wheel snakes" that hold their tails in their teeth and roll along like wheels, stealing small children and drowning them in the lake.

### Lake Sandnesvatet

In northern Norway, another *vasstrollet* (the Norwegian word for "lake monster") haunts Lake Sandnesvatet on Hamaroy Island. On a summer evening in 1910, a woman rowing on the lake

### No Mystery Here

It's hard to imagine how, or why, a fourteenth-century chronicler and a nineteenth-century farmer in Iceland would have made up a description of a creature so like Nessie and the other lake serpents. Perhaps—just perhaps—there's something more to the stories than the skeptics allow.

collided with a large, dark animal just under the surface. At first she thought it was a log, but then she touched it: it was soft. It appeared to be 5 to 6 meters (15 to 20 feet) long and about as wide as the rowboat. The monster has been sighted—and occasionally struck by other boats—every summer since then. At another lake about six miles away, a story is told that Lapps bringing their reindeer to graze in the area found the carcass of a large, unknown animal by the shore.

### The Skrimsels

Several Icelandic sagas refer to an animal called the "skrimsel." The earliest description comes from a chronicle in 1345 that recounted the sighting of a mysterious thing, like a great animal, in a lake called the Lagarflot. As described in the chronicle, "At times it seemed like a great island, and at others, there appeared humps, with water between them."

In 1860, an English student of Norse sagas visiting Iceland got a description and a sketch of a skrimsel from some farmers in a remote village. They described the creature as 42 feet long overall with an 18-foot tail and a 6-foot neck and head. The drawing showed an animal with serpent-like humps but with whiskers like those of a seal on its muzzle.

# The Rest of the World

Most continents seem to have at least one monster lurking in their wetlands. Eastern Siberia has the dinosaur-like beast of Lake Vorota, reportedly 6 feet wide and 30 feet long with a large fin on its back. Australia has the Bunyip, with a head like a dog's and a hairy body. In Argentina, there are stories of a creature with humps and a swan-like neck living in Lago Nahuel Huapi, the Lake of the Tigers.

In Africa, where, some people believe, dinosaurs may still roam the swamps and jungles of the continent's interior, the Congo has its own lake monster, Mokele-Mbembe. Stories of Mokele-Mbembe can be confusing because the name "Mokele-Mbembe" is sometimes used generically to describe any one of a number of mysterious beasts that haunt the swamps of sub-Saharan Africa.

They all describe creatures that are very unusual indeed. In 1919, a Belgian official supervising a railroad construction project reported that a monster had chased him and attacked a village, killing five natives. The beast the survivors described wasn't a classic lake serpent, though, but a beast identical to the Triceratops, a stubby land dinosaur with three horns and a ruff on its head, that lived about 70 million years ago.

In 1932, two other Europeans encountered Mokele-Mbembe: one on land, the other in a river. Each described a huge creature—about 15 to 20 feet long—with a long neck. To experts, the animal described sounded a lot like a type of dinosaur called a sauropod.

A number of expeditions have been sent to look for Mokele-Mbembe, but they have returned with only one or two distant sightings and grainy, inconclusive photographs along with lots of local folk tales of the beast. No one has yet proved the existence of Mokele-Mbembe or any other dinosaurs on the continent.

# The Tasmanian Tiger and Other Big Cats

Australians feel a little guilty about what happened to the Tasmanian tiger. It wasn't a tiger, really, but an animal that looked more like a middle-sized dog, about two feet tall at the shoulder and weighing about 60 pounds. Like kangaroos and wallabies, it was a marsupial, carrying its young in a pouch under its belly. But it was a carnivore, a hunter and possibly a carrion eater, the marsupial equivalent of a wolf or a big cat. Its scientific name is *thylacine*; the tiger nickname came about because it had stripes—probably for camouflage—along its back.

When the English started raising sheep on the island of Tasmania in the nineteenth century, they thought the thylacine was a sheep-killer. So, like wolves in other parts of the world, thylacines were systematically exterminated. Bounties were paid for killing them, and they were shot, snared, trapped, and poisoned until by the early twentieth century there were hardly any to be found, outside of zoos.

In the 1930s, the Australian government woke up to the fact that one of the country's unique animals was in serious danger of becoming extinct. In 1936, the government passed a law protecting thylacines. This was the same year, ironically, that the last one known to exist, a captive in a Tasmanian zoo, died.

*One of the last photographs of one of the last thylacines in a Tasmanian zoo.*

321

Officially, all that remains of the Tasmanian tiger are a few skins and stuffed specimens and some photographs. Officially, it has been declared extinct, but people keep seeing it around—sometimes disappearing into the woods at a distance, sometimes flashing into view in the headlights of a car on a lonely road.

Are there actually some left, living furtively in the mountains of Tasmania? Or are Australians in denial, refusing to believe that the thylacine is gone forever? On one hand, there have been hundreds of sightings, many quite convincing; there have even been a couple of photographs taken after its supposed extinction. Tasmania has lots of rugged wilderness in which an animal species could live for a long time without interacting with humans. On the other hand, photos can be doctored and eyewitnesses can be mistaken. In 65 years, no one has ever found any unambiguous physical evidence of wild thylacines—no bodies or bones, no definite clumps of hair. So for now, the thylacine is still a phantom, one of the many animals that may, or may not, exist.

### The Mystery Deepens

Big cats in general seem to be a popular animal for sightings. Sightings of thylacines have been reported on the Australian mainland, where they have been extinct as far as anyone knows, for 3,000 years. Australians also claim to occasionally spot another marsupial predator, the so-called Queensland tiger (thylacoleo), which supposedly became extinct about 16,000 years ago.

# Missing Links

They live on every continent, it seems, except Australia and Antarctica—shadowy, human-like creatures, hiding on the fringes of human civilization. Different names have been given to them—Sasquatch, Bigfoot, Yeti, Yeren, Nguoi Rung—but the descriptions of them are remarkably similar. They're tall, up to seven feet or more, and their bodies are covered in dark hair. They walk upright. Their arms are long, their necks short, their faces ape-like. They have a distinctive set of howls, they smell terrible, and they are immensely strong.

The fossil record shows that modern humans—*Homo sapiens*—make up only one branch of a family tree of *hominids* that have lived on the earth during the past three million years. Most died out long ago, but at least one, Neanderthal man, lived side by side with us for tens of thousands of years. It could be that we have a very shy and reclusive relative living still in the less explored corners of the world.

# Yeti

In the Himalayan Mountains, so tall that they are referred to as "the roof of the world," there is said to live a creature called "Yeti" by the Tibetans and "the Abominable Snowman" by Westerners. This doesn't seem like a friendly thing to call a creature that has done no harm to anyone and that seems to spend a good deal of its time avoiding us. It is reported as being about seven feet tall and covered with black or red hair. It's also supposed to be bad tempered and unfriendly, although there is one 1938 report of it saving a climber, Captain d'Auvergue, the curator of the Victoria Memorial in Calcutta, India. Captain d'Auvergue had become snow blind and almost froze to death; the creature nursed him to health before sending him back down the mountain.

The first report of the Yeti to reach the West was from J.W. Fraser in 1820. Then in 1903, a climber named Hugh Knight reported seeing one. In 1925, N.A. Tombazi, a Greek photographer with a British geological expedition, had one pointed out to him in the distance when the group was at an altitude of about 15,000 feet. "Unquestionably, the figure in outline was exactly like a human being, walking upright and stopping occasionally to uproot or pull at some dwarf rhododendron bushes," Tombazi reported. "It showed up dark against the snow and, as far as I could make out, wore no clothes." Tombazi had no time to take a picture, but he went over to check out the area where he had seen it and found footprints in the snow. "They were similar in shape to those of a man, but only six to seven inches long by four inches wide at the broadest part of the foot. The marks of five distinct toes and the instep were perfectly clear, but the trace of the heel was indistinct."

### What Does This Mean?

**Hominids** are the scientific term for the ancestors of modern human beings and any side branches that we might not be directly related to, but which are, anthropologically speaking, our cousins.

### No Mystery Here

The Himalayan Mountains form the border between India, Nepal, and Tibet. They are high, remote, and for the most part uninhabited. Mount Everest, the tallest peak in the world at 29,028 feet, straddles the border between Nepal and China, and the main industry in the area is catering to the climbing parties that come to try to scale Everest.

Yeti tracks were photographed by British mountain climbers Eric Shipton and Michael Ward in 1951. They spotted them on the southwestern slope of a glacier about 20,000 feet up between Tibet and Nepal. The prints were bigger than the ones Tombazi inspected, being about 18 inches long and 13 wide.

Several native Tibetans have reported close encounters with the creature. Sen Tensing, a Sherpa mountain guide, saw one at a religious festival on Mount Everest. He said it was about 5 feet tall and was entirely covered with hair except for the face. A Lama at Rongbuk Monastery in Tibet, which sits at 16,000 feet, making it one of the highest inhabited spots in the world, saw it close up and commented on its extremely bad smell, something that has been noted by other observers.

Tenzing Norgay, the Sherpa guide who accompanied Sir Edmund Hillary to the top of Everest in 1953, making them the first two human beings to stand at the highest spot in the world, has never seen the Yeti, but he has seen its footprints. His father saw it twice in 1935 and heard it whistling. "We Sherpas invent no other animal," he is quoted as saying. "Why should we invent the Snowman?"

# Bigfoot

We here in North America have a mysterious man-like creature of our own, and we call him Bigfoot. He is found—well, actually he isn't found, but if he were, it would be in the Pacific Northwest of the United States and in Western Canada. In Canada, he is called Sasquatch, which is a mispronunciation of the Salish (a Native American language) word for "wild men."

Bigfoot is said to be six to eight feet tall; he walks upright, probably weighs more than 300 pounds, is covered with dark fur, has a very bad smell about him, and—like his cousin the Yeti—is very shy. The British explorer David Thompson, the first European to travel the length of the Columbia River, was also the first European to run across a set of Sasquatch footprints, back in 1811.

### The Mystery Deepens

The Victoria, British Columbia, *Daily Colonist* newspaper reported the capture of a Sasquatch back in 1884. A train crew captured the creature along the Frazer River. They described it as " ... something of the gorilla type, standing four feet seven inches in height and weighing 127 pounds. He has long black, strong hair and resembles a human being with one exception, his entire body, excepting his hands (or paws) and feet are covered with glossy black hair about one inch long ... he possesses extraordinary strength, as he will take hold of a stick and break it by wrenching it or twisting it, which no man could break the same way."

The train crew named the creature "Jacko." Its description is so unlike the usual description of a Sasquatch and is so much like a chimpanzee that it seems probable that a chimpanzee, perhaps escaped from a carnival, is what they caught.

There have been scattered sightings of Bigfoot through the years. In 1924, a group of miners complained that, after they shot at a Bigfoot during the day, their cabin was surrounded by Bigfoots (Bigfeet?) that night. The creatures threw stones at the building and pounded on the walls. In 1958, Jerry Crew, a bulldozer operator in Humboldt County, California, found large Bigfootprints around the area he had been working. He took a plaster cast of one of the prints, and a picture of him holding the cast made it into newspapers all over the country. It was the big footprint he was holding that gave the name "Bigfoot" to the creature.

## The Patterson Picture

In 1967, Bigfoot enthusiasts Roger Patterson and Bob Gimlin took a short movie, about five or six seconds' worth, of what they claimed was a Bigfoot sighting. The creature on the film is definitely not an animal. Whether it is a Bigfoot or a man in a funny suit is still being debated.

*A frame from the Patterson movie of Bigfoot.*

Sightings and footprint findings continue at the rate of several hundred a year, and if Bigfoot is there to be found, sooner or later someone will find him.

## Bigfeet Elsewhere

Creatures or wild men like Bigfoot and Yeti have been reported all over the world. There's the Florida Everglades Skunk-ape, the Wild Man in Vietnam, and the Almas in Siberia. Russian scientist Boris Porshnev has suggested that they could all be surviving remnants of Neanderthal man, but few scientists are willing to take him up on it.

# Chupacabra

A new animal has joined the cryptozoo: the chupacabra ("goat sucker"). Reported in Mexico and Puerto Rico, this mysterious beast is said to puncture the necks of goats and suck out their blood. It has been described as a small, alien-dinosaur crossbreed with quills running down its back. It has also been described as a hopping animal with a very bad smell.

One theory is that alien visitors have created a hybrid creature that either escaped or was released deliberately. Veterinarians who have seen the supposedly mutilated goats say there is nothing in their death that is not consistent with a wild dog or possibly a panther attack.

# Examining the Unknown

The most difficult challenge of investigating the unknown, whether it's sightings of cryptids or of something else, is to remain objective, weighing the evidence as it comes in and forming an opinion that you aren't afraid to change if new facts show you to be wrong.

Of course, none of us can really do that. The best we can do is grudgingly accept new evidence that contradicts what we really want to believe. Many people can't even manage to do that. Look at all the people who refuse to believe in evolution. Old beliefs are comfortable, like old shoes, and we don't like having to break in a new pair. But if there's one thing that's certain, it's that over the next 20 years (starting from whenever you like), something that most of us are certain is true will be shown to be false. And it's just as certain that many people won't believe it. And the legends will live on. Anyway, that's what we believe.

---

### The Least You Need to Know

➤ Cryptozoology is the study of cryptids—animals not yet proven to exist.

➤ Sightings of the Loch Ness monster date from the sixth century.

➤ The thylacine, or Tasmanian tiger, was supposedly extinct in the 1930s, but sightings continue to be reported.

➤ Yetis and Yeti tracks have been seen in Nepal for hundreds of years, but nobody has gotten a good photograph of one or other physical evidence.

➤ There is a photo of the North American Bigfoot, but it may be a hoax.

---

# Chapter 26

# Will the Real William Shakespeare Please Stand Up?

### In This Chapter

➤ The mysterious William Shakespeare

➤ Who wrote the plays?

➤ The case for Sir Francis Bacon

➤ Edward de Vere, the Earl of Oxford

➤ Christopher Marlowe

➤ The case for Shakespeare

It may come as a surprise that there is a continuing controversy as to whether William Shakespeare actually wrote the plays attributed to him. There's no doubt that there really *was* a William Shakespeare. And even the doubters concede that William Shakespeare, the man from Stratford-on-Avon, moved to London where he became a minor actor and theater manager. But was he the man who wrote *Hamlet* and *Macbeth* and 35 more of the world's greatest dramas—or was it someone else writing in his name?

To make the question even more interesting, even the people who think the author was not William Shakespeare can't decide among themselves who the writer was. Everyone of any importance in the Elizabethan world has been suggested as the real author, from Queen Elizabeth to a secret committee of noble men and women parceling out different scenes in each play among themselves.

### No Mystery Here

There's a continuing controversy between English professors and drama professors as to whether Shakespeare's plays were meant to be performed or read as literature. Well, despite the fact that the plays are, in a real sense, literature, they were written to be performed. The scenes are too carefully crafted with the needs of actors in mind for it to be otherwise (with the possible exception of *Troilus and Cressida*). We're glad to be able to settle that for you!

### No Mystery Here

As a matter of fact, there were several dozen plays published with Shakespeare's name on them that scholars now generally agree were not written by Shakespeare—whoever he was. We'll offer a possible explanation for this later in the chapter.

"Why should there be any doubt who wrote the plays?" you may well ask. After all, isn't it logical to assume that William Shakespeare wrote the plays attributed to William Shakespeare? Some of the plays were published during his lifetime, and the rest were published during the lifetimes of people who must have known him. The printed plays had his name on the title page. Surely someone would have said something if his name was being put on plays he didn't really write.

All very logical and possibly true. But the sixteenth century was not the twentieth century. There were no copyright laws back then to protect literary property, and there were social, political, and legal reasons why some of the possible authors of the plays might not have wanted their names on the title page. Or so say the doubters.

## Why the Fuss?

There's one thing critics, writers, and professors of literature and drama generally agree on: Whoever wrote the plays attributed to William Shakespeare is the greatest writer and dramatist that the English-speaking world has yet produced. The Microsoft ENCARTA Encyclopedia, for example, says:

> Throughout the Western world [Shakespeare] is held to be the greatest dramatist ever, and his plays are still performed and inspire much new and experimental theatre. His plays communicate a profound knowledge of the wellsprings of human behavior as revealed in his masterful characterizations of humanity. The skilful use of poetic and dramatic means to create a unified aesthetic effect out of a multiplicity of vocal expressions and actions is recognized as an achievement unequalled in other literature.

But what do we know about William Shakespeare, the man who supposedly wrote all those plays? Surprisingly little.

To make our investigation easier to follow, we'll call Shakespeare the man by his name, and we'll call whoever wrote the plays The Playwright.

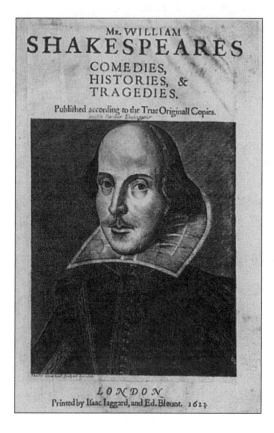

*William Shakespeare. Did this man write those plays?*

## Why Not Shakespeare?

A basis of the argument of the anti-Shakespeare bunch is that we don't really know much about Shakespeare. Here's pretty much all we know about him:

➤ 26 April 1564—Born. On this date is written in the baptismal register of the Stratford parish church, "Gulielmus filius Johannis Shakspere" ("William, son of John Shakspere").

➤ 27 November 1582—Married Anne Hathaway.

➤ 26 May 1583—Daughter Susanna baptized.

➤ 2 February 1585—Hamnet and Judith, twins, baptized.

➤ 15 March 1595—Shakespeare, William Kempe, and Richard Burbage paid by the Treasurer of the Royal Chamber for "two comedies or interludes" performed before the queen by the Lord Chamberlain's players the previous December.

➤ 11 August 1596—Hamnet died at 11 years old, buried in Stratford.

➤ 29 November 1596—Shakespeare and Francis Langley named in a petition for sureties of the peace—sort of like a restraining order by one William Wayte, who must have had some reason to be afraid of them.

➤ 4 May 1597—Bought a house and garden (named "New Place") in Stratford for 60 pounds.

➤ 1598—Name listed as an actor in the cast of Ben Johnson's *Every Man in his Humour.*

➤ 1599–1611—Named on various documents as one of the tenants of the Globe Theatre.

➤ 1 May 1601—Paid 320 pounds for 107 acres of land with grazing rights on the common pasture near Stratford. Also bought a cottage across the street from New Place.

➤ 19 May 1603—Listed as principal comedian in Ben Johnson's *Sejanus his Fall.* One of nine actors issued a Royal Patent allowing them to stage plays at the Globe Theatre.

➤ 15 March 1604—Received four and a half yards of red cloth from the Great Wardrobe to make clothing suitable for appearing as a groom of the King's Chamber in King James's coronation procession.

➤ 23 April 1616—Died. Left most of his property to his elder daughter, Susanna Hall, and his second-best bed to his wife Anne. Buried in Stratford as "Will Shakspere gent."

We've left out some commercial transactions, but essentially that's it. That's all the documented evidence that William Shakespeare ever existed.

Notice one interesting thing about the list—nowhere on it is there any hint that he ever wrote anything beyond signing his name. Not one play, not one poem, nothing. There is even some doubt as to whether he could write at all since his signature is almost illegible and his name is spelled several different ways.

And then there's his will, in which he is careful to list even his "second-best bed." But nowhere in it does he mention a single book. Books were of some value in Shakespeare's day. Is it reasonable to assume that the greatest playwright in the English language would not own a book, not even the reference books he used to work out the plots of his historical plays? And, if he did own books, wouldn't he have listed these valuable possessions in his will to pass on to his beloved daughter or to distribute among his fellow playwrights?

## And Besides ...

The preceding information is the main part of the argument against Shakespeare being The Playwright, but there's more. The plays of The Playwright show an immense knowledge of numerous fields. The Playwright ...

➤ Used military terms like a soldier.

➤ Used naval terms like a sailor.

➤ Knew courtly etiquette and court manner-isms.

➤ Knew legal language and the operation of law courts like a lawyer.

➤ Must have been fluent in Latin and Greek since several of the works he used for reference in his historical dramas had not yet been translated into English.

We could go on like that, but you get the idea.

What the anti-Stratfordians ask is simply this: How could William Shakespeare, the son of a middle-class glove-maker in a small town with nothing but a local free-school education (if that—there is no record of him actually attending school), have picked up the necessary knowledge to have become The Playwright?

And, the literary forces assembled against Shakespeare point out, when Shakespeare died, not one Elizabethan poet or playwright wrote so much as an ode in his memory. If he were that important, if he shone brighter than all the rest, why wouldn't they have honored his memory? Particularly when he was dead, so they didn't have to feel jealous any more?

**No Mystery Here**

Some of the variant spellings that have been found for the name Shakespeare: Chaksper, Sackesper, Saxspere, Schackspeare, Schachespeare, Scackspeer, Schackspire, Shagspere, Shakaspeare, Shakespar, Shakespare, Shakespeere, Shakesper, Shakespeye, Shakespeyre, Shakesspere, Shakspeare, Shakspeere, Shaksper, Shakspeyr, Shakspeyre, Shakspurre, Shakysper, Shaskespeare, Shaxberd, Shaxeper, Shaxkespere, Shaxpeare, Shaxper, Shaxpere, Sheakspeare, and Shexpere.

Perhaps this is because this Will Shakespeare fellow wasn't a person of any artistic consequence at all. But if Shakespeare wasn't The Playwright, who was?

# Sir Francis Bacon

The first contender for the quill of The Playwright is Sir Francis Bacon (1561–1626), philosopher, statesman, lawyer, legal scholar, and inventor of the Bi-literal *Cipher*, also called the Baconian Cipher. It is at least partly because of the cipher—and the possibility that Bacon used it to hide messages in the plays of The Playwright to prove that he wrote them—that the idea of his authorship is so popular. It gives people who like this sort of thing a lifelong game they can play: hunting for the cipher message that will prove once and for all that Sir Francis wrote the plays. The secret message doesn't even have to be in the form of the Bi-literal Cipher; after all, if Bacon invented one cipher, he could have invented two.

## The Mystery Deepens

People who defend the real William Shakespeare as The Playwright call themselves the Stratfordians, from Shakespeare's birthplace, Stratford-on-Avon. The anti-Stratfordians divide themselves up as the Baconians, who think Sir Francis Bacon wrote the plays; the Oxfordians, who believe the Earl of Oxford was The Playwright; the Rutlanders, who root for the Fifth Earl of Rutland; the Marlovians, who believe Christopher Marlowe rose from the dead to write the plays; and the Groupies, who think a group of aristocrats took turns writing the plays. And there are easily a dozen more candidates.

Bacon was certainly bright enough to be considered a contender, and his educational background, on the surface, was more extensive than Shakespeare's. Bacon studied under private tutors when he was a child, learning Greek, Latin, French, German, and probably a few other languages as well as the works of the classical authors, science, history, music, rhetoric, and religion. He went to Cambridge at the age of 12 but was soon dissatisfied, complaining that the professors didn't know as much as he did.

Bacon studied law at Gray's Inn, was a member of Parliament, and served King James I as solicitor general, attorney general, privy counselor, Lord Keeper, and Lord Chancellor. After a scandal in which he was accused of taking bribes—probably trumped-up charges—Bacon retired from public life. He spent his remaining years becoming the philosopher that he felt God and his nature had always intended him to be.

### What Does This Mean?

A **cipher** is a type of secret writing where the individual letters of the message are either transposed (moved around) or substituted (one letter takes the place of another).

Bacon never showed any ability or inclination to write plays for the common folk, and his writing is a bit stuffy and humorless. But perhaps he reserved the warmth and humor for the plays and didn't sign his own name to them because he thought it beneath his dignity as a scholar to write such common stuff. Perhaps.

In the mid-nineteenth century, an American woman named Delia Bacon became the standard bearer for the theory that Francis Bacon was The Playwright. She was probably influenced by the fact that she shared a name with the great scholar, although she was no relation. Delia went to Stratford in 1856 to dig up

Shakespeare's body, convinced that she would find the original manuscripts of all the plays buried with him along with a note saying something like, "I wrote these. Francis Bacon." The local authorities refused to allow her to dig. Late in life, Mark Twain became convinced that Shakespeare couldn't have written the plays and wrote a short book called *Is Shakespeare Dead?* to prove his point. His thesis was that it would have required more learning than Shakespeare was known to have, and he decided it was probably Bacon who had done the job.

## The Cipher

Let's look at one of the key arguments—the Baconian Cipher. Bacon called it the Bi-literal Cipher because it's made up of two elements that, for now, we'll call the letters a and b. Each letter of the alphabet is designated by a five-letter combination of the two elements, as follows (note that the alphabet he used was only 24 letters: I and J were counted as one letter, and there was no U):

**No Mystery Here**

The passage of time has made much Elizabethan English obscure to us today. At the time they were written, the plays were instantly understandable and enjoyed by the masses. The English at the time had a love of language, and what they didn't understand they would have enjoyed anyway as long as it "rolled mellifluously off the tongue."

| | | |
|---|---|---|
| A = aaaaa | I/J = abaaa | R = baaaa |
| B = aaaab | K = abaab | S = baaab |
| C = aaaba | L = ababa | T = baaba |
| D = aaabb | M = ababb | V = baabb |
| E = aabaa | N = abbaa | W = babaa |
| F = aabab | O = abbab | X = babab |
| G = aabba | P = abbba | Y = babba |
| H = aabbb | Q = abbbb | Z = babbb |

To turn this system into a form of secret communication, Bacon suggested setting a book in type using two slightly different fonts. In those days, metal fonts were expensive, and a printer would often use two or more fonts if he didn't have enough of one to make up the pages for a book. So the appearance of slightly different fonts in a printed book was not uncommon.

One font would be designated the "a" font and the other the "b" font, and the message would be set accordingly. In the following example, we'll use normal text for the "a" font and italic letters for the "b" font. Spaces between words are ignored.

Let's say the message is "Attack at dawn," and the text to be set is Hamlet's famous "To be, or not to be" soliloquy. We'll only need the first few lines:

> To be, or not to be: that is the question:
> Whether 'tis nobler in the mind to suffer
> the slings and arrows of Outrageous fortune,
> Or to take arms against a sea of troubles,
> And by opposing end them?

| A | T | T | A | C | K |
|---|---|---|---|---|---|

Tobeo / *rnott* / *obeth* / atist / heque / *stion*

| A | T | D | A | W | N |
|---|---|---|---|---|---|

Wheth / *ertis* / *noble* / rinth / *emind* / tosuf / fer

As a cipher, it is more of an intellectual exercise than a workable means of hiding information. For one thing, if the message is an urgent one, such as "attack at dawn," you're not going to be able to take the time to set it in a book, print the book, and distribute it. For another, if the two fonts are too different, the book will look strange and invite suspicion, but if they are too similar the letters will be very hard to tell apart.

There were two fonts, maybe more, used in the First Folio edition of Shakespeare's plays. They were probably used because it was a big book and the printer needed a lot of type. But maybe, for a few pages, the type was very carefully set, and the fonts were mixed to form a Bi-literal Cipher. Maybe somewhere it says, "My name is Sir Francis Bacon and I wrote these words."

### Mysterious Comments

"It is not clear whether Bacon wrote Shakespeare, but it is well established that Shakespeare ate bacon."

—Professor Irwin Corey, The World's Foremost Authority

# The Earl of Oxford

Another contender for the title of The Playwright is Edward de Vere, the Seventeenth Earl of Oxford (1550–1604). de Vere had the aristocratic birth, the extensive education, and the reputation as a talented poet to recommend him as a possible contender. J. Thomas Looney thought so and wrote a book called *"Shakespeare" Identified* to prove his point.

Looney had analyzed the writings of The Playwright and had come up with nine "general features" that the author of the works must have possessed along with nine "special characteristics" that would help identify him. With regard to the general features, the author must have been ...

1. A mature man of recognized genius.

2. Apparently eccentric and mysterious.

3. Of intense sensibility—a man apart.

4. Unconventional.

5. Not adequately appreciated.

6. Of pronounced and known literary tastes.

7. An enthusiast in the world of drama.

8. A lyric poet of recognized talent.

9. Of superior education—classical—the habitual associate of educated people.

### Here There Be Dragons

Poor Mr. Looney wrote *"Shakespeare" Identified* in 1918, but the publisher he brought it to refused to accept it because of his name—Looney. The publisher told him that he would be a figure of fun and suggested that he use a *nom de plume*. But Looney refused, insisting that his name was pronounced "Loney" and was common on the Isle of Man. It wasn't until 1920 that he found a publisher to take his book, name and all.

And as far as special characteristics, he must have been ...

1. A man with feudal connections.

2. A member of the higher aristocracy.

3. Connected with Lancastrian supporters.

4. An enthusiast for Italy.

5. A follower of sport including falconry.

6. A lover of music.

7. Loose and improvident in money matters.

8. Doubtful and somewhat conflicting in his attitude toward women.

9. Of probable Catholic leanings but touched with skepticism.

Upon investigating the possible Elizabethan poets who fit this profile, Looney stumbled upon Edward de Vere. In his poem "Women," de Vere had described them as follows:

> These gentle birds that fly from man to man,
> Who would not scorn and shake them from the fist
> And let them fly, fair fools, which way they list?

**No Mystery Here**

One thing Looney failed to recognize was that the traits he listed were intensely subjective. A writer often uses material in which he doesn't personally believe or is not expert. He does this by getting advice from someone who is an expert. We, ourselves, have done this on occasion and have been complimented on how well we understood a subject that we, in fact, knew little about. (It's our secret—don't spread it around.)

That description corresponded pretty well with what Looney thought The Playwright thought of women. The poem is written in a style not unlike that of The Playwright's style in the Sonnets. And the imagery in "shake them from the fist" is straight from falconry. Further research by Looney showed that it was probable that de Vere had written plays but that none of them had survived. At least, none that were published or performed under his name.

De Vere might have chosen to conceal his identity, had he indeed written the plays. Playwrighting was not considered a profession for a nobleman in those days, and had he written anything that displeased the queen, he had a lot to lose.

But the Oxfordians have one serious difficulty to overcome—the fact that the Earl died in 1604. *Antony and Cleopatra, King Lear, Macbeth, Coriolanus, Cymbeline, Pericles, Timon of Athens, The Winter's Tale, The Tempest,* and *Henry VIII* were all first performed after 1604. We would have to believe that the plays were all finished, or mostly finished, before de Vere died. But it's hard to believe that a playwright who was much in demand would have stockpiled 10 major works.

# Christopher Marlowe

The one Elizabethan playwright who most experts agree could be The Playwright if it wasn't the guy called Shakespeare was Christopher Marlowe. Marlowe was the author of *Tamburlaine, The Jew of Malta*, and *The Tragical History of Dr. Faustus*, plays that are so good that, if it wasn't for The Playwright, those years might be known as the Age of Marlowe. But for years, Marlowe wasn't even considered a possibility. And for one good reason—he was murdered in 1593 at the age of 29, before so much as one play written in the name of Shakespeare had been published.

Yet several experts think they see the hand of Marlowe in some of the early works of The Playwright. *Titus Andronicus, Richard II, Richard III*, and *Henry VI* (parts I, II and

III) are most commonly mentioned. Perhaps, were it not that they knew he was dead, they would admit to seeing his hand in some of the later plays as well. It is generally agreed that Marlowe's work was a strong influence on The Playwright.

### The Mystery Deepens

In 1901, Dr. Thomas Mendenhall, a distinguished scientist, compared word length frequencies (how many one-letter words, how many two-letter words, and so on) between lengthy manuscripts and discovered that authors stay consistent in this measurement from work to work but different authors vary considerably from each other. He compared a sample of over 200,000 words from Bacon's works with a similar sample of The Playwright's works and found them quite different. Bacon used more two- and three-letter words and more long words from seven letters and up but fewer four-, five-, and six-letter words. Then Mendenhall compared the works of Marlowe with The Playwright and, to his astonishment, found that they matched exactly.

## Dead Is Dead—or Is It?

Suppose Marlowe didn't die when everyone thinks he did. The story is that he was killed in a fight. There are several different versions of whom he was fighting and why, but the official version, found in the Public Record Office in 1925, where it had sat for 332 years, was that he was in the house of a Mrs. Bull with three companions when they got into a fight. Marlowe was stabbed in the head by one of the three, a man named Friser. The only witnesses were his three companions. Friser was held briefly for breaching the peace but was let go with a Royal Pardon a month later, whereupon he went back to work for his master, Thomas Walsingham. The other two witnesses were also agents of Thomas Walsingham.

I use the word "agents" advisedly. Walsingham's cousin, Sir Francis Walsingham, had been the head of Queen Elizabeth's secret service until his death in 1590, and there is strong reason to believe that Thomas worked for him and that Marlowe had been one of his agents.

At the time of his supposed murder, Marlowe was under investigation by the *Court of the Star Chamber* in London for the offense of atheism, for which he could have been tortured to death. Walsingham couldn't get the charges dismissed or overlooked, but he could get Marlowe out of the country. If he was still useful to Walsingham—or even out of friendship—it could well be that the "murder" was arranged, and Marlowe was spirited out of England for a few years, probably with Queen Elizabeth's knowledge and possibly with her covert assistance.

If so and if he was still writing plays, he certainly couldn't publish them or have them produced under his own name. Maybe his friend, the actor and producer William Shakespeare, let him use his.

# The Case for Will

Now let's look at the possibility that William Shakespeare really was the author of the plays attributed to him. It's true that we don't know a lot about Shakespeare's life, but that doesn't mean he didn't spend part of it writing plays. It just means there is no direct proof that he wrote them, just as there is no direct proof that he *didn't* write them.

If one of the other suspects (and there are many more, such as the poet Sir Edward Dyer; Sir Walter Raleigh; Robert Cecil, first Earl of Salisbury; and Queen Elizabeth herself ) had been The Playwright, then the chances are great that many people would have known about it. Everyone connected with the Globe Theatre, where many of the productions were first staged, would certainly have known.

This means that, in short order, everyone connected with the London theatre scene would have known. The publisher and printer of the plays would have known or at least would have known that the true identity of the author was being kept from them. And nobody said anything about it—not then, not later.

There's also the fact that several plays Shakespeare probably didn't write were definitely attributed to him, among them *Edward III*, *The Life of Sir John Oldcastle*, *The London Prodigal*, and *A Yorkshire Tragedy*. Some take this as a sign that, if he didn't write them, he didn't write any of the others. But we think there's another, stronger explanation. Shakespeare was so highly regarded as a playwright that, when a publisher wanted to sell a play and he didn't know who wrote it, he would stick Shakespeare's name on it to help sales.

One of the arguments used over and over by the anti-Stratfordians is that The Playwright must have been a professional scholar and probably a professional lawyer, a member of the nobility, or a diplomat who spent years abroad; in other words, he would have had to lead six different lives to fulfill all the qualifications The Playwright obviously possessed. As far as we know there have been very few great literary works written by scholars, and none written by members of the nobility, at least not in English; there is a Japanese novel written by a princess that's very impressive.

We'll leave you with a story. John Manningham, a young law student, wrote the following in his diary for 13 March 1601:

Upon a time when Burbidge played Richard III there was a citizen grew so far in liking him that, before she went from the play, she appointed him to come that night unto her by the name of Richard the Third. Shakespeare, overhearing their conclusion, went before, was entertained and at his game ere Burbidge came. Then, message being brought that Richard the Third was at the door, Shakespeare caused return to be made that William the Conqueror was before Richard the Third.

After which Manningham added, "Shakespeare's name William."

The story is probably apocryphal, but the point of it for us is that Shakespeare must have been well-known at the time or the story wouldn't be worth telling.

And so the mystery remains. It's somehow ironic that the person recognized as the greatest writer in the English language should be such an enigma. Perhaps it was Queen Elizabeth herself who wrote the plays, and ... But no, let's stop here. Perhaps we weren't intended to know. Perhaps it's better that it remains a mystery.

**No Mystery Here**

There are several snide comments by contemporaries of Shakespeare that the anti-Stratfordians take to mean that Shakespeare was not The Playwright. There was the nasty pamphlet written by dramatist Robert Green in which he calls "the only Shakescene in a country" an "upstart crow" and hints that he is a plagiarist. But to be a plagiarist one must have written something, even if only to steal someone else's words, which means, at the very least, that Shakespeare could indeed write and had written plays of some sort. It sounds more like professional jealousy to us.

**Mysterious Comments**

"GOOD FRIEND FOR JESUS SAKE FORBEARE
TO DIGG THE DUST ENCLOASED HEARE;
BLEST BE THE MAN THAT SPARES THESE STONES,
AND CURST BE HE THAT MOVES MY BONES"

—The epitaph over William Shakspere's tomb at Stratford, said to have been written by him

### The Least You Need to Know

➤ There is a question as to whether William Shakespeare had the background knowledge necessary to have written the plays attributed to him.

➤ Sir Francis Bacon had the necessary knowledge to write the plays, but he was not a great poet, and he lacked a sense of humor.

➤ Edward de Vere, the Seventeenth Earl of Oxford, is another popular candidate, but he died too early to have written some of the plays.

➤ Christopher Marlowe, who also died early, is another possibility, but only if his death was staged.

➤ William Shakespeare is still the most likely candidate to have written Shakespeare's plays.

# Glossary

**Area 51**   Also known as Groom Lake, Area 51 is alleged to be a secret Air Force base about 90 miles north of Las Vegas. It is supposedly where top-secret military aircraft, from the U-2 to the stealth fighter, were test flown.

**aspects**   The aspects of the planets on a horoscope chart are their distance apart and the angles formed by connecting them.

**astrology**   The practice of attempting to foretell or influence the outcome of an event or to assess the character, behavior, or fortune of a person by studying the inter-relationship of the sun, the planets, and the stars.

**back-engineering**   This is a technician's term for taking something apart to see how it works and how to make more.

**Bermuda Triangle**   An area in the Atlantic Ocean bounded by Bermuda and the coast of North America from Florida to as far north as whoever is using the term chooses to claim, in which ships and planes are said to disappear at a larger than nor-mal rate.

**biosphere**   The totality of life on a planet from the smallest microbe to the largest whale, from the highest drifting seed pod or spore in the atmosphere to the microbes buried deepest beneath the earth or at the bottom of the deepest ocean trench.

**Black Hand**   An extortion and terror organization that preyed on Sicilian immi-grants. Members would send a demand for money to shopkeepers and would threaten to burn down the store, destroy merchandise, or kidnap the victim's wife or children if they were not paid. The note would be signed with the device of a crudely drawn black hand.

**brigantine**   A two-masted sailing ship in which the forward mast is square-rigged (with square sails) and the main mast is schooner-rigged (with triangular sails).

**century**   In addition to its usual meaning of 100 years, this term also denotes one of the collections of 100 quatrains containing the prophecies of Nostradamus.

**Cayce, Edgar** (1877–1945)   American prophet and psychic healer whose prophecies have inspired hundreds of books.

**clairaudience**   The ability to hear by psychic ability what cannot be heard by ordinary means.

**clairvoyance**   The ability to see into the future, or at a great distance by psychic ability or aid from the spirit world.

**Deuxeime Bureau**   Also known as the Second Bureau of the French Army, this was the French spy and counterspy service.

**dirigible**   A lighter-than-air craft with a rigid, usually cigar-shaped frame filled with hydrogen or helium gas and a passenger compartment called a gondola suspended beneath it. The Goodyear blimp looks like a dirigible but doesn't have a rigid frame and collapses like a giant balloon when emptied of gas.

**divination**   The act of foretelling, or attempting to foretell, the future by magical or occult means.

**Doppler effect**   The name for the apparent shift in the frequency of sound or light waves when the object emitting them is going toward or away from the observer. When an object is approaching, the light or sound waves have the speed of the object added to their natural frequency the crests arrive more often, making the frequency seem higher than it actually is. When the object is retreating, the waves seem longer. The usual example is the rising and falling sound a train whistle makes as the train passes a listener.

**ephemeris**   A yearly table of the location of the different planets in the heavens. (The plural is ephemerides; it's Greek.) To compile a horoscope, it is necessary to have an ephemeris of the birth year of the subject. There are now computer programs that do this automatically.

**ESP**   *See* extra sensory perception.

**extra sensory perception**   the ability to see or sense objects or events by means of psychic abilities outside of the normal five senses. Includes **clairaudience, clairvoyance, telekinesis, telepathy,** and other senses.

**folie deux**   French for "madness of two," this term is used in clinical psychology to describe a common delusion shared by two people when one of them seems to have influenced the other.

**Halys**   The ancient name for the river, now called Kizil Irmak, that flows through Turkey into the Black Sea. In order to cross the Halys, Croesus would have had to attack Persia.

**homeopathy**   From the Greek words *homeo* (similar) and *pathos* (suffering), this a system of medical treatment that assumes the symptoms of a disease are the body's efforts to cure the disease. Thus, if an illness is accompanied by a fever, a substance that causes a fever can cure the illness. Because too much of something that mimics disease symptoms can be dangerous, homeopaths dilute the substance greatly. Indeed, the dilutions are so great, sometimes less than one part per million, that it is doubtful that their use can have anything beyond a placebo effect.

**horoscope**   A geocentric (earth-centered) map of the solar system at a particular moment in time. The most common are the "natal charts," which show the heavens at the moment of a person's birth.

**misanthrope**   Someone who doesn't like people very much.

**Nachrichtendienst**   Literally translated as "information service," this was the name of the German military secret service during World War I.

**naturopathy**   Uses natural remedies, such as sunlight supplemented with diet and massage, to cure disease.

**Nostradamus**   Latin name of Michel de Notredame (1503–66), a medical doctor who is widely known as a prophet because of the hundreds of obscure quatrains he wrote predicting future events.

**oracle**   A person who acts as a voice for the gods to predict the future or advise on a course of action, or a place where such people give their revelations.

**osteopathy**   A branch of medicine started in 1892 by Dr. Andrew T. Still. At first concentrating on physical manipulation of the body as a cure for all disease, it has since become respectable. A course of study at osteopathic schools is much like those in regular medical schools.

**Pillars of Heracles (or Hercules)**   This is what the Greeks called the Straits of Gibraltar, the narrow straits at the West end of the Mediterranean Sea that provide an outlet to the Atlantic Ocean and that separate Europe from Africa by a scant nine miles.

**Project Blue Book**   The Air Force project that investigated claims of UFO sightings from 1952 to 1969.

**prophecy**   The foretelling of future events by a prophet. Often the prophecy involves the dire results of evil behavior.

**prophet**   One who has been divinely selected to bring the word of the gods (or in the case of Biblical prophecy, the One God) to the people.

**quatrains**   Verses of four lines, the pattern Nostradamus used to write his prophecies.

**Roswell**   The town in New Mexico where a UFO might or might not have crashed in 1947.

**343**

**sardonic**   Scornful and bitter, expecting that no good will come of whatever is happening.

**seismologist**   A person who studies earthquakes.

**Shaman**   A doctor. Priest, and/or magician in a tribal culture.

**Sibyls**   The priestess prophets who received the messages from the gods and passed them on to the priests. They took their name from Sibyl, a great prophetess of ancient legend.

**spectroscope**   The device that splits a beam of light into its various colors.

**spectrum**   The rainbow of colors that a beam of white light can be broken into when it is passed through a prism.

**tables of houses**   Compilations based on latitude for finding the location of the "houses" in a person's horoscope. The houses are 12 divisions of the heavens based on the location of the birthplace of the person whose chart is being done.

**telekinesis**   The ability to move objects by psychic means.

**telepathy**   Mind reading or communicating by mental energy

**UFO**   An acronym for unidentified flying object, the term was coined by the Air Force in 1947 to give it something more official-sounding to call the objects than "flying saucers."

**UFOlogist**   A person who studies reports of UFOs to try to determine how authentic the reports are and just what it was that was seen.

**Zodiac**   The imaginary belt in the heavens that contains the plain of the ecliptic. Along this belt lie the 12 signs of the Zodiac. (If you draw an imaginary line from the center of the sun to the center of the earth and then keep the line tight as the earth circles the sun, you would have created a flat surface in space called the plain of the ecliptic. The orbits of all the planets except Pluto lie on or fairly close to this plane if you extend it far enough.)

# Astrological Information

For a fuller explanation of how these astrological elements are combined and used, see Chapter 14, "An Astrology Primer."

## The Signs of the Zodiac

The astrological year begins on March 21 and ends on the following March 20. The following table contains the signs of the Zodiac. These signs represent the area of the sky that the sun enters on these dates.

| Astrological Sign | Associated Dates |
| --- | --- |
| Aries (the Ram) | March 21 through April 19 |
| Taurus (the Bull) | April 20 through May 19 |
| Gemini (the Twins) | May 20 through June 20 |
| Cancer (the Crab) | June 21 through July 22 |
| Leo (the Lion) | July 23 through August 21 |
| Virgo (the Virgin) | August 22 through September 22 |
| Libra (the Scales) | September 23 through October 22 |
| Scorpio (the Scorpion) | October 23 through November 21 |
| Sagittarius (the Archer) | November 22 through December 21 |
| Capricorn (the Goat) | December 22 through January 20 |
| Aquarius (the Water Carrier) | January 21 through February 19 |
| Pisces (the Fish) | February 20 through March 20 |

# The Qualities Attributed to the Signs of the Zodiac

Each of the Signs has various qualities associated with it, which are used in developing the individual horoscope. The various schools of astrology differ a bit in their attribution of these qualities, but in general they agree on those listed below.

| Astrological Sign | Associated Qualities |
| --- | --- |
| Aries | Courage, energy, impatience, leadership |
| Taurus | Patience, persistence, obstinacy, consolidation |
| Gemini | Cleverness, superficiality, mobility, instability |
| Cancer | Sensitivity, parenthood, inspiration, elusiveness |
| Leo | Dignity, self-confidence, libido, pretentiousness |
| Virgo | Care, tidiness, authority, etiquette, pedantry |
| Libra | Harmony, justice, precision, testing, trivia |
| Scorpio | Endurance, egoism, profundity, passion, brutality |
| Sagittarius | Spirituality, propriety, yearning, striving |
| Capricorn | Self-awareness, independence, industry, stubbornness |
| Aquarius | Optimism, adaptability, conviction, helpfulness |
| Pisces | Compassion, sensitivity, tolerance, vagueness, intuition |

# The Planets and What They Represent

As with the Signs, the Planets have qualities associated with them, which are used in reading the horoscope.

| Planet | Associated Qualities |
| --- | --- |
| Sun | The masculine principle, the living being, vitality, psychic energy |
| Moon | The feminine principle, the soul or psyche, change or fluctuation (the tides, the months), fecundity, the mother |
| Mercury | Intellect, reason, judgment, mediation, movement |
| Venus | Love, art, harmony, attraction; girl or maiden, sweetheart or mistress |
| Mars | Action, energy, impulsiveness, aggressiveness, brutality; soldiers, athletes, surgeons |
| Jupiter | Harmony and law, humor, riches, health; bankers, the upper classes, fortune hunters |
| Saturn | Concentration, limitation, inhibition, solemnity, sobriety, maturity, old age; farmers, miners, realtors |

| Planet | Associated Qualities |
|---|---|
| Uranus | Suddenness, revolution transmutation, violence, the occult arts, creativity; magicians, astrologers |
| Neptune | Fantasy and imagination, mysticism, impressionability, vagueness, deception and self-deception |
| Pluto | The masses, power, higher power, invisible forces, propaganda; demagogues and dictators |

# The 12 Houses and What They Represent

As with the Signs and Planets, the Houses have qualities. All of these taken together—Signs, Planets, and Houses—combine to form a pattern that can be read by a skillful astrologer.

| House | Associated Qualities |
|---|---|
| First | Childhood, personality, physical condition |
| Second | Money and things material, gain or loss |
| Third | Family, communications, writing and documents |
| Fourth | The home, birthplace, mines and underground places; in a man's chart, his mother; in a woman's chart, her father |
| Fifth | Sex, especially nonmarital; pleasure, education, gambling |
| Sixth | Health, servants, food, clothing, small animals |
| Seventh | Partnership, marriage, agreements, open enemies; the husband in a woman's chart; the wife in a man's chart |
| Eighth | Death, inheritances, wills, loss, accidents, a partner's wealth |
| Ninth | Spirituality and philosophy, sea voyages and other travel, foreign countries, religion |
| Tenth | Vocation or job, profession, employer, superior, business, government |
| Eleventh | Wishes or hopes, society, friends, companions, counselors, the wealth of employers |
| Twelfth | Secret enemies, prisons, hospitals, plots, unseen difficulties, large animals |

# Reporting UFOs

Air Force Regulation 200-2 specifies a report form for UFO sightings. It went through several revisions. The following are selected portions of the 12 August 1954 version, as cited in Major Donald E. Kehoe's book, *The Flying Saucer Conspiracy:*

**INTELLIGENCE**

Unidentified Flying Objects Reporting (Short Title: UFOB)

(1) Purpose and Scope. This Regulation establishes procedures for reporting information and evidence pertaining to unidentified flying objects and sets forth the responsibility of Air Force activities in this regard. It applies to all Air Force activities.

(2) Definitions:

   a. Unidentified Flying Objects (UFOB)—Relates to any airborne object which by performance, aerodynamic characteristics, or unusual features does not conform to any presently known aircraft or missile type or which cannot be positively identified as a familiar object.

   b. Familiar Objects—Include balloons, astronomical bodies, birds, and so forth.

(3) Objectives. Air Force interest in unidentified flying objects is two-fold: First, as a possible threat to the security of the United States and its forces, and secondly, to determine technical aspects involved.

... ... ...

(4) Responsibility:

   a. Reporting. Commanders of Air Force activities will report all information and evidence that may come to their attention including that received from adjacent commands of the other services and from civilians.

b. Investigation. Air Defense Command will conduct all field investigations within the ZI [Zone of the Interior (the continental United States)] to determine the identity of any UFOB.

c. Analysis. The Air Technical Intelligence Center (ATIC), Wright-Patterson Air Force Base, Ohio will analyze and evaluate: All information and evidence reported within the ZI after the Air Defense Command has exhausted all efforts to identify the UFOB, and all information and evidence collected in oversea areas.

d. Cooperation. All activities will cooperate with Air Defense Command representatives to insure the economical and prompt success of an investigation, including the furnishing of air and ground transportation when feasible.

... ... ...

(7) Reporting. All information relating to UFOBs will be reported promptly.

... ... ...

d. Report Format. Reports will include the following numbered items:

1. Description of the object(s):
    a. Shape.
    b. Size compared to a known object (use one of the following terms: Head of a pin, pea, dime, nickel, quarter, half-dollar, silver dollar, baseball, grapefruit, or basketball) held in the hand at about arm's length.
    c. Color.
    d. Number.
    e. Formation, if more than one.
    f. Any discernible features or details.
    g. Tail, trail. Or exhaust, including size of same compared to size of object(s).
    h. Sound. If heard, describe sound.
    i. Other pertinent or unusual features.

2. Description of course of object(s):
    a. What first called the attention of observer(s) to the object(s)?
    b. Angle of elevation and azimuth of the object(s) when first observed.
    c. Angle of elevation and azimuth of the object(s) upon disappearance.

d. Description of flight path and maneuvers of object(s).

e. Manner of disappearance of object(s).

f. Length of time in sight.

3. Manner of observation:

   a. Use of one or any combination of the following items: Ground-visual, ground-electronic, air-electronic. (If electronic, specify type of radar.)

   b. Statement as to optical aids (telescopes, binoculars, and so forth) used and description thereof.

   c. If the sighting is made while airborne, give type aircraft, identification number, altitude, heading, speed, and home station.

4. Time and Date of Sighting:

   a. Zulu time-date group of sighting.

   b. Light conditions (use one of the following terms): Night, day, dawn, dusk.

5. Locations of observer(s). Exact latitude and longitude of each observer, or Georef position, or position with reference to a known landmark.

6. Identifying information of all observer(s):

   a. Civilian—Name, age, mailing address, occupation.

   b. Military—Name, grade, organization, duty, and estimate of reliability.

7. Weather and winds-aloft conditions at time and place of sightings.

   a. Observer(s) account of weather conditions.

   b. Reports from nearest AWS or U.S. Weather Bureau Office of wind direction and velocity in degrees and knots at surface, 6,000', 10,000', 16,000', 20,000', 30,000', 50,000', and 80,000', if available.

   c. Ceiling.

   d. Visibility.

   e. Amount of cloud cover.

   f. Thunderstorms in area and quadrant in which located.

8. Any other unusual activity or condition, meteorological, astronomical, or otherwise, which might account for the sighting.

9. Interception or identification action taken (such action may be taken whenever feasible, complying with existing air defense directives).

10. Location of any air traffic in the area at time of sighting.

11. Position title and comments of the preparing officer including his preliminary analysis of the possible cause of the sighting(s).

12. Existence of physical evidence such as materials and photographs.

(8) Evidence. The existence of physical evidence (photographs or materiel) will be promptly reported.

    a. Photographic:

        1. Visual. The negative and two prints will be forwarded; all original film, including wherever possible both prints and negatives, will be titled or otherwise properly identified as to place, time, and date of the incident (see "Intelligence Collection Instructions" (ICI) June 1954).

        2. Radar. Two copies of each print will be forwarded. Prints of radarscope photography will be titled in accordance with AFR 95-7 and forwarded in compliance with AFR 95-6.

    b. Materiel Suspected or actual items of materiel which come into possession of any Air Force echelon will be safeguarded in such a manner as to prevent any defacing or alteration which might reduce its value for intelligence examination and analysis.

(9) Release of Facts. Headquarters USAF will release summaries of evaluated data which will inform the public on this subject. In response to local inquiries, it is permissible to inform news media representatives on UFOB's when the object is positively identified as a familiar object (see paragraph 2b), except that the following type of data warrants protection and should not be revealed: Names of principles, intercept and investigation procedures, and classified radar data. For those objects which are not explainable, only the fact that ATIC will analyze the data is worthy of release, due to the many unknowns involved.

BY ORDER OF THE SECRETARY
OF THE AIR FORCE

Tyromancy: Divination by observing the coagulation of cheese.

# Divination Techniques

There are more divination techniques than you can shake a stick at. (Shaking a stick, incidentally, could be considered a form of either dowsing or rhabdomancy.) The following is a list of some of the many ways of appealing to the gods or the fates to determine the future.

**aeromancy**   Divination by atmospheric phenomena

**alectromancy** or **alectryomancy**   Divination by a rooster

**aleuromancy**   Divination by slips of paper baked into cakes

**alomancy**   Divination by salt

**alphitomancy**   Truth-telling by eating barley cakes

**amniomancy**   Divination by means of the caul (a membrane that covers the heads of some newborn babies)

**anthropomancy**   Divination by human sacrifice

**apantomancy**   Divination by chance meeting with any object

**arithmomancy**   Divination by numbers (numerology)

**armomancy**   Divination by the shoulders

**aspidomancy**   Divination by revelation

**astragalomancy**   Divination by casting dice

**astrology**   Divination by the stars and planets

**austromancy**   Divination by studying the wind

**axinomancy**   Divination by driving an axe into a post or by balancing a stone on the axe blade

**belomancy**   Divination by the fall of arrows

**bibliomancy**   Divination by books, particularly the Bible

**botanomancy**   Divination by observing the smoke and flame from burning briar or vervain branches

**caloptromancy**   Divination by mirrors

**capnomancy**   Divination by smoke rising from a fire

**causinomancy**   Divination by objects placed in a fire

**cerainoscopy**   Divination by observing lightning

**cephalomancy**   Divination using the boiled skull or head of a goat

**ceroscopy**   Divination by pouring molten wax into cold water

**chalcomancy**   Divination by listening to the tones made by striking metal bowls with a mallet

**chresmomancy**   Divination by listening to the ravings of a lunatic

**cleidomancy**   Divination by dangling a key over a Bible

**cleromancy**   Divination by casting stones, pebbles, or dice

**coscinomancy**   Divination by sieve and tongues

**critomancy**   Divination by studying barley cakes

**cromniomancy**   Divination by observing the growth of special onions

**crystallomancy**   Divination by peering into crystals

**cyclomancy**   Divination by studying a turning wheel

**dactylomancy**   Divination by dangling a ring over an alphabet board

**dacryomancy**   Divination by tears and crying

**daphnomancy**   Divination by listening to the crackling of burning laurel

**demonomancy**   Divination through the aid of demons

**dictiomancy**   Divination by a dictionary

**dowsing**   Finding underground water by using a forked stick

**eromancy**   Divination by air

**extispicy**   Divination by entrails (anthropomancy)

**felidomancy**   Divination by watching cats

**floromancy**   Divination by flowers

**gastromancy**   Divination by speaking in a low voice while in a trance

**geloscopy**   Divination from the tone of someone's laughter

**geomancy**   Divination by drawing signs on the earth

**graphology**   Character analysis by studying handwriting

**gyromancy**   Divination by rapidly dancing or turning in circles until exhausted

**halomancy**   Divination by watching burning salt

**haruspication**   Divination by examining the entrails of animals

**hippomancy**   Divination by studying the motion of horses

**hydromancy**   Divination by studying various aspects (color, rate of flow, and so on) of water

**icthyomancy**   Divination by examining the entrails of fish

**kephalonomancy**   Divination by the head of an ass

**lampodomancy**   Divination by observing a lamp flame

**lecnomancy**   Divination by peering into a basin of water

**libanomancy**   Interpreting omens by studying burning incense

**lithomancy**   Divination by studying light reflected by colored stones

**macharomancy**   Divination by swords or knives

**margaritomancy**   Determining guilt or innocence by bouncing pearls in a pot

**meteoromency**   Divination based on meteors and other aerial phenomena

**metagnomy**   Divination while in a hypnotic trance (comparatively recent)

**metoposcopy**   Reading character from the lines of the forehead

**moleosopy**   Studying moles on the skin as an indication of a person's character

**myomancy**   Divination by observing rats and mice

**necromancy**   Divination by calling up the spirits of the dead

**nephelomancy**   Prophecy by the shape and motion of clouds

**numerology**   Divination by numbers (arithmomancy)

**oenomancy**   Divination by studying the appearance of wine or wine dregs

**omphalomancy**   Contemplation of one's own navel

**oneiromancy**   Dream interpretation

**onemancy**   Divination by the questioning of the Angel Uriel

**onomancy**   Divination by interpreting names

**onychomancy**   Divination by examining fingernails in the sunlight

**oomancy, oomanlia,** or **ooscopy**   Divination by eggs

**ophiomancy**   Divination by observing serpents

**ornithomancy**   Divination by the flight and songs of birds

**palmistry**   Divination by the lines of the hand

**parthenomancy**   Divination by thread (used to test virginity)

**passomancy**   Divination by studying pebbles

**pegomancy** or **pessomancy**   Divination by spring water or bubbling fountains

**phyllorhodomancy**   Divination by rubbing rose leaves between your palms and listening to the sound

**psychomancy**   Divination by questioning spirits

**pyromancy**   Divination by fire (causinomancy)

**rhabdomancy**   Divination by rods, sticks, or staffs

**rhapsodomancy**   Divination by poetry

**scapulomancy**   Divination by the bones of the shoulder

**sciamancy**   Divination by evocation of the dead

**scrying**   Peering into mirrors or crystal balls to read the future

**selenomancy**   Divination by observation of the moon

**sideromancy**   Divination by dropping dry straw on a hot skillet

**sortilege**   Divination by casting lots

**splanchomancy**   Divination by the entrails of human sacrifices

**spodanomancy**   Divination by writing in ashes

**stoicheomancy**   Bibliomancy using the books of Homer or Virgil

**sycomancy**   Divination by the leaves of a fig tree

**tephramancy**   Divination by the ashes of a sacrificial fire

**theomancy**   Divination by the evocation of sacred names

**tiromancy** or **tyromancy**   Divination by cheese

**transataumancy**   Foretelling the future by overheard conversation

**xylomancy**   Divination by fallen or burning wood

# Selected Bibliography

Much of the information in *The Complete Idiot's Guide to Unsolved Mysteries* was taken from the following books, which will prove useful to anyone interested in delving a little deeper into specific topics of interest.

## General

Baring-Gould, Sabine. *Strange Survivals*. London: Methuen & Co, 1892.

Cooper-Oakley. *The Count of Saint-Germain*. Blauvelt, New York: Rudolf Steiner Publications, 1970.

Fort, Charles. *The Books of Charles Fort*. New York: Henry Holt, 1941.

Mackay, Charles. *Extraordinary Popular Delusions and the Madness of Crowds*. London: Harrap, 1956 [reprint of 1852 edition].

Somerlott, Robert. *Here, Mr. Splitfoot*. New York: Viking, 1971.

Wilson, Colin. *From Atlantis to the Sphinx*. New York: Fromm International, 1996.

——. *Mysteries*. New York: Putnam's, 1978.

Zolar. *The Encyclopedia of Ancient and Forbidden Knowledge*. Los Angeles: Nash, 1970.

## Archaeology and Crypto-Archaeology

Bord, Janet and Colin. *Mysterious Britain*. St. Albans, Great Britain: Paladin, 1974.

de Camp, L. Sprague. *The Ancient Engineers*. New York: Ballantine, 1974.

Hawkins, Gerald. *Stonehenge Decoded*. New York: Dell, 1966.

Lewis, H. Spencer, Ph.D. *The Symbolic Prophecy of the Great Pyramid.* San Jose: The Rosicrucian Press, 1936.

Niel, Fernand. *The Mysteries of Stonehenge.* New York: Avon, 1975.

Pochan, A. *The Mysteries of the Great Pyramids.* New York: Avon, 1971.

# Astrology

Heindel, Max. *Simplified Scientific Astrology.* Oceanside, CA: The Rosicrucian Fellowship, 1926.

Levi, Eliphas. *Transcendental Magic* (translation by A.E. Waite). London: Rider & Co., 1896.

Lewi, Grant. *Astrology for the Millions.* New York: Doubleday, 1969.

MacNeice, Louis. *Astrology.* London: Aldus Books, 1964.

Saint-Germain, Comte de. *Practical Astrology.* Chicago: Laird & Lee, 1901.

# Atlantis

de Camp, L. Sprague. *Lost Continents: The Atlantis Theme.* New York: Gnome Press, 1954.

Ley, Willy. *Another Look at Atlantis.* New York: Bell, 1969.

Osborn, Chase Salmon, B.S., L.L.D. *The Earth Upsets.* Baltimore: Waverly Press, 1927.

Plato. *The Dialogues of Plato* (translated into English by B. Jowett, M.A.). New York: Random House, 1937 (original copyright 1892).

# Mata Hari

Coulson, Major Thomas, O.B.E. *Mata Hari: Courtesan and Spy.* New York: Blue Ribbon Books, 1930.

Howe, Russell Warren. *Mata Hari: The True Story.* New York: Dodd, Mead, 1986.

Ostrovsky, Erika. *Eye of Dawn: The Rise and Fall of Mata Hari.* New York: Macmillan, 1978.

# Prophecy

Collier, Robert. *Something to Hope For.* New York: The Book of Gold, 1942.

Forman, Henry James. *The Story of Prophecy.* New York: Farrar & Rinehart, 1936.

Stearn, Jess. *Edgar Cayce, The Sleeping Prophet.* New York: Doubleday, 1967.

Sugrue, Thomas. *There is a River: The Story of Edgar Cayce.* New York: Henry Holt, 1943 (revised 1945).

# Shakespeare Authorship

Bowen, Catherine Drinker. *Francis Bacon: The Temper of a Man.* Boston: Little, Brown, 1963.

Chute, Marchette. *Shakespeare of London.* New York: Dutton, 1949.

Harbage, Alfred. *William Shakespeare: A Reader's Guide.* New York: Farrar Straus and Giroux, 1963.

Michell, John. *Who Wrote Shakespeare?* London: Thames and Hudson, 1996.

Rowse, A.L. *William Shakespeare.* New York: Harper and Row, 1964.

Schoenbaum, S. *Shakespeare's Lives.* London: Oxford University Press, 1991.

# Spiritualism

Feilding, Evrard. *Sittings With Eusapia Palladino & Other Studies.* New York: University Books, 1963.

Jackson, Herbert G., Jr. *The Spirit Rappers.* New York: Doubleday, 1972.

Porter, Katherine H. *Through a Glass Darkly: Spiritualism in the Browning Circle.* New York: Octagon Books, 1972.

# Strange Happenings

Baring-Gould, Sabine. *The Book of Werewolves.* New York: Causeway Books, 1973.

Berlitz, Charles. *The Bermuda Triangle.* New York: Doubleday, 1974.

Copper, Basil. *The Vampire in Legend and Fact.* New York: Citadel, 1993.

Hill, Douglas. *The History of Ghosts, Vampires & Werewolves.* New York: Harrow, 1973.

Kusche, Lawrence David. *The Bermuda Triangle Mystery—Solved.* New York: Harper & Row, 1975.

# UFOs

Condon, Dr. Edward, et al. *Scientific Study of Unidentified Flying Objects* [The Condon Report]. New York: Bantam, 1969.

Fuller, John G. *The Interrupted Journey.* New York: Dell, 1966.

Kurland, Michael. *The Complete Idiot's Guide to Extraterrestrial Intelligence.* New York: Alpha Books, 1999.

Randle, Kevin D. & Donald R. Schmitt. *UFO Crash at Roswell.* New York: Avon, 1991.

# Index

## SYMBOLS

12 Houses
associated qualities, 347
casting horoscopes, common themes, 180-181

## A

A.R.E. (Association for Research and Enlightenment), 96
*Abduction: Human Encounters with Aliens* (Mack), 296
abductions
alien encounters, story of Betty and Barney Hill, 291-296
increase after publication of Hills' experience, 296-297
abilities (persons with ESP), 52
Abominable Snowman, 323
Adar (god associated with Saturn), Chaldean astrology, 161
Air Force investigation
Betty and Barney Hill, alien encounter, 292
Project Sign, flying saucer reports, 273-274
Roswell incident, 280-281
airship sightings, 268
Hamilton, Alex (farmer), 269
Texas windmill, 269-270
*Alien Autopsy*, 284

alien encounters, 291
Betty and Barney Hill, 291-292
Air Force investigation, 292
claim to examination by aliens, 294-296
inability to account for two hours, 293
hypnotherapy, 297-298
increase in claims of abduction, 296-297
*Roswell incident*, 284
almanac, astrological (Lilly), 164-166
Amburgh, Charles Van ("expert" witness in Braintree crime), 224
anagrams, 83
Anakim tribe, Gilgal Refaim monument, 113
anarchists, Sacco and Vanzetti (events of Braintree), 224
"expert" witnesses, 224-225
Lowell Commission investigation, 225-226
ancient Egyptian books, *Nostradamus*, 84
anecdotal evidence (ESP), 53-55
Grant, Julia (wife of Ulysses Grant), 55-56
Lincoln, Abraham, 55-56
Twain, Mark, 55
animal magnetism (Mesmer), 191-192
Anti-Alien readings (*Roswell Incident*), 284
Antichrist, 68

Anwari (Persian poet and astrologer), prediction of the "great tempest", 163
Aquarius (the Water Carrier) zodiacal sign, 177
archaeology books, 357-358
Area 51 (Groom Lake), 283
Aries (the Ram) zodiacal sign, 174
Arnold, Kenneth (private pilot), sighting of flying saucer, 270-271
arrest for espionage, Mata Hari, 257
articles of faith, *Roswell Incident*, 282
Ashley Place Levitation, 195
assertions of Donnelly regarding Atlantis, 135-137
associated qualities
planets, 346-347
signs of the zodiac, 174, 346
Aquarius (the Water Carrier), 177
Aries (the Ram), 174
Cancer (the Crab), 174
Capricorn (the Goat), 177
Gemini (the Twins), 174
Leo (the Lion), 175
Libra (the Scales), 176
Pisces (the Fish), 177
Sagittarius (the Archer), 176
Scorpio (the Scorpion), 176
Taurus (the Bull), 174
Virgo (the Virgin), 175
Association for Research and Enlightenment. *See* A.R.E.

asteroid crash (fate of the universe), 127
astrologers, 159
  Chaldean priests
    development of constellations, 160
    gods associated with planets, 161
    *post hoc ergo propter hoc*, 160-161
    *Zodiac*, 162
  Dixon, Jeane, 170
    Jeane Dixon effect, 170
    role for FBI, 170
  learned, 163
    Brahe, Tycho, 163-164
    Kepler, Johannes, 164
    Lilly, William, 164-166
  royal, 162
astrological almanac (Lilly), 164-166
*Astrological Predictions* (Lilly), 164
astrology, 157-172
  12 Houses, associated qualities, 347
  books, 358
  casting horoscopes, 172-182
    12 Houses, 180-181
    drawing lines to determine aspects, 181
    ephemeris, 178-179
  changing view of the solar system, 167
  Dixon's predictions, 170
    Jeane Dixon effect, 170
    role for FBI, 170
  Hitler, 167-168
  medieval world, 162
    learned astrologers, 163-166
    royal astrologers, 162
  parallelism, 171-172
  planets, associated qualities, 346-347
  science of "cold reading", 158-159

signs of the Zodiac, 173, 345
  associated qualities, 174-177, 346
  cusps, 177
*Astrology: The Space Age Science* (Goodavage), 171
*Atalanta*, Bermuda Triangle legend, 20-21
Athens (Greek city to stop Atlantis), 130
Atlantis, 129
  books, 358
  Cayce, Edgar, 99
  Columbus, 134
  Donnelly, 135
    assertions, 135-137
    collection of facts, 138
    evidence for existence, 137
  origins, 132-134
  Plato, dialogues, 130-131
  post-Donnelly seekers, 138
    Blavatsky, 139
  Root Races of Mankind, 139
    Cayce, Edgar, 139-140
    Galanapoulos, Anghelos, 140
*Atlantis: The Antediluvian World* (Donnelly), 135
Aurelianus, Ambrosius (Stonehenge, theory of erection), 111
axeman (New Orleans) crime, 226
  axeman hysteria, 228-229
  Besumer, Louis (grocer or spy), 227-228
  murder of Joseph Mumfre, 231-233
  role of Rosie Cortimiglia, 229
  Schneider, 228
  *Times-Picayune* letter, 229-231
  victims, 231

# B

back-engineering, 283
background radiation, 123
Bacon, Sir Francis (contender for the quill of *The Playwright*), 331-332
  Baconian Cipher, 331-334
Bailey, F. Lee (lawyer for Sam Sheppard case), 236
balloon analogy (why the universe is retreating), 122
Balsamo, Giuseppe (idol), 200
Bathurst, Sir Benjamin, mystery of disappearance, 24-25
beginning of the universe, 118
  conceptual framework, 118-119
  stars, 119-120
Berlitz, Charles (coauthor of *The Roswell Incident*), 281-282
Bermuda Triangle legends, 18-21
  "Devil's Triangle", 19
  disappearing Avengers, 18-19
  Flight 19, 20
  *H.M.S. Atalanta*, 20-21
  missing DC-3, 21
  *Scorpion*, 21
  *U.S.S. Cyclops*, 21
Besumer, Louis (grocer or spy), New Orleans axeman crime, 227-228
Bierce, Ambrose, disappearing persons story, 26
Big Bang theory, 122-123
Bigfoot (human-like creatures), 324-325
  Patterson picture, 325
biosphere, 143-144
  conditions for life to exist on other planets, 146
    generation stars, 147
    right mix of stars and planets, 147

Doctor Drake's equation, 150
  Milky Way example, 151-154
Fermi paradox, 147-149
formation of planets from stars, 144
  detecting Earth-size planets, 146
  wobble technique, 145
lack of evidence for extra-terrestrial life existence, 148-149
radio signal detection of extraterrestrial life, 154
  Project Ozma, 154
  Project Phoenix, 154-155
  SERENDIP, 155-156
  SETI League, 155
birth charts, casting a horoscope, 178
  12 Houses, 180-181
  drawing lines to determine aspects, 181
  ephemeris, 178-179
*Black Hand* (New Orleans axeman crime), 226
Blavatsky, Helena Petrovna (mystic and spiritualist), Root Races of Mankind, 139
bluestone (Stonehenge), 110
book resources
  archaeology and crypto-archaeology, 357-358
  astrology, 358
  Atlantis, 358
  general, 357
  prophecy, 358-359
  Shakespeare authorship, 359
  spiritualism, 359
  strange happenings, 359
  UFOs, 359
Borden, Lizzie, 237-240
  death of father Borden, 240-241
  death of stepmother Borden, 241-242
  human fascination with mysteries, 5

investigation, 242
  Borden burglary, 244
  clues and suspects, 242
  facts, 243
trial, 244
  burning of a dress, 245-246
  defense team, 246-247
unanswered questions, 247-248
Brahe, Tycho (learned astrologer), 163-164
Braintree crime, anarchists Sacco and Vanzetti, 224
  "expert" witnesses, 224-225
  Lowell Commission investigation, 225-226
Breckenridge, Colonel Henry (role in Lindbergh baby kidnapping), 211
brigantine, 14
Bunyip (lake serpent), 320

## C

Cagliostro, Count, 200-203
  elixir of youth, 202
  Paris, 203-204
character traits (signs of the zodiac). *See* associated qualities, signs of the zodiac
cairns, 46
Cancer (the Crab) zodiacal sign, 174
Cape of Good Hope, *Flying Dutchman*, 12
Capital building sightings (UFOs), 274
Capricorn (the Goat) zodiacal sign, 177
Captain Van der Decken, *Flying Dutchman*, 12
carbon dating, potsherds, 112
casting horoscopes, 172-182
  12 Houses, common themes, 180-181
  drawing lines to determine aspects, 181
  ephemeris, 178-179

Cayce, Edgar (prophet)
  A.R.E. (Association for Research and Enlightenment), 96
  Atlantis, 99, 139-140
  diagnoses and treatments, 98
  psychic readings through self-induced trance, 96-97
Cenozoic Era, 125
centuries (groups of quatrains), 83
Chaldean priests (astrologers)
  development of constellations, 160
  gods associated with planets, 161
  *post hoc ergo propter hoc*, 160-161
  *Zodiac*, 162
"Champ" (lake serpent), 318
cheating mediums, 196
Chicxulub structure (fate of the universe), 127
China, Great Pearl, ancient pastime UFOs, 267
*Choir Gaur, the Grand Orrery of the Ancient Druids*, 111
chupacabra ("goat-sucker"), 326
ciphers, 332
Circle of Fire (Pharoah Thuthmosis III), ancient pastime UFOs, 267
clairaudience, 52
clairvoyance, 52, 192
"cold reading" (astrology), 158-159
colonels, Lindbergh baby kidnapping, 211-212
Columbus, Atlantis, 134
communicating with the dead, 185
  Hydesville sisters and spiritualism, 186-187
    digging for the rapper, 187
    public lecture of Leah Fox, 188-189

mediums, 193
cheating, 196
Home, Daniel Dunglas, 193-195
seances, 190
Davis, Andrew Jackson, 192-193
Deacon Strong, 189-190
Mesmer, Dr. Friedrich Anton, 191-192
Swedenborg, Emanuel, 190-191
*Complete Idiot's Guide to Astrology, The*, 178
composition of the stars, 120-121
conceptual framework, beginning of the universe, 118-119
Condon, Dr. John F. (role in Lindbergh baby kidnapping), 213
rejection syndrome, 218
Conjunction aspect, 181
constellations, Chaldean priests (astrologers), 160
Copt, 103
Cortimiglia, Rosie (role in New Orleans axeman crime), 229
Count Cagliostro, 200-203
elixir of youth, 202
Paris, 203-204
Count de Saint-Germain, 197
facts and legends, 198
life after death, 199-200
Court of the Star Chamber, 338
crashing asteroid (fate of the universe), 127
Crater, Judge Joseph Force, disappearing persons story, 29-30
creatures, 303
chupacabra, 326
cryptids, 315-316
lake leviathans, 316-321
examining the unknown, 326

ghouls, 311
Dahmer, Jeffrey, 313
Gein, Ed, 311-312
human-like, 322
Bigfoot, 324-325
Yeti, 323-324
Tasmanian tiger, 321-322
vampires, 304-305
Paole, Arnold, 306-308
Roma lamia, 305-306
werewolves, 308
lycanthropy, 310
salve, 309
cremation, Paole, Arnold, 307-308
crimes, 223
Braintree, 224
"expert" witnesses, 224-225
Lowell Commission investigation, 225-226
Lizzie Borden story, 237-240
death of father Borden, 240-241
death of mother Borden, 241-242
investigation, 242-244
trial, 244-247
unanswered questions, 247-248
New Orleans axeman, 226
axeman hysteria, 228-229
Besumer, Louis (grocer or spy), 227-228
murder of Joseph Mumfre, 231-233
role of Rosie Cortimiglia, 229
Schneider, 228
*Times-Picayune* letter, 229-231
victims, 231
Sam Sheppard case, 233
retrial, 235-236

role of Dr. Leland Kirk, 234
"surgical instrument", 234
Croesus oracle, 66-67
cryptids, lake leviathans, 315-321
"Champ" (Lake Champlain), 318
Flathead Monster (Lake Flathead), 319
Lake Sandnesvatet, 319-320
Loch Ness Monster, 316-317
Ogopogo (Lake Okanagan), 319
skrimsel, 320
crypto-archaeology books, 357-358
cryptozoology, 316
*Crystal Enlightenment* (Raphaell), 138
crystals, science of crystals, 138
cusps, signs of the zodiac, 177
*Cyclops* (Bermuda Triangle legend), 21

## D

Dahmer, Jeffrey (ghoul), 313
*Dakar* submarine, 22
dance, Hindu temple dancing of Mata Hari, 251-252
dates associated with astrological zodiacal signs, 345-346
dating
carbon, potsherds, 112
Sphinx, 108
Davidson, David, history of mankind through interpretation of Great Pyramid, 105-106
Davis, Andrew Jackson (subject of mesmerism), 192-193
Day, Flight-Lieutenant W.T., disappearing persons story, 27

DC-3 missing (Bermuda Triangle legend), 21
*De nova stella* (Brahe), 164
*De Vliegende Hollander. See Flying Dutchman*
Deacon Strong, séance example, 189-190
dead persons (communicating with), 185
  Hydesville sisters and spiritualism, 186-187
    digging for the rapper, 187
    public lecture of Leah Fox, 188-189
  mediums, 193
    cheating, 196
    Home, Daniel Dunglas, 193-195
  seances, 190
    Davis, Andrew Jackson, 192-193
    Deacon Strong, 189-190
    Mesmer, Dr. Friedrich Anton, 191-192
    Swedenborg, Emanuel, 190-191
deaths (Lizzie Borden story), father Borden, 240-241
  stepmother Borden, 241-242
decans (signs of the Zodiac), 178
Declaration of Principles Concerning Activities Following the Detection of Extraterrestrial Intelligence, 155
definitions (UFOB report form), 349
Delphic oracle, 66-67
Denvignes, Colonel Joseph (role in Mata Hari conquest of Kalle), 256-257
*Derfliegende Hollander* (opera), legend of the *Flying Dutchman*, 12
detecting Earth-size planets, 146

*Deuxieme Bureau* (French spy service), Mata Hari's offer to work, 253-254
"Devil's Triangle", Bermuda Triangle legend, 19
diagnoses, Edgar Cayce's psychic readings, 98
dialogues (Plato)
  *Kritias*, 131
  *Timaios*, 130-131
dinosaurs, 126
dirigible sightings, 268
  Hamilton, Alex (farmer), 269
  Texas windmill, 269-270
disappearances
  *Erebus* (ship in search for the Northwest Passage), 42-48
    evidence of missing expedition, 44
    McClintock, Captain Frances (expedition), 46-47
    Rae, John (overland search), 44-45
    speculation, 47-48
  Eric the Red, 35
  people, 23
    Bathurst, Sir Benjamin, 24-25
    Bierce, Ambrose, 26
    Crater, Judge Joseph Force, 29-30
    Hoffa, James, 30-32
    officers Day and Stewart, 27
    Picard, Pauline, 28-29
    Ross, Charles, 25-26
    Small, Ambrose, 26-27
    unfound persons, 32
  planes, 11
    legends of the Bermuda Triangle, 18-21
  Roanoke colony settlers, 37-41
  ships, 11
    *Flying Dutchman*, 12

    legends of the Bermuda Triangle, 21
    *Mary Celeste*, 13-17
    *Rosalie*, 17-18
    *Terror* (ship in search of the Northwest Passage), 42-48
      evidence of missing expedition, 44
      McClintock, Captain Frances (expedition), 46-47
      Rae, John (overland search), 44-45
      speculation, 47-48
disbanding of Project Blue Book, 277-278
Dixon, Jeane (astrologer), 170
  Jeane Dixon effect, 170
  role for FBI, 170
Dodona oracle, 65
dolmens, 112
dolorite. *See* bluestone
Donnelly, Ignatius T.T., Atlantis, 135
  assertions, 135-137
  collection of facts, 138
  evidence for existence, 137
Donovan, Colonel William Joseph (role in Lindbergh baby kidnapping), 211
Doppler effect, 146
dowsing, 52
Drake, Dr. Frank (professor of astronomy and astrophysics), Doctor Drake's equation, 150-154
drawing lines, horoscope charts, 181
Druid Temple, 110

# E

Earl of Oxford (contender for the quill of *The Playwright*), 335-336 ecosphere, 145

*Edward Gein: America's Most Bizarre Murderer* (Gollmar), 312

Einstein's General Theory of Relativity, 121

elixir of youth (Count Cagliostro), 202

empirical proof versus eyewitness evidence (UFOs), 299-300

ephemeris, casting horoscopes, 178-179

*Erebus* (ship in search for the Northwest Passage), disappearance, 42-48

  evidence of missing expedition, 44

  McClintock, Captain Frances (expedition), 46-47

  Rae, John (overland search), 44-45

  speculation, 47-48

Eric the Red (explorer who discovered Greenland), 33-34

  disappearance, 35

  Little Ice Age, 34-35

ESP (extrasensory perception), 51

  abilities, 52

  anecdotal evidence, 53-55

    Grant, Julia (wife of Ulysses Grant), 55-56

    Lincoln, Abraham, 55-56

    Twain, Mark, 55

  precognition evidence, 56-58

  sensory organs, 53

  testing, Rhine deck of cards, 58-60

espionage, Mata Hari's arrest, 257

ETI (extraterrestrial intelligence) event, 154

  procedures to follow if signal detected, 155

  Wow!, 154

*Eurydice* submarine, 22

evidence

  alien body, *Roswell Incident*, 284

  anecdotal, ESP, 53-56

  Borden, Lizzie, story, 242-244

  existence of Atlantis (Donnelly), 137

  Franklin expedition for the Northwest Passage, 44

  lack of for extraterrestrial life, 148-149

  Lindbergh baby kidnapping, 211

    presented at trial, 220

  precognition, Robertson, Morgan (author *Futility*), 56-58

ExNPS (Exploration of Neighboring Planetary Systems), 146

"expert" witnesses, events of Braintree, 224-225

Exploration of Neighboring Planetary Systems. *See* ExNPS

explorers, 33

  Eric the Red, 33-34

    disappearance, 35

    Little Ice Age, 34-35

  Franklin expedition (search for the Northwest Passage), 42-48

  Roanoke colony, 36

    disappearance, 37-41

    Fernandez split from White, 39

    Indian fights, 36-37

    Raleigh, Sir Walter, 36

    tensions between White and Fernandez, 38

extinctions, 126

extrasensory perception. *See* ESP

extraterrestrial intelligence event. *See* ETI event

extraterrestrial life, 143-156

  conditions for life to exist on other planets, 146

generation stars, 147

  right mix of stars and planets, 147

Doctor Drake's equation, 150

  Milky Way example, 151-154

Fermi paradox, 147-149

formation of planets from stars, 144

  detecting Earth-size planets, 146

  wobble technique, 145

lack of evidence, 148-149

radio signal detection, 154

  Project Ozma, 154

  Project Phoenix, 154-155

  SERENDIP, 155-156

  SETI League, 155

eyewitness evidence versus empirical proof (UFOs), 299-300

Ezekiel, ancient pastime UFOs, 266

**F**

fate of the universe, 123-128

  Chicxulub structure, 127

  crashing asteroid, 127

  dinosaurs, 126

  first mystery, 124-125

  geologic eras, 125

    Cenozoic Era, 125

    Mesozoic Era, 125

    Paleozoic Era, 125

    Precambrian Era, 125

  mass extinctions, 126

  Nemesis, 127-128

  role of gravity, 124

Fatima, 90

  glowing globe, 91

  proof of existence, 91

  three secrets of Lady of Light, 92

    glimpse into hell, 92-93

third secret, 94
unknown light, 93-94
white mist, 90
FBI, Jeane Dixon's role, 170
female spy (Mata Hari), 249-251
arrest for espionage, 257
*Deuxieme Bureau* French spy service, 253-254
German conquest of Kalle, 255
return to Paris, 257
role of Denvignes, Colonel Joseph, 256-257
Hindu temple dance, 251-252
intercepts, 257-260
lovers, 252
Madrid, 255
mistaken identity in Falmouth, 254-255
myths, 260-261
offer to work for *Nachrichtendienst* German consul, 252-253
Fermi, Enrico (physicist), Fermi paradox, 147-149
Fernandez, Simon (Roanoke colony pilot for White), 38
first mystery, role in fate of the universe, 124-125
first-generation stars, 147
Flathead Monster (lake serpent), 319
Flight 19 (Bermuda Triangle legend), 20
Florida Everglades Skunk-ape, 325
*Flying Dutchman* (legendary ghost ship), 12
flying saucers (sightings), 270
alien encounters, 291
Hill, Betty and Barney, 291-296
hypnotherapy, 297-298
increase in claims of abduction, 296-297

Arnold, Kenneth (private pilot), 270-271
eyewitness evidence versus empirical proof, 299-300
Mantell, Captain Thomas, death of, 271-272
Project Blue Book, 275
disbanding, 277-278
Robertson Panel, 275-276
reports of trained observers, 273
Capital building sightings, 274
Project Sign (Air Force), 273-274
"flying silver cigars", 268
Hamilton, Alex (farmer), 269
Texas windmill, 269-270
*folie a deux*, 294
Fox, Leah (one of the Hydesville sisters), public lecture, 188-189
Franklin, Sir John (search for the Northwest Passage), disappearance of the ships, 42-48
evidence of missing expedition, 44
McClintock, Captain Frances (expedition), 46-47
Rae, John (overland search), 44-45
speculation, 47-48
Freedom of Information Act Web site, 221
*Fugitive, The*, 235

# G

Galanapoulos, Anghelos (Greek professor), seeker of Atlantis, Santorini collection, 140
Ganzfeld technique, testing for psi powers, 60-61
Gein, Ed (ghoul), 311-312

Gemini (the Twins) zodiacal sign, 174
generation stars, conditions for life to exist on other planets, 147
first generation, 147
second or third generation, 147
geologic eras (fate of the universe), 125
Cenozoic, 125
Mesozoic, 125
Paleozoic, 125
Precambrian, 125
ghouls, 311
Dahmer, Jeffrey, 313
Gein, Ed, 311-312
gibbets, 304
*Gift of Prophecy: The Phenomenal Jeane Dixon, A* (Montgomery), 170
Gilgal Refaim, 112
Anakim tribe, 113
summer solstice, 112
unique structure, 112
Giza
Great Pyramid of Khufu at Giza, 103
Great Sphinx, 107
glowing globe, events at Fatima, 91
gods associated with planets, Chaldean astrology, 161
Golden Cage prediction, *Nostradamus* verse, 83-84
Goodavage, Joseph, parallelism, 171
Grant, Julia (wife of Ulysses Grant), anecdotal evidence for ESP, 55-56
gravity, role in fate of the universe, 124
*Great Cryptogram, The* (Donnelly), 137
Great Pearl, ancient pastime UFOs, 267
Great Pyramid, 102
history of mankind, 105-106

relationships of inside markings, 104-105

Taylor's interpretation, 102-104

*Great Pyramid, Why was it built and Who built it?, The*, 102

"great tempest" prediction (Anwari), 163

Greek oracles, 64-67
Croesus and Delphic, 66-67
Dodona, 65

Greenland, Eric the Red, 33-35
disappearance, 35
Little Ice Age, 34-35

Grenville, Sir Richard (Roanoke expedition leader), 36-37

Groom Lake (Area 51), 283

# H

*H.M.S. Atalanta*, Bermuda Triangle legend, 20-21

Hamilton, Alex (farmer), airship sighting, 269

Hauptmann, Bruno (arrest for Lindbergh baby kidnapping), 219

Hawkins, Gerald S. (Stonehenge, theory of erection), 111

hell, glimpse through Lady of Light, 92-93

Heracles (Greek hero), 131

Hill, Betty and Barney, alien encounter, 291-292
Air Force investigation, 292
claim to examination by aliens, 294-296
inability to account for two hours, 293
increase in claims of abduction, 296-297

Hindu temple dance, Mata Hari, 251-252

history of mankind, Great Pyramid, 105-106

Hitler, Adolf, decisions with the aid of astrologers, 167-168

hits, Rhine deck of cards, 59-60

Hoffa, James (boss of the Teamsters Union), disappearing persons story, 30-32

Home, Daniel Dunglas (prince of physical mediumship), levitation abilities, 194-195

homeopathy, 99

hominids, 323

horoscopes, 158, 172-182
casting, 172-182
12 Houses, 180-181
drawing lines to determine aspects, 181
ephemeris, 178-179
"cold readings," 158-159
signs of the Zodiac, 173
associated qualities, 174-177
cusps, 177

Houses (12)
associated qualities, 347
casting horoscopes, 180-181

Howe, Ellic (author), investigated Hitler's possible use of atrologers, 167

Hoyle, Fred (astronomer), Steady State theory, 122

Hubble, Edwin (astronomer), Hubble's Constant, 122

human fascination with mysteries, 5
Borden, Lizzie, story, 5

human-like creatures, 322
Bigfoot, 324-325
Patterson picture, 325
Yeti, 323-324

Hydesville sisters
spiritualism, 186-187
digging for the rapper, 187
public lecture of Leah Fox, 188-189

hypnosis, Fatima, 90-94
glowing globe, 91
proof of existence, 91-92
three secrets of Lady of Light, 92-94
white mist, 90

hypnotherapy, alien encounters, 297-298

hypnotic regressions, 298

hypnotic trances, 298

# I

*I Love a Mystery*, 4

idols
Balsamo, Giuseppe, becomes Cagliostro, 200-201
Count de Saint-Germain, 197
facts and legends, 198
life after death, 199-200
Rasputin miracles, 205-207

Indian fights (Roanoke colony), 36-37

intercepts, Mata Hari story, 257-260

interferometry, 146

International Academy of Astronautics, 155

*Interrupted Journey, The* (Fuller and Hill), 294

investigations
Borden, Lizzie, 242
Borden burglary, 244
clues and suspects, 242
facts, 243
Majestic-12 operation, *Roswell Incident*, 288

*Is Anyone Out There? The Scientific Search for Extraterrestrial Intelligence* (Drake and Sobel), 150

Ishtar (god associated with Venus), Chaldean astrology, 161

*Isis Unveiled* (Blavatsky), 139

## J

Japanese Pyramid, 106
  circle of smaller steps, 107
  cultural knowledge and
    intellect, 107
  structure, 106-107
Jeane Dixon effect (astrology
  predictions), 170
Jones, Inigo (Stonehenge, theory of erection), 111
Judge Joseph Force Crater, disappearing persons story,
  29-30

## K

Kanda Swandi (cult of Mata
  Hari), 250
Kepler, Johannes (learned
  astrologer), 164
Khufu at Giza, 103
kidnappings
  Lindbergh baby, 209-210
    arrest of Bruno
     Hauptmann, 219
    colonels, 211-212
    communication with
     the kidnappers,
     214-215
    Condon, Dr. John F.,
     213, 218
    discovery of the body,
     216
    evidence, 211
    follow-up ransom notes,
     212-213
    Lindbergh bills, 218
    money drop, 215-216
    Parker, Ellis (detective),
     role, 217-218
    question of current exis-
     tence, 221
    ransom note, 210-211
    trial, 219-221
  Ross, Charles, 25-26
Kirk, Dr. Leland, role in Sam
  Sheppard case, 234
*Kritias* dialogue (Plato), 131

## L

Lady of Light (events at
  Fatima), 90
  glowing globe, 91
  proof of existence, clearing
   of the sky, 91-92
  three secrets, 92
    glimpse into hell, 92-93
    unknown light, 93-94
  white mist, 90
Lady of Medjugorje visions,
  95-96
lake leviathans, 316-321
  "Champ" (Lake
   Champlain), 318
  Flathead Monster (Lake
   Flathead), 319
  Lake Sandnesvatet,
   319-320
  Loch Ness Monster,
   316-317
  Ogopogo (Lake Okanagan),
   319
  Scandinavia, 319
  skrimsel, 320
Lake of the Tigers serpent,
  320
lamia (vampires), 305-306
learned astrologers, 163
  Brahe, Tycho, 163-164
  Kepler, Johannes, 164
  Lilly, William, astrological
   almanac, 164-166
legends, 12
  Bermuda Triangle, 18-21
    Devil's Triangle, 19
    disappearing Avengers,
     18-19
    Flight 19, 20
    *H.M.S. Atalanta*, 20-21
    missing DC-3, 21
    *Scorpion*, 21
    *U.S.S. Cyclops*, 21
  Merlin, 68-69
Leo (the Lion) zodiacal sign,
  175
levitation, Daniel Dunglas
  Home, Ashley Place
  Levitation, 194-195

Libra (the Scales) zodiacal
  sign, 176
life after death, Count de
  Saint-Germain, 199-200
life on other planets, necessary conditions, 146
  generation stars, 147
  right mix of stars and
   planets, 147
*Lignum Vitae*, 70
Lilly, William (learned
  astrologer), astrological
  almanac, 164-166
Lincoln, Abraham, anecdotal
  evidence for ESP, 55-56
Lindbergh Archives, 221
Lindbergh baby kidnapping,
  209-210
  arrest of Bruno
   Hauptmann, 219
  colonels, 211-212
  communication with the
   kidnappers, 214-215
  Condon, Dr. John F., 213
   rejection syndrome, 218
  discovery of the body, 216
  evidence, 211
  follow-up ransom notes,
   212-213
  Lindbergh bills, 218
  money drop, 215-216
  Parker, Ellis (detective),
   role, 217-218
  question of current existence, 221
  ransom note, 210-211
  trial, 219
    conviction, 221
    evidence, 220
line drawing, horoscope
  charts, determining aspects,
  181
lintel stones (Stonehenge),
  110
Little Ice Age, Eric the Red,
  34-35
Loch Morar, 318
Loch Ness Monster, 316-317

Looney, J. Thomas (anlysis of the writings of The Playwright)
  identification of special characteristics, 335
  nine general features, 335
lovers of Mata Hari, 252
Lowell Commission investigation, events of Braintree, 225-226
lycanthropy, 309-310

# M

MacLeod, Sir Campbell (husband of Mata Hari), 250-251
Madrid, Mata Hari, 255
Majestic-12 operation (*Roswell Incident*), 284-288
  investigation, 288
  open questions, 288-290
Malachy (prophet), 69
  list of prophesied popes, 70-73
Mantell, Captain Thomas (flight leader), death of, 271-272
Marduk (god associated with Jupiter), Chaldean astrology, 161
Marlowe, Christopher (contender for the quill of *The Playwright*), 336
*Mary Celeste* (ship), 13
  analysis of the facts, 16-17
  court of inquiry, 15-16
  embellishments, 15
  final voyage, 14-15
  reasonable explanations, 17
  story, 13
mass extinctions, 126
mass hypnosis (Fatima), 90
  glowing globe, 91
  proof of existence, 91-92
  three secrets of Lady of Light, 92-94
  white mist, 90

Mata Hari mystery, 249-251
  alone in Madrid, 255
  *Deuxieme Bureau* French spy service, 253-254
  German conquest of Kalle, 255
    arrest for espionage, 257
    return to Paris, 257
    role of Denvignes, Colonel Joseph, 256-257
  Hindu temple dance, 251-252
  intercepts, 257-260
  lovers, 252
  mistaken identity in Falmouth, 254-255
  myths, 260-261
  offer to work for *Nachrichtendienst* German consul, 252-253
McClintock, Captain Frances (expedition to find members of Franklin expedition of Northwest Passage), 46-47
*Meadows of Gold and Mines of Gems*, 103
medieval astrology, 162
  learned astrologers, 163
    Brahe, Tycho, 163-164
    Kepler, Johannes, 164
    Lilly, William, 164-166
  royal astrologers, 162
medieval prophecy, 68-75
  Merlin, 68-69
  Mother Shipton, 76
    Cardinal Wolsey prediction, 76
    predictive verses, 77-80
  *Nostradamus*, 80-81
    ancient Egyptian books, 84
    Golden Cage prediction, 83-84
    obscure verse, 81-83
    prophecy revealed through wandering, 81
    quatrains, 84-88

St. Malachy, 69
  list of prophesied popes, 70-73
mediums (communicating with the dead), 193
  cheating, 196
  Home, Daniel Dunglas, levitation, 193-195
Medjugorje visions, 95-96
megaliths, 102
Merlin (prophet/wizard), 68-69
*Merlinus Anglicanus Junior* (Lilly), 164
Mesmer, Dr. Friedrich Anton (animal magnetism), 191-192
mesmerism (animal magnetism), Davis, Andrew Jackson, 191-193
Mesozoic Era, 125
metaphysical, 124
mFTs (Multi-Channel Fourier Transform Spectrometer), 146
middens, 35
Milky Way, plugging into Doctor Drake's equation, 151-154
*Minerve* submarine, 22
miracles of Rasputin, 205-207
*Mirror of Magic, The* (Seligmann), 204
mistaken identity in Falmouth, Mata Hari, 254-255
modern prophecy, 89
  Cayce, Edgar, 96
    *Atlantis*, 99
    diagnoses and treatments, 98
    psychic readings through self-induced trance, 96-97
  Fatima, 90
    glowing globe, 91
    proof of existence, 91-92

three secrets of Lady of Light, 92-94
  white mist, 90
Our Lady of Medjugorje, 95-96
Mogul balloons, link to *Roswell Incident*, 283
Mokele-Mbembe (lake serpent), 320
money drop (Lindbergh baby kidnapping), 215-216
monoliths, 102
monuments, 101-102
  engineering ability, 113
  Gilgal Refaim, 112
    Anakim tribe, 113
    summer solstice, 112
    unique structure, 112
  Great Pyramid, 102
    history of mankind, 105-106
    relationships of inside markings, 104-105
    Taylor's interpretation, 102-104
  Japanese Pyramid, 106
    circle of smaller steps, 107
    cultural knowledge and intellect, 107
    structure, 106-107
  megaliths, 102
  monoliths, 102
  Sphinx, 107
    dating, 108
    investigating interior, 108-109
  Stonehenge, 110
    stones, 110
    theories of erection, 111
Moore, William (coauthor of *The Roswell Incident*), 281-282
Mother Shipton (medieval prophet), 76
  Cardinal Wolsey prediction, 76
  predictive verses, 77-80

Multi-Channel Fourier Transform Spectrometer. *See* mFTs
Mumfre, Joseph (New Orleans axeman crimes), 231-233
murder
  Borden family story, 237-240
    death of father Borden, 240-241
    death of stepmother Borden, 241-242
    investigation, 242-244
    trial, 244-247
    unanswered questions, 247-248
  Mumfre, Joseph, New Orleans axeman crime, 231-233
mysteries
  answers lost in the past, 8
  defined, 3
    human fascination with, 5
    universal interest in, 4
  increased mysteriousness with each solution, 7-8
  Mata Hari, 249-251
    alone in Madrid, 255
    arrest for espionage, 257
    *Deuxieme Bureau* French spy service, 253-254
    German conquest of Kalle, 255-257
    Hindu temple dance, 251-252
    intercepts, 257-260
    lovers, 252
    mistaken identity in Falmouth, 254-255
    myths, 260-261
    offer to work for *Nachrichtendienst* German consul, 252-253
  solved with several solutions, Shakespeare's plays, 7

unknown versus unknowable, 6-7
mysteries of the universe, 117
  balloon analogy, 122
  beginning, 118
    conceptual framework, 118-119
    stars, 119-120
  Big Bang theory, 122-123
  composition of the stars, 120-121
  fate of the universe, 123-127
    Chicxulub structure, 127
    crashing asteroid, 127
    dinosaurs, 126
    first mystery, 124-125
    geologic eras, 125
    mass extinctions, 126
    Nemesis, 127-128
    role of gravity, 124
  red shift of the stars, 121
  Steady State, 122
myths, Mata Hari story, 260-261

## N

*Nachrichtendienst* German consul, Mata Hari, 252-253
natal (birth) charts, casting a horoscope, 178
  12 Houses, 180-181
  drawing lines to determine aspects, 181
  ephemeris, 178-179
naturopathy, 99
Nebo (god associated with Mercury), Chaldean astrology, 161
Nemesis (fate of the universe), 127-128
Nergal (god associated with Mars), Chaldean astrology, 161

Nessie. *See* Loch Ness Monster

New Age Atlantis, 138

New Orleans axeman crime, 226
- axeman hysteria, 228-229
- Besumer, Louis (grocer or spy), 227-228
- murder of Joseph Mumfre, 231-233
- role of Rosie Cortimiglia, 229
- Schneider, 228
- *Times-Picayune* letter, 229-231
- victims, 231

Norse, Eric the Red, 33-34
- disappearance, 35
- Little Ice Age, 34-35

Northwest Passage search, 42
- Franklin expedition, 42-43
  - disappearance of the ships, 43
  - evidence of missing expedition, 44
  - Rae, John (overland search), 44-45
- McClintock, Captain Frances (expedition), 46-47
- speculation, 47-48

*Nostradamus* (medieval prophet), 80-81
- ancient Egyptian books, 84
- Golden Cage prediction, 83-84
- obscure verse, 81-83
- prophecy revealed through wandering, 81
- quatrains, 84-88

Novykh, Grigory Yefimovich. *See* Rasputin miracles

# O

Objectives (UFOB report form), 349

obscure verse, *Nostradamus*, Golden Cage prediction, 81-84

Ogopogo (lake serpent), 319

"Old Fox". *See* Parker, Ellis (detective in Lindbergh baby kidnapping), 217

Opposition aspect, 181

oracles, 64-66
- Croesus and Delphic, 66-67
- Dodona, 65
- Sibylline Books, 67-68

origins, Atlantis, 132-134

orrery, 111

Our Lady of Medjugorje visions, 95-96

# P

Paleozoic Era, 125

Paole, Arnold (vampire story), 306-307
- cremation, 307-308
- disinterring of his body, 307

Parallel aspect, 181

parallelism (astrology), 171-172

Parker, Ellis (detective in Lindbergh baby kidnapping), 217-218

Patterson picture, Bigfoot, 325

people, disappearances, 23
- Bathurst, Sir Benjamin, 24-25
- Bierce, Ambrose, 26
- Crater, Judge Joseph Force, 29-30
- Hoffa, James, 30-32
- officers Day and Stewart, 27
- Picard, Pauline, 28-29
- Ross, Charles, 25-26
- Small, Ambrose, 26-27
- unfound persons, 32

Pharoah Thuthmosis III (Circle of Fire), ancient pastime UFOs, 267

philosopher's stone, 201

physical mediums (communicating with the dead), 193
- cheating, 196
- Home, Daniel Dunglas, levitation, 193-195

Picard, Pauline, disappearing persons story, 28-29

Pillars of Heracles, 131

Pisces (the Fish) zodiacal sign, 177

planes, disappearances, 11, legends of the Bermuda Triangle, 18-21

planets
- associated qualities, 346-347
- conditions for life to exist on other planets, 146
  - generation stars, 147
  - right mix of stars and planets, 147
- formation from stars, 144
  - detecting Earth-size planets, 146
  - wobble technique, 145
- gods, Chaldean astrology, 161

Plato dialogues, Atlantis, 130-131

Playwright (Shakespearean plays)
- known information about William Shakespeare, 329-330
- necessary knowledge base, 330-331
- who wrote the plays, 328-329
  - contender Earl of Oxford, 335-336
  - contender Marlowe, Christopher, 336-337
  - contender Sir Francis Bacon, 331-334
  - Shakespeare himself, 338-339

popes, prophesied by St. Malachy, 70-73

*post hoc ergo propter hoc*, Chaldean priests, 160-161

potsherds, carbon dating, 112
Precambrian Era, 125
precognition evidence, 52
    Robertson, Morgan (author *Futility*), 56-58
predicting the future (prophecy), 64
predictive verses, Mother Shipton (medieval prophet), 77-80
priests, Chaldean (astrologers)
    development of constellations, 160
    gods associated with planets, 161
    *post hoc ergo propter hoc*, 160-161
    *Zodiac*, 162
*Principles of Nature, Her Divine Revelations, and a Voice to Mankind* (Davis), 192
Pro-Alien readings (*Roswell Incident*), 283-284
Proctor, Captain William ("expert" witness in Braintree crime), 225
Project Blue Book, 275
    disbanding, 277-278
    Robertson Panel, 275-276
Project Mogul, link to *Roswell Incident*, 283
Project Ozma, 154
Project Phoenix, 154-155
Project Sign (Air Force), investigation of flying saucer reports, 273-274
proof of existence, events at Fatima, clearing of the sky, 91-92
prophecy, 63
    Antichrist concern, 68
    books, 358-359
    medieval, 68-75
        Merlin, 68-69
        Mother Shipton, 76-80
        *Nostradamus*, 80-88
        St. Malachy, 69-73
    modern, 89
        Cayce, Edgar, 96-99

Fatima, 90-94
    Our Lady of Medjugorje, 95-96
    predicting the future, 64
    prophecy of the six M's (Kepler), 164
psi powers, testing, Ganzfeld technique, 60-61
psychic readings, Edgar Cayce, self-induced trance, 96-97
Purpose and Scope regulation (UFOB report form), 349
pyramidologist, 103
pyramidology, John Taylor, 103
pyramids
    engineering ability, 113
    Gilgal Refaim, 112
        Anakim tribe, 113
        summer solstice, 112
        unique structure, 112
    Great Pyramid, 102
        history of mankind, 105-106
        relationships of inside markings, 104-105
        Taylor's interpretation, 102-104
    Japanese Pyramid, 106
        circle of smaller steps, 107
        cultural knowledge and intellect, 107
        structure, 106-107
    Sphinx, 107
        dating, 108
        investigating interior, 108-109
    Stonehenge, 110
        stones, 110
        theories of erection, 111

**Q**

quarks, 124
quatrains, *Nostradamus*, 83-88

**R**

radio signal detection of extraterrestrial life, 154
    Project Ozma, 154
    Project Phoenix, 154-155
    SERENDIP, 155-156
    SETI League, 155
Rae, John (overland search for missing ships of Northwest Passage search), 44-45
*Ragnarok, the Age of Fire and Ice* (Donnelly), 137
Raleigh, Sir Walter (Roanoke colony), 36
ransom note, Lindbergh baby kidnapping, 210-211
Rasputin miracles, 205-207
readings, *Roswell Incident*, 283
    Anti-Alien, 284
    Pro-Alien, 283-284
red shift (stars), 121
regression (hypnosis), 298
reporting UFOs
    Project Blue Book, 275
        disbanding, 277-278
        Robertson Panel, 275-276
    trained observers, 273
        Capital building sightings, 274
        Project Sign (Air Force), 273-274
    UFOB report form, 349-350
*Republic, The* (Plato), 130
resources, 357
    archaeology and crypto-archaeology, 357-358
    astrology, 358
    Atlantis, 358
    general books, 357
    prophecy, 358-359
    Shakespeare authorship, 359
    spiritualism, 359
    strange happenings, 359
    UFOs, 359

Responsibility (UFOB report form), 349-350
retrial, Sam Sheppard case, 235-236
Rhine, Dr. Joseph Banks
  deck of cards, 58-59
    hits, 59-60
    symbols, 59
    testing ESP, 58-59
rhyming couplets, Mother Shipton (medieval prophet), 77-80
Roanoke colony, 36
  disappearance, 37-40
  Fernandez split from White, 39
  first indian fights, 36-37
  Raleigh, Sir Walter, 36
  tensions between White and Fernandez, 38
Robertson Panel (panel of scientists to consider UFO question), 275-276
Robertson, H.P. (head of Robertson Panel), 275
Robertson, Morgan (author *Futility*), evidence for precognition, 56-57
  link to the sinking of the *Titanic*, 57-58
Rokeby (poem by Sir Walter Scott), legend of *Flying Dutchman*, 12
Roma lamia, 305-306
Rommie (lake serpent), 319
Root Races of Mankind, *Secret Doctrine* (Blavatsky), 139
*Rosalie* (ship), 17-18
Ross, Charles, story of his kidnapping, 25-26
*Roswell Incident, The* (Moore and Berlitz), 281-282
*Roswell Incident* (UFOs), 279
  Air Force investigation, 280-281
  alien body evidence, 284
  articles of faith, 282
  Majestic-12 operation, 284, 288

  investigation, 288
  open questions, 288-290
  Project Mogul, 283
  readings, 283
    Anti-Alien, 284
    Pro-Alien, 283-284
  story of Berlitz and Moore, 281-282
royal astrologers, 162
Ruppelt, Captain Edward J. (head of Project Blue Book), 275

**S**

Sacco, Nicola (Italian anarchist), 224
  "expert" witnesses against Sacco, 224-225
  Lowell Commission investigation, 225-226
Sagittarius (the Archer) zodiacal sign, 176
salve, werewolves, 309
Sam Sheppard case, 233
  retrial, 235-236
  role of Dr. Leland Kirk, 234
  "surgical instrument", 234
Samas (god associated with the sun), Chaldean astrology, 161
Sandnesvatet lake serpent, 319-320
Santorini collection, Atlantis, 140
sarsen stone (Stonehenge), 110
Scandinavia lake monsters, 319
  Lake Sandnesvatet, 319-320
  skrimsel, 320
Scherer, Chrstopher (prefect of canton in Switzerland), sighting, 267-268
Schwarzkopf, Colonel H. Norman (role in Lindbergh baby kidnapping), 211

"science of"
  astrology, "cold reading", 158-159
  crystals, 138
Scorpio (the Scorpion) zodiacal sign, 176
*Scorpion*, Bermuda Triangle legend, 21
Scott, Sir Walter (novelist), *Rokeby*, 12
seances, 190
  Davis, Andrew Jackson, 192-193
  Deacon Strong, 189-190
  Foxes of Hydesville, 188-189
  Mesmer, Dr. Friedrich Anton, 191-192
  Swedenborg, Emanuel, 190-191
Search for Extraterrestrial Intelligence. *See* SETI
Search for Extraterrestrial Radio Emissions from Nearby Developed Intelligent Populations. *See* SERENDIP
search for the Northwest Passage, 42
  Franklin expedition, 42-43
    disappearance of the ships, 43
    evidence of missing expedition, 44
    Rae, John (overland search), 44-45
  McClintock, Captain Frances (expedition), 46-47
  speculation, 47-48
second-generation stars, 147
*Secret Doctrine, The* (Blavatsky), Root Races of Mankind, 139
Secret *Life* (Jacobs), 297
secrets, Lady of Light, 92
  glimpse into hell, 92-93
  third secret, 94
  unknown light, 93-94

sensory organs, ESP, 53
SERENDIP (Search for Extraterrestrial Radio Emissions from Nearby Developed Intelligent Populations), 155-156
SETI (Search for Extra-terrestrial Intelligence), 154
  League (radio signal detection of extraterrestrial life), 155
Sextile aspect, 181
Shakespeare, William, 327-328
  known information about him, 329-330
  Playwright's knowledge, 330-331
  who wrote the plays, 328-329
    contender Earl of Oxford, 335-336
    contender Marlowe, Christopher, 336-337
    contender Sir Francis Bacon, 331-334
    Shakespeare himself, 338-339
Sheppard, Sam Reese (son of Sam Sheppard), 236
ships, disappearances, 11
  *Flying Dutchman*, 12
  legends of the Bermuda Triangle, 21
  *Mary Celeste*, 13-17
  *Rosalie*, 17-18
Shipton, Mother (medieval prophet), 76
  Cardinal Wolsey prediction, 76
  predictive verses, 77-80
Sibylline Books, 67-68
sightings
  ancient pastime UFOs, 266
    Circle of Fire (Pharoah Thuthmosis III), 267
    Ezekiel, 266
    Great Pearl, 267

Scherer, Christopher (prefect of canton in Switzerland), 267-268
dirigible, 268
  Hamilton, Alex (farmer), 269
  Texas windmill, 269-270
flying saucers, 270
  Arnold, Kenneth (private pilot), 270-271
  Mantell, Captain Thomas (death), 271-272
Project Blue Book, 275
  disbanding, 277-278
  Robertson Panel, 275-276
reports of trained observers, 273
  Capital building sightings, 274
  Project Sign (Air Force), 273-274
signs of the Zodiac, 172-177, 345
  associated qualities, 174, 346
    Aquarius (the Water Carrier), 177
    Aries (the Ram), 174
    Cancer (the Crab), 174
    Capricorn (the Goat), 177
    Gemini (the Twins), 174
    Leo (the Lion), 175
    Libra (the Scales), 176
    Pisces (the Fish), 177
    Sagittarius (the Archer), 176
    Scorpio (the Scorpion), 176
    Taurus (the Bull), 174
    Virgo (the Virgin), 175
  cusps, 177
Sin (god associated with the moon), Chaldean astrology, 161
Sir Benjamin Bathurst, mystery of disappearance, 24-25
skrimsel (lake serpent), 320

sleeping prophet (Cayce, Edgar), 96-97
Small, Ambrose, disappearing persons story, 26-27
Smith, Charles Piazzi (Astronomer Royal of Scotland), 105
  history of mankind through interpretation of Great Pyramid, 105-106
  relationships of inside markings of Great Pyramid, 104-105
Smith, Dr. John (Stonehenge, theory of erection), 111
spectrograph, 145
spectroscope, 146
spectrum, 120, 146
Sphinx, 107
  dating, 108
  investigating interior, 108-109
*Spirit Rappers, The* (Jackson), 189
spiritualism
  books, 359
  Hydesville sisters, 186-187
    digging for the rapper, 187
    public lecture of Leah Fox, 188-189
  mediums for communicating with the dead, 193
    cheating, 196
    Home, Daniel Dunglas, 193-195
  seances, 190
    Davis, Andrew Jackson, 192-193
    Mesmer, Dr. Friedrich Anton, 191-192
    Swedenborg, Emanuel, 190-191
spotted dolorite. *See* bluestone
Square aspect, 181
St. Malachy (prophet), list of prophesied popes, 69-73

stars
    beginning of the universe, 119-120
    composition, 120-121
    conditions for life to exist on other planets, 146
        generation stars, 147
        right mix of stars and planets, 147
    formation of planets, 144
        detecting Earth-size planets, 146
        wobble technique, 145
    red shift, 121
Steady State theory, 122
Stewart, Pilot Officer D.R., disappearing persons story, 27
stone monuments, 101-102
    engineering ability, 113
    Gilgal Refaim, 112
        Anakim tribe, 113
        summer solstice, 112
        unique structure, 112
    Great Pyramid, 102
        history of mankind, 105-106
        relationships of inside markings, 104-105
        Taylor's interpretation, 102-104
    Japanese Pyramid, 106
        circle of smaller steps, 107
        cultural knowledge and intellect, 107
        structure, 106-107
    megaliths, 102
    monoliths, 102
    Sphinx, 107
        dating, 108
        investigating interior, 108-109
    Stonehenge, 110
        stones, 110
        theories of erection, 111
*Stonehenge Decoded*, 111
stones of Stonehenge, 110
    bluestone, 110
    sarsen, 110
    Welsh sandstone, 110

Straits of Gibraltar, 131
strange happenings, books, 359
summer solstice, Gilgal Refaim, 112
"surgical instrument", Sam Sheppard case, 234
Surid (king of Egypt), 103
suspects, Lizzie Borden story, 242
Swedenborg, Emanuel (communication with the dead), 190-191
symbols, Rhine deck of cards, 59

## T

Tasmanian tiger, 321-322
Taurus (the Bull) zodiacal sign, 174
Taylor, John (mathemetician and publisher), Great Pyramid, 102-104
    contribution to pyramidology, 103
    relationships of inside markings, 104-105
telekinesis, 52
telepathy, 52
temperature inversions, 274
Terrestrial Planet Finder. *See* TPF
*Terror* (ship in search for the Northwest Passage), disappearance, 42-43
    evidence of missing expedition, 44
    McClintock, Captain Frances (expedition), 46-47
    Rae, John (overland search), 44-45
    speculation, 47-48
testing
    ESP, Rhine deck of cards, 58-60
    psi power, Ganzfeld technique, 60-61

Texas windmill, airship sighting, 269-270
Theory of Evolution, 145
Theory of Relativity (Einstein), 121
third-generation stars, 147
*Thresher* submarine, 22
thylacines, 321-322
*Timaios* dialogue (Plato), 130-131
*Times-Picayune* letter, New Orleans axeman crime, 229-231
*Titanic* link to Morgan Robertson's *Futility*, evidence for precognition, 57-58
TPF (Terrestrial Planet Finder), 146
trained observers, UFO reports, 273
    Capital building sightings, 274
    Project Sign (Air Force), 273-274
trial
    Borden, Lizzie, 244
        burning of a dress, 245-246
        defense team, 246-247
    Lindbergh baby kidnapping, 219
        conviction, 221
        evidence, 220
Trine aspect, 181
Twain, Mark, anecdotal evidence for ESP, 55

## U

*U.S.S. Cyclops*, Bermuda Triangle legend, 21
UFOlogist, 266
UFOs, 265
    alien encounters, 291
        Hill, Betty and Barney, 291-296

hypnotherapy, 297-298
increase in claims of abduction, 296-297
ancient pastime, 266
  Circle of Fire (Pharoah Thuthmosis III), 267
  Ezekiel, 266
  Great Pearl, 267
  sighting of prefect Christopher Scherer, 267-268
books, 359
dirigible sightings, 268
  Hamilton, Alex (farmer), 269
  Texas windmill, 269-270
eyewitness evidence versus empirical proof, 299-300
flying saucers, 270
  Arnold, Kenneth (private pilot), 270-271
  Mantell, Captain Thomas (death), 271-272
Project Blue Book, 275
  disbanding, 277-278
  Robertson Panel, 275-276
reports of trained observers, 273
  Capital building sightings, 274
  Project Sign (Air Force), 273-274
*Roswell Incident*, 279
  Air Force investigation, 280-281
  alien body evidence, 284
  articles of faith, 282
  Majestic-12 operation, 284-290
  Project Mogul, 283
  readings, 283-284
  story of Berlitz and Moore, 281-282

UFOB report form, 349
  Definitions, 349
  Objectives, 349
  Purpose and Scope regulation, 349
  Responsibility, 349-350
Unidentified Flying Objects, Reporting. *See* UFOs, UFOB report form
universal interest in mysteries, 4
universe mysteries, 117
  balloon analogy, 122
  beginning, 118
    conceptual framework, 118-119
    stars, 119-120
  Big Bang theory, 122-123
  composition of the stars, 120-121
  fate of the universe, 123-128
    Chicxulub structure, 127
    crashing asteroid, 127
    dinosaurs, 126
    first mystery, 124-125
    geologic eras, 125
    mass extinctions, 126
    Nemesis, 127-128
    role of gravity, 124
  red shift of the stars, 121
  Steady State theory, 122
unknown light, secret of Lady of Light, 93-94
*Urania's Children: The Strange World of the Astrologers* (Howe), 167

Van der Decken, Captain, *Flying Dutchman*, 12
Vanzetti, Bartolomeo (anarchist), 224
  "expert" witnesses against Vanzetti, 224-225
  Lowell Commission investigation, 225-226
verses
  Mother Shipton, predictive verses, 77-80
  *Nostradamus*, Golden Cage prediction, 81-84
Virgin Mary, Lady of Light prophecy, 92
  glimpse into hell, 92-93
  third secret, 94
  unknown light, 93-94
Virgo (the Virgin) zodiacal sign, 175

# W

Wagner, Richard (*Derfliegende Hollander* opera), legend of the *Flying Dutchman*, 12
Welsh sandstone (Stonehenge), 110
werewolves, 308
  lycanthropy, 310
  salve, 309
white mist, events at Fatima, 90
White, John (Roanoke colony settler), split from Fernandez, 38-39
Wild Man in Vietnam, 325
Wion, Arnold (French monk), *Lignum Vitae*, 70
wobble technique, planets and stars, 145
Wolsey, Cardinal, prediction of Mother Shipton, 76
Wow! ETI event, 154

# V

Vagrancy Act of 1824, 166
vampires, 304-305
  Paole, Arnold, 306-307
    cremation, 307-308
    disinterring of his body, 307
  Roma lamia, 305-306

# X-Z

Yeti (human-like creatures),
  323-324

Zelle, Magaretha Gertrude. *See*
  Mata Hari mystery
ziggurats, Japanese Pyramid,
  106
    circle of smaller steps, 107
    cultural knowledge and
      intellect, 107
    structure, 106-107
*Zodiac*, Chaldean astrology,
  162
Zodiacal signs, 172-177, 345
    associated qualities, 174,
      346
        Aquarius (the Water
          Carrier), 177
        Aries (the Ram), 174
        Cancer (the Crab), 174
        Capricorn (the Goat),
          177
        Gemini (the Twins), 174
        Leo (the Lion), 175
        Libra (the Scales), 176
        Pisces (the Fish), 177
        Sagittarius (the Archer),
          176
        Scorpio (the Scorpion),
          176
        Taurus (the Bull), 174
        Virgo (the Virgin), 175
    cusps, 177